# Language Rights and Political

# Language Rights
# and Political Theory

Edited by

WILL KYMLICKA

and

ALAN PATTEN

OXFORD
UNIVERSITY PRESS

# OXFORD
UNIVERSITY PRESS

Great Clarendon Street, Oxford OX2 6DP

Oxford University Press is a department of the University of Oxford.
It furthers the University's objective of excellence in research, scholarship,
and education by publishing worldwide in

Oxford New York

Auckland Bangkok Buenos Aires Cape Town Chennai
Dar es Salaam Delhi Hong Kong Istanbul Karachi Kolkata
Kuala Lumpur Madrid Melbourne Mexico City Mumbai Nairobi
São Paulo Shanghai Taipei Tokyo Toronto

Oxford is a registered trade mark of Oxford University Press
in the UK and in certain other countries

Published in the United States
by Oxford University Press Inc., New York

British Library Cataloguing in Publication Data

Data available

Library of Congress Cataloging in Publication Data

Data available

ISBN 0-19-926290-X (Hbk.)
ISBN 0-19-926291-8 (Pbk.)
1 3 5 7 9 10 8 6 4 2

Typeset by Newgen Imaging Systems (P) Ltd., Chennai, India
Printed in Great Britain
on acid-free paper by
Biddles Ltd., Guildford & King's Lynn

# Acknowledgements

This volume grew out of a workshop on language rights held at Queen's University, Kingston, Ontario, in March 2001, where many of these chapters were first presented. We'd like to thank Idil Boran for helping to organize the workshop, John Edwards for his participation, Jacob Levy for his suggestions, Michael James for his excellent copy-editing, and Dominic Byatt for his enthusiastic support. Special thanks to Julie Bernier for her speedy and efficient work in providing background research, harmonizing the formatting of the various chapters, and compiling the references.

Funding for this project was received from the Faculty of Arts and Science at Queen's University and the Social Sciences and Humanities Research Council of Canada. Two of the chapters have been published previously in slightly different forms: Thomas Pogge's chapter was first published in Jorge Gracia and Pablo de Greiff (eds), *Hispanics/Latinos in the United States: Ethnicity, Race, and Rights* (New York: Routledge, 2000), 181–200; Philippe Van Parijs' chapter was published in *Policy, Philosophy, and Economics*, 1 (2002), 59–74. We are grateful for permission to reprint these chapters.

*Will Kymlicka, Kingston*
*Alan Patten, Montreal*
*November 2002*

# Contents

*List of Figures*                                                                  ix

*List of Tables*                                                                   ix

*Notes on Contributors*                                                            x


1. Introduction: Language Rights and Political Theory:
   Context, Issues, and Approaches                                                 1
   *Alan Patten and Will Kymlicka*

2. Language Rights: Exploring the Competing Rationales                             52
   *Ruth Rubio-Marín*

3. A Liberal Democratic Approach to Language Justice                              80
   *David D. Laitin and Rob Reich*

4. Accommodation Rights for Hispanics in the United States                        105
   *Thomas W. Pogge*

5. Misconceiving Minority Language Rights:
   Implications for Liberal Political Theory                                       123
   *Stephen May*

6. Linguistic Justice                                                              153
   *Philippe Van Parijs*

7. Diversity as Paradigm, Analytical Device, and Policy Goal                      169
   *François Grin*

8. Global Linguistic Diversity, Public Goods, and the
   Principle of Fairness                                                           189
   *Idil Boran*

9. Language Death and Liberal Politics                                            210
   *Michael Blake*

10. Language Rights, Literacy, and the Modern State                               230
    *Jacob T. Levy*

11. The Antinomy of Language Policy                                                250
    *Daniel M. Weinstock*

12. Beyond *Personality*: The Territorial and Personal Principles of
Language Policy Reconsidered                                           271
*Denise G. Réaume*

13. What Kind of Bilingualism?                                            296
*Alan Patten*

*References*                                                              322
*Index*                                                                  340

# List of Figures

7.1  The diversity clover                                        175
7.2  Diversity: benefits and costs                              188
13.1  Perfect concentration                                     300
13.2  Imperfect concentration                                   303
13.3  Bilingual districts                                       303

# List of Tables

6.1  Al, An, and Bo under four compensation regimes             159
6.2  Variable number of speakers of the dominant language       163

# Notes on Contributors

ALAN PATTEN is Associate Professor of Political Science and William Dawson Scholar at McGill University. He has a BA (McGill) and MA (Toronto) in Economics, and an M.Phil. and a D.Phil. (Oxford) in Politics. In 2001–2 he was a Laurance S. Rockefeller Visiting Fellow at the University Center for Human Values, Princeton University. He is the author of *Hegel's Idea of Freedom* (OUP, 1999), which won the First Book Prize awarded by the Foundations of Political Theory Organized Section of the American Political Science Association, and the Macpherson Prize awarded by the Canadian Political Science Association. His articles include 'Political Theory and Language Policy', *Political Theory* (2001) and 'Democratic Secession from a Multinational State', *Ethics* (2002). He is currently writing a book on political theory and language policy.

WILL KYMLICKA is the author of five books published by Oxford University Press: *Liberalism, Community, and Culture* (1989), *Contemporary Political Philosophy* (1990; second edition 2002), *Multicultural Citizenship* (1995), *Finding Our Way: Rethinking Ethnocultural Relations in Canada* (1998), and *Politics in the Vernacular: Nationalism, Multiculturalism, and Citizenship* (2001). He is also the editor of *Justice in Political Philosophy* (Aldershot: Edward Elgar, 1992), *The Rights of Minority Cultures* (OUP, 1995), and co-editor of *Ethnicity and Group Rights* (New York University Press, 1997), *Citizenship in Diverse Societies* (OUP, 2000), and *Can Liberal Pluralism Be Exported? Western Political Theory and Ethnic Relations in Eastern Europe* (OUP, 2001). He is currently a Professor of Philosophy and Political Studies at Queen's University and a Visiting Professor in the Nationalism Studies Program at the Central European University in Budapest.

RUTH RUBIO-MARÍN is Professor of Constitutional Law at the University of Seville. Her interests include immigration, minority rights, language rights, gender, and constitutional law. She is the author of *Immigration as a Democratic Challenge* (Cambridge University Press, 2000) and co-author of *Igualdad y Mujer: la norma y su aplicacion* [Equality and Women: The Rule and its Application] (Seville: Instituto Andaluz de la Mujer, 1999). She has also published articles in English and Spanish dealing with nationality, citizenship, and human rights. She holds a law degree from the Seville Law School and a Ph.D. in Law from the European University Institute in Florence. She was a Visiting Fellow in the Law and Public Affairs Program at Princeton University in 2001, and has been invited as a Visiting Global Law School Faculty at New York University.

DAVID D. LAITIN is Professor of Political Science at Stanford University. He received his Ph.D. from University of California at Berkeley in 1974. He has conducted field research in Somalia, Nigeria, Spain, and Estonia. His books include *Politics, Language and Thought: The Somali Experience* (University of Chicago Press, 1977), *Hegemony and Culture: Politics and Religious Change among the Yoruba* (University of Chicago Press, 1986), *Language Repertoires and State Construction in Africa* (Cambridge University Press, 1992), and *Identity in Formation: The Russian-Speaking Populations in the Near Abroad* (Cornell University Press, 1998). He is currently working in collaboration with James Fearon on a project seeking to account for civil war incidence throughout the world since 1945.

ROB REICH is Assistant Professor of Political Science and Ethics in Society at Stanford University. His main interests are in political philosophy, and his recent work focuses on the moral status of children in liberal democracies. He is the author of *Bridging Liberalism and Multiculturalism in American Education* (University of Chicago Press, 2002). Reich received a 2002 Spencer Foundation Postdoctoral Fellowship, and is currently enjoying a fellowship at the Stanford Humanities Center. Before attending graduate school, Rob was a sixth grade teacher at Rusk Elementary School in Houston, Texas.

THOMAS W. POGGE is Professor of Philosophy at Columbia University. He is the author of *Realizing Rawls* (Cornell University Press, 1989), and the editor of *Global Justice* (Blackwell, 2001). He has published many articles on justice, democracy, and nationalism in journals such as *Philosophy and Public Affairs*, *Ethics*, *Journal of Political Philosophy*, and *Ethics and International Affairs*. His next book on global justice will be published as part of the Oxford Political Theory series.

STEPHEN MAY is Foundation Professor and Chair of Language and Literacy Education in the School of Education, University of Waikato, New Zealand. He has written widely on ethnicity, nationalism, and multiculturalism, with a particular focus on their implications for language and education. His recent major publications include *Critical Multiculturalism* (Routledge Falmer, 1999), and *Language and Minority Rights: Ethnicity, Nationalism, and the Politics of Language* (Longman, 2001). He is a founding editor of the international and interdisciplinary journal *Ethnicities*.

PHILIPPE VAN PARIJS holds a Ph.D. in the social sciences (Louvain 1977) and a D.Phil. in philosophy (Oxford 1980). He is a professor at the Université Catholique de Louvain, where he directs the Hoover Chair of Economic and Social Ethics. His books include *Evolutionary Explanation in the Social Sciences* (Rowman and Littlefield, 1981), *Qu'est-ce qu'une société juste?* (Seuil, 1991), *Marxism Recycled* (Cambridge University Press, 1993), *Real Freedom for All* (OUP, 1995), and *What's Wrong with a Free Lunch?* (Beacon Press, 2001).

FRANÇOIS GRIN is Adjunct Director of the Unit for Education Research (SRED) and Senior Lecturer at the University of Geneva. From 1998 to 2001, he was Deputy Director of the European Centre for Minority Issues, to which he remains affiliated as a Senior Fellow. His research focuses on the economics of language, the economics of education, and the evaluation of language and education policies. He is the author of some 150 publications in these fields.

IDIL BORAN completed her PhD in philosophy at Queen's University in 2001. She is currently a postdoctoral fellow of the Social Sciences and Humanities Research Council of Canada at McGill University and was previously a postdoctoral fellow at the Chaire Hoover d'éthique économique et sociale. Her writing on issues of linguistic and cultural rights has appeared in *Critical Review of International Social and Political Philosophy, Language Problems and Language Planning*, and *The Schoolfield: International Journal of Theory of Education*.

MICHAEL BLAKE is Assistant Professor of Public Policy and Philosophy at Harvard's John F. Kennedy School of Government. He has previously been affiliated with the University Center for Human Values at Princeton and with the Department of Philosophy at Harvard. His work focuses on the relationship between group affiliation and liberal neutrality, with a special emphasis on the issues of international justice and multicultural policy. His writing has appeared in *Public Affairs Quarterly, Law and Philosophy*, and *Philosophy and Public Affairs*.

JACOB T. LEVY is Assistant Professor of Political Science at the University of Chicago. He is the author of *The Multiculturalism of Fear* (OUP, 2000). His other publications include 'Classifying Cultural Rights', in W. Kymlicka and I. Shapiro (eds), *Ethnicity and Group Rights* (New York University Press, 1997), 'The Multiculturalism of Fear', in *Critical Review* (1996), 'Three Modes of Incorporating Indigenous Law', in W. Kymlicka and W. Norman (eds), *Citizenship in Diverse Societies* (OUP, 2000), as well as a number of essays and reviews on developments in Australian Aboriginal land rights law.

DANIEL M. WEINSTOCK holds the Canada Research Chair in ethics and political philosophy in the Département de philosophie de l'Université de Montréal, and is the founding Director of the Centre de recherche en éthique de l'Université de Montréal. He has published widely on issues surrounding the accommodation of multiculturalism and value pluralism within the liberal democratic framework, as well as on the moral and political philosophy of Immanuel Kant.

DENISE G. RÉAUME is Professor of Law at the University of Toronto. She has published several articles in the areas of language rights and the role of law in arbitrating disputes in a multicultural society, including: 'Common Law Constructions of Group Autonomy', in Shapiro and Kymlicka (eds), *Ethnicity and Group Rights* (New York University Press, 1997), 'Justice Between Cultures: Autonomy and the Protection of Cultural Affiliation', *University of British Columbia Law Journal* (1995), 'The Group Right to Linguistic Security: Whose Rights, What Duties?', in J. Baker (ed.), *Group Rights* (University of Toronto Press, 1994), 'Moral and Legal Responses to the Multi-Cultural, Multi-Ethnic State', *Rechtstheorie* (1993), 'The Constitutional Protection of Language: Security versus Survival', in D. Schneiderman (ed.), *Language and the State: The Law and Politics of Identity* (Yvon Blais, 1991), and 'Second-Class Rights? Principle and Compromise in the Charter' (co-authored with L. Green), *Dalhousie Law Journal* (1990). Her research interests include discrimination law and multiculturalism, in addition to language rights, and bring together substantive legal questions and theoretical debates.

# 1

# Introduction
# Language Rights and Political Theory:
# Context, Issues, and Approaches

ALAN PATTEN AND WILL KYMLICKA

Political theory in the last decade has been awash with discussions of cultural diversity and ethnic, racial, and religious pluralism, with books exploring 'the ethos of pluralization', 'strange multiplicity', and 'the politics of recognition'. Yet there is one form of diversity which has received relatively little attention from political theorists: linguistic diversity. To our knowledge, there has not been a single monograph or edited volume which examines the issue of language rights from the perspective of normative political theory.

This is a striking gap when compared with the many important volumes by political theorists dedicated to issues of race (Mills 1997; Cochran 1999; Gutmann and Appiah 1996), indigenous people (Ivison, Sanders, and Patton 2000; Poole and Kukathas 2000; Tully 1995), immigration (Bauböck 1995; Cole 2000; Bader 1997; Rubio-Marín 2000), nationalism (Tamir 1993; Canovan 1996; Miller 1995; 2000; Miscevic 2000; Moore 2001); and religion (Audi 2000; Rosenblum 2000; Spinner-Halev 2000). In each of these areas, there is a vibrant debate amongst political theorists about how rights claims relating to these forms of diversity connect with liberal-democratic principles of freedom, justice, and democracy. There are well-developed 'liberal theories of immigration' or 'liberal theories of nationalism', for example, as well as criticisms of such theories by communitarians, feminists, civic republicans, postmodernists, and others.[1] By contrast, one would be hard-pressed to know where to look to find an articulation of a normative theory of language rights, whether liberal, communitarian, post-colonial, or otherwise.

Fortunately, this surprising gap is now being remedied. The past few years have witnessed the publication of several articles and chapters on the implications of normative principles of freedom and equality for language policy (for example, Van Parijs 2000a; 2002; Carens 2000: 77–87; Bauböck 2001;

---

[1] See, for example, the feminist and post-colonial critiques of liberal theories of nationalism and multiculturalism in Narayan and Harding (2000), Okin (1999), Shachar (2001), Yuval-Davis and Werbner (1999), and Deveaux (2001).

Réaume 2000; May 2001: Ch. 4; Patten 2001; N. Levy 2001; Green 1987 is a valuable earlier article). At the same time, some sociolinguists and political scientists who specialize in language policy in particular countries have also started to examine the normative dimensions of their field of study, and to consider the extent to which the policies they study conform to various normative principles (for example, Branchadell 1999, Costa 2003 on Spain; Schmidt 2000, Rhee 1999 on the US; MacMillan 1998, Coulombe 2000 on Canada).

While the debate over normative theories of language rights is still quite new, we believe it is possible to identify the emerging approaches and to suggest some of the likely areas for future theoretical development. Our aim in this volume is to provide the reader with an up-to-date statement of the contending positions in the debate, and also to push the debate forward. We have brought together some of the most prominent political theorists and social scientists who work in the field, with the aim of exploring how political theorists can conceptualize issues of language rights and contribute to public debates on language policy.

In this introduction, we begin by exploring several of the factors that have fuelled the new interest in language rights (section 1). We then survey some of the issues that need to be addressed by a theory of language policy (section 2), before turning to the idea of 'language rights' and some of the key distinctions that have been proposed in theorizing such rights (section 3). The four sections that follow then consider some of the principal normative approaches that are advanced in this volume and elsewhere. We first explain why language controversies cannot be adequately resolved by recourse to ideas of 'benign neglect' and 'linguistic human rights' (section 4). We then consider two prominent normative models of language—the 'nation-building' and 'language preservation' models—and draw attention to some shortcomings of each approach (sections 5 and 6). We conclude by outlining a range of 'procedural' approaches that emerge in a number of the contributions to the volume (section 7). Although this all makes for a rather lengthy introduction, we hope that it gives the reader a sense of why language rights are important in political theory today, of what language debates are really about, and of what some of the dominant positions are in those debates. This will help situate the more detailed arguments developed in subsequent chapters.

# 1. The Context

Why have language rights and language policy become an issue for political theorists now? We can identify both practical and theoretical factors that have spurred reflection on language issues. At the practical level, we have seen a growing range of political conflicts and challenges throughout the world that are centred on linguistic diversity. At the theoretical level, a series of internal developments within the field of political theory itself have converged on questions of language rights and language policy.

Let's start with some of the practical conflicts and challenges. Linguistic diversity has emerged as a major source of political controversy in several distinct political contexts, affecting the stability and sustainability of a wide range of political communities. We can distinguish at least five such contexts.

1. *Eastern Europe.* For some people in the West, reflection on the political significance of linguistic diversity was first stimulated by the experience of eastern European countries after the fall of communism in 1989. Optimistic assumptions about a rapid spread of liberal democracy to the region were quickly shattered by the outbreak of ethnic conflicts, many of them along linguistic lines. Countries that had accorded a range of minority language rights (at least on paper) under the Communist regime often shifted to a policy of official monolingualism. Indeed, laws declaring the majority language as the sole official language were often the very first laws adopted by the newly independent countries of the former Soviet Union or Yugoslavia.[2] Linguistic minorities understandably felt threatened by the perceived loss of status and rights implied by such laws, and responded with a range of mobilizations, from peaceful protest to violent secession.

This surge of ethnolinguistic conflict in eastern Europe was a shock to the broad public in the West, partly because it shattered hopes for a rapid transition to liberal democracy in the region, and partly because it was physically so close to the West. But the underlying lesson was already quite familiar to specialists in democratization around the world. In many countries in Asia and Africa, efforts to construct common institutions and a shared identity have been severely complicated by linguistic diversity and demands for recognition by numerous language groups (Weinstein 1990). There is an increasing consensus that language policy plays a vital role in the process of democratic transition (Grin and Daftary 2003). It has become clear, in short, that the practical challenge of promoting democratization around the world requires attending to issues of linguistic diversity.

In response to fears about the spread of ethnolinguistic conflict in eastern Europe, various Western organizations sought to develop standards for how 'good' liberal democracies resolve these issues. These include the Council of Europe's European Charter for Regional or Minority Languages (1992) and its Framework Convention for the Protection of National Minorities (1995), as

---

[2] Taras (1998: 79) discusses the 'paradox' that formerly monolingual countries in the West are moving towards greater respect for diversity, whereas formerly multilingual countries of the Soviet Union are 'pressing ahead with unilingualism'. A familiar joke in the region stated that under the Communists, you could talk in whatever language you liked so long as you praised the Communist Party; under the new regime, you can voice any political opinion you like so long as you say it in the majority language.

well as the Organization for Security and Cooperation in Europe's Oslo Recommendations on Linguistic Rights of National Minorities (1998). These declarations of minimum standards and best practices regarding linguistic diversity were intended to guide east European countries in their efforts to 'rejoin Europe', and indeed meeting these standards is a precondition for admittance to the European Union (EU) or NATO.

But this raises an obvious question: what are the 'minimum standards' and 'best practices' of Western democracies regarding linguistic diversity? The need to formulate standards as a guide for democratizing countries in eastern Europe required Western scholars and policy makers to reflect on their own historic practices and contemporary policies. And this quickly led to the realization that linguistic issues are far from being 'resolved' in the West either.

2. *Regional languages/minority nationalisms*. There are in fact several different kinds of unresolved linguistic issues in the West. Historically, the most important and bitter have been conflicts between a dominant language group and various smaller but still powerful regionally concentrated and historically rooted language groups. Examples include regional language groups in Belgium (Flanders), Spain (Catalonia and the Basque Country), Canada (Quebec and parts of several other provinces), Italy (the German-speaking South Tyrol), United States (Puerto Rico), and Switzerland (the French- and Italian-speaking cantons).

These are the closest analogues in the West to the sorts of conflicts we see in eastern Europe, which also typically involve conflicts between dominant national groups and regionally concentrated historically rooted linguistic minorities. As in eastern Europe, these conflicts in the West have been most intense when the dominant national group attempts to impose its language as the state language on all parts of the country, including those regions which the minority views as its historic homeland. Such attempts have typically generated strong resistance, from peaceful protest to secessionist movements.

The outcome of these conflicts has varied widely from country to country, although we can see a clear trend in the West towards granting increased language rights to such regional linguistic groups. Indeed, in all of the aforementioned cases, the regional language has been accorded the status of an official language, at least within the region of the country where it is concentrated. In some cases, the regional language has a co-equal status, alongside the dominant majority language; in other cases, the regional language is in fact the only official language within the region. In either case, the result has been to enable speakers of the regional language to access a wide range of public institutions— schools, courts, the media, local government—in their own tongue.

One could argue that this is now the 'norm' for how Western democracies deal with regional languages,[3] and that these sorts of accommodations should

---

[3] Amongst the Western democracies, France and Greece have strongly resisted this trend to according official status to regional languages. However, even France has now moved in that direction, particularly with respect to Corsica, leaving Greece as the main exception to the trend.

be seen as either minimum standards or best practices for dealing with regional language groups. After all, the countries that have moved in this multilingual direction are amongst the most peaceful, prosperous, free, and democratic societies around.[4] Yet it is interesting to note that none of the recent international declarations on language rights asserts that there is a right to official language status, or even recommends such a policy. On the contrary, there has been great reluctance to view policies of official bilingualism or multilingualism as 'rights' rather than pragmatic accommodations.

Part of the complexity here is that debates over regional languages are never just debates over language. For regional language groups, in both the East and the West, are almost always also 'national' groups: that is, they see themselves not just as having a distinct language, but also as forming a distinct 'nation' within the larger state. They mobilize behind nationalist political parties with nationalist goals of self-government. Language rights are part of a larger programme of sub-state nationalism.

As a result, debates over the status of a regional language are also debates over nationhood. For the minority language group, recognition of its language is seen as a symbol of recognition of its nationhood. For the minority group, official multilingualism is desired in part because it is a symbol of, and a step towards, acceptance that it is a multination state, a partnership of two or more nations within a single state.

Yet this is precisely what members of the dominant group typically wish to avoid. For accepting that a regional language group is also a 'nation' has potentially far-reaching consequences. Assertions of nationhood typically involve not only claims to protection of a group's language and culture, but also a claim to territory (the nation's 'homeland') and a claim to self-determination over that territory, perhaps even its secession. This is one reason why most Western countries were until recently quite unwilling to accord official status to regional languages: they knew it was tantamount to, or a step towards, accepting the claim to nationhood by the regional group, and hence opening up claims to territorial self-government.[5]

The shift towards official language rights in the West, therefore, is intimately tied up with increased acceptance of the legitimacy of minority nationalism.[6]

---

[4] For a more detailed defense of the 'success' of these examples of multilingual federations, see Kymlicka (2001a: Ch. 5).

[5] Conversely, attempts to impose a single state language throughout the territory of the state are often attempts to impose a hegemonic national identity on all citizens, and to entrench the idea that the state is a nation-state belonging to the dominant group and embodying its right to self-determination. Majority support for official monolingualism, as much as minority demands for bilingualism, are typically manifestations of nationalist projects.

[6] However, some advocates of official languages policies have seen these policies as part of a nation-building alternative to accepting the multination state. It is sometimes said that the 'Trudeau vision' of Canada involved the implementation of an official languages policy as part of an effort to forge a coast-to-coast Canadian national identity (McRoberts 1997: Ch. 4; Kymlicka 1998: 133–5).

Dominant groups in the West have learned to accept the idea that their country contains groups that see themselves as distinct and self-governing nations and that may even view themselves as having a right to secede.[7] Yet this acceptance remains hesitant and somewhat reluctant, and there is no eagerness to enshrine it in international norms, let alone to attempt to impose it on countries in eastern Europe, where the idea of minority nationalism remains anathema. In eastern Europe, and indeed much of the world, demands for official language status for minorities are still resisted in part because the majority is unwilling to accept any language claims which could be seen as acknowledging the minority's 'nationhood', and/or as opening up the door to broader nationalist claims for territorial autonomy and secession.

In short, language conflicts are inextricably related to nationalist conflicts, and so addressing issues of linguistic diversity is central to the larger political project of 'containing nationalism' (Hechter 2000). The link between nationhood and language is complex.[8] Having a distinct language is clearly not a necessary condition for a group to view itself as a distinct nation (for example, nationalist conflict in Northern Ireland or Serbia). And even where a regional group does ground its distinct national identity on a distinct language, it is not always clear how the two are related. National groups often demand self-government on the grounds that it is needed to protect their language and culture. Yet some commentators argue that the causal relationship goes in the other direction: that is, national minorities do not seek self-government in order to preserve their language but rather they want to preserve their distinct language as one of the conditions necessary for the successful exercise of rights to self-government (for example, Bauböck 2000: 384–6; 2001: 332–5). In either case, however, the practical challenge of defusing nationalist conflicts must grapple with the issue of linguistic diversity.

So far, we have discussed two practical challenges—assisting democratization and dealing with regional minority nationalisms—and suggested that linguistic diversity has emerged as a central issue for each. In a way, this should not be a surprise: the role of language in these issues is quite evident. The interesting question is why it has taken so long for people to recognize the centrality of language to these debates.

There are undoubtedly several factors at work here, but part of the answer may be that neither of these issues has directly affected the day-to-day lives of the four Western countries that have been most powerful and influential in

---

Arguably, Switzerland is a more successful example of a state that has used a form of official multilingualism to foster and reinforce a common sense of nationhood.

[7] For a discussion of the striking level of tolerance for secessionist political mobilization in the West, and how this relates to larger patterns of acceptance for minority nationalism, see Kymlicka (2002).

[8] For recent discussion, see Barbour and Carmichael (2000) and Taras (1998).

setting the post-war intellectual agenda: the US, UK, France, and Germany. Public institutions in all four of these countries have effectively been monolingual for a century or more, with no significant movement challenging the hegemonic position of the majority language. France and the US both contain a linguistically distinct regional nationalist movement—in Corsica and Puerto Rico, respectively—but these islands are peripheral, literally and figuratively, to the political life of the country, barely registering in the everyday political consciousness of most French or American citizens. And while the UK confronts significant cases of minority nationalism in Scotland, Wales, and Northern Ireland, these are not primarily rooted in linguistic differences.[9] None of these countries faces the sort of linguistic/national divisions found in Canada, Spain, Switzerland, or Belgium, not to mention Russia or Yugoslavia.

As a result, scholars from these four countries have often written as if one could simply take for granted that people in a political community share a common language. They have often written as if this were the 'normal' or 'natural' condition for a 'mature' democratic political community. Not surprisingly, much of the initial literature on language rights emerged from countries where this assumption could not be made.

Yet even in the countries where the majority language retains a more or less undisputed hegemonic position, two recent political developments have heightened interest in linguistic diversity. The first concerns trends in immigrant integration; the second concerns attempts to build transnational institutions.

3. *Immigrant integration*. Many Western countries now contain large numbers of immigrants. This is nothing new for the traditional 'countries of immigration', like the US, Canada, and Australia, but is a more recent phenomenon for 'Old World' countries like the UK, France, or Germany. Unlike the case of regionally concentrated and historically rooted national minorities, immigrant groups are unlikely to demand either territorial self-government or official language status. It is assumed that immigrants will learn the dominant language of their new country, and indeed this is a requirement to gain citizenship in almost all Western countries. Immigrants know before they arrive that the public institutions of their new society operate in a particular language, and do not generally seek to challenge that, except in very specific contexts and often only on a transitional basis.

Since this expectation of linguistic integration has been widely shared both by native-born citizens and immigrants themselves, it has not historically been a source of major conflict. Some immigrants pass on their mother tongue to their children, and use it in their home and church, but these children rarely pass the language on to their own children, so that the ancestral language is lost by the third generation. This pattern of immigrant language shift has become so

---

[9] Welsh nationalists are concerned with reviving the use of Welsh, but English remains the dominant language of interaction amongst the Welsh, as amongst the Scots and Irish republicans.

familiar and expected that, until recently, many people assumed that it was almost inevitable.

However, several recent trends in immigration are questioning this historic pattern. One of these is the rise of immigrant 'transnationalism', that is, the tendency of immigrants to maintain regular connections back to their country of origin, aided by improved transportation and communications technologies.[10] Another is the rise of the ideology of 'multiculturalism', that is, the idea that immigrants should not have to abandon or hide their ethnic identity in order to integrate, as in older models of assimilation or 'Americanization', but rather should be able to visibly and proudly express their ethnic identity in public, and have public institutions accommodate this.[11] These two changes, combined with the sheer size of certain immigrant groups, have led some people to fear that the old patterns of language shift will no longer occur. This has led to speculation about the growth of permanent immigrant 'enclaves' or 'ghettos', where even the second and third generations of immigrant groups will live and work predominantly in their ancestral language, with only a minimal or non-existent command of the state language. The potential for such self-segregated enclaves is seen as both a problem for the immigrants themselves, whose lack of fluency in the dominant language condemns them to political marginalization and economic disadvantage, and potentially a threat to the larger society, since learning the dominant language is often seen as vital for establishing a sense of patriotism and loyalty to the larger society. If the traditional patterns of immigrant language shift break down, national unity and political stability may ultimately be threatened.[12]

Since immigrant language shift is no longer assumed to be natural or inevitable, many commentators argue that it needs to be buttressed by new state policies aimed at encouraging or compelling language shift. This is one of the impetuses behind the 'English-only' movement in the United States, which has waged a campaign to remove a number of entitlements previously enjoyed by linguistic minorities and to declare English the official language of the country (Schmidt 2000; Crawford 2001). It is also reflected in more moderate proposals to strengthen the language tests for naturalization (Pickus 1998; Piller 2001), and/or to provide greater government support for language learning (Bloemraad 2002), and/or reforms to programmes of transitional bilingual education for immigrant children. Similar proposals have surfaced in Western Europe, where difficulties in immigrant integration are often blamed on the inability or unwillingness of immigrants to learn the state language. In some

---

[10] On immigrant transnationalism, see Ong (1999), Basch, Glick Schiller, and Szanton Blanc (1994), and Castles (2000).

[11] On immigrant multiculturalism in the US, see Glazer (1997); in Canada, see Kymlicka (1998).

[12] For feverish speculations along these lines, see Schlesinger (1992), Lind (1996), and Brimelow (1996).

European countries, there is even talk about legally requiring immigrants to attend language classes as a precondition for access to social benefits.

Critics argue that such policies are illiberal and a return to discredited assimilationist policies. Others argue that they are unnecessary, since the traditional intergenerational patterns of language shift remain valid (Portes and Rumbaut 2001). The very passion of the debate confirms, however, that language now occupies a central place in the larger debate on immigrant integration. It is widely accepted that any response to the practical challenge of integrating immigrants must include an explicit focus on issues of language.

4. *European union/transnational democracy*. The centrality of language has also surfaced in another important context, namely, attempts to construct transnational political communities such as the European Union. The European Union is often cited by commentators as a model for new forms of transnational democracy and post-national citizenship that will gradually replace the old Westphalian model of the nation-state. It is difficult to dispute the need for such transnational political institutions, given the number of problems that transcend national boundaries and require international coordination and regulation: for example, environmental issues; international security; refugees.[13]

Yet it has become increasingly clear that one of the most important obstacles to building a stronger sense of European citizenship is linguistic diversity. The EU has been widely criticized for its 'democratic deficit', and studies show that the general public in most European countries feel little sense of connection to the European Parliament. Attempts to encourage greater public identification with and participation in pan-European political institutions have not yet found a solution to the problem of linguistic diversity.

There are really two different problems here. One concerns the vertical linkage between individual citizens and the EU itself. It is impossible for the institutions of the EU to conduct all aspects of their business in every language spoken by EU citizens.[14] It would be prohibitively expensive for the EU to provide interpretation services for every meeting amongst civil servants or for it to translate every internal memo or briefing paper into all of the languages spoken by EU citizens or even into the eleven official languages recognized by the EU. Instead, the EU has gradually come to distinguish between external and internal aspects of communication. The external dimension involves communication with ordinary citizens or amongst ministers or heads of government. In these contexts, people have a right to use any of the eleven official EU languages. In the internal workings of the Commission, however, officials work in a small number of languages—French,

---

[13] For discussions of the desirability/necessity of constructing transnational forms of democracy, see Held (1995) and Young (2000: Ch. 7). For the EU as a model or harbinger of transnational democracy, and its democratic deficit, see Lehning and Weale (1997), Nentwich and Weale (1998), and Schmitter (2000).

[14] For an up-to-date discussion of European language policy, see Nic Shuibhne (2002).

English, and, to a lesser extent, German—and everyone is expected to be proficient in one or several of these languages. In a few areas, such as the new European Patent Office, a smaller number of languages is designated for external communication, and in almost no area of EU activity are accommodations made for the regional and minority languages of member states.[15] But not all EU citizens are fluent in one of the official or working languages, and even if they are they may prefer to identify and interact with domestic political institutions that can communicate with them in their own language.

The second problem concerns the horizontal linkage between citizens themselves. Democratizing the EU presupposes that citizens throughout Europe can form a single 'demos', that is, that they can deliberate and act together as a single political community, whose decisions would reflect 'the will of the people' or 'popular opinion'. Yet it is very difficult to imagine how this sort of collective deliberation, agency, and will-formation can occur at a pan-European level. How can Danes and Italians come together to deliberate about the issues confronting the EU? Not only do they not share a common language, they do not read the same newspapers or watch the same TV news programmes. While there is a growing elite that can participate effectively at the pan-European level, the only forms of political participation and deliberation that are truly popular (that is, easily accessible to the mass of citizens) remain specific to each country, conducted in the national language(s). Put another way, politics seems to be most participatory and democratic when it is 'politics in the vernacular', conducted in the language of the people (Kymlicka 2001a). In short, any response to the practical challenge of building new forms of transnational democracy must grapple with the issue of linguistic diversity.

5. *Indigenous languages/biodiversity.* Finally, public awareness of language issues has also been heightened by recent studies predicting the rapid disappearance of most of the world's languages—up to 90 per cent of the world's languages are now considered 'endangered' (Nettle and Romaine 2000; Crystal 2000). Most of these threatened languages are indigenous languages, and concern for their disappearance is related to larger trends towards rethinking the rights and status of indigenous peoples. Such staggering rates of linguistic loss are also seen as a symbol of the more general crisis of biodiversity, since indigenous languages are seen as containing within them a wealth of ecological information that will be lost as the language is lost. Saving endangered languages is now widely seen as an important part of the larger challenge of preserving biodiversity.

Given these various practical challenges, it was perhaps inevitable that political theorists would be called upon or inspired to take up the challenge of developing a normative theory of language rights. But there are also reasons

---

[15] The priority given to 'state' languages is particularly galling to Catalan speakers, who outnumber speakers of Danish and Finnish.

internal to the discipline of political theory that have spurred interest in the topic. A concern with language rights can be seen as a natural outgrowth of some of the larger debates that have preoccupied political theorists over the last two decades. We will briefly mention two such debates, relating to ideas of multicultural citizenship and deliberative democracy.

The first debate, over multicultural models of citizenship, can be seen as one of the successors to the liberal-communitarian debate that dominated the field in the 1980s. This earlier debate is too complex to summarize here, but for our purposes it can be seen as raising two sets of issues. One concerns the relationship between the individual and the community, as liberals defended the rights and freedoms of the individual against the encroachment of society, and communitarians defended the integrity and cohesiveness of society against the unrestricted choices of individuals. A second set of issues concerns the relationship between universalism and particularism, as liberals defended universal principles of freedom and equality, whereas communitarians insisted that morality was always local and tied to shared cultural meanings.

Much of the work in political theory in the last 20 years can be understood as attempting to break down these stark dichotomies between individual/community and universalism/particularism. One strategy, popular amongst both liberals and communitarians, is to argue that, even if we start with liberal assumptions about the universal value of individual freedom and democracy, these values can in fact be upheld only if they are embodied within the institutions and traditions of particular political communities, which in turn can be upheld only if citizens have a strong sense of identification with and membership in these particular communities. The health of a liberal democracy requires not only that citizens believe in certain universal values—for example, the Universal Declaration of Human Rights—but also that they feel a sense of identification with, loyalty to, and membership in a particular national political community. Citizens must feel that they belong together in a single polity, must have the desire to deliberate and act together as a self-governing community, and must be willing to accept special responsibilities for co-citizens that go beyond the responsibilities we have for all human beings around the world. In all of these ways, universal liberal values depend on particularistic feelings of political identity and community membership.

This insight has generated a vast array of new ideas in the political theory literature in the 1990s, including theories of liberal nationalism (Tamir 1993; Miller 1995; Canovan 1996), civic republicanism (Oldfield 1990; Skinner 1998), patriotism (Blattberg 2000; Viroli 1995; Habermas 1995), and civic virtue (Galston 1991; Glendon and Blenkenhorn 1995). There are significant differences amongst these various authors and schools of thought, but they share the concern that democracy presupposes certain kinds of communal identities amongst citizens. Citizenship identities are seen as a bridge between the universal values of freedom and democracy endorsed by liberals and the particularistic values of community and culture endorsed by communitarians. And, for most writers, it is assumed that the sort of community citizens should identify with is, in the first instance, the *national* political community.[16]

Yet this recognition of the importance of citizenship and civic identities was complicated by the simultaneous awareness that traditional models of citizenship were hopelessly inadequate for the context of modern pluralistic societies. Traditional conceptions of citizenship, inherited from ancient Rome or Renaissance city-states, were defined to suit a narrow group of white, heterosexual, Christian, property-owning males. Critics from a range of perspectives— feminist, postmodernist, post-colonial, critical race studies, and others—have demonstrated the need to dramatically reform our idea of citizenship if it is to accommodate the identities, aspirations, and capacities of all citizens. This has spurred the ongoing quest to develop new 'multicultural' or 'group-differentiated' models of citizenship, including the ideas of 'strange multiplicity', 'ethos of pluralization', and 'politics of recognition' that we mentioned at the beginning of our introduction.[17]

This search for a model of citizenship that can build common civic identities, while simultaneously affirming cultural diversity, has been one of the central goals of political theory in the last decade. The resulting literature has worked out with considerable sophistication the connections between the underlying principles of liberal democracy and the various ways in which public institutions can respond to differences of culture and nationality.[18] And yet, until very recently, the specific issue of linguistic diversity was rarely explored in depth. Some of the concepts that figure prominently in these discussions are clearly relevant to debates about language policy, and language is often referred to as an example. But there have been relatively few attempts to apply systematically the insights from these theories to specific controversies over language or to formulate the theories in ways that take into account particular facts and social theories relating to language acquisition, language use, and language shift. The existing body of normative work on citizenship and cultural diversity has not engaged extensively with country-specific studies of language policy (for example, McRae 1983; 1986; 1997; Coulombe 1995; Levine 1997; MacMillan 1998; Schmidt 2000; Grillo 1989) or with contemporary work in sociolinguistics (Fishman 1991; Edwards 1985; Phillipson 1992; Nettle and Romaine 2000; May 2001) or with comparative political science (Laponce 1984; Laitin 1992; 1998).

[16]  This in turn has led to growing interest amongst political theorists in the sort of citizenship education that might inculcate the desired identities (Callan 1997; Macedo 2000; Feinberg 1998; Reich 2002).

[17]  For 'multicultural citizenship' and 'group-differentiated citizenship', see Kymlicka (1995a) and Young (1990) respectively. For 'strange multiplicity', 'ethos of pluralization', and 'politics of recognition', see Tully (1995), Connolly (1995), and Taylor (1992) respectively.

[18]  In addition to the works cited in note 14, see also Tamir (1993), Spinner (1994), Miller (1995), Carens (2000), Barry (2001), and Kymlicka (2001a).

Yet it is increasingly clear that linguistic diversity is central to any larger theory of multicultural citizenship. Language plays a complicated role with respect to the building of civic identities. On the one hand, linguistic homogenization has been one of the central mechanisms that states have used to inculcate a common civic identity within diverse societies. Indeed, a common language can be seen as a uniquely appropriate basis for building common civic identities. In a liberal society, the state cannot ground a common civic identity in a particular religion or way of life: this would violate what Rawls calls 'the fact of reasonable pluralism', according to which citizens in a free society will inevitably have different and often competing conceptions of the good life. But nor can the state hope to ground a common civic identity in purely universal values of freedom or democracy, since these values do not explain why citizens should feel any particular sense of attachment to one liberal-democratic country rather than any other. Promoting a common language is sometimes seen as a way out of this conundrum: it helps to unite people into a single political community without imposing a particular conception of the good life. A common national language helps to promote a common civic identity without denying the 'fact of reasonable pluralism' or the liberal commitment to neutrality regarding conceptions of the good life.

On the other hand, as we discussed earlier, such attempts to impose a common state language can often generate intense resistance, particularly where they involve depriving a regionally concentrated and historically rooted language group of its traditional rights to maintain public institutions operating in their own language. In such contexts, policies of linguistic homogenization can be a recipe for nationalist conflict. Even in contexts of immigration, where there may be little explicit challenge to the principle of long-term linguistic integration, there can nonetheless be divisive debates about the relationship between language and civic identity. Excessive emphasis on language as the key to civic identity and community membership can be seen as a manifestation of nativism or as a return to old-fashioned cultural assimilation. Immigrants may fear that expectations of linguistic integration are a code for, or prelude to, expectations that they give up their cultural practices and ethnic identities more generally. Assumptions about a common language may also be insensitive to the distinctive needs of recent immigrants, for whom fluency in the state language is often a long-term goal but not yet a present reality. In all of these ways, language is a central but contested element in any theory of civic identity.

Issues of language have also arisen within political theory for another reason. There has been an important shift in contemporary democratic theory from 'vote-centric' to 'talk-centric' theories of democracy. In much of the post-war period, democracy was understood almost exclusively in terms of voting. Citizens were assumed to have a set of preferences, fixed prior to and independent of the political process, and the function of voting was simply to provide a fair decision-making procedure or aggregation mechanism for translating these pre-existing preferences into public decisions, either about who to elect (in standard elections) or about what laws to adopt (in issue-specific referendums).

But it is increasingly accepted that this 'aggregative' or 'vote-centric' conception of democracy cannot fulfil norms of democratic legitimacy. For one thing, since preferences are assumed to be formed independently of and prior to the political process, it provides no opportunity for citizens to try to persuade others of the merits of their views or the legitimacy of their claims. Similarly, it provides no opportunity for citizens to distinguish claims based on self-interest, prejudice, ignorance, or fleeting whims from those grounded in principles of justice or fundamental needs. There is in fact no public dimension to the process at all. While citizens may need to physically leave their homes to go to the ballot box, the aggregative vote-centric model does not expect or encourage citizens to meet in public to discuss and debate their reasons for the claims they make. Indeed, with new technology, it is quite possible to have a form of aggregative democracy in which citizens never leave their home, and vote through the Internet.

As a result, the outcome of the aggregative model has only the thinnest veneer of legitimacy. It provides a mechanism for determining winners and losers, but no mechanism for developing a consensus or shaping public opinion, or even formulating an honourable compromise. Many studies have shown that citizens will accept the legitimacy of collective decisions that go against them, but only if they think their arguments and reasons have been given a fair hearing and that others have taken seriously what they have to say. But if there is no room for such a fair hearing, then people will question the legitimacy of decisions.

To overcome these shortcomings of the vote-centric approach, democratic theorists are increasingly focusing on the processes of deliberation and opinion-formation that precede voting. Theorists have shifted their attention from what goes on in the voting booth to what goes on in the public deliberations of civil society. Dryzek (2000: v) calls this the 'deliberative turn' in democratic theory, which he dates to around 1990.[19] A more deliberative democracy would, it is hoped, bring several benefits. The benefits for society would include better decisions, since the decision-making process would draw forth the otherwise

---

[19] For discussions of this shift from an 'aggregative' to a 'deliberative' conception of democracy, see Young (2000: Ch. 1), Dryzek (1990: Ch. 1), Christiano (1996: 133–50), Cohen (1997: 143–55), Miller (2000: Ch. 1), and Phillips (2000). Not everyone uses the labels of 'aggregative' and 'deliberative' democracy to describe these two models. Dryzek and Young object to the term 'deliberative' democracy, since they think it suggests an overly rationalist picture of the nature of political communication. Dryzek prefers the term 'discursive democracy', and Young prefers the term 'communicative democracy'. They are, however, equally committed to the 'talk centric' conception of democracy. The older aggregative model is also sometimes known, particularly within American political science, as the 'pluralist' model—a term which dates back to the 1950s. This is potentially misleading today, since the sort of 'pluralism' it refers to concerns organized interest groups, not the identity-groups which underlie contemporary debates about 'pluralism'. For different senses of pluralism, see Eisenberg (1995).

unarticulated knowledge and insights of citizens, and since citizens would test and discard those assumptions or beliefs which were found in public debate to be wrong or short-sighted or otherwise indefensible. It would also lead to greater unity and solidarity in society. For one thing, political decision making would be seen as more legitimate since everyone would have a fair chance to have their views heard and considered. Moreover, the very fact that people share the experience of deliberating in common provides a tangible bond that connects citizens and encourages greater mutual understanding and empathy. In a deliberative democracy, we would seek to change other people's behaviour through non-coercive discussion of their claims rather than through manipulation, indoctrination, propaganda, deception, or threats. This is a sign of mutual respect (Dryzek 2000: 2) or indeed of civic friendship (Blattberg 2000).

So 'deliberative democracy' promises benefits to the larger society. But it offers particular benefits to minority or marginalized groups. If such groups are to have any real influence in a majoritarian electoral system, and any reason to accept the legitimacy of the system, it will be through participating in the formation of public opinion rather than through winning a majority vote. As Simone Chambers (2001: 99) puts it, 'voice, rather than votes, is the vehicle of empowerment'. This seems clear from the recent advances made by groups such as gays and lesbians, the deaf, or indigenous peoples, who account for less than 5 per cent of the overall electorate. Their empowerment has largely come about through participating in a public debate that has transformed the pre-existing assumptions held by members of the larger society about what is right and fair for these groups. If democracy is to help promote justice for these groups rather than leaving them subject to the 'tyranny of the majority' (or the indifference and neglect of the majority), then democracy will have to be more deliberative. As a result, a wide range of theorists—liberals, communitarians, critical theorists, feminists, multiculturalists—have identified the need for greater deliberation as one of the key priorities for modern democracies.[20]

Much more could be said about this new deliberative model of democracy. The key point for us, however, is that this shift to a deliberative model of democracy makes the issue of language even more central and also more contested. On the one hand, these attractive models of deliberative democracy all seem to presuppose that people share a common language. Virtually all existing models of deliberative democracy simply take for granted that everyone shares a common language. Establishing a common language of public debate, therefore, can be seen as one of the preconditions for the sort of inclusive and justice-promoting democracy we seek.

[20] For liberals, see Rawls (1999: 574), Dworkin (2000: 364–5), and Gutmann and Thompson (1996); for communitarians, see Sandel (1996); for critical theorists, see Habermas (1996) and Chambers (1996); for feminists, see Fraser (1992) and Phillips (1995: 145–65); for multiculturalists, see Williams (1998; 2000) and Young (2000).

On the other hand, the very process of selecting a single language can be seen as inherently exclusionary and unjust. Where political debate is conducted in the language of the majority group, linguistic minorities are at a disadvantage, and must either invest the time and effort needed to shift as best they can to the dominant language or accept political marginalization. Dominant groups often express puzzlement at the reluctance of some minorities to shift to the dominant language, but, as we noted earlier, the experience of the EU shows that dominant groups exhibit the very same reluctance. They would prefer to continue debating politics in their own national language rather than participate in a pan-European debate conducted in a foreign language. Indeed, the hope of achieving a common language seems quite utopian in such transnational contexts. The issue of whether and when language shift can legitimately be expected or required in order to promote a more deliberative democracy remains unresolved. Here again, there is growing recognition that any plausible theory of deliberative democracy has to grapple with issues of linguistic diversity.

So a confluence of theoretical developments has pointed political theorists in the direction of linguistic diversity. Political theory journals in recent years have been dominated by theories of citizenship, nationhood, multiculturalism, and deliberative democracy. As these theories have evolved, it has become increasingly clear that all of them rest on—often implicit—presuppositions about people's language repertoires, and all have—often unstated—consequences for language policy and language rights. Further progress on these theories requires excavating these implicit presuppositions about language repertoires, and clarifying and evaluating their unstated consequences for language policies.

## 2. The Issues

Disputes over language policy are connected then with some of the big theoretical questions of the day and with important macro developments in politics and society. Some theorists examine language as a way of enriching our understanding of larger theories of citizenship and democracy. For others it is a way into the study of ethnonationalism, globalization, democratization, and other broad phenomena that have captured the attention of the academy and the general public.

At the same time, language policy has a very concrete dimension pertaining to day-to-day communication in a range of different areas of social life. Conflicts over language policy are concerned with the rules that public institutions adopt with respect to language use in a variety of different domains. What language or languages do public officials have a right or duty to use in speaking amongst themselves or with the publics that they serve? Should a person's linguistic status or competences influence what other entitlements he or she can claim? Should public institutions get involved in regulating or directing linguistic behaviour in the private realms of the market, family, and civil society?

The answers that one gives to these questions are a reflection, of course, of one's understanding of the broader issues at stake, and so we have sought to foreground these concerns and will return to them again as the chapter progresses. But it would be a mistake to consider language solely from an abstract theoretical and macro-political perspective and to ignore the fine-grained issues and distinctions that are often central to real-world language disputes. In this section and the next, we try to give a sense of some of these concrete issues and distinctions by, first, surveying a number of different domains in which language policy choices get made and, then, introducing the idea of 'language rights' and considering four key distinctions that are helpful in theorizing different possible language rights regimes.

## Internal Usage

Public institutions are sites of constant communication amongst employees and officials. Managers give instructions to their subordinates. Civil servants hold meetings together, write memos to one another, and keep records. Police, fire, and ambulance officials work in teams and take orders from their superior officers. And so on. Public institutions would not be able to do the jobs we expect of them unless the employees and officials that staff them are able to communicate effectively with one another.

This need for effective internal communication raises important questions for language policy. Should public institutions adopt a policy of 'laissez-faire' concerning internal language usage—allowing different employees and officials to work out for themselves, in the particular contexts they find themselves in, the language they will use to communicate with one another? Or should such institutions adopt a more prescriptive approach—for instance, insisting through hiring and promotion criteria that employees have certain language competences, or mandating the use of particular languages in internal communications and record-keeping? Given that the government is one of the largest employers in modern societies, these decisions have a significant impact on individual employment opportunities.

It is hard to think of any state that is completely laissez-faire on these questions. Most states require, as a minimum, that their public employees and officials be competent in some state or official language, whether it be formally or informally designated as such. In the United States, for example, although there is no formally designated official language at the federal level, it is a de facto requirement for employment in the federal public sector that the applicant speak English. Although the European Union recognizes eleven 'official and working' languages, only three of these—French, English, and, trailing well behind, German—are de facto languages of internal communication within the Commission (Kraus 2000).

Some governments go even further in explicitly designating some particular language or languages for internal communications. The 1991 Law on the Languages of the Peoples of the Russian Federation (arts. 3.1 and 11.1) requires that all work by federal government bodies be carried out in Russian. Estonia's 1995 Languages Act (art. 3.1), Catalonia's Act No.1 on Language Policy of 7 January 1998 (Ch. 1, arts. 9 and 10), and the 1994 Constitution of The Federal Democratic Republic of Ethiopia (art. 5) have similar requirements with respect to Estonian, Catalan, and Amharic respectively.[21] Canada's Official Languages Act (1969; 1988) gives employees of federal government institutions the right (subject to certain qualifications) to work in either English or French, and Belgium has similar provisions facilitating linguistic diversity within the central administration, often setting up parallel French- and Dutch-language sections of the same office (McRae 1986: 189–202).

## Public Services

Public officials and employees do not communicate only amongst themselves, of course; they also deal with the public. They give advice and information; they enforce the law; they offer health care in public facilities; they conduct public meetings and hearings; and so on.

A second kind of language policy decision that must be faced, then, concerns what language or languages public institutions should operate in when they are serving the general public. These decisions can have dramatic effects on a person's access to public services and social rights. The editors of a recent volume on 'linguistic human rights' describe several situations in which public authorities refused, or were unable, to communicate with members of the general public in their own language (Skutnabb-Kangas and Phillipson 1994: 19). They recount the story of a Finnish immigrant who committed suicide in a Swedish hospital after the non-Finnish-speaking staff were unable to understand him when he sought to explain his symptoms. And they tell the story of a school class of Sámi speakers in Norway who wrote a letter in their own language to the local police requesting permission to organize a bazaar, only to have the letter returned with a note saying that it should have been written in Norwegian.

Should the public authorities have been able to deal with the public they serve in their own languages in these cases? Given the particular facts of these cases— the proximity of Finland to Sweden, the fact that 90 per cent of the population of the municipality in question were Sámi-speaking—it is tempting to say 'yes'. But how far should this obligation to accommodate linguistic diversity in the provision of public services extend? Does it extend to *any* possible language that hospital patients might speak or that members of the public might use in

---

[21] The Russian, Estonian, and Ethiopian laws include provisions for the use of other languages in local or regional administration.

correspondence with the police? And does such an obligation require that the health service, or police, employ members of staff who can themselves provide the service in the minority language, or would it be enough for them to have interpreters and translators on hand who can ensure adequate communication where necessary?

Assuming that there is no obligation to provide a full set of services in *every* language that members of the public might speak, how should a public authority decide when to make services accessible to speakers of some particular language? Do the numbers count? Does it matter whether the language in question is that of an immigrant group or of an established 'national' or indigenous group? Are certain facts about the language itself ever relevant—for instance, whether it is a language of wider (international) communication, or whether it could reasonably be considered a dialect of some other language that is recognized in the provision of public services? Would Norwegian public authorities have the same obligations towards Finnish- or Sámi-speakers if those individuals could also speak Norwegian?

Not surprisingly, different countries and public authorities have approached this cluster of issues in a variety of ways. One approach, as we have already suggested in section 1, has been explicitly to designate certain 'official' languages and then to say that members of the public have a right, sometimes subject to a 'where numbers warrant' qualification, to receive public services and communications in those languages. Sometimes this right to communicate with public institutions in a particular language is enjoyed across the country (the 'personality principle') and sometimes it is restricted to specific territories of the country (the 'territoriality principle') (for more on these principles, see section 3 below).

A different approach is to designate some particular language as the normal language of public communication, but then to make specific accommodations for people who lack proficiency in that language. In the United States, for instance, English is the normal language in which federally funded public services are delivered. But an Executive Order signed by President Clinton on 11 August 2000 requires that all federally funded service providers make arrangements to provide effective service to people with limited English proficiency.[22] These arrangements may involve hiring bilingual staff who can provide the service in the recipient's own language, or arranging for translation services to facilitate the delivery of the service by an English-speaker.

## Courts and Legislatures

Courts and legislatures are bodies that meet in public and are subject to close public scrutiny. As with the internal deliberations of the bureaucracy, to a considerable extent the communication that takes place in these spheres is

---

[22] The Executive Order derives its authority from a section of the 1964 Civil Rights Act that prohibits discrimination in the provision of public services on the basis of 'national origin'.

amongst elites. But these institutions also interact with ordinary citizens (for example, litigants, individuals appearing at public hearings), they issue laws and decisions to the general public, and their formal deliberations are held in public. Decisions about language use in these areas can have significant effects on the ability of people to exercise their most basic rights, including rights of democratic participation (concerning the legislature) and the protection of their fundamental civil rights (concerning the courts).

The language policy issues raised in these spheres concern the freedom to use particular languages in these public bodies, the availability of translators to facilitate the use of particular languages, and the language(s) in which official versions of laws and judicial decisions are recorded. In some countries, legislators must speak in a designated official language of the state or in a language designated for use by the legislature's customary rules of procedure. Until recently in Spain, for instance, all deliberations in the national parliament were required to be held in Spanish. Now, use of Spain's three principal regional languages—Catalan, Basque, and Galician—is permitted, but only on one special day of the year.

In the US Congress, by contrast, legislators have the liberty to speak in any particular language of their choice but cannot expect their utterances to be translated into languages understood by other legislators or the general public.[23] In other jurisdictions, however, not only can legislators speak in a variety of different languages, but interpretation services are offered to facilitate their doing so and minutes and decisions recorded in any of these languages are considered equally official. At meetings of the European Union's Council of Ministers, for instance, ministers can speak in any of the eleven state languages of EU member states, and interpreters must manage 110 different translation pairs. The rules of procedure for the European Parliament go even further, allowing for simultaneous interpretation from one of the eleven official languages into a non-official language (European Parliament 1999: Ch. XVI).

A variety of approaches is also discernible in the area of language policy in the judicial process. Most jurisdictions will provide a translator for certain persons appearing before the court—for example, defendants, witnesses—who do not speak the usual language of the court. Some jurisdictions will allow litigants appearing before the court to choose which amongst several recognized languages to use and will provide translators to facilitate general understanding. In the European Court of Justice, the language of the case can be any of the eleven official European languages (or Irish), at the discretion of the applicant, and the Court maintains a staff of interpreters to facilitate general understanding. And in some countries, for instance in Canada, an accused person who speaks a designated official language has a right, not only to understand the charges against him and the court proceedings (something that could be ensured through an

---

[23] Thanks to Ronald Schmidt and James Crawford for correspondence about this point.

adequate translation service), but also to a trial that is substantially *in* his own language—that is, to a trial in which the judge and jury are able to understand his language and issue instructions in this language, where court transcripts are recorded in this language, and so on (*R. v. Beaulac*;[24] Réaume 2000). Moreover, these rights are not regarded as conditional on the accused person being unable to understand the usual language of the court. They require the court to accommodate his preference to use his own language even where he could quite comfortably use another.

## Education

Education is a particularly important area of language controversy around the world (Skutnabb-Kangas 2000; May 2001: Ch. 5; Porter 1996). Language policy choices in this area are relevant not just to the effective delivery of a public education but also to the future patterns of language use by the generations of children whose linguistic repertoires are shaped by the school system. Most of the controversies concern what the main language medium or media of public education should be, but increasingly there are also disputes about what additional languages should be taught as subjects in the public school curriculum. How these issues are resolved can profoundly shape not only the individual student's language skills but also the ability of linguistic groups to reproduce themselves over time.

Faced with a linguistically diverse student population, educational policy makers have a number of options with respect to the medium of instruction. They could, for instance, designate a single language as the main medium of public education and offer special immersion programmes for children who enter the school system with limited proficiency in this language. Alternatively, they could designate a single language of instruction but introduce a programme of transitional bilingualism for children with limited proficiency in this language. In such a programme, students take certain subjects in their home language while they are acquiring proficiency in the designated language, and then are eventually channelled into the mainstream system that operates in the designated language. Both of these approaches are quite common in the United States, although legislation and popular initiatives in some states, such as California's Proposition 227 (1998), have sought to limit the use of transitional bilingualism (Schmidt 2000; Crawford 2001).

Public education systems can go even farther than this in accommodating language diversity. A third option is what American educators call 'bilingual-bicultural maintenance' programmes (Young 1990: Ch. 6). These involve a concerted effort to use both the majority language—in the US case, English—and

---

[24] 1 S.C.R. 768.

the student's home language as a medium of instruction in different parts of the curriculum throughout the student's time in the public school system, or at least for some significant portion of it. A final option would be to establish parallel school systems for a variety of designated languages in which those languages would serve as the main medium of instruction (teaching the majority language as a second language subject for those students for whom it is not the medium of instruction).[25] As with other public services, any of these options could be offered on the basis of the personality principle (same options no matter where you are in the country) or the territoriality principle (the options made available depend on what region of the country you reside in).

A language policy for public education must not only decide which medium-of-instruction options to make available; it must indicate what degree of choice parents will be allowed with respect to those options. Is the normal expectation or requirement that parents send their children to the majority-language system except where limited proficiency in that language indicates that some special provision should be made? Or should parents be able to choose more liberally from amongst the various options that are offered? If parallel public education systems are set up in several designated languages, should all parents have the choice of which system to send their children to, or can access legitimately be restricted to members of the language group? For example, Quebec has established a publicly funded school system for the long-settled anglophone minority in the province, but immigrants are required to place their children in the French-language system (Levine 1990; Coulombe 1995; MacMillan 1998).

Second-language instruction has also become a major political issue in some jurisdictions, especially in multilingual countries such as Switzerland and Belgium. In the past, these countries privileged their national languages to teach as second-language subjects—that is, the Flemish in Belgium would learn French as a second language and the French would learn Dutch. Today, however, members of each language group would often prefer to learn English rather than the language of their co-citizens. As a result, Belgians now have greater access to the global economic and cultural resources made available by fluency in English, but have reduced access to the cultural and political life of their own co-citizens. A similar situation has arisen in Switzerland, where German-speakers would prefer to learn English rather than the French or Italian of their co-citizens, and vice versa. How should the goals of maximizing individual opportunity in a globalized economy be weighed against the goal of promoting mutual understanding within a particular country?

Issues can also arise about the timing of second-language teaching. In a jurisdiction such as Quebec, where French is regarded as vulnerable to pressures

---

[25] The separate-schools approach can be found, for instance, in a number of provinces in Canada and in Finland (where Swedish-speakers have access to their own schools in many areas (McRae 1997: 287)).

from English, is it legitimate to postpone the teaching of English as a second language to ensure that French is firmly established in the student's linguistic repertoire? Even in countries such as Sweden, where the majority language is relatively secure, there is a question about how much time and emphasis should be devoted to teaching in English. There is concern that Sweden's bilingual, Swedish-English school option might be hampering children—especially those with a home language other than Swedish—from fully mastering Swedish.

## Private Language Usage

So far our survey of language policy issues has focused on language use by and within public institutions. We have been concerned with the different kinds of language rules that might be adopted by bureaucracies, government-funded agencies and service-providers, courts, legislatures, public schools, and so on. A further set of policy questions arises with respect to language use away from the public sector. To what extent should the state regulate, or impose restrictions on, language use in various non-public settings—such as in the home or on the street, in the associations and activities of civil society, or in the business of private firms and corporations?

Most states regulate non-public language use to some degree. For example, it is standard for states to insist that products marketed by private firms have commercial packaging, warning labels, and so on, written in certain languages—typically, the official languages of the state or, if there is no official language, the language of the majority. It would be hard to argue that these regulations pose any threat to basic individual liberties, but they are not entirely uncontroversial. In the 1970s and 1980s, it was common for English-speaking Canadians to complain about 'bilingual cereal boxes' and, more recently, the European Court of Justice has considered whether linguistic packaging requirements amount to a non-tariff barrier in violation of the European Union's commitment to the free movement of goods.[26]

Historically, much more severe restrictions on private language use have not been uncommon. To take an extreme case, in Spain during the Inquisition, gypsies who were found guilty of speaking their own language had their tongues cut out (Laitin 1992: xi). In 1918, the state of Iowa sought to prohibit the speaking of languages other than English in public places, on the telephone, and on the railways (Kloss 1977: 52). These sorts of restrictions are now more or less unthinkable, but other significant restrictions can still be found. More recently in the United States, the 'disparate impact' provisions of the 1964 Civil Rights Act have been interpreted by the courts as limiting the right of private businesses to ban the use in the workplace of languages other than English—for

[26] *Hermann Josef Goerres*, Case C-385/96, Judgment of 14 July 1998; *Yannick Geffroy v. Casino France SNC*, Case C-366/98, Judgment of 12 September 2000.

example, in informal conversations amongst employees or during breaks (Schmidt 2000: 24–8). France's law no. 94-665 ('Loi Toubon') of 4 August 1994 makes the use of French compulsory in a number of spheres of language use—typically, with the right to use other languages as well—including formal communications between firms and their employees, commercial advertising, public signs, and materials circulated at meetings and conferences. Another French law, no. 94-88, of 1 February 1994 mandates that 40 per cent of all songs played on FM radio in France must be in French, and the Catalan language legislation of 1998 requires similar Catalan-language content quotas. Quebec's *Charte de la langue française* (1993 [1977], Title 1, Ch. 7, Sec. 58) not only mandates the use of French in a variety of contexts but goes one step further and restricts the presence of languages other than French on commercial signs—requiring, under the current law, that French have marked predominance in all such signs. And in certain cantons of Switzerland, the local authority prohibits the establishment of private schools in a language other than the designated language of the canton.

## Immigration, Naturalization, and Enlargement

Up to this point, the discussion has focused on the rules regarding language use that are applied with respect to a given group of people—the citizens and residents of the state—on a fixed territory—the territory of that state. Decisions about language policy also arise in thinking about admitting new people to the state or to citizenship and about enlarging the state (or political community) by incorporating new territories.

Countries that accept immigrants typically have certain criteria by which they judge particular applicants, such as family reunification, professional skills, and so on. To what degree should proficiency in some particular language be one of these criteria? In Canada, for instance, applicants for immigration are selected according to a point system that awards points for a variety of qualifications, including knowledge of one of Canada's official languages. Quebec, which operates its own immigration scheme, also has a points system, but awards more points for knowledge of French than for knowledge of English.

Once immigrants (and refugees) have taken up residence in a country, the question then arises whether they should be required to learn the majority or official language of their adopted country. Several countries, including Austria, are proposing to make attendance at language classes a legal requirement for newcomers (Fermin 2001; Bauböck 2003), and many states make language proficiency—for example, in an official language of the state, or in the majority language—a criterion, or even a necessary condition, for immigrants and refugees to be 'naturalized' to the status of citizen.

The incorporation of new territories into the state is less common than the admission and naturalization of immigrants but, when it is being considered, it too gives rise to questions about language. In the United States, for instance, decisions about state borders, or about when to admit territories as states, have been explicitly made with the aim of ensuring that there would be an anglophone majority (Kymlicka 1995a). Territories in the American south-west and Hawaii were offered statehood only when non-anglophones in those areas were outnumbered by English-speaking settlers and immigrants, and Puerto Rico's 'fitness' for statehood is often questioned on the grounds that it will never have an anglophone majority (Barreto 2001). Decisions about enlarging the European Union are also sensitive to linguistic issues. With eleven state languages already officially recognized by the EU, the question arises whether it would be legitimate to ask prospective new members to waive the right to have their languages recognized as well. A different aspect of the EU accession process is the requirement imposed on new members that they extend certain language rights to their own linguistic minorities (Nic Shuibhne 2002).

## Official Declarations

Official language declarations typically have both a substantive and a symbolic aspect. Substantively, they give people rights to government services in particular languages, to use certain languages in the courts, and so on. The substantive implications of such declarations can be analysed under the various headings surveyed above. But, even once all the substantive policy decisions have been settled, a residual symbolic question remains. Is it legitimate for a state or jurisdiction to make the explicit symbolic gesture of declaring some language or languages to be official? Although purely symbolic, these decisions can profoundly affect whether and how members of different groups identify with the state and/or their own linguistic group.

Some countries—for instance, the United States and Japan—have resisted the temptation of formally declaring their usual language of government business to be official. But elsewhere such declarations are relatively common. By 1999, 22 states of the United States had passed 'official English' declarations, many of which are purely symbolic in character (Schmidt 2000: 29). The EU has eleven official languages, and the South African Constitution of 1996 formally recognizes the same number. India officially recognizes Hindi and English but allows state legislatures to officially adopt other languages (so far 18 have been adopted). Switzerland has three official languages, plus a special status for a fourth; Belgium has two, plus a special status for a third; and Canada has two. A 1992 amendment to France's constitution declared French to be 'the language of the republic', and Italy is now considering a similar constitutional amendment. Spain has only one official language—Spanish (Castilian)—but allows other languages to be declared official by its autonomous communities.

## 3. Language Rights

In the previous section we have surveyed some of the kinds of issues that a language policy must address. As the discussion indicates, some of them can be framed as questions about 'language rights'. The question as to whether public services should be offered in some language X, for instance, is often analysed as a question about whether X-speakers should have a legal right to receive public services in their own language.

It is worth emphasizing that these two formulations are not identical, however, and that the questions about language policy are not exhausted by those concerning language rights. It is quite possible that a government office could adopt a policy of serving people in language X, of hiring only employees who are competent in X, and so on, without it being the case that X-speakers could be considered to have a right to X-language services or could take anyone to court if services were not provided in X. That said, the creation of legal rights or entitlements is one of the central ways in which language policy decisions about issues such as those listed above get shaped and implemented in practice. It is an obvious way for governments committed to the recognition of language minorities to bind their own officials and agencies to comply, and to make it difficult for future governments to reverse course in the future.

In view of the different language policy issues we have been surveying, it is possible to organize the various policy / rights options according to four distinctions:

(1) tolerance- vs promotion-oriented rights;
(2) norm-and-accommodation vs official-languages rights regimes;
(3) personality vs territoriality rights regimes; and
(4) individual vs collective rights.

Let us take a closer look at each of these pairings.

### *Tolerance- vs Promotion-Oriented Rights*

The distinction between tolerance-oriented and promotion-oriented language rights was introduced by Heinz Kloss (1971; 1977) and has become one of the most influential ways of approaching language rights in the literature. Tolerance rights are protections individuals have against government interference with their private language choices. Rights that permit individuals to speak whatever languages they like—free from government interference—in their homes, in the associations and institutions of civil society, in the workplace, and so on, are all examples of what Kloss means by tolerance rights. Promotion-oriented rights involve the use of a particular language by public institutions. They are rights that an individual might have to the public use of a particular language—in the courts, the legislature, the public school system, the delivery of public services, and so on. Many of the rights and policy areas discussed in the previous section seem to fall into Kloss's second category, except for the rights raised in the subsection on private language usage, which involve decisions about the degree of private linguistic autonomy that individuals should enjoy.

Kloss and others have invoked this distinction mainly as a tool for differentiating the claims of different kinds of language groups from one another. Kloss distinguishes, for instance, between 'immigrant' language groups and groups that have been present within a state for at least several generations and have maintained their language (roughly, what theorists today refer to as 'national' groups) (Kloss 1971: 259–62). In Kloss's view, immigrant languages should enjoy tolerance rights but not promotion rights. The state should not prevent immigrants from using their native languages in the home, in civil society, and so on, but nor should it accord immigrants the right to the use of their languages by public institutions and authorities. By contrast, national groups should, in Kloss's view, enjoy both tolerance and promotion rights.

It is clear from the discussion earlier that alternatives to Kloss's principle of assigning rights to different groups are possible as well. One could hold, as France for instance is sometimes said to, that only the language of the national majority should enjoy promotion rights, and that all other languages should be limited to tolerance rights. Whereas Kloss's principle locates the key distinction between immigrant and national groups, this second principle would locate it between the national majority's language and all other linguistic groups. Alternatively, one could claim that all languages, be they 'immigrant' or 'national', should, in principle, be eligible for both tolerance and promotion rights. Since it would be impossible to extend the full set of promotion rights to all linguistic groups, a proponent of this approach to assigning rights might then advocate denying promotion rights to certain languages on the basis of factors other than 'national' or 'immigrant' status—such as numbers, territorial concentration, suitability as a language of international communication, and so on. And, of course, as we saw earlier, there is nothing written in stone about the idea that all groups should enjoy even a full set of toleration rights. In a number of jurisdictions around the world, at least some restrictions on toleration rights are enforced.

## Norm-and-accommodation vs Official-languages Rights Regimes

As Ruth Rubio-Marín argues in her contribution to this volume, there is an important sense in which Kloss's distinction is too crude. Consider, for instance, the right of an accused person lacking proficiency in the usual language of the court to a court-appointed interpreter. This language right is clearly not a tolerance-oriented right as that term has just been defined. But nor is it clearly a promotion-oriented right either. There is no real attempt to promote the accused person's language; rather, the aim is to ensure that the accused can understand the court proceedings. Moreover, it is unlikely that Kloss would want to reserve this sort of right to national groups and deny it altogether to immigrants.

What is needed, this suggests, is a further distinction, this time between two different sorts of non-tolerance-oriented rights, or two different ways in which the speakers of particular languages can be accommodated in public situations. Our survey of some of the main language policy issues, and the ways in which actual states have responded to those issues, indicates a distinction along these lines between two approaches.

The first, which we call the 'norm-and-accommodation' approach, involves the predominance of some normal language of public communication—typically, the majority language of the jurisdiction concerned. Unless some special circumstance arises, this language is used in the courts and legislatures, in the delivery of public services, as the medium of public education, and so on. Special accommodations are then made for people who lack sufficient proficiency in this normal language. These accommodations could take a variety of different forms depending on the circumstances. They might involve the provision of interpreters, the hiring of bilingual staff, and the use of transitional bilingual and/or intensive immersion educational programmes to encourage rapid and effective acquisition of the normal language of public communication. The key priority is to establish communication between the public institution and citizens or residents with limited proficiency in the usual language of public business, so that the latter can access the rights and benefits to which they are entitled.

The other approach is to designate certain selected languages as 'official' and then to accord a series of rights to speakers of those languages. In contrast with the norm-and-accommodation approach, this approach typically involves a degree of equality between the different languages that are selected for official status. In a situation of perfect equality, any public service that could be received in one official language could also be received in the other; any piece of public business could be transacted in any of the official languages; laws, judgments, and records are kept in all the official languages and have the same legal status; and so on. Unlike the special accommodations offered under the norm-and-accommodation approach, the enjoyment of official language rights is not contingent on a lack of proficiency in the majority or usual language of the society. A person is free to exercise her official language rights in a minority language even if she is quite fluent in the majority language. In contrast with a norm-and-accommodation rights regime, then, an official-languages rights regime is not just about facilitating communication. There is a further 'non-instrumental' or 'intrinsic' goal or value—to use terminology proposed by Rubio-Marín and Réaume respectively in their chapters in this volume—that is being defended in the establishment of such a regime. This goal, as we suggested in section 1, is, in practice, often connected with a recognition of speakers of the language as constituting a distinct nation or people.

In practice, no state extends official status to every single language spoken on its territory. This means that the official-languages approach to dealing with linguistic diversity is typically supplemented by some application of the norm-and-accommodation approach for those languages not designated as official. The key policy divide, therefore, is between those jurisdictions that rely entirely on the norm-and-accommodation approach and those that deal with linguistic diversity, at least in part, through the recognition of certain official languages.

Of course, it is quite possible that a jurisdiction could refuse *any* accommodation to speakers of certain languages. A state could simply insist that certain public communications will take place in a given language and refuse to offer any translation or transitional assistance for those who lack proficiency in this language. As we will see below, this kind of attitude towards language minorities can involve grave injustice and is a circumstance in which it is sometimes appropriate to talk of the violation of 'linguistic human rights'.

## Personality vs Territoriality Rights Regimes

A third important distinction in thinking about the main language policy options is between the 'personality' and 'territoriality' principles of language rights (Royal Commission on Bilingualism and Biculturalism 1967; McRae 1975; Laponce 1984; and see the chapters by Réaume and Patten in this volume). The distinction is quite general, and there is no reason why it could not be applied to the norm-and-accommodation approach, but it is usually discussed in the context of official languages rights. The personality principle is the principle that citizens should enjoy the same set of (official) language rights no matter where they are in the country. The opposing principle, that language rights should vary from region to region according to local conditions, is generally labelled the 'territoriality principle'. On the first principle, language rights follow *persons* wherever in the state they may choose to live; on the second, they depend on what part of the *territory* of the state persons find themselves in. The territoriality principle typically (but not invariably—see the discussion of 'bilingual districts' by Patten in this volume) involves an attempt to divide a multilingual state into a series of unilingual regions, in which only the local majority language gets used in a variety of public contexts.

Canada is a good example of a country that follows—to a considerable degree—the personality principle. Federal government services are made available in either English or French anywhere in the country so long as numbers warrant, and parents have a right to send their children to public school in their own official language, again subject to the proviso that there be a minimum level of demand. Belgium and Switzerland, by contrast, are good examples of countries that follow the territoriality principle. With some exceptions and qualifications, the two main provinces of Belgium—Wallonia and Flanders—are unilingual in French and Dutch respectively, whereas the Brussels Capital area is officially bilingual. In Switzerland, most decisions pertaining to language are made at the cantonal level, and most cantons have opted to operate unilingually in the language of their own local majority.

### Individual vs Collective Rights

Further complicating any discussion of language rights are the various distinctions that get drawn between *individual* and *collective* language rights. One distinction associated with this vocabulary is between 'universal' and 'group-differentiated' rights. Universal rights are rights that everyone in the relevant jurisdiction has, irrespective of the particular language group to which they belong. Group-differentiated rights, by contrast, are rights that can be exercised only by members of designated language groups. In Quebec, for instance, the *Charte de la langue française* (Title I, Ch. 8) grants a universal right to a French-medium public education—any resident of Quebec can exercise this right—but a group-differentiated right to an English-medium public education—roughly, only children with at least one parent educated in English in Canada can exercise this right.

In other contexts, the individual / collective distinction centres on whether or not there must be some minimum demand for a service or accommodation if any particular individual is entitled to claim it as a right. According to this variant of the distinction, an individual language right is one that an individual can claim irrespective of the number of co-linguists residing in the state or jurisdiction that is relevant to the exercise of the right. A collective language right, by contrast, is one that is triggered only when some threshold level of demand for the service or accommodation is reached. In the United States, for example, the speakers of a language other than English have a right, under the Voting Rights Act, to a ballot printed in their language only if at least 10,000 voters in the same electoral district are speakers of that language (Schmidt 2000: 20–2). By contrast, a non-English-speaker has a right in court proceedings to a court-appointed translator no matter how many other speakers of his or her language live in the jurisdiction covered by the court. According to this version of the individual/collective distinction, then, the (bilingual ballot) voting right is a collective right and the (access to interpreters) judicial right an individual one.

By far the most common distinction tracked by the individual / collective vocabulary, however, focuses on who the bearer of the right is. Some rights are clearly held by individuals. It is the individual who exercises the right, and it is the individual's interests that are protected by the right and, indeed, that are considered sufficiently important, taken in isolation, to place others under the particular duties that are correlated with the right. Other rights are more naturally assigned, not to an individual, but to some group of individuals—for example, an ethnic, national, or linguistic group—or to a corporate body—such as a trade union, church, or business. These rights can be exercised only by some body or

official acting on behalf of the group, and they protect the accumulated interests of many individual members of the group or, on some accounts, the interests of the group as such (Réaume 1994).

Collective rights in this third sense of the term typically figure in discussions
of language policy when it is claimed that there is a right, enjoyed by particular
language groups, to 'linguistic security' (the right to the provision of certain
public arrangements that support the security and flourishing of a particular
language) or to 'linguistic survival' (the right that a language community survive over time) (Green 1987; Réaume 1991; 1994). These rights, if they exist,
would not be exercised by a single individual, nor would they be grounded in the
urgency of protecting the interests of some particular individual taken in isolation. Rather, they would be exercised by bodies and officials acting on behalf of
the group as a whole in order to protect the accumulated interests of all of the
group's members and/or the interests of the group as such.

It is often suggested that there is a fundamental opposition between individual and collective rights, but this is only partly true.[27] Individual rights do
place limits on the sorts of policies officials and public bodies can implement in
order to realize the goals associated with certain possible collective rights. If individual members of some minority language group have a right to public education in their own language medium, for instance, then this would conflict with an
attempt by the majority to protect a right to linguistic survival through a policy
of mandatory majority-language-medium education. Some collective rights do
not conflict with individual rights, however, but are instead respected *through* the
recognition of certain individual rights. According to one view of the group right
to linguistic security, for instance, respect for such a right is constituted by a policy that establishes certain (individual) rights for members of the group—for
instance, rights to public education in the group's language medium, or rights to
receive public services in the group's language, and so on.[28] Whether or not there
is a tension between individual and collective rights depends entirely on what
individual and collective rights people are said to possess.

Talk of a conflict between individual and collective rights is usually just an
awkward way of raising a set of basic normative questions about language
policy. How should the various policy issues that we have been discussing be
addressed? Which tolerance and promotion rights should be enjoyed by which
individuals, belonging to which language groups? Should a state endorse the
norm-and-accommodation approach or the official-languages approach? When
is a collective goal, such as group linguistic survival or security, sufficiently
important to entail that certain individual rights should or should not be
recognized? To address these kinds of questions, a closer look at some of the
normative principles underlying decisions about language policy is needed.

[27] For criticism of this position, see Kymlicka (1995*a*: especially 45–8).
[28] This is one way of reading Green (1987).

## 4. The Need for a Normative Theory of Language Rights

The chapters in this volume offer a wide range of approaches to these normative questions. Before we examine them, however, it might be useful briefly to
consider two approaches that seem superficially attractive, but that in the end
are not credible options.

1. *Benign neglect*. The first of these is the idea of 'benign neglect'.[29] Liberalism
as a political theory is sometimes associated with ideas such as 'minimal
government' and 'benign neglect'. Applied to disputes about language policy,
these ideas would seem to suggest that the state should refuse to do anything
that would encourage or discourage particular linguistic choices by its citizens.
Just as many liberals believe that disestablishment is the best response to religious
conflict, the same is true, it is sometimes said, for language. For those who hold
this view, the state should not recognize, endorse, or support any particular
language or language group any more than it should recognize, endorse, or
support a particular church or religion.

The normative issues underlying language rights start to become interesting
as soon as it is realized that this superficially attractive solution is incoherent. If
one thing is clear from the discussion in the two previous sections, it is that the
idea of linguistic disestablishment is an illusion. Although the state can avoid
regulating, or interfering with, the language choices people make away from
public institutions—it can respect a set of 'tolerance-oriented' rights—there is
no way for it to avoid taking a stand on a whole series of other language policy
issues (Pool 1991a: 496; Kymlicka 1995a: 111; Carens 2000: 77–8; Patten 2001:
693). Public services have to be offered in some language(s) or other, and the
same is true of public education. Because there is simply no way of disengaging
from language choices in these policy contexts, it is possible to talk of a 'fact of
linguistic establishment' (Bauböck 2001).

It might, in principle, be possible for the state to avoid general linguistic
policies regarding internal language use in government offices (government
employees could be left free to work it out for themselves on a case-by-
case basis), or language use in courts or legislatures (everyone could speak
in whatever language they wished). But, even if conceivable, these policies
would hardly be desirable. It is important that government employees
be able to communicate effectively with one another and that legislators and
litigants be able to understand and participate in the political and legal
proceedings they are involved in. Nobody would favour 'benign neglect' or
'minimal government' if it meant that air traffic controllers could not
understand one another or if it meant that defendants could not understand the
charges against them.

---

[29] For further discussion of this idea, see Kymlicka (1995a: 107–15).

Of course, a state can do without an 'official languages' policy if by this it is meant a formal declaration that a particular language or set of languages is to be regarded as official. As we mentioned earlier, there are well-known examples of countries, including the United States, that have declined to adopt such a policy. But no country, including the United States, can or should avoid having a language policy in the broader sense of taking a position on a range of the issues sketched in section 2 above. A state can also do without an 'official languages' policy—again the United States is an example—if this approach is understood in contrast with what we earlier called the 'norm-and-accommodation' approach. But the norm-and-accommodation approach—which involves establishing a usual language of public communication and then making specific transitional accommodations for those who lack proficiency in this language—comes no closer to 'minimum government' or 'benign neglect' than an official languages policy, and thus cannot be defended as more in tune with a supposed liberal commitment to these ideals. The idea of benign neglect, therefore, has a useful role to play in thinking about tolerance rights with respect to the private use of language, but cannot provide any sort of guidelines for thinking about language policy with respect to public institutions, which is the central issue confronting any normative theory of language rights.

2. *Linguistic human rights*. Once the naïve 'benign neglect' model is discarded, we are left with the challenge of identifying more promising normative approaches to language policy. One recently popular approach invokes the idea of 'linguistic human rights'. Human rights represent a widely, if not universally, accepted normative standard that has the great advantage of being partially integrated into international legal practice. If a particular regime of language rights could be shown to follow from, or be in some way 'integral' (de Varennes 1996; 2001) to human rights, then this would offer an impressive normative and political foundation for that regime.

This is an intuitively attractive approach, in part because it offers a universal standard that applies to all individuals, wherever they are. It thereby seems to avoid the arbitrariness of singling out particular groups or languages for official language status, or collective rights, or accommodation rights on the grounds of their numbers, history, or 'nationhood'.

One difficulty, however, is that existing human rights declarations in fact say very little about language rights.[30] Existing international standards set only minimal limits on domestic language policies. They primarily protect certain

---

[30] To be sure, human rights standards do place constraints on how certain language policy objectives are pursued by governments. Governments sometimes adopt as a goal the diffusion of a single language across the whole of the state (we discuss this 'nation-building' approach to language policy in the next section). As Weinstock and Levy mention in their contributions to this volume, historically governments have often pursued this objective with methods that clearly violate human rights standards and/or standards that would be widely considered to be part of a minimally liberal or

tolerance rights, that is, the right of members of linguistic minorities to publish their own magazines, or to establish their own private schools, or to form their own cultural organizations, and the right not to be discriminated against on the basis of one's mother-tongue. These rights can be seen as part and parcel of traditional individual rights to freedom of speech, freedom of the press, freedom of association, and non-discrimination. For example, the Universal Declaration of Human Rights (United Nations 1948) recognizes rights to freedom of expression (art. 19), to a fair trial (art.10), and not to be 'subjected to arbitrary interference with ... privacy, family, home or correspondence' (art. 12). These rights arguably entail language rights such as the right to publish books and newspapers in one's own language, the right to a court-appointed interpreter in certain circumstances, and the right to assign one's child a personal name associated with one's own language.

International declarations are far less clear on the extent of promotion rights: for example, the right to public funding of minority language schools or of minority language radio/TV, or the right to use one's language in dealing with public officials, or the right to have judicial proceedings in one's language or to receive government documents in one's language, or the right to official language status. Yet it is precisely these promotion rights which are at the heart of most language conflicts around the world.

As a result, existing international norms are clearly inadequate to resolve most of the disputes discussed in this volume. Some commentators have pushed to strengthen these international standards and/or to reinterpret them, so as to be more responsive to the demands of linguistic minorities. One version of this movement is the campaign for 'linguistic human rights' associated with some high-profile sociolinguists—for example, Skutnabb-Kangas and Phillipson (1994).

But it is doubtful that international law will ever be able to do more than specify the most minimal of standards. The members of various linguistic groups have quite different needs, desires, and capacities, depending on their size, territorial concentration, and historic roots. A set of guidelines that is

---

decent political order. Cutting out the tongues of Spanish gypsies is one clear example that we mentioned earlier. Or consider the English colonial practice of punishing children in Kenya for using a native language in the vicinity of the school: 'The culprit was given corporal punishment—three to five strokes of the cane on bare buttocks—or was made to carry a metal plate around the neck with the inscription: I AM STUPID or I AM A DONKEY' (Ngugi 1985, cited in Skutnabb-Kangas and Phillipson 1994: 19). By any reasonable standard, such a practice is humiliating, cruel, and grossly illiberal. Whatever the legitimate goals of language policy might be, they are not legitimately pursued by means of policies that violate basic rights to personal security and privacy, or that undermine the social bases of self-respect. It is not clear from the Kenyan example, however, whether a *language* right is at stake or not. Does our intuitive reaction to the example indicate that children have a right to speak their own language in the vicinity of the schoolyard (this would be a language right) or, rather, that the government should not pursue a policy of this kind through such cruel and humiliating methods (there would be an important right indicated here, but not a language right)?

satisfactory to a small, dispersed immigrant group will not satisfy a large, concentrated historic minority. The right to public funding for mother-tongue university education, for example, might be meaningless for the former, but might be seen as essential to the latter. Any attempt to define a set of rights that applies to all linguistic groups, no matter how small and dispersed, is likely to end up focusing on relatively modest claims. For example, the 'linguistic human rights' movement has focused primarily on securing a universal right for publicly funded mother-tongue primary education. This is hardly trivial, but it falls far short of what is at stake in most linguistic conflicts around the world, where groups are fighting over the use of languages in public administration, higher education, and public media. Both majority and minority groups want much more than is, or could reasonably be, guaranteed in international law.[31]

This problem seems unsolvable within the linguistic human rights framework. Its very attraction—namely, that its standards apply universally to all individuals regardless of history, numbers, or nationhood—is precisely its weakness. The only sorts of language rights that can be defined in this universal way are minimal rights, primarily tolerance rights plus a few very modest promotion or accommodation rights (to court interpreters, for example). Even if we agree that there are such universal linguistic human rights, they are unable to address the real policy questions that are at the heart of linguistic conflict around the world, which invariably centre around more extensive rights-claims, by both minorities and majorities, that are conditional on size, history, and national self-determination. In this way, linguistic human rights, while certainly an important part of a larger theory, are insufficient to ensure linguistic justice or to provide guidelines for resolving linguistic conflict.

The right to a court-appointed interpreter, for example, falls well short of the kinds of judicial rights that many proponents of minority language rights call for or indeed of the rights that are found in a number of countries with significant linguistic minorities (Réaume 2000). As we observed earlier, in some jurisdictions an accused person who speaks a designated language has a right not only to understand the charges against him and the court proceedings—something that could be ensured through an adequate translation service—but also to a trial that is substantially *in* his own language, where the judge's instructions are issued in his language, where court transcripts are recorded in his language, and so on. Moreover, these rights are not regarded as conditional on the accused person being unable to understand the usual language of the court. They

---

[31] The Council of Europe's Charter for Regional and Minority Languages attempts to deal with this problem of the variable situations of minority language groups by adopting an 'à la carte' approach, which offers a menu of 67 measures from which a minimum of 35 must be adopted. Ideally, the measures chosen from the menu would be tailored to match the situation of different minority groups. However, nothing in the Charter requires states to adopt more robust language rights for more sizeable / concentrated groups, and many states have refused to do so.

require the court to accommodate his preference to use his own language even where he could quite comfortably use another.

This stronger set of language rights in the context of the judicial process— 'official languages' rights rather than 'norm-and-accommodation' rights—does not obviously follow from, or conflict with, widely accepted understandings of human rights. We need, therefore, a more sophisticated normative account of language policy that can tell us whether such rights should be recognized and, if so, for what languages and language groups.

A similar point can be made about language rights in the context of public education. There is likely to be very widespread agreement that some methods should not be used in or around schools as a means of getting children to acquire some particular language competence. Any minimally liberal and human-rights sensitive political morality will insist that certain means—particularly those that involve violence, cruelty, and humiliation—ought never to be used in pursuit of educational ends, even where those ends are valid ones. There is much less agreement, however, on whether non-oppressive means could legitimately be used in pursuit of those same ends. Would it be legitimate for the state to require all children to attend a school in which the main medium of education is the majority language of the state, or some other language designated as official? Or, if this requirement is still considered too draconian because of its implications for the freedom of parents to choose certain private schooling options, would it at least be legitimate for the state to insist that the medium of all public schooling be the majority or official language? Alternatively, should (certain) linguistic minorities be accorded a right to public education in their own language medium?

As we mentioned, linguistic humans rights activists answer these questions by positing a human right to mother-tongue-medium primary education. But this claim, however attractive it might be, seems more like the conclusion of an argument than the argument itself. If someone challenges the claim—by arguing, for instance, that all children should be educated in a common state-wide language of citizenship, or, more weakly, that all immigrant children should be educated in the predominant language of the host state or in one such language if there are several—what resources is the human-rights perspective left with to respond? Like the controversy over language rights in the judicial process, the debates about language and education cannot be settled by simply inspecting basic human rights standards.

In the end, both the 'benign neglect' approach and the 'linguistic human rights' approach suffer from the flaw of attempting to avoid the unavoidable. They both fail to confront the fact that language policies inevitably involve privileging a limited set of languages, and that the goal of a theory of linguistic rights must therefore be to provide standards for evaluating the decision about which languages to privilege in which contexts.

As we observed at the outset of this chapter, surprisingly little attention has been given by political theorists to articulating and developing a normative account of language rights. In the absence of a well-worked-out normative theory of language policy, much of the discussion, both in academia and in public debate, has tended to operate implicitly with a simple dichotomy. On the one side, some people assume that language policy should aim to promote linguistic assimilation so as to ensure a single common language within each country. This goal of linguistic convergence, which is associated with nation-building projects of the nineteenth and twentieth centuries, is said to be necessary to achieve national unity and social cohesion, or to enable democratic deliberation, or to ensure equal opportunities. On the other side, there are commentators who assume that language policy should aim to prevent linguistic assimilation so as to maintain linguistic diversity and preserve weak languages. The preservation of linguistic diversity is said to be a public good in everyone's interest—like the preservation of ecological diversity—and/or a right of individual speakers of threatened languages.

Both of these approaches find some sympathy amongst the contributors to the present volume. Many of the contributions, however, identify a range of difficulties with these two familiar approaches, and several propose alternative ways of thinking normatively about language rights. Whereas both the nation-building and diversity-preserving approaches are outcome-oriented, these alternative proposals are more procedural in character: they focus not on the outcome in terms of people's eventual language repertoires, but rather on the appropriate conditions and procedures under which those repertoires are formed. Some of the normative standards proposed include democratic fairness (Laitin and Reich), anti-discrimination (Blake), 'minimalism', 'anti-symbolism', and 'revisability' (Weinstock), the 'counter-balancing' of unjust nation-building (Levy), facilitating 'collective choice' (Réaume), and the fairness of 'background conditions' under which speakers of different languages can further their language-related identities and ambitions (Patten).

In the next three sections we take a closer look at some of these different normative approaches to language policy. We begin by reviewing the 'nation-building' approach that sees the main goal of language policy as the promotion of state-wide linguistic convergence (section 5). We then turn to the 'diversity' or 'language maintenance' approach, which emphasizes, as ends in themselves, the goals of preserving linguistic diversity and weak or vulnerable languages (section 6). Finally, some of the new approaches that emphasize procedural standards of evaluation are briefly described (section 7).

## 5. Nation-Building and Language Policy

Historically, all liberal democracies have engaged in a process of nation-building. They have adopted a range of policies to promote a common language and a common sense of national identity and membership. In some situations, convergence on a common language and identity has been the intended objective of the policies selected, as when the state insists that all public education shall be in a single language medium or when it refuses to offer public services in other languages. Elsewhere this convergence has been the unintended but foreseeable consequence of other state policies. Policies that reduce social isolation—such as the building of roads and railways—and enable nationwide communication—such as literacy campaigns or the establishment of radio and television broadcasting—tend to engender linguistic convergence, even if their primary objectives lie elsewhere. In many countries, mandatory military service has been an important promoter of linguistic uniformity.

These nation-building projects are sometimes perceived as expressing an attitude of cultural imperialism and ethnocentric prejudice. Although this attitude is certainly reflected in some of the statements of key nineteenth century proponents of nation-building—think of Mill's notorious remarks about the Basques and Bretons 'sulking on their rocks' (Mill 1991: 431)—not to mention the actual practice of nation-building—think of Franco's efforts to eradicate Spain's regional and minority languages (Conversi 1997: Chs 4–5)—it would be a mistake to simply dismiss nation-building on the grounds that it is 'insensitive to difference'.

One reason for this has just been hinted at. Sometimes language convergence is a (predictable) side-effect of policies that are themselves not difficult to justify. The building of roads and railways that link towns and regions of a country promotes economic development and expands the options and opportunities open to people who had formerly lived in relative isolation (Weber 1976: Ch. 6). But, of course, once people start to have regular contact with other parts of the country—through travel, migration, trade, and so on—their patterns of language use will inevitably change, and it is not surprising when their language repertoires begin to converge.

As Levy shows in his contribution to this volume, a similar point can be made about literacy. Even the strongest critics of nation-building presumably do not object to state-sponsored literacy campaigns. And yet these campaigns, which were often part of nineteenth and twentieth century nation-building projects, carry with them important ramifications for the language repertoires of ordinary people. In part, this is because only a subset of spoken languages have a written form or have textbooks published in them. As a practical matter, a state concerned to promote literacy is often forced to direct its energies at encouraging people to acquire some particular language—a language that is both spoken by at least some people in the state and is available in written form. Literacy also brings individuals into a kind of virtual contact, or 'imagined community', with people in other parts of the country (and world). It makes it more likely that they will read the same books and newspapers, consume the same products, learn from the same textbooks, and so on—all of which may encourage a convergence on a common, national language.

Even if we focus on deliberate attempts by nation-builders to diffuse a single common language across the state, it is clear that important goals can be associated with such a project. For example, standardized public education in a common language has often been seen as essential if all citizens are to have an equal opportunity to work in the modern economy—and, conversely, if businesses are to have at their disposal a labour force possessing the linguistic competences necessary for flexibility, trainability, and mobility in the modern workplace (Gellner 1983). Minority-language communities can easily become ghettoized when their members are unable or unwilling to master the majority language of the state. Their economic opportunities will be limited by the work available in their own language, and they will have trouble accessing the culture of the larger society or participating meaningfully in its political life. A nation-building policy that seeks to integrate speakers of less widely spoken languages into the majority language community can enhance social mobility by offering new options and opportunities to people raised in minority language communities.

This concern for the social mobility of minority-language speakers is a theme in a number of contributions to the present volume. In his paper on Spanish-language accommodations in the United States, Thomas Pogge proposes that the ongoing controversies concerning the use of Spanish in public education should be adjudicated according to a fundamental normative principle stipulating that 'the best education for each child is the education that is best for this child'. Taking aim at the proposition that people should have, as part of the respect owed to them as members of a cultural community, the opportunity to have a public education in their own language, Pogge argues that respecting the wish of parents to educate their children in their home language may have an adverse impact on their children. Since English is overwhelmingly the language of opportunity and mobility in the United States, the interests of children lie in achieving full competence in English. While acknowledging the complexity of the empirical questions raised by his framework of analysis, Pogge suggests that the urgency of learning English indicates a preference for 'English first' rather than 'bilingual' education policies (see also Rodriguez 1982: Ch. 1; Porter 1996; Barry 2001). The chapters by Levy, Laitin and Reich, and Patten also appeal to social mobility considerations to defend majority-language education policies in specific empirical situations.

Convergence on a common national language can also be seen as important for generating the sort of solidarity, or social cohesion, required by a democratic welfare state. It is hard to carry out a programme of social justice when the political community is fragmented into identity groups that do not share the affective bonds of common citizenship and see cooperation with one another solely as an instrument of mutual advantage. A successful nation-building project can help to ensure that language no longer serves to separate citizens into distinct and mutually antagonistic groups, but would become one of the defining bonds of a common identity.

Moreover, as we emphasized towards the end of section 1, a common language has been seen as essential to democracy. How can 'the people' govern together if they cannot understand one another? Democracy involves not only a formal process of voting (a 'vote-centric' process) but an ongoing, informal activity of deliberation and discussion (a 'talk-centric' process). As Patten discusses in his contribution to the volume, linguistic diversity can be a significant barrier to the full flourishing of this deliberative dimension of democracy. If citizens cannot understand each other, or if they seek to communicate only with co-linguists, then democratic politics is likely to be compromised. A successful nation-building project that brings about a common national language of political dialogue can eliminate this obstacle to the flourishing of democracy.

Several of the contributors to the volume take issue with aspects of the nation-building model. Citing a body of research from sociolinguistics and education studies, Stephen May contests the claim that US bilingual education leaves children worse off in social mobility terms than English immersion. A number of studies suggest that bilingual education does as well as, or even outperforms, English immersion at imparting proficiency in English to students and equipping them to enter the labour force. Moreover, even where the results of bilingual education are disappointing, May suggests, it is hard to know how much of this can be traced back to language policy decisions about medium of instruction and how much it reflects discrimination encountered by Spanish-speakers in the workplace. If May's arguments are sound, then there may not be a trade-off between the nation-builder's goal of promoting linguistic convergence and support and recognition for minority languages, through the public education system for example. Minority language speakers may be able to learn the dominant language and generally equip themselves for success in the modern economy even while receiving a significant portion of their schooling in their home language (see also the discussion of social mobility by Patten in this volume).

A further limitation on the social mobility argument for nation-building is that some language minorities are sufficiently large and institutionally complete—they constitute their own 'societal cultures' (Kymlicka 1995a; 2001a)—that individual members can find a relatively full range of economic, social, and cultural options and opportunities in their own language. The clearest examples are the regionally concentrated and historically rooted 'national' groups we discussed earlier, such as the Québécois, Catalans, or Flemish. In these cases, the argument for nation-building loses its force, since minority language speakers cannot be described as 'ghettoized' if they choose to remain within their own linguistic communities (see also the discussion of the 'threshold' condition by Laitin and Reich in this volume).

In such cases, nation-building efforts to construct a common language-based national identity and political forum not only lose their justification, they are also likely to be counter-productive. They will be regarded by the national minority as an attempt by the majority to dominate the state, rather than as good-faith attempts to promote a common good. As a result, they almost invariably stimulate a defensive nationalist response from the national minority, reinforcing their desire for greater territorial self-government or perhaps even secession.

More generally, we can say that whether nation-building is a viable strategy depends, at least in part, on whether there is a competing nationalist movement within the state. The nation-building strategy has proven quite effective in the case of immigrant groups (even large ones), but has typically been strongly resisted by groups which see themselves as forming 'nations within', with the accompanying rights of national self-government. Where states confront this sort of minority nationalism, the best way to promote a common identity and to encourage the practice of deliberative democracy may be to adopt policies that recognize and institutionalize a degree of national and linguistic difference. Indeed, one could argue that the choice between the 'norm and accommodation' approach and the 'official languages' approach is, in effect, a choice between a state that continues to think of itself as a (tolerant, diverse) nation-state and a state that accepts that it is and will remain a multination state. Here again, it is impossible to separate language policy choices from larger debates about the relationship between nations and states, and the appropriate way of managing the phenomenon of competing nationalisms within a single state.

The chapter by Van Parijs is also relevant to a consideration of the nation-building approach to language policy. Like nation-builders, Van Parijs draws attention to a good that can be achieved when people speak a common language. When two people can speak the same language, this opens up the possibility of a range of utility-enhancing communications and interactions. For communication to take place, however, it is obviously not necessary that each person learn the other's language. It is enough that everyone have some common lingua franca as part of their linguistic repertoire. But this means that there will be a significant asymmetry between those people who happen to speak the designated lingua franca as their native language and those who must learn it as a second (or third, etc.) language. The former group does not have to devote any resources or time to learning the lingua franca and they find themselves in the happy situation of having a great deal of important business transacted in their own language. The latter group, by contrast, must incur the costs involved in learning the lingua franca or find themselves excluded from significant economic, political, and social affairs.

Van Parijs's analysis draws attention, then, to a significant issue that nation-builders must address. Assuming that nation-builders are correct to emphasize the value of having a common public language for state-wide communications—and the same goes for international communications—what is the just way of distributing the language-learning costs that are entailed by the establishment of such a language? According to Van Parijs, speakers of other languages who learn the lingua franca are creating a public good that native speakers of the lingua franca willingly benefit from whenever they communicate in the lingua franca with those who have learned it. For native speakers of the lingua franca to contribute nothing to the costs of producing this public good would amount to free-riding. Van Parijs argues that, as a rule of thumb, 'linguistic justice' requires that native speakers of the lingua franca pay for half the costs of learning the lingua franca faced by speakers of other languages, including both the explicit cost of language tuition and the opportunity cost of devoting time to learning the language.

## 6. Maintaining Languages and Language Diversity

The nation-building approach to language policy is frequently hostile towards the preservation of minority languages and the maintenance of linguistic diversity. Policies that are designed to diffuse a common language throughout the state, such as a requirement that all public education be conducted in a single state language, make it difficult for minority language communities to sustain themselves. Even where the goals of nation-builders are consistent with accommodations towards minority languages—for example, because language convergence can still be achieved when schooling is conducted in a minority-language medium—nothing in the nation-building framework indicates whether or why such accommodations might be normatively desirable.

To many people who write and think about language policy, this hostility or indifference towards minority languages is unacceptable. The world's languages, they point out, are dying. According to one recent estimate, about half of the world's languages have disappeared in the past 500 years (Nettle and Romaine 2000: 2). With many of the world's 6,000 or so languages spoken by relatively few people—including about 2,000 that are spoken by fewer than a thousand people—everything points to an acceleration of this trend (see Boran, this volume). As The Economist (2001) put it, 'of the world's 6,000 or 7,000 languages, a couple go out of business each week'. It is true that new languages and dialects also appear from time to time—consider the various Englishes that are now spoken around the world—but it is unlikely that these new forms of speech will be sufficient to offset the global loss of languages.

Even where entire languages are in no danger of disappearing, particular language communities often are. This tendency is sometimes referred to as 'linguistic genocide' (Skutnabb-Kangas 2000), but it does not typically involve the members of these communities literally being killed. Rather, it means that those individuals have a tendency either to adopt new habits of language use or to move to parts of the country or world where their language community is relatively secure. Social scientists have for some time now described a process of territorialization in patterns of language use (Laponce 1984: Ch. 5; Kymlicka 2001a: 212–13). Languages have a tendency to concentrate themselves into well-defined territories and to disappear from regular use outside of these places. Following Ernest Gellner (1983: 139–40), Philippe Van Parijs (2000a: 239) has compared this tendency to a move from Kokoschka to Modigliani. Where a linguistic map of many parts of the world would once have resembled a Kokoschka portrait, with its 'riot of diverse points of colour', increasingly such a map looks like a painting by Modigliani: a patchwork of neatly separated and clearly demarcated areas of uniform colour with little shading or overlap.

A final, and in some ways more striking, aspect of language loss is the tendency for certain languages to become marginalized. Although communities of people continue to use their own languages in certain areas of life, they increasingly turn to some second language in other contexts of communication. A typical pattern, which linguists refer to as 'diglossia' (Ferguson 1959; Fishman 1972: 91–2), sees the speakers of a marginalized language using their own language in contexts of intimacy—with family, friends, and close associates—but switching to some other, higher-status language in more prestigious public domains. The most obvious sign of language marginalization is the growing use of English in certain areas of life by non-native-English-speakers. English has rapidly established itself as the international language of business, telecommunication, diplomacy, education, pop culture, science, scholarship, and travel. Since so many day-to-day activities take place in a context of global interconnectedness—from listening to the radio, to reading a college textbook, to holding a meeting in a corporate office—English impinges on the lives of people in non-English-speaking countries on a regular basis, even if a great deal of everyday life still takes place in local languages. Teaching English as a second language is now a vast global industry worth billions of dollars a year and employing tens of thousands of people (Phillipson 1992). According to *The Economist* (2001), as many as one billion people are learning English and perhaps half the world's population will have some proficiency in it by 2050.

For nation-builders, these tendencies—the wholesale disappearance of some languages, the territorial concentration of others, and the increasing marginalization of virtually every language other than English—are not necessarily to be regretted. If these tendencies imply a gradual convergence on a common lingua franca, then they should be applauded, for, as nation-builders emphasize, there are very great advantages to having a common language. To many other people, however, these tendencies represent an alarming and threatening phenomenon. The disappearance and marginalization of languages and language communities is a pernicious feature of modernity, and one that should galvanize policy makers into action.

For many who hold this view, the maintenance or preservation of minority languages is a fundamental requirement of a normative theory of language policy. The strongest conceivable version of this position makes the preservation of vulnerable languages the supreme goal of all language policy, a goal that trumps all other objectives and possible side-constraints. Moderate versions of the language-maintenance approach regard the preservation of vulnerable languages as an important goal of language policy, but one that should only be pursued subject to respecting certain rights held by speakers both of the vulnerable languages themselves and of dominant languages. And weak versions of the position accept not only these rights-based side-constraints but also the validity of the language-convergence goals promoted by nation-builders. Weak language maintainers seek to preserve vulnerable languages as far as possible, consistent with respecting the rights of all concerned and making room for the emergence of a state-wide lingua franca.

Leslie Green (1987: 653) has suggested that ensuring the preservation of vulnerable languages is the 'implicit value assumption of nearly every linguistic demographer and sociolinguist' who has written on the subject of language rights. In this volume, the chapter by François Grin takes as its point of departure the premise that linguistic diversity is a good and then explores the consequences for analytic work, and policy making, of accepting this assumption. Grin acknowledges that his is a philosophically contentious value assumption but suggests that there is a degree of social consensus surrounding it. Very often others who adopt such a value assumption make little or no effort to justify it, but simply take it to be obviously true. But as we have seen in our discussion of the nation-building approach, it is not obvious to everyone. It is thus legitimate and important to ask why we should care about the preservation of vulnerable languages. Why does it matter if some languages or language communities disappear or get marginalized? Indeed, why does it matter so much that language policy makers are normatively required to take steps to counteract such a tendency?

Where political theorists and sociolinguists have addressed these questions, they have developed a variety of different kinds of answers. For instance, one approach emphasizes the value of diversity itself. Fewer languages means less global linguistic diversity, and global linguistic diversity is, according to this view, itself something that is valuable.

An argument of this kind is developed and assessed by Idil Boran in her contribution to the volume. She considers the popular argument that a decline of linguistic diversity is somehow akin to a decline in biodiversity, so that justifications of language maintenance policies can be modelled after the justifications advanced on behalf of the conservation of species (see also Nettle and Romaine 2000). According to Boran, biodiversity and linguistic diversity are of value to people in several kinds of ways. One kind of value they instantiate is broadly aesthetic in character. A world with more species and languages is more colourful, interesting, and dynamic than one with less diversity. Languages, for instance, are vehicles of cultures, and cultures create new forms of social life and 'experiments in living' that are then available for anyone to adopt (Van Parijs 2000a). Another way in which biodiversity and linguistic diversity are valuable is more narrowly scientific in character. A diverse natural world contains species that may be of great utility to progress in science and medicine. In the same way, a diverse linguistic world contains different ways of talking about the world and thus may hold clues to techniques or uses of the natural world that are unfamiliar to speakers of the world's dominant languages.

These values give us a reason to care about the preservation of global linguistic diversity. Moreover, Boran argues, linguistic diversity, like biodiversity, is a public good, one that people in general can enjoy even if they have not contributed to its production or maintenance. This means that the costs of preserving linguistic diversity should not just be left to speakers of vulnerable languages but should be shared more broadly amongst everyone in the globe who profits from the scientific (and other) innovations that diversity facilitates.

A second kind of reason for caring about the disappearance of languages points to something intrinsically valuable about particular languages (taken one by one) besides the contribution they make to global linguistic diversity. There are a variety of ways of articulating the intrinsic value of particular languages. Denise Réaume (2000) has argued that languages are valuable as collective human accomplishments and ongoing manifestations of human creativity and originality. Each language is a unique form of expression with its own distinctive way of framing and conceptualizing the world. Like a living organism, it evolves and adapts to its environment, often in strikingly imaginative ways that no individual could have predicted or directed. Réaume and others also emphasize the ways in which a language acts as a repository for a particular culture's history, traditions, arts, ideas, and so on (Crystal 2000). In the same way that an archive or museum is valuable—because of the value of what it contains and preserves—a language is valuable as well.

The intrinsic value of particular languages, understood along these lines, provides a reason why we should want to avoid the disappearance of languages. Just as we are generally disposed to respect and protect expressions and bearers of human creativity, history, and so on, the argument is that we should adopt a similar attitude towards languages.

A third argument in favour of language preservation policies is perhaps the most popular one found in the literature. It is a commonplace in the literature on language rights that language is not just a tool of communication. It is also, for some people, a central and defining feature of identity. Many people self-identify with the (local) community of speakers of their language. They are proud of their language and the cultural achievements that have been expressed through it, and they take pleasure in using the language and encountering others who are willing to use it. They hope that the language community will survive and flourish into the indefinite future. And, in some contexts, they feel respected and affirmed when others address them in their language and denigrated when others impose their own linguistic preferences.

To many theorists, these facts about the importance of language to individual identity ground an argument on behalf of language maintenance policies. The best-known formulation of this position is perhaps Charles Taylor's essay 'The Politics of Recognition' (1992). According to Taylor, public institutions must ensure that individuals enjoy adequate recognition if they are to enjoy and express their identities in a free and undistorted manner. For Taylor, there are two main models of how this recognition might be established. The 'politics of universalism' offers recognition by extending equal rights to all citizens and otherwise adopting a 'difference-' or 'culture-blind' stance vis-à-vis the particular attitudes and commitments that citizens embrace. The 'politics of difference', by contrast, requires a respect for fundamental rights but, within the constraints set by this requirement, then calls for public institutions to actively protect vulnerable cultures in order to give those cultures the tools they need to ensure survival. Taylor's sympathies clearly lie with this second model of recognition. 'If we're concerned with identity', he argues, 'then what is more legitimate than one's aspiration that it never be lost?' (1992: 40).

In a contribution to the present volume, Stephen May endorses a version of this identity argument. Drawing on the position he develops more fully in a recent book (2001: Ch. 4), he argues that, even if language is a merely contingent factor in identity, it is nevertheless a significant and 'constitutive' one. From this premise, that 'languages ... provide their speakers with significant individual and collective forms of linguistic identity', May argues for language protection policies. Since majority language speakers enjoy a secure language and identity as a matter of course, it would be unjust to refuse these same goods to speakers of minority languages.

A fourth and final argument worth mentioning in favour of language maintenance policies returns to some of the 'social mobility' and 'equal opportunities' considerations raised in our earlier discussion of nation-building. In that discussion, we suggested that it was important to distinguish between cases in which a linguistic minority does not have access to a fairly full range of options (a societal culture) in its own language and those cases in which it does. It is only in the former sort of case that an argument for nation-building grounded in an appeal to social mobility can get off the ground, since in the latter kind the linguistic minority already forms a 'nation within'.

In his contribution to the volume, Patten suggests that there may be an important intermediate kind of case, which he terms 'vulnerable societal cultures' (see also Patten 2001). In these cases, a linguistic minority does have access to a fairly full set of options in its own language, but it is in danger of losing this access as more and more important language domains shift to the majority or dominant language. When this happens, members of the linguistic minority who lack full fluency in the more dominant language risk being stranded. They may no longer have at their disposal the 'context of choice' they need for individual autonomy. It is conceivable that the solution to this problem could be a more aggressive nation-building policy that works to ensure that everyone is fluent in the dominant language. In many situations, however—particularly when nationalist dynamics are in play—this solution may not be realistic. A public policy of combating the marginalization of the minority language may have more chance of success than a policy of diffusing the majority language throughout the entire minority community.

A number of chapters in the volume challenge one or several of these arguments for language maintenance policies. A general theme in many of the critical responses is a concern that such policies may end up being too onerous or disadvantageous for speakers of vulnerable languages themselves. Weinstock makes this point, for instance, in the context of an assessment of the intrinsic-value defence of language protection policies. Theorists who appeal to the intrinsic value of particular languages do so with the objective of defending certain rights for speakers of those languages. Weinstock argues, however, that, if we really take seriously the ideas that languages are intrinsically valuable and that anything that is intrinsically valuable should be respected and protected, then we should acknowledge that speakers of vulnerable languages have not just rights to maintain their language but also duties to do so. They should be encouraged, and perhaps even compelled, to maintain their language, even if some of them are not interested in doing so. And this implication of the intrinsic value approach, Weinstock implies, is unacceptable. The 'latitude' or freedom that goes with having a right disappears when one is constrained by duty to exercise the right in certain ways.

The concern that language preservation policies may entail imposing serious restrictions on speakers of vulnerable languages themselves is developed further in the chapters by Levy, Boran, and Laitin and Reich. As Levy emphasizes, one reason why some language communities survive is their relative social and geographic isolation from mainstream society. All else being equal, a distinct language is more likely to survive when its speakers have a low level of literacy, when they live in geographically isolated communities, when they do not participate in the mainstream economic and social life of the state in which they live, and so on. If taking language preservation seriously means adopting policies that prevent the spread of literacy or block access to mainstream society and economy, then this seems too high a price to pay. Indeed, for many liberals there is a positive obligation to extend literacy, education, training for the modern workplace, and so on, to all citizens.

Implicit in this criticism of the language maintenance approach is the idea that linguistic survival is as much about the choices and dispositions of speakers of a language as it is about the behaviour and structures imposed by outsiders. Sometimes languages disappear or become marginalized because of oppressive actions by outside agencies—usually an imperial power or a central state firmly in the control of speakers of the dominant language. But even in the absence of oppression, there is no guarantee that a particular language will survive. The attitudes, dispositions, and preferences of speakers of the vulnerable language, and the opportunities and options available in the majority or dominant language, may mean that the prospects for the vulnerable language are bleak even if nobody is oppressively imposing the majority language (Edwards 1985; 1994). Laitin and Reich suggest that the case of Wales and the Welsh language may be a good illustration of this possibility. Many people who live in Wales, including many who are descendants of Welsh-speakers, have no real orientation to the Welsh language. On any plausible view of what an absence of oppression would consist in, there is no reason to think that these people would generally choose to learn Welsh or to use it on a regular basis. Liberals, Laitin and Reich argue, should respect these internal group differences concerning the value and choiceworthiness of the language and should not seek to impose the attitudes and preferences of one sub-group onto everybody. The strength of the identity interest in language is variable within and between groups, and any plausible theory of language rights must respect and accommodate this variability.

Blake makes a similar point by considering a thought experiment involving two different stories about how a language might die. In the first story, members of an isolated language community change, over the course of generations, the vocabulary and syntax of their language, until there comes a point at which the original language that they spoke can be considered dead. In the second story, the members of a language community come into contact with another language and gradually adopt its patterns of speech, until, eventually, their original language is dead. Blake suggests that we have quite different intuitive reactions to these two stories, even though they are both cases of language death. The first case, Blake believes, is relatively harmless and almost nobody would favour intervening to prevent the kind of linguistic change it involves from occurring. The second case, by contrast, arouses our suspicions, because we cannot help but wonder whether the contact with the foreign language community involved some kind of relationship of discrimination or oppression.

In Blake's view, this thought experiment points to two distinct ways in which language change and language death can occur. Such outcomes can result from oppression or from what Blake terms 'the free exercise of the human imagination'. A liberal approach to language policy should concern itself with the former and not the latter kind of change. The problem, then, with many of the arguments that are made on behalf of language preservation policies is that they are too blunt. Because they make general appeals to identity, or intrinsic value, or diversity, they do not capture the normative significance of this distinction between the two kinds of cases.

## 7. Procedural Approaches

A striking feature of the nation-building and the language-maintenance approaches is that they each formulate the fundamental normative requirement for language policy makers in terms of the realization of a certain sort of outcome. For nation-builders, that outcome is one in which a single common language is diffused amongst all citizens of the state. For language maintainers it involves the preservation of languages that are vulnerable to disappearance or marginalization.

As we have seen, a number of objections can be raised against both of these traditional approaches. It is not clear that the arguments for nation-building completely crowd out the possibility of minority-language accommodations. Sometimes the goods emphasized by nation-builders can be realized within minority language communities and there is no great urgency to establish a state-wide language. In other situations, the achievement of a common state language is possible even when various minority language accommodations are made. And sometimes a nation-building project is likely to encounter such significant resistance that it is better, perhaps as a matter of 'second-best', to focus on developing the minority-language community instead. On the other hand, the language-maintenance approach does not seem to formulate the issues quite correctly either. Preserving vulnerable languages seems like a worthwhile cause when the speakers of those languages are facing, or have faced, various forms of oppression and injustice. It is less clear that it is a worthwhile cause when it goes against the choices and preferences of significant numbers of people in the vulnerable language community or involves imposing significant restrictions on their opportunities or mobility.

A number of the chapters in the volume seek to avoid the problems arising from the two traditional approaches by articulating a procedural, or non-outcome-based, account of basic normative principles governing language policy. On these views, we do not assess possible language policies, or language rights regimes, by asking whether certain desirable outcomes will be generated, such as convergence on a common language or the preservation of threatened languages. Rather, we ask whether certain procedural standards have been satisfied in the generation of whatever outcomes happen to come about.

Various chapters suggest different possible procedural standards. Laitin and Reich emphasize democratic legitimacy, for instance. In their view, language protection schemes should be seen as analogous to certain public goods that are provided by the state. Language security belongs in a class of goods the provision for which out of general tax revenues is neither required nor prohibited by considerations of justice. For these goods, the correct level of provision by the state is a function of what the democratic process decides. If, after due deliberation, a majority wish to devote public resources to protecting a particular language, then it is reasonable and legitimate for the state to pursue such a goal. If, on the other hand, the majority is uninterested in language preservation, then no fundamental norm is being violated if the language subsequently dies out or is marginalized. The key point is not whether a certain language outcome is generated, but whether the standards of democratic legitimacy are satisfied or not.

Weinstock also suggests a series of non-outcome-related standards by which to assess possible language rights regimes. In his view, an acceptable language policy must satisfy three separate standards. First, the state should, as far as possible, leave it up to citizens themselves to rank the various goods at play in language disputes, intervening only where it is necessary to ensure effective communication in the public domain ('minimalism'). Second, the state should avoid attaching or suggesting—for example, through its pronouncements—any symbolic significance to the language policy decisions that it must necessarily make ('anti-symbolism'). And third, the state's language policies should always be open to revision, so that, if new patterns of language use emerge in society, the state's language choices can be adapted accordingly ('revisability').

Blake's position flows out of his critique of existing language preservation arguments. In his view, as we have seen, the key issue is not whether the language dies but whether language change, including language death, takes place in a context of oppression and injustice. His paper considers a number of different accounts of what should count as 'oppression' and 'injustice' for the purposes of a normative theory of language rights. He argues that past and present discrimination on the basis of language should count as oppressive in such a theory, but that a refusal to grant a language official language rights should not, nor should the fact that some languages carry with them more options and opportunities than others.

Levy also proposes a procedural view of language rights, one that focuses on establishing conditions that 'counterbalance' the predictable tendency of modern states to engage in unjust nationalizing projects. Like Weinstock, Levy is alert to the variety of oppressive, violent, and illiberal methods that modern states have employed to try to turn their citizens into nations sharing common languages. Levy appeals to the political theory of constitutionalism to argue that, where there is good reason to suspect that the state will engage in a particular sort of injustice, institutional safeguards and mechanisms ought to be introduced that will lean against this tendency. Language rights can act as just this sort of bulwark. They give institutional weight and power to members of linguistic minorities and thereby make it difficult for the state to run roughshod over their basic interests. For Levy, then, we assess a regime of language rights, not according to its success at diffusing a common language or at preserving vulnerable languages, but on the basis of its capacity to check and counterbalance predictable excesses of the modern state.

In her contribution to the volume, Réaume explicitly argues against 'consequentialist' theories of language rights that seek to justify such rights in terms of goals such as general communication, social cohesion, language survival, political stability, encouraging diversity, and so on. She suggests that these theories tend to see language in excessively instrumental terms and ignore the 'intrinsically valuable dimension' of language and, in particular, the value that each language community places on its own language. Instead, she argues, a normative theory of language rights ought to proceed from the value of individual participation with others in acts of creating and sustaining language communities. A language rights regime should include both negative liberties and positive accommodations that protect spaces in which these 'collective choices' can be made.

Finally, Patten suggests a procedural standard to govern the 'recognition' that is owed to language-based identities. Individuals do not have a right, he argues, that their language-related identity should succeed or flourish, since any such right might easily collide with the same right held by the speakers of a different language (on the assumption that there is a limit to the number of languages that can flourish in a given community). Nor do people have a right to the equal success of their identity, since some people adopt identities that are rather easy to realize whereas others have difficult-to-satisfy identities. What people can legitimately claim, however, is that their language-related identity be dealt with by public institutions in an even-handed way, so that everyone can strive to realize and advance his or her identity under background conditions that are fair. If certain rights and accommodations are extended to one language, then even-handedness requires that they also be extended to others. Patten suggests that this sort of argument can be marshalled in defence of minority language rights and the personality principle, so long as certain countervailing conditions are not engaged.

We hope that this introduction has given readers a sense of where the normative debate about language rights is currently at. We've tried to sketch a picture of the political and theoretical contexts in which this debate is taking place, to identify some of the concrete issues and fine-grained distinctions that much of the debate turns on, and to suggest some of the new approaches being developed. As we emphasized at the start of this chapter, the field of language rights is a relatively new one for normative political theorists, and to some extent we are still sorting out the relevant questions, let alone identifying the answers. A fully adequate theory of language rights will undoubtedly have to consider other contexts, distinctions, and approaches. We hope that this volume will provide a stimulus and a resource for further reflection on the normative issues surrounding language policy.

# 2

# Language Rights: Exploring the Competing Rationales

RUTH RUBIO-MARÍN

## 1. Introduction

Language rights, as moral and legal categories, have thus far received little theoretical reflection. As the debate on multiculturalism gains in strength, this is most likely to change. In many ways, language diversity poses the most serious challenge to some orthodox liberal principles. In the face of increasing cultural diversity, tolerance as non-intervention—for some, the paradigmatic liberal response to the challenge of peaceful coexistence in religiously diverse societies—simply does not seem to be an alternative. Even those who argue that there is still a lot that the state can do in order to ensure cultural fairness by way of disestablishing the preferences of the dominant majorities recognize that, when it comes to language policy, there are some limits; the state simply needs to function in some language (Walker 1999: 154). The state's reliance on law for the articulation and limitation of power makes it an essentially linguistic enterprise. Also, as a project of collective political deliberation and collective pursuit of socio-economic well-being, the state simply rests on the possibility of communicative exchanges.

On the other hand, the intimate relationship between language and culture is widely recognized. Language is a means of communication but not a culturally neutral one. In fact, language is one of the most recurrent features that commentators of nationalism refer to when listing, however tentatively, the set of objective criteria by which different national cultures and peoples can be identified. Indeed, over the last decade, in most cases of state disintegration linked to nationalist claims the rallying point of divergent identity has been language (Coulombe 1995: 71). It is therefore not surprising that national minorities, often the speakers of a minority language within a state, have traditionally

I would like to thank the editors of this volume and Gerry Neuman for insightful comments on a previous draft, and Pablo de Greiff for helpful discussions on many of the issues addressed in the chapter.

articulated language claims as part of their nationalist agenda. Think of Basque or Catalan speakers in Spain or the Francophone speakers in Quebec. Language rights, from this perspective, are articulated as acts of cultural defence against the eroding impact of an economically and/or politically dominant language, the majority language that is endorsed by the state.

Yet, because the linguistic dimension of the state is inevitable, one can always formulate a defence against the charge of cultural assimilationism when it comes to state language policy. Privileging a certain language as a public language, whether it be expressly sanctioned as the official language or simply used for most public and private transactions, can in principle be explained as the result of functional demands. Modern economies require a mobile, trained, and easily retrainable workforce, which is difficult to imagine without a standardized education in a common language. Similarly, it can be said that political legitimacy, understood in terms of the will of the people and the gradual consolidation of forms of representative democracy, demands a process of joint and ongoing deliberation that cannot function without a common language. Ultimately, the notion of the state as a community of destiny, resting on different forms of civic solidarity, trust, and loyalty, is difficult to picture without the possibility of a common language.

It has indeed been argued that this kind of functional requirement which supported linguistic homogeneity played a significant role in the consolidation of nationalism as a modern phenomenon (Taylor 1999). But linguistic nationalism has not succumbed or been reduced to a state logic. In spite of plausible considerations of general interests, and of some obvious benefits that national minorities could derive from assimilating into the majority language, many such groups have consistently shown a strong resistance to doing so. Thinking about language rights as ways of accommodating the needs of such minorities within the state requires, therefore, understanding the primordial importance that people attach to their cultures and linguistic environments.

On the other hand, whether contested or not in terms of its cultural impact on linguistic minorities, we know that the state has to function in a limited number of languages. For some people this will always create obstacles to linguistic access. This is why, apart from instruments of cultural protection, we also need to think of language rights in terms of rights that enable the citizen to overcome such obstacles. From that perspective, the concern is not with cultural defence per se, but with setting the conditions that allow for the enjoyment of the sphere of bounded equality which state membership entails while avoiding liabilities linked to linguistic capabilities. And this is where the notion of instrumental language rights comes into play.

In this chapter I propose giving up the more or widely endorsed classification of tolerance verus promotion–oriented language rights (Section 1 for one that distinguishes between instrumental and non-instrumental language rights and briefly explore the concept and typology of non-instrumental language rights (section 3). I then analyse the concept of instrumental language rights (section 4), assess to what extent the right and/or duty to learn the majority language can be a valid substitute for the recognition of such rights (section 5), and finally assess a range of reasonable limits to such recognition (section 6), exemplifying how they would apply to the case of the right to bilingual ballots for Hispanics in the US Southwest (section 7). In doing so, I hope to contribute to the self-awareness around existing state practices of linguistic accommodation by bringing to the surface the normative basis upon which some of those practices rest. In my view this normative basis can and ought to be expanded to cover additional linguistic claims and, to that purpose, I focus on the potential of the notion of language rights as instrumental rights.

## 2. Language Rights in Tolerance versus Promotion-Oriented Language Regimes: A Classification of Doubtful Usefulness

Before going into the elaboration of the instrumental/non-instrumental distinction as applied to language rights, let us pause briefly on a different analytical tool that some commentators have used in their attempt to grapple with this new notion of language rights. Connecting such rights with possible language rights regimes, some authors have distinguished between the rights recognized in a tolerance-based language regime and those granted in a promotion-oriented regime (for all, MacMillan 1991: 61). A tolerant language regime is generally defined as one that ensures that the state will not interfere to restrict the spontaneous expression of linguistic preferences in civil society. At the most, in terms of active participation, the state will be expected to engage in the fight against societal prejudices.

This kind of linguistic regime, it is argued, does not really require conceptualizing new forms of rights. Indeed, what one could call 'tolerance language rights' are just specific ways in which more of the traditionally recognized freedoms can be enjoyed. Think, for instance, of freedom of speech as covering the right to choose the language of expression and not just the contents of such expression, or the right to family privacy as empowering people to freely decide which language to use at home for family interactions. The same could be said about freedom of the press covering the language of the media, and of the right to education as the right of parents to privately fund their children's education in their preferred language. All of these are negative freedoms which, in a tolerant regime, are supposed to ensure the state's cultural neutrality. In that respect, they fit best with the philosophical conception of the liberal state claiming that the state should remain neutral with regard to cultural options, which are simply expected to compete freely in the cultural marketplace.

In contrast, it is said that promotion-oriented language regimes represent a model in which the state is actively committed to the protection of a certain language or certain languages. The most characteristic sign of such a regime is the express recognition of a certain language or, eventually, several languages as the official language(s) of the state. Rather than remaining neutral, the state engages in the protection of a certain language or certain languages as a defining element of its public culture. This is why in such regimes negative rights do not exhaust the category of language rights and all sorts of positive accommodations are recognized.

As I see it, there are at least three reasons why the distinction between tolerance- and promotion-oriented language regimes, with its connection to negative linguistic freedoms and positive linguistic rights, is not likely to be a useful analytical tool. First of all, it seems to imply that a pure tolerance regime is a much more feasible option than it really is. And this has nothing to do with whether or not a state recognizes some language as official and whether or not it declares, as one of its express purposes, that of satisfying the claims of language promotion of citizens. As mentioned above, while the state can, in principle, guarantee religious neutrality by not embracing any official religion, it cannot guarantee perfect linguistic neutrality (Kymlicka 1995a: 111; Carens 2000: 77–8; Bauböck 2001: 321). Because the state needs to function in some language, pure linguistic disestablishment is simply not an option. The state will rely on a language or, in any event, a limited number of languages to provide social services and schooling. It will have a parliament and governmental and judicial institutions using that same language. And whether intended or not, this will inevitably favour the community or communities whose language the state decides to operate in, in myriad ways. Symbolic recognition is definitely at stake. So is the possibility to meaningfully enjoy the whole set of rights, services, and employment and social mobility opportunities that the large apparatus of the modern state provides. The chances of cultural reproduction are also compromised.

Second, the distinction seems to imply that, whenever the state actively accommodates a certain language, especially when this is a minority language, its main aim is to protect and promote the language and the culture to which it belongs. And again, this is not necessarily true. Many states accommodate linguistic diversity in many ways and to different degrees. Think for instance of the right to translation services in criminal trials that many contemporary democracies recognize as part of formal due process guarantees. It would be far-fetched to suggest that by recognizing such a right the state is necessarily endorsing, as its primary underlying aim, that of protecting the identity of linguistic minorities.

Finally, and conversely, the distinction seems to suggest that, when the state protects individual spaces of freedom and autonomy through non-interference rights, allowing for such spaces to be used as spaces of cultural and linguistic expression is simply an inevitable corollary, not something that the state actively pursues in order to protect or promote certain languages and cultures. And that, again, is not necessarily true.

## 3. Non-Instrumental Language Rights

It seems to me that a more interesting analytical tool for addressing the question of language rights is the distinction between instrumental and non-instrumental language rights. Although the distinction between the instrumental interest in language as a means of communication and the expressive interest in language as a marker of identity has been discussed in the literature,[1] the potential of this distinction to construct a theory of language rights needs to be further explored. Some courts, such as the Canadian Supreme Court, have also noticed the different nature of the interests that language rights can serve,[2] but are still far from offering clarity as to the normative grounds and implications (Green and Réaume 1990).

### The Nature of Non-Instrumental Language Rights

The main distinguishing feature of the non-instrumental category is the protected good, and not whether the right at stake is a negative freedom or a positive action right. The instrumental/non-instrumental divide distinguishes between, on the one hand, those language claims that aim at ensuring a person's capacity to enjoy a secure linguistic environment in her/his mother tongue and a linguistic group's fair chances of cultural self-reproduction which we could call language rights in a strict sense, and, on the other, those language claims that aim at ensuring that language is not an obstacle to the effective enjoyment of rights with a linguistic dimension, to the meaningful participation in public institutions and democratic process, and to the enjoyment of social and economic opportunities that require linguistic skills. Language is indeed an essential instrument of communication, but people's attachment to their language cannot be reduced to its utility in communication. 'Language is

---

[1]   Denise Réaume (1991) and Leslie Green (1987) have been pioneers in exploring the connection between these two different types of interests served by language and the relevance of the distinction for understanding language rights. I owe much inspiration to their insightful distinction.

[2]   About one-third of the rights recognized in the Canadian Charter of Rights and Freedoms (1982) are language rights. Most of them are language rights in the non-instrumental or strict sense of the word, that is, rights that aim to protect anglophone and francophone minorities across the country, and thus recognize as a constitutional task the accommodation of at least these two national and linguistic cultures in the Canadian geopolitical space. There are also some language rights of the instrumental kind, such as the right of the parties and witnesses in a trial to the assistance of an interpreter if they cannot understand the language in which the trial takes place (art. 14). The Supreme Court has indeed understood this kind of right as of a different nature. It has referred to this guarantee as part of the right to a fair trial and full defence that applies to everyone as a principle of universal justice. Language rights (meaning what I call here non-instrumental language rights), as the Supreme Court has systematically recognized, are different in their origin and function, their aim being to protect the official language minorities and to ensure the equal status of French and English. See, for all, *R. v. Beaulac*, 1 S.C.R. 768.

a marker of identity, a cultural inheritance and a concrete expression of community' (Green 1987: 659). And it is this dual nature of language that the divide between instrumental and non-instrumental language rights tries to capture.

The underlying idea behind the notion of non-instrumental language rights is the commitment, on the part of the state, to help a certain collectivity achieve the goal of protecting its language. Because the majority will probably see its expressive needs taken care of through mainstream institutions, language rights, as rights that trump majority interests, become a tool for the protection of minorities from the political and economic power of the culturally dominant majority. Language rights are mainly concerned with people's linguistic and cultural identity. They rest on the recognition of people's right to live in their language and to enjoy a secure linguistic environment knowing that 'their language group may flourish and that one may use one's language with dignity' (Green 1987: 658). The recognition of this kind of right is best supported by those theses that argue for the protection of cultural membership as necessary for the fulfilment of individual autonomy and as a basis for self-respect (Taylor 1992; Kymlicka 1995a; Tamir 1993; Margalit and Raz 1995). In other words, what such rights do is allow a certain language minority to avoid the trade-off between state citizenship and cultural identity by ensuring that its speakers can live in their language in every relevant sphere, including the public sphere.

Non-instrumental language rights, as defined here, and regardless of how narrowly or generously recognized, are always group rights. Membership of the recognized linguistic community is what makes one a holder of the right at stake (Green 1987). Indeed, thinking of non-instrumental language rights as individual rights makes little sense because the good that such rights try to serve is a public good that is both collectively generated and collectively enjoyed (Réaume 1991: 48).[3] The protection of one's membership in a language community, as a protection of a certain context of choice and sense of identity provided by its culture, is meaningful only as a communal experience. There have to be sufficient people committed to speaking that language and nurturing the culture it represents. Non-instrumental language rights focus on the cultural dimension of language, and such a dimension loses its meaning without the community experience that makes of language a cultural-identity marker.

Most of the countries which do specifically recognize language rights in their constitutions expressly refer to the languages and the communities that the protection covers. Exceptionally, some countries refer simply to a numerical threshold leaving the question open as to which, exactly, the protected language

---

[3] Notice that this has nothing to do with whether the right at stake can be exercised individually (for example, the right to address the courts in one's language) or only collectively (the right of a community in which a language group is a majority to have its own language policy or schooling system).

groups will be.[4] In strict terms the prior definition of the protected groups is not mandated by the group nature of these rights. It is simply generally assumed that the state is obliged, if at all, to accommodate only its autochthonous language groups. Beyond cost considerations or concerns with the limits of accommodation in view of the purpose of preserving state unity, there is a general sense whereby a world order organized around states allocates geo-political spaces to different cultural groups which are recognized as autochthonous in each place, however artificial and historically contingent the underlying narratives may be.

## A Proposed Typology

Looking for an analytically useful typology we could say that language rights as cultural protections can be of three sorts. All of them rest on the assumption that a minority language group cannot flourish if it cannot take part in public life in its language, and if it lacks the basic means of cultural reproduction (Réaume 1991: 52; Kymlicka 1995a: 78). One type satisfies the demands that the state and its institutions accommodate language minorities in both practical and symbolic ways. The recognition of an official status to a language other than the majority language is one of the most common mechanisms of minority accommodation.[5] Such recognition is often linked to other rights even though these may also be recognized independently. Some of these rights include the right of citizens to learn the declared official language; to use it in their interaction with public officials such as the judiciary, administrative, or parliamentary authorities; to have the public officials use it to address them individually or collectively—think of the right to have statutes published in several official languages; to have a certain presence in publicly funded media; and to have it as the language of public education.[6]

---

[4] As way of example, article 7 of the Constitutional Law on Human Rights and Freedoms and the Rights of National and Ethnic Communities or Minorities in the Republic of Croatia provides that, where a minority represents more than 50% of the population, the relevant minority language becomes official in the concerned area.

[5] From this perspective the extension of an official status to the majority language would in principle be nothing but the expression of the status of the language of the majority as such. There is only one way in which it could be referred to as a language group right, namely, when there is a disconnection between the size of the language group and its social and political power. In those cases where the majority of the country's population speaks a certain native language which has nevertheless not been the language of common use in the public or social institutions, its assertion as an official language can be seen as a remedial action to help the language group recover from the kind of discrimination which, in spite of its numerical power, it obviously suffered in the past.

[6] The Canadian Charter of Rights and Freedoms contains one of the most detailed lists of constitutional language rights. Article 17.1 recognizes everyone's right to use French or English in Parliament; article 18.1 provides that federal statutes be in both English and French; article 19.1 contemplates the right to use English or French in federal courts; article 20.1 refers to language rights in the administration of services; and article 23 contemplates a regime of language rights in the realm of education.

The second type of non-instrumental language rights consists of language minorities' powers of self-government that enable them to protect their own linguistic environment. Think of Canada. Quebec's power to collectively pursue its own linguistic policy, to have its own public institutions, schools, and media using French as a vernacular, and its power to influence the immigration policy of the country so as to protect the cultural identity of the province can all be seen as non-instrumental language rights of the francophone minority in Canada, given that such a minority holds a majority position within Quebec, where about 80 per cent of the population is Francophone.

In this regard, it is clear that a federal or in any event decentralized form of government is, in principle, much more accommodating of such rights than its centralized counterpart.[7] However, the exact extent to which decentralized territorial government embodies collective language rights will depend mainly on two things: first, on whether the borders of the federated units ensure that ethnolinguistic minorities form local majorities and, second, on the precise powers accorded to these units and their linguistic relevance.[8]

Finally there is a third type of language right, namely, promotional rights to assist the linguistic minority in its attempt to assert itself and fight against the assimilation pressure of the dominant language. Think, for instance, of qualified access to public funding to promote the use of minority languages in the media, in technology, or in the arts. Whereas the first two types of language rights are in a sense *inevitable*—the state, as a public machinery, *must* function in some language and it *must* have some form of territorial distribution of power—the likelihood that different states will accommodate this third type of right hinges on two things: their willingness to protect minority languages and their more general views about the state's role in correcting social power differences even when they are not directly linked to a present or even past form of state discrimination.

## Some Relevant Clarifications

It should be clear that, as conceived here, these are rights that protect minorities from the majority's political and economic power and the subsequent external

[7] One of the best articulations of this idea in constitutional reasoning can be found in *Reference Re Secession of Quebec*, 2 S.C.R. 217.

[8] In this respect it is interesting to note that the Congress of Local and Regional Authorities of Europe (1998), one of the main promoters of the European Charter for Regional or Minority Languages, in its Recommendation 43 has encouraged the Council of Ministers to adopt in their states two separate sets of recommendations: (1) where administrative subdivisions are already established, and where minorities constitute a substantial proportion of that population, competencies should be delegated to local communities in the linguistic field together with others which are found of greatest significance for the preservation of the minorities' identity; and (2) where member states are planning to change their system of administrative subdivisions, to avoid gerrymandering with regard to minorities, administrative subdivisions should be established which prevent the dispersal of the minority members so that they can be afforded effective protection, and the population should be consulted in the marking of the territorial boundaries.

pressure to assimilate. They are not rights to perpetuate a group's cultural hegemony in any given state at any given moment, or to ensure the survival of a threatened language per se. This is why the English Only movement in the US, as a movement which tries to ensure that English remains the only language which is publicly accommodated, cannot be interpreted as a call for language rights of the English-speaking majority.[9]

A different question is which unit should be taken as the framework of reference to determine a group's majority or minority status. In principle, nothing speaks for granting the state the monopoly as a referential community. Back to our Canadian example: nothing prevents the autochthonous Anglophone speakers in Quebec from being conceptualized as an ethnolinguistic minority. And, indeed, the English-speaking community enjoys such rights under the Canadian Charter. The Charter has de-territorialized language rights by attaching them to speakers of both French and English rather than to Provinces, recognizing thereby minority status to both the Francophone minorities outside Quebec and the Anglophone minority inside Quebec. In my view, the relevant factor for normative purposes should be the extent to which the Francophone public system and society in Quebec really constitutes an obstacle to the collective attempt of the Anglophone community to remain such. Given the predominance of English in the rest of the country, this seems questionable. Things are quite different when similar claims for cultural preservation are made by other minority groups such as the native communities living in Quebec.

The answer to this sort of question is, then, likely to be highly contextual. In principle, because a strong structure of decentralized powers can reproduce many of the assimilation pressures at a sub-national level, nothing speaks against characterizing minorities within minorities as such. That said, it is almost certain that the degree of protection that such a minority might need to safeguard its linguistic environment will be significantly less when, at a country level, it enjoys a majority position.[10]

Whether the language at stake is threatened with extinction as a world language is in itself irrelevant. To stay with our Canadian example, the fact that

[9] In this respect, when the movement demands the recognition and constitutional entrenchment of English as an official language, with the aim of prohibiting the use of other languages in public domains, it actually attempts to take the official status not as a defence of a threatened language group—though this is far too often the rhetoric used—but as an excuse for not accommodating minority language claims.

[10] Note, however, that the European Charter for Regional or Minority Languages of 26 June 1992, which entered into force on 1 March 1998 and is the first international treaty of general application dealing comprehensively with the issue of linguistic diversity in Europe, precludes this possibility. Article 1 of this Charter defines 'regional or minority languages' which fall under the scope of its protection as those 'traditionally used within a given territory of a State by nationals of that State who form a group numerically smaller than the State's population'.

French is likely to be viable, as a world language, even without a French-speaking Quebec, or that English is certainly viable without an English-speaking minority inside of Quebec, is relevant only to the extent that this has a direct impact on the experience of linguistic security and identity for the relevant minorities within their societies. Nowadays this is most likely to be the case with English, as a language that enjoys a hegemonic position as a world trade language and corresponding prestige. Be that as it may, it is not languages but language speakers that language rights, as defined here, try to protect.[11]

Because the recognition of minority status to ethnocultural groups is often a highly sensitive political question, in practice some states have found it easier to commit themselves to a more diffuse idea of linguistic diversity. There is nothing wrong with embracing linguistic diversity as a collective aim to serve the interests of society as a whole and not only or mainly of certain language speakers in having a rich and diverse cultural environment which enhances the practical relevance of individual autonomy. On the other hand, there may be a certain danger in resting any theory of language rights on such diffuse general interests only (Green 1987: 656). In my view, the main concern has to do with the likelihood that any attempt to do so will end up subverting the order of rights and duties and fall into the temptation of making language minorities the holders of the primary responsibility for language maintenance for the good of the general and diffuse interest of language diversity, which may result in the oppression of dissident members of such minorities. Furthermore, we should keep in mind that there are also strong general interests that would be better served by linguistic homogeneity even in a pluralist democracy; and it is not clear why these should not prevail over the benefits of language diversity (Bauböck 1999). Think of the interest in the lower costs that multilingualism in the administration of public services would entail, or the interest in furthering a common identity which will then enhance solidarity among citizens, or, simply, the importance of having a common language as a means of communication for a transparent political process (Green 1987: 64; Réaume 1991: 41; Kymlicka 1995a: 77).

The truth of the matter is that even those states that adhere to the goal of linguistic pluralism often do so rather rhetorically. When one looks then at the specific mechanisms states devise for linguistic protection, one can perceive that they are keen to apply them only to those languages spoken by autochthonous groups as opposed to, say, immigrant groups. This shows that their concern is

---

[11] Thus it is important that the use of this terminology which refers to instrumental and non-instrumental approaches to language rights does not lend itself to misapprehension. By a non-instrumental rights approach I do not mean that the protection of a certain language becomes the goal in itself, regardless of how it can instrumentally serve the interests of its users. In other words, this is not a survivalist approach that focuses on the need to protect language diversity per se, as if languages themselves were the beneficiaries of rights to ensure their survival. In a way, both types of language rights, as conceived here, are instrumental in a strict sense. They always serve instrumentally the interests of their speakers.

much more with accommodating minorities cultural claims than they are often willing to recognize. They simply try to do so in what they perceive to be the least politically divisive way: accommodation without explicit recognition of a group's national identity.[12]

## 4. Language Rights from an Instrumental Perspective

Instrumental language rights respond to different concerns. Sometimes they are expressly sanctioned in national constitutions. One of the most common rights is the right to the assistance of an interpreter in criminal proceedings as part of a larger set of procedural guarantees.[13] But, even when such rights are not explicitly recognized, some courts have read them into other rights. Often, they are simply recognized as a matter of administrative practice. That these rights are of a distinct nature is revealed by the fact that even some of the states which have traditionally been most opposed to assuming the protection of a specific language per se as part of the state's legitimate role—such as the US, which has debated and rejected the idea of sanctioning English as the official language—have recognized some forms of language rights.[14] Elaborating on the underlying rationale for such recognition may thus offer interesting insights about the grounds upon which language claims can be asserted even when the idea of language identity and security as primary goods which deserve specific protection is publicly rejected.

---

[12]  So, for instance, it is a well-known fact that the European Charter for Regional or Minority Languages has focused on the protection of languages and linguistic diversity, rather than on the protection of the language users, as a way of defeating the resistance shown by some states, like France, to the recognition of minority rights. On the other hand, article 1 expressly excludes the languages of migrants, and the Explanatory Report of the Charter dwells on this point by indicating that the purpose of the Charter is not to resolve the problems arising out of recent immigration.

[13]  See, for instance, article 14 of the Canadian Charter of Rights and Freedoms; article 14 (3) of the International Covenant on Civil and Political Rights; and article 6.3 of the European Convention on Human Rights.

[14]  See, for instance, *Lau v. Nichols*, 414 US 563, where the Supreme Court found that instruction in English is detrimental only to students having a limited knowledge of English and amounts to a denial of equal opportunity in education, since 'English deficient' students are so disadvantaged that the education they do receive is almost useless. Granted, the Court did not say that education in their own language was mandatory, and expressly left open the choice between that and special education to help students learn English. But to say that, as a matter of right, providing education only in English when students cannot understand it constitutes a violation of the principle of non-discrimination is important. Also, extending the instrumental reasoning, one could imagine another Court embracing empirical evidence showing the importance of some mother-language instruction for optimal cognitive development to make the case that not providing for it would amount to discrimination. None of this would require the Court to assert immigrants' general right to cultural self-reproduction through the school system.

The idea that feeds the notion of instrumental language rights is that language should not be a liability in the enjoyment of one's general status of civil, social, and political rights and opportunities in society. This is why we prefer to call them instrumental. Obviously, in a sense every right can be described as instrumental to the protection of some good. But the reason behind calling these language rights instrumental is that their primary purpose is to help *instrumentally* in the protection of the goods that other rights which have been generally recognized are primarily concerned with. Precisely because most of the goods that are at stake have been embraced in different ways and to different degrees by liberal democratic states as primary goods that deserve rights protection, this conceptualization will allow for these derivative linguistic rights to be perceived mostly as a matter of consistency with already accepted premises of legitimacy.

The starting assumption is the liberal commitment not to punish people for traits that they do not choose, traits that say nothing about their moral worth and at the same time may be essential to their sense of identity. Among the many things that people do not choose in life is their native language, the language of their primary socialization. The learning of a second language is more or less difficult depending on many factors, including the mastery of one's first language, the age at which the learning process starts, people's linguistic talents, and the availability of adequate resources. And some people are never able to successfully complete the process.

Moreover, even people who learn a second language, unless this happens at a very early age, rarely lose their foreign accents. Now, one of the problems is that certain accents are not simply perceived as more or less exotic accents, epitomizing cultural diversity as an asset of humankind. Rather, because language often functions as a proxy for ethnicity, and some ethnic groups are associated with low social profiling, retaining a certain language or its accent can have a tremendous and often permanent stigmatizing impact. Furthermore, even when a certain language is not per se attached to a certain set of stigmatizing stereotypes, when listening to an adult who speaks a dominant language poorly, it is almost inevitable to relate such talk to that of a child or to the talk of the most poor and illiterate in society. Relevant information about the person's background or overall skills can certainly change this initial impression. But such knowledge is generally lacking in most casual and daily social interactions.[15]

In this regard the first and foremost instrumental language right should be the right not to be discriminated against because of one's language or accent.

---

[15] Presumably, different circumstances will have an impact on these social experiences of perception. In multinational states, where people have long had to live and struggle with the fact of cultural diversity, people may be less inclined to make the connection between accents and class or education. Immigrant societies like the US may also come to accept that the majority language is above all, a lingua franca, so that the standard expectation in linguistic exchanges is that it indeed be able to fulfil this role, and not that it provide some relevant information as to the social status or educational skills of the person to be measured through the correctness or accuracy of his or her use of the language.

Nothing can be more threatening to a person's ability to enjoy on equal terms the rights, freedoms, and opportunities generally recognized than being subject to systematic discrimination. In fact, many constitutions and international human rights documents explicitly prohibit discrimination on the basis of language.[16] Arguably, because language groups are often the targets of generalized prejudice, the state should not only refrain from discriminating on the basis of language but actively participate in eradicating discrimination patterns in civil society, just as it often feels compelled to take an active role in the eradication of racial or religious discrimination. Presumably, the degree of commitment of the state to notions of substantive equality[17] will determine the scope of protection that is afforded to language groups subject to generalized social prejudice.[18]

In my view, part of the eradication process will necessarily have to consist in some degree of public accommodation of the languages of the discriminated groups, so that the latter come to be respected as holders of a cultural identity. Only through such accommodation will the speakers of the dominant language, who may have never experienced obstacles of linguistic access themselves, perceive language minorities as more than 'poor speakers' of the dominant language; as people who have their own culture and are in the process of supplementing it with elements of a new one; as people facing the challenge of learning to become fluent in a second language. Giving the option to learn these languages in public schools to both their native speakers and the other students, making the learning of some second language mandatory, and making sure that the minority languages have some access to the media would all be legitimate anti-discrimination measures in this regard and could arguably give rise to language rights claims. Facilitating the process of acquisition of the

---

[16] See, for instance, article 2.1 of the International Covenant on Civil and Political Rights; article 14 of the European Convention on Human Rights; article 3 of the Italian Constitution; and article 3 of the German Basic Law.

[17] By this I mean the commitment to ensure the conditions that enable people to enjoy their formal rights or freedoms in an effective manner, and this entails an effort to remove the obstacles that disadvantaged groups may encounter in civil society.

[18] This, of course, is not to say that language can never be used as a legitimate ground for differentiation. So, for instance, it is common and in my view perfectly legitimate that certain public administrations will require some kind of linguistic competence as a condition for qualification. Indeed, such a policy can be said to serve the right the general public has to address and be addressed by the public administration in a certain language. That said, there have to be limits on how competence criteria can be defined, otherwise they could become a form of discrimination against those who are not native speakers of a given language. There have been constitutional cases in Spain about when such language requirements could or could not amount to discrimination. Generally, the Spanish Constitutional Court has decided that there has to be some significant connection and proportionality between the kind of language skill that is demanded as a condition for public employment and the specific skills that the adequate performance of the work actually requires. See, for all, *Sentencia del Tribunal Constitucional* (decision of the Constitutional Court) 46/1991. Arguably, similar criteria ought to apply in private sector employment.

dominant language for language minorities cannot replace the need for some accommodation of the minority languages, however minimal. Some degree of public visibility is needed to enhance the capacity for empathy of the average citizen who may have never experienced linguistic exclusion himself or herself.

Purposeful discrimination is only the most blatant form of language liability and does not exhaust by any means the notion of instrumental language rights.[19] Because language skills are so crucial to functioning in society, to participating in the political process, and to interacting with state authorities, there are many ways in which lack of knowledge of the public and dominant language(s) can diminish people's chances even where this is not linked to discrimination. In those instances where the interaction at stake is considered of sufficient relevance to be accorded the status of a right, we have the basis for instrumental language rights claims.

Think about the right to education. Whatever else we may say, if one simply does not understand the language in which education takes place, education itself becomes meaningless. As with many other rights, the right to education rests for its minimal fulfilment on the possibility of comprehensible linguistic interactions. The same applies to the right to a fair trial, which requires that one be able to understand and be understood. Think also of the right to vote, which may be of little use if one cannot understand the options expressed in monolingual ballots. Bilingual ballots may be required to overcome this obstacle. Again, take the case of access to social rights or public benefits. The right to public health can be meaningless in many instances if one is not able to communicate with a physician. In general, language difficulties will create big obstacles to access to many of the benefits provided by the state that have to be applied for through

---

[19] As a matter of fact, calling the right not to be discriminated against because of one's language an instrumental language right implies an improper use of the notion of instrumentality, as defined above. It is true that in a way such a right can be phrased as the paradigmatic instrumental language right. Being the object of prejudice and discrimination obviously sets limits to the enjoyment of other rights and freedoms. However, here the instrumentality is inherent to the right to equality and does not refer to the connection between language and the enjoyment of a right which rests on the possibility of comprehensible linguistic interactions. Thus, one could argue that the notion of non-discrimination can also be instrumentally used to defend non-instrumental language rights, that is, one's equal right to the protection of one's linguistic identity. Indeed, some commentators have proposed relying on the notion of human rights in general, and specifically on the right to non-discrimination, to accommodate language minority claims instead of using language of minority rights (de Varennes 1996). The problem with this is that, if states are not willing to recognize people's cultural goods as objects that deserve autonomous and heightened protection, the right to equality loses many if its teeth, as any test of equality has to allow for the possibility of what are generally called *reasonable, rational*, or *objective differentiations*. I do not mean to say that the right to equality and the non-discrimination clause do not have a great strategic potential, especially when one considers how widely accepted they are and how great the resistance of states to cast cultural accommodations in terms of minority rights is. Much to the contrary. I merely mean to say that the same reasons that explain such resistance are likely to come up phrased as *reasonable justifications* for limiting cultural accommodation claims under the pertinent equality test.

official forms which some people will simply not understand. The freedom to choose one's profession is also recognized in liberal democracies and sometimes even entrenched as a constitutional right.[20] But lack of skills in the dominant language, as one of the most basic skills required for most forms of employment, will without a doubt diminish tremendously one's professional opportunities.

Because in this view language guarantees rest on the importance of other rights, what makes a certain degree of linguistic accommodation mandatory is the recognition of such rights. As the moral primacy granted to different rights will vary, one can expect the primacy given to derivative language rights to vary accordingly. But the least one could expect is some degree of internal consistency. The higher a given state places the enjoyment of a certain right, the more willing it should be to support those language rights that are instrumental to its enjoyment.[21]

One can expect that there will be reasonable disagreement as to which overall language policies best address these linguistic concerns. Also, it will not always be easy to tell, just by looking at a specific language accommodation, whether it embodies an instrumental or a non-instrumental language right. The determining factor for the distinction will be the rationale, or the grounds upon which the linguistic claim is made and granted, more than the concrete form of right itself.

Imagine the claim to have education in one's mother tongue during one's early years. Would this be an instrumental or a non-instrumental language right? It depends. As a non-instrumental language right the force of the claim would have to be sustained by the claim that such education is crucial to ensure a successful linguistic socialization process in one's language. Arguably one could also say that on a larger scale this right makes cultural reproduction for the group possible, and, that part of what it is to be able to live in one's language in every relevant sphere is to enjoy the communal experience of education in one's language. Also, a language community with its own institutions will have greater visibility and, hence, social respectability (Réaume 1991: 52). However, the same language claim could be grounded on the evidence of sociolinguistic studies that point to the importance of mastering one's mother tongue for further optimal cognitive development, including the kind of development required to learn a second language; and thus it could be argued that this should be recognized as a language right that derives instrumentally from the general right to education. If, on the other hand, the right that was claimed was the right to continued

---

[20] See, for instance, article 12 of the German Basic Law.

[21] Of course, this is not to say that we should limit the normative aspirations phrased around the notion of language rights claims to simply match the normative claims that different states have already recognized. Ultimately, the claim about instrumental language rights is not a claim about the rights that states ought to recognize *because* they have already recognized other rights which require the possibility of comprehensible linguistic interaction, but a claim about the rights that states ought to recognize *and* the language claims that they ought to accept as part of what that recognition entails.

education in one's mother tongue at later stages of development, it would be much less plausible to articulate such a right on purely instrumental grounds.

Although their ultimate rationales differ, it is obvious that instrumental and non-instrumental language rights are far from being unrelated. If a language group is systematically discriminated against, and if it can have access to meaningful options of all sorts only by abandoning its language and learning how to function in the majority language, the chances of it surviving over time are slim, given the pressures on their speakers to abandon the language for the sake of greater opportunities of all sorts (Réaume 1991: 46–7). Conversely, although language rights conceived in the strict sense focus more on the use of language as the expression of a certain cultural identity than on its purely communicative aspects, the two cannot be completely separated. After all, language is first and foremost a tool of social interaction and communication. Using it as a way of asserting one's cultural identity when the language itself does not serve as a meaningful tool of interaction or communication makes little sense and more than anything has the potential to undermine the self-esteem of its users, who come to be seen by the majority community as vain and absurd fanatics.[22]

To summarize, from the description of a specific language guarantee it may not be possible to immediately decide whether we are encountering an instrumental or non-instrumental right. Also, there may be reasonable disagreement as to what exactly is required in order to accommodate one or the other type of claims. But clarity on the rationale upon which the different language claims are based is still important for deciding which rights to recognize and, presumably, who should be accorded them.[23] The identification of legitimate ends still does not dictate the chosen means, as we shall see. But being able to rule out from the start the normative validity of the end to be achieved will help us cover at least part of the distance.

---

[22] So it is important both to make the distinction and to understand the relationship between both rationales. The Canadian Supreme Court, one of the few courts to have embraced in an explicit manner the distinction between different types of language rights, has not always kept the interconnection between them in mind. Thus, for instance, it has interpreted the right to choose English or French before the Courts established by the Canadian Parliament, provided for in article 19.1 of the Canadian Charter of Rights and Freedoms, as a right to choose the preferred language but not as a right to be understood in such language. See *MacDonald v. City of Montreal*, 1 S.C.R. 460, and *Société des Acadiens du Nouveau-Brunswick v. Association of Parents for Fairness in Education*, 1 S.C.R. 549. But it would be foolish to expect a language minority to heroically sacrifice the effective enjoyment of rights as fundamental as the right to a fair trial for the sake of asserting the right to use its own language as a symbol of cultural affirmation. When there is no obligation to actively accommodate the minority language by making sure that there are sufficient judges who are proficient in both languages or in each of the languages, insisting on using the minority language is likely to be perceived as a gesture of burdensome and costly vanity.

[23] Thus, multinational states may be willing to accommodate non-instrumental language rights for autochthonous national minorities as a way of ensuring their right to preserve their cultural identity, but strongly opposed to doing the same for immigrant groups which are ultimately expected to integrate into mainstream society. On the other hand, they may be much more willing to grant what is instrumentally required to facilitate that integration process and to do so on grounds of justice.

## 5.  The Right or Duty to Learn the Dominant Language(s) as an Alternative Response

The instrumental approach to language rights only makes the case for achieving a certain aim: to avoid linguistic obstacles that may curtail the enjoyment of rights, freedoms, and opportunities that rest on the possibility of comprehensible linguistic interactions. In order to determine which specific claims can be derived from such goals, one still needs to establish the connection between the purpose to be achieved and the means used. Also, as long as the means used are well suited to get us to the desired end, it is legitimate to make a case for those means that are the least harmful to other general interests that may be at stake.

### The Right to Learn the Dominant Language

Applied to the notion of instrumental language rights, given that our concern is with language as a tool of communication, what this means is that every time we can articulate an instrumental language claim we can make a case that the optimal way of serving such interest would be to facilitate people's learning of the dominant language, rather than devising mechanisms to assist them in their own language. This is mainly for two reasons: first, because fluency in the dominant language will in most cases be the best way of overcoming obstacles to language access; and second, it will also be the means that best help society's general interest in reducing the costs of accommodating linguistic diversity, in preserving its national identity through a common language, and in avoiding the risks of divisiveness which, some will say, are inherent in some different forms of linguistic accommodation. This is indeed the main difference between an instrumental and a non-instrumental approach. Only the latter approach requires, as a matter of principle, institutionalized accommodation of the minority languages.[24]

Given all that has been said, one may argue that instead of generically talking about instrumental language rights we should focus on articulating the right of every member in society to learn the state language(s). Indeed, some constitutional courts have recognized that the right to learn it derives directly from the language's official status and the right of citizens to use it in their interactions with public authorities.[25] One could also argue that it flows instrumentally from

---

[24] Again, this should be qualified with the caveat that a minimal public accommodation of the minority languages may be required as the only effective means to fight against generalized patterns of discrimination and thus to enhance the possibility of effective integration. Note then the inherent weakness of grounding the non-instrumental language claims of national minorities as identity claims on purely instrumental reasons of linguistic access, as some language rights advocates commonly do.                    [25] See *Sentencia del Tribunal Constitucional* 6/82.

the recognition of those other rights and freedoms that require linguistic capabilities. But probably the best defence would be simply that it should be part of what any conception of the more generic right to education should encompass in a linguistically plural state committed to notions of democracy, the rule of law, and distributive justice.

There is no doubt that, in general, the right to education is connected to the need to ensure equal opportunities of access to socially valuable skills and knowledge, which are key for the achievement of social prestige, economic well-being, and professional self-fulfilment. Such a right is also strictly tied to the need to prepare citizens to participate in the political process in an informed and responsible way. The reason why there has not been a greater need to spell out this right to learn the dominant language as an essential element of the right of education probably has to do with the fact both compulsory education and the use the official or public language(s) of the state as vernacular languages in the education system are generally accepted, so that most people naturally come to learn them.

But there are many ways in which this right could become controversial. Think of the situation in which people live with several public languages whether they be officially recognized or not.[26] Or think of the situation in which a certain language enjoys a dominant position in the economy even though it is not recognized as an official language. In these cases, there should be a prima facie duty of the state or the educational public authorities to teach all the relevant languages. Even in multinational societies with mechanisms designed for the permanent protection of ethnolinguistic identities, such a right ensures a minimal exit option for individuals who may not be willing to forgo the possibilities linked to the knowledge of the dominant languages.

Another interesting issue is whether such a right should assist adults as well as children, given that often the right to public education is understood to apply only to the period of compulsory education. The issue is clearly most relevant for immigrant adults. In my view, a case could be made for such an extension. The right to public education until a certain age makes sense if we start with the assumption that new members of society are born and educated within it. But a society which accepts new members on an ongoing basis needs to ensure that the conditions for their equal access to rights and opportunities are also secured. As well, the needs of citizens who, for some reason or other, might have spent their childhood outside of their country and then return as adults should be taken into account.

[26] So for instance, the Spanish Constitution accords to Castilian the status of official language in the whole of the country and, to the other languages of Spain, such as Catalan, Basque, or Galician, a co-official status within their respective territories. Citizens living in one of those territories are then subject to a regime of two official languages. Think further of the additional challenge posed by the use of English and French as working languages in some European institutions, even though all EU national languages officially have equal status.

Part of the reason why this right to learn the dominant language(s) is bound to be controversial when spelled out in the context of a linguistically diverse society confronted with the renewed challenge of incorporating immigrants is that, even if agreement can be reached in the domain of principles, there will probably be disagreement as to what the fulfilment of such a right exactly requires, even for children. Indeed, the existence of competing linguistic theories on the best way to learn a second language inevitably makes the decision as to how to fulfil this right a controversial one. Much of the language debate in the US specifically turns on this issue, namely, whether bilingual education or the sink-or-swim approach of full immersion is the more efficient way to help children from an immigrant household learn sufficiently good English to be able to function in society.[27]

If what has been said is right, one of the things we may conclude is that the cogency with which instrumental language rights other than the right to learn the dominant languages can be claimed may vary depending on the context. The more strongly the state is committed to ensuring an effective right to learn the majority language, the less compelling the demands for accommodation in other languages will be. But this does not mean that, as long as the state does indeed provide for a meaningful right to learn the language, it can fully discharge any other responsibility for accommodating instrumental language needs. The policy of encouraging and facilitating linguistic integration may well be legitimate and yet insufficient to achieve the state's ends. Several factors may account for this. Unfortunately, shortcomings in the educational system will be one of the most common. But ultimately the main reason why the right to learn a second language cannot cancel out other instrumental rights to ensure comprehensible linguistic interactions is that, no matter how genuinely committed the state may be, the learning of a second language may well be beyond what many people can achieve even under largely favourable conditions.

## The Duty to Learn the Dominant Language

Some people would readily concede most of what I have said concerning the political relevance of obstacles to linguistic access, and yet object to the defence of instrumental language rights by reference to such obstacles as resting on a fatal flaw, namely, that of reversing the terms and calling a right what in reality ought to be conceived of as both a right and a duty. People should regard the acquisition of the language(s) of the state as a civic duty and not just a right, given the overall relevance of learning the language for the proper functioning of a democratic society committed to the rule of law. However contested such a duty may be on other grounds, it seems that a fundamental general interest is served when the official language(s) can function as lingua francas to enable

---

[27] See Crawford (1992b: Part V).

understanding, trust, and cohesion, all of which are essential for the preservation of healthy democratic institutions, and that such an interest is served when citizens regard learning the official language(s) as a civic duty.[28]

Sometimes such a duty is expressly spelt out in the legal order.[29] More often, it is recognized in indirect ways. As mentioned above, people born in the country are subject to compulsory education which will typically include the learning of the language in which public institutions function. As for immigrants, sometimes as a condition for their initial entry, but more frequently as a condition for naturalization, they will be asked to show linguistic competence in the (or one of the) national language(s). Granted, such an obligation does not always cover everyone. Left out are native-born citizens who may have lived outside the country, immigrants who have not become naturalized, short-term visitors, and, in countries where there is more than one official language, citizens who may have been brought up and educated in a minority official language or newcomers who may have been scrutinized for their competence in such a language even though the majority language may still be the language predominantly used by the central or federal institutions.

Now, clearly, when one is born in a society, there has to be a right attached to such a duty, as there is no guarantee that people will in fact be able to learn such a skill at home, or, in any event, to do so sufficiently to realise all the personal and collective interests attached to the knowledge of the language. Linking the right and duty to education to a right and duty to learn the dominant languages at school is therefore defensible. With adults it is a different matter. If they were born in society, one can say that they already ought to have learned the language through the means provided by the state. If, more likely, they joined as immigrants at a later stage, they themselves are to be held primarily responsible for acquiring the required linguistic skills. The fact that language criteria for naturalization are generally accepted reflects the intuition that, before they can join as full members, it is legitimate to ask immigrants for proof that they will be able to function as members of the state community.

The relevant question, however, remains whether the existence of a civic duty to be competent in the majority language can exonerate the state from

[28] Even the European Charter for Regional or Minority Languages in its sixth preambular paragraph considers that 'the protection and encouragement of regional or minority languages should not be to the detriment of the official languages and the *need to learn* them' (my emphasis). And the Explanatory Report of the Charter states that the Charter by no means seeks to foster any kind of partitioning off of linguistic groups, recognizing that in every state it is necessary to know the official language or one of the official languages.

[29] Article 3 of the Spanish Constitution sanctions the right *and duty* of every Spaniard to know Castilian as the official language in Spain. Other national minority languages have been recognized as co-official languages together with Castilian within their regions, but no equivalent duty to know them has been constitutionally sanctioned. Although still far from articulating a clear justification for the distinction, the Spanish Constitutional Court seems call on the function of Castilian as the lingua franca to account for it. See *Sentencia del Tribunal Constitucional* 84/1986.

accommodating instrumental language needs when indeed people fail to fulfil such a duty and what is at stake is so important as to deserve rights protection. In other words, failure to observe the duty to be competent in the language does not have to lead to automatic penalties. In principle, only the most serious infringements of civic duties, such as the duty to abide by the criminal law, can trigger a limitation of one's general rights and freedoms, and even that often in a way that is strictly connected to other people's enjoyment of their rights and freedoms. That would not be as certain in the case with the duty to know the language in which the public institutions function, and where, at best, the society could claim only general and diffuse public interests. More importantly, because the fulfilment of the duty does not exclusively depend on individual disposition and is often linked to insufficient commitment of the state to facilitate such knowledge, one should be wary of 'punishing' with further exclusion those who have presumably failed. Ultimately, one may argue, the state may be more or less demanding in imposing such a duty on newcomers who intend to stay; but once they are in, often for good, to allow their rights to be de facto limited by obstacles to linguistic access seems to be largely objectionable.[30]

It is commonly objected that supporting instrumental language rights can actually contribute to the failure to learn the majority language because it discourages people to learn it, thinking they can get by without it. In addition, even though instrumental and non-instrumental rationales may differ, they are not disconnected. Indeed, one can expect instrumental language rights to have cultural spillover effects. When otherness is acknowledged and partially accommodated, people are more likely to be proud than ashamed of their distinctiveness. And this national pride may also predispose people against linguistic assimilation to the extent of hindering their chances of meaningful social integration. Because only linguistic assimilation can truly guarantee equality in the enjoyment of rights and freedoms and of social and economic opportunities, the recognition of instrumental language rights—at least, of any right other than the right to learn the majority language, whatever we want to call it—is ultimately self-defeating, or so the argument goes.

In my view, the concern proceeds from a questionable assumption. Indeed, one may argue that the opposite is more likely to be true. One could say that, because immigration is generally triggered by a desire to enjoy the larger

---

[30] The Spanish experience offers a relevant example. The Constitutional Court has inferred two main implications from the constitutional duty to know Castilian: first, the obligation on the part of the public authorities to teach Castilian, and second, the presumption that, when such authorities address the citizenry in Castilian, for example by using it as the language for statutory drafting, they are being understood so that, in principle, one cannot claim ignorance of Castilian as an excuse for ignoring the law. However, it has not been willing to infer that, in concrete instances of inter-subjective interaction, the state can call on the generic duty to know Castilian to deny language assistance when the effective enjoyment of a constitutional right is at stake, such as, for instance, the right to due process which may require the assistance of an interpreter in trial (*Sentencia del Tribunal Constitucional* 74/1987).

opportunities that the receiving society has to offer and the acquisition of linguistic skills is indeed a precondition for such enjoyment, one can in principle assume that immigrants will be motivated to learn the majority language.[31] If this is the case, making such knowledge a condition for even minimal enjoyment of those rights that require linguistic interaction may aggravate their reality of exclusion and marginalization. Yet most of the time it is precisely the reality of exclusion that lies at the root of the difficulty in acquiring the relevant language tools to function properly in society. The already disempowered should not be further disempowered. We should be wary of facilitating the creation of subcultures of marginalization under paternalistic pretences. If effective inclusion is the leading concern, instrumental language rights and the right and opportunity to learn the majority language should coexist with, not compete against, each other. In general, economic domination and oppression are amongst the most secure routes to cultural pluralism. Preventing members of certain groups from having access to the dominant institutions of society and enjoying the full set of rights and freedoms will almost certainly make them retain their different culture (Spinner 1994: 63).

## 6. Reasonable Limits to Instrumental Language Claims

If, as I have argued, the right to learn the state language(s) cannot cancel out the reasons for instrumental language rights, it is also clear that no order would resist an endless multiplication of instrumental language claims, such as, for instance, the right to have access to every governmental benefit in every existing language, or the right to have the education system or the judiciary functioning in every language spoken in society. There have to be limits on what we can reasonably expect a state to accommodate even in an instrumental way.

The necessity of identifying some of the criteria for pondering the specific weight of instrumental language rights claims becomes even more urgent when we realise that, once we are willing to recognize the distinction between instrumental and non-instrumental language rights, there is no reason to limit the instrumental rights to autochthonous national minorities, no matter how broad the consensus that only those groups should be accorded non-instrumental language rights. Since what is at stake is the effective enjoyment of non-linguistic

---

[31] Granted, the reality of immigration is broad enough to include much diversity in the range of expectations. Some immigrants may come with the expectation of eventually returning to their countries of origin, or only on temporary basis, and may be less motivated to invest in learning the majority language. However, there is something odd in taking what seems to be the exception as the norm and grounding on it the set of rules that are to govern the majority of the cases. In any event, even if it were true that some immigrants were genuinely uninterested in learning the language of the receiving society, one would still need to answer the question for those who might be willing to do so but are not able because of the lack of either adequate support or individual capabilities.

rights and freedoms that are otherwise accorded to immigrants, there would be no reason to exclude them.[32]

Now, from what has been said thus far, some limits to and priorities within the legitimate range of language claims can be articulated. First of all, let us recall that, because of their instrumental nature, these language claims will derive their strength from that of the right on which they are grounded. Thus, there may be a stronger basis for the right to be educated in a language one can understand, or the right to the assistance of an interpreter at one's trial, than the right to have some other social benefit delivered in that language, if and when the right to education is considered of more importance than the right to whatever other social benefit we are talking about.

Moreover, it is not only the relevance of the right per se that must be taken into account, but what the linguistic conditions for its minimally effective enjoyment are. Think of the difference between the right to bilingual social services and the right to translation in one's trial. Intuition tells us that the latter should take primacy over the former. One reason this is so is that we imagine that the goods at stake in one's trial, such as personal freedom, may be of higher importance than the economic stake in a certain social service. But this may not account for every relevant aspect. Perhaps a fine, and not a prison sentence, is what is at stake in the judicial process, and the economic stake could well be less significant than that linked to the social service, say, public funding for housing. However, the fact is that one's trial consists mainly of a linguistic exercise that takes place in a very concrete place and time, and where the linguistic acts that take place are taken to provide evidence of the highest relevance to determining the outcome. The same is generally not true of social services which often require some form of linguistic interaction, often through a written application, a procedure that is sometimes expanded over a period of time, and typically allows for the possibility of correcting formal mistakes, such as those that may be linked to insufficient knowledge of the language in which the procedure or the application process takes place.

An additional limitation comes from keeping in mind the *telos* or purpose that these rights serve, especially when compared with those of non-instrumental language rights. Once again, the aim of instrumental language rights is not the protection of one's linguistic or cultural identity but the overcoming of

---

[32] Note that we are not specifically addressing the question of the relevance of citizenship as a formal condition for such enjoyment. The distinction is made on the basis of whether the ethnic group is part of the founding state or predated it, through links to the territorial domain which it now occupies, or whether it has been formed mainly through the addition of immigrant newcomers. Thus, an immigrant may be denied an instrumental language right, not because she is not part of a given foundational or pre-existing ethnic community, but because of her lack of citizenship when and if the instrumental language right at stake is derived from another right which requires citizenship as a condition for its recognition. Take, for instance, the right to vote as a political right which is generally accorded to only citizens and the instrumental language right of bilingual ballots that we could imagine deriving from it in a given setting.

language obstacles so as to enjoy in a minimally significant way a given right or freedom that rests on the possibility of linguistic interactions. So, if we think of language rights in the judicial realm, a right to use and be understood in one's language by the courts or the jury may be a non-instrumental right, but the instrumental rationale would be satisfied simply by the right to a translator.

Granted, in theory one could always argue that only by being able to use and to be understood in one's language can the effectiveness of the enjoyment of whatever right is at stake be maximized. To go back to our example, relying on a translator can be only a second-best option as it deprives the judicial process of some of its purity. There is a whole cultural background shared by the speakers of a language which is relevant to giving full meaning to the linguistic expression. Using translations curtails the immediacy of the process too. But if carried to its ultimate conclusion, this way of reasoning would obliterate the difference between instrumental and non-instrumental language rights. Because the aim of the former is to establish a minimum of rights of universal application, such a conceptualization requires sacrificing the optimal for the feasible and hence subjecting instrumental language rights claims to the strict purpose of making sure that the linguistic exchange is actually comprehensible. The 'minimally effective enjoyment' standard should therefore apply.

This brings us to the larger question of the relevance that another feasibility constraint, namely, that of the monetary costs involved, ought to play. Clearly, this cannot be the determining factor in the recognition of the right at stake because that would defeat the argument that instrumental language rights are rights in the strict sense. But it can and ought to play some role in determining the scope and the institutional choice for accommodating the underlying claim. In this respect two factual considerations ought to be mentioned: numbers and geographical concentration. When the numbers of speakers of a language are high, and when these speakers are geographically concentrated, it is more feasible to accommodate their language needs. Think of the possibility of having a school system that teaches children of the largest minorities in their language during the first schooling years as a way of supporting their cognitive development and hence their overall educational skills. Or think of facilitating the right to vote or to access social benefits through bilingual ballots and application forms in those languages most widely spoken in the concerned area.

The regrettable but inevitable limitations that derive from cost considerations can only make the right to learn the state language(s) even more compelling. Indeed, one could make the case that cost considerations should in principle not be acceptable as limitation criteria unless there is a strong commitment on the part of the state to facilitate the learning of such language(s), as arguably the least burdensome means of satisfying the interests at stake. Also, because the different criteria for the legitimate limitations of instrumental language rights claims should all be considered jointly, one could still make the case that the importance of some instrumental language rights, such as the right to translation in criminal trials, is such that monetary constraints should be accorded no weight at all.

Feasibility or cost considerations account for only part of the intuition that numbers matter. This is because rights, of whatever kind, do not exhaust the conditions of legitimacy in the exercise of state power. Some of those conditions are actually expressed through general commitments to principles of legitimization, such as a system based on the rule of law, a democratic form of government, or redistributive notions in the framework of a social state which themselves already have a linguistic dimension.[33] This is why the disenfranchisement of large segments of society, or the exclusion of large pools of children from meaningful education by language obstacles, poses a greater legitimacy problem than can be captured by the idea of multiple infringements of individual rights. And in this way numbers matter too.

## 7. A Right to Bilingual Ballots for Hispanics in the US Southwest?

So many possible factors have been raised here that it may seem difficult to assess the potential of this instrumental approach to language rights to advance specific language rights claims in real contexts. Presumably, in virtually every real-world case the various factors will point in different directions. So let us take the claim to bilingual ballots for the Hispanic population in the US Southwest to see how the proposed framework for the evaluation of instrumental language rights could actually be applied to a specific case.

To evaluate this claim, we would first ask whether the right at stake is of a fundamental nature, so as to support resting on it a language right of the instrumental kind. Clearly that is the case with suffrage in virtually all democratic constitutional regimes, including the US. The right to suffrage embodies the state's commitment to a democratic form of government. It plays a crucial role in allowing citizens to protect the rest of their rights and freedoms and to advance their interests and views in society.

---

[33] So it is interesting to see how in a legal order with a relatively precarious articulation of rights, like the European Union, it is still possible to make a strong case for the recognition of a set of language rights stemming directly from the Union's commitment to the principles of democracy and the rule of law and the related requirements of openness, transparency, and sound administration (Nic Shuibhne 2002). Granted, the recognition of some rights is directly connected to the demands of such commitments. Think of the connection between the commitment to a democratic form of government and the right to suffrage; the commitment to the rule of law and the rights that derive from the principle of legal certainty; or the commitment to a social form of state and the right to public education.

Next, we may want to ask ourselves to what extent language can be an obstacle to the meaningful exercise of suffrage. The large Spanish-speaking presence in civil society may ensure that there are enough media to keep people in the Southwest who are not fluent in English sufficiently informed about the political agenda at any given point in time. However, when it comes to voting, being able to cast an informed vote when the options expressed in the ballot— think for instance of a referendum—are written only in English depends on the capacity to understand this language sufficiently. In that sense, language can be and often is an obstacle to the exercise of voting rights.

Third, we should ask ourselves whether the means for learning English are properly provided, both for children of school age and for adults. In fact there is a history in the US of linking first the validity of English-literacy requirements and then the need for bilingual ballots to the experience of unequal educational opportunities of some discriminated groups. Thus, the 1965 Voting Rights Act nullified the English-literacy requirement for voting contained in the New York State constitution to enfranchise Puerto Ricans. Congress acted in the awareness that Puerto Ricans were persons educated in American-flag schools in which the predominant classroom language was one other than English and extended the ban nationwide in 1970. Going one step further in 1975, after hearing testimony about the denial of equal educational opportunities by State and local governments, which had left groups such as Hispanics, Asian Americans, and American Indians illiterate in English, Congress declared that it was 'necessary to eliminate such discrimination by prohibiting English-only elections and by prescribing other remedial devices'.[34]

Whatever the educational means provided, we would then need to check whether any substantial numbers of people nonetheless do not know the language well enough, since, if so, that would automatically strengthen the case for a right to bilingual ballots. The educational system may not be successful in meeting the needs shaped by the specific acculturation process that takes place in Spanish-speaking households and communities. Immigrants might have little time or resources to devote to learning the language or enormous difficulties in learning English as a second language after a certain age. One may argue that, because naturalization requires knowledge of English, such knowledge should be presupposed as a condition for exercising voting rights. After all, only naturalized immigrants are entitled to vote. But this assumes, as Tresviña has rightly argued (1992: 263), that there is only one level of literacy for all contexts, whereas, according to Tresviña, to pass the naturalization test requires about a third-grade level of English; education experts generally designate fifth-grade English skills as the dividing line between functional literacy and illiteracy; and voting materials, especially the explanations of ballot propositions, are written at levels as high as college English.

[34] See 2 U.S.C. 1973a, cited in Tresviña (1992: 256).

Finally, what makes the case for bilingual ballots for the Spanish speaking population of the Southwest especially resistant to cost considerations that may be alleged against it in favour of less costly alternatives, such as, presumably, improving the educational system, is the fact that we are talking about a large population which is geographically concentrated. Those factual conditions make the provision of translated written materials and oral voter assistance more feasible. Also, in terms of legitimacy, having a large pool of disenfranchised citizens should stir the democratic conscience in a system of government which is committed to the will of the majority in a particularly compelling way.

It is interesting to note that the 1975 Voting Rights Act amendments which, for the first time, introduced bilingual ballots in the US were indeed sensitive to almost all the considerations mentioned above. Indeed, Congress incorporated bilingual election provisions of voting rights requiring that written materials and oral voter assistance be made available in languages other than English under certain circumstances: a single language-minority group must account for at least 5 per cent of a jurisdiction's voting-age citizens and (1) the English literacy rate must be below the national average, or (2) the jurisdiction must have conducted the 1972 election only in English and have attracted the participation of fewer than 50 per cent of potential voters. Numbers, demographic concentration, low rates of English literacy, and the assumption of the link between monolingual elections and particularly low electoral turnouts in some areas were all taken into account in shaping this highly controversial policy. The question here is whether these conditions ought to ground the right to bilingual ballots as derivative from the constitutional right to suffrage and the constitutional commitment to a democratic form of government, as I have argued here.

## 8. Conclusion

The notion of language rights is gaining force as a way for ethnocultural minorities to articulate some of their most essential concerns about the preservation of their cultural and linguistic environment within the state. However, language rights are also relevant within the reading of liberalism that denies the state's duty to protect specific cultural rights of minority groups. This becomes clear as soon as we are willing to recognize the inevitable linguistic dimension of both the state apparatus and the modern nation construct. Language obstacles can indeed hinder the effective exercise of many traditional rights and freedoms that rest on the possibility of comprehensible linguistic interactions and limit the possibilities of economic and professional success in a society that functions in a dominant language.

It is time to start articulating some language claims as language rights, and perhaps also some civic language duties, on grounds other than the claim to cultural self-reproduction. Among them are: everyone's right to learn the dominant language(s) on the state's account which is not limited to the age of compulsory education, and, when different languages coexist, everyone's duty to learn a second language for the sake of ensuring cultural empathy; the right to receive some education in one's mother tongue in the earliest years; the right to some presence in the public media of the languages most widely used in society; the right not be discriminated against because of one's language or accent in seeking access to employment, services, and goods; the right to a translator as part of the right to a legal defence; the right to bilingual or multilingual ballots, administration of essential services, and statutory drafting at least where numbers warrant and conditions of geographical concentration of the language speakers make these feasible options.

In each of these cases, access to some meaningful good without liabilities linked to language skills is at stake. When the numbers of people affected by linguistic obstacles to access are sufficiently broad, the reality becomes troubling not just from the perspective of the enjoyment of their individual rights, but also from that of the overall commitment of the state to legitimization principles such as the rule of law or a democratic form of government. Law is a linguistic creature. Participating in its deliberation process and in its creation, complying with it, and being able to shape one's expectations according to it requires the law and law-making process to be minimally transparent to the members of society. Hence the challenge to articulate what this implies in a multilingual society. An exercise of recognition and consistency is called for: recognition of the existence of linguistic obstacles to access to basic goods linked to morally irrelevant features such as one's mother tongue, and consistency in addressing such obstacles in view of the basic premises of equality.

# 3

# A Liberal Democratic Approach to Language Justice

DAVID D. LAITIN AND ROB REICH

Linguistic diversity is a social fact that raises important normative questions about justice. Since most states are linguistically diverse—by which we mean that the political boundaries of the state circumscribe a territory in which persons do not share the same native tongue—the state must have language policies, either explicit or implicit, that answer questions such as: what language(s) should be used in public institutions?; should linguistic minorities receive education in their native language, and, if so, should the state fund it?; can the state mandate or prohibit the use of some language(s) in public or non-public domains?; and can linguistic communities within the state mandate or prohibit the use of some language(s) within given zones or territories?

We seek to provide a framework to address questions of this sort within liberal political theory. Liberalism, in both its classical and contemporary formulations, aspires to ideals of justice, freedom, and equality that are universal in reach, and it justifies these ideals by appeal either to the innate capacities of all human beings or to heuristics such as Rawls's original position. The problem faced by liberals in answering questions about linguistic justice is that universal theories tend to strip human beings of virtually all social contingencies. Until the recent burst of work on multiculturalism, the liberal tradition has ignored ethnic and national groups or, more strongly, had advocated some kind of difference blindness as a matter of principle. Liberalism, in short, is more often than not anthropologically bare (Mehta 1999). To put actual humans into our liberal framework, we listen to the voice and syntax from the tongues of the abstract human beings who are the typical subjects of liberal theory. But we do so without renouncing aspirations towards universalism or denouncing the original position.

As a prelude to our approach, we evaluate three broad approaches within contemporary political thought to questions about language policy. One approach situates linguistic justice within a redistributive paradigm. In this view, justice requires attempting to determine what distributions are necessary to compensate

The authors acknowledge incisive comments from Josep Costa, James Fearon, Claudine Gay, Will Kymlicka, Isabela Mares, Susan Moller Okin, Alan Patten, and Anne Wren on earlier drafts of this chapter.

individuals for any unfairness suffered by virtue of not knowing how to speak the dominant or politically preferred language. Two kinds of questions are relevant here: what is owed to individuals who, through no fault of their own, speak a language or dialect that limits their social mobility and disables their participation in public institutions?; and what are the fair terms of cooperation among linguistic groups in the production of the public good of a common language? The focus is on the costs of attaining linguistic convergence. This *compensatory approach to linguistic justice* is self-consciously at the core of liberal thinking.

A second approach looks to history and the ugly record of injustices done to linguistic minorities. In this view, justice requires asking how historical injustices that marginalized once-thriving language communities can be remedied, so that marginalized languages, and the value of these languages to the identities of their speakers, can be restored. The focus here is on revitalizing languages that have waned in use over generations. Bringing these languages back to life requires an intrusive state that can limit the free choices of parents and children as to what language will be used in schools, offices, and even on the street. Because this view is most often promoted by representatives of national minority groups, we call this the *nationalist approach to linguistic justice*. As will become apparent, advocates of this approach deviate some from liberal principles.

A third approach sees linguistic justice as rooted in the claim that individuals can be free only when they have access to a culture which is both flourishing and their own. In this view, culture and language are intimately bound up with one another, and justice demands that minority groups receive external protections from the state—among them a slate of language rights—to sustain their culture. The rights of minority groups are limited, however, by the respect owed first and foremost to individuals, not groups. Minority rights exist here within a liberal framework. Groups are permitted neither to abridge the autonomy of their members to challenge certain traditions or beliefs, nor to undermine the civil and political rights of those who challenge their tradition. Borrowing from Kymlicka, we call this the *liberal culturalist approach to linguistic justice*. Kymlicka's project has been to reformulate the nationalist perspective so that it remains consistent with liberal principles.

While not denying the importance and cogency of the perspectives on language policies that come from these three approaches, this chapter finds that all ignore vital elements of empirical reality. Furthermore, all ignore or downplay the fundamental indeterminacy of liberal principles of justice in coming to grips with competing language claims. The standard approaches, therefore, miss seeing in competing justice claims an opportunity for opening up a genuine and valuable space for liberal democratic politics. To develop our argument, we first explore each of the three approaches. Next we present and defend our *liberal democratic* approach to linguistic justice. We then address potential objections and conclude with reflections about the limits of liberal justice with respect to language policies.

## 1.  Three Approaches to Language Justice

*Compensatory Justice*

Why might the fact of linguistic diversity be a problem that requires compensation? The reason is that individuals have no influence over the language of their
parents, yet their parents' language, if it is a minority one in a polity, constrains
social mobility and, if the language is not officially recognized, the opportunity
to participate politically. Since those who speak a minority (or dominated)
language are more likely to stand permanently on the lower rungs of the socio-
economic ladder in any polity, something like the Rawlsian difference principle
would require compensation for those in the minority language community for
learning the dominant language. If they learn it, they are paying a price to produce the joint good of a language community, from which members of the
dominant language group benefit. From this point of view, it is unfair for members of the dominated language community to pay all the costs themselves for
the production of this joint good. Having set up the problem this way, the goal
becomes how to create compensatory schemes to maximize fairness (Pool
1991*a*; Van Parijs, this volume).

Empiricists are likely to be perplexed as to whether those forwarding compensatory claims have set up the problem correctly. In a wide range of concrete
examples of language politics, people either ignore or eschew opportunities
for compensation. Consider the case of Catalonia. In the medieval and early
modern eras, one of the dominant languages of this region of the Iberian peninsula was Catalan, as Catalonia was a vibrant trading centre in the Mediterranean
world. Barcelona, capital of Catalonia, was the first city on the peninsula to get
the Gutenberg printing press, and Catalan became a widespread literary language. But, increasingly incorporated into a centralizing Spanish empire, nearly
all Catalans developed a facility in Castilian, the dominant Spanish language. By
the early eighteenth century, virtually all publications in Catalonia were in
Castilian (Laitin, Solé, and Kalyvas 1994). Catalans could now effectively communicate not only with all other Catalans but with Castilian speakers spread all
over the globe. Yet in the late nineteenth century (in the so-called 'renaissance'),
again in the 1930s (in the second republic), and finally in the post-Franco period
since 1975, Catalans enthusiastically participated in efforts to revive their language in order to make it the principal medium of official and educational affairs
in their region of Spain.

Using the language of remedying historical injustice, Catalan leaders were
asking for state compensation not for their children to learn Castilian (to help in
the production of the joint good, a language community), but to revive Catalan!
Catalans were expending their own resources to further a linguistic programme
that would, to the extent that their children would become less competent
to speak and write Castilian, *decrease* their range of communication possibilities.

In the context of Spain, they were paying a heavy opportunity cost, risking their children's future linguistic marginalization. From a compensatory justice perspective, Catalan seekers of 'linguistic normalization' are happy slaves.

A similar tale can be told about contemporary Ghana. Many Ghanaians have expressed an interest in having for their country a common language (a joint good) that is unique to Ghana. The problem is in coordinating on one of the indigenous languages, none of them sufficiently dominant to serve as a 'focal point' for coordination. When researchers suggested compensatory schemes for purposes of creating the joint good of a language community, respondents were, to say the least, sceptical. To be sure, some respondents felt that no compensation would be sufficient given the costs of learning the language of a neighbouring group. But most respondents saw compensation to be a nefarious bribe for matters that were not subject to calculation. About the suggestion that a common Akan (the plurality language group of the country, encompassing a set of related languages) serve as Ghana's official language with hefty compensation for speakers of other languages, one respondent asked, 'Is the fellow who designed the questions an Akan? He is biased.' When a Ga respondent was asked if he would accept a compensation offer for learning Ewe (a minority language in the east of the country) he pleaded, 'I cannot sell my birthright . . . You just can't kill one language and use it as a manure for another' (Laitin 1994: 628). If respondents refuse to consider pay-offs as compensation for their efforts in the production of a collective good, it is worth considering whether the differential life chances associated with one's mother tongue are best approached with compensatory and redistributionist aims.

Consider now the situation of professional parents living in the small European democracies such as the Netherlands, Sweden, Norway, and Denmark. Assume that these parents have advanced skills enabling them to apply for jobs in many countries. Assume as well that limiting a job search to one's home country constrains lifetime earnings. Finally, assume that, if they remain in their own country, their children will develop mastery of the locally dominant language with reasonable skills in English; meanwhile, if they work outside their country, their children will develop mastery of English with diminished skills in their parents' language. If these parents were motivated to broaden mobility options for themselves and their children, we should expect to see them seeking to maximize their children's exposure to English through emigration and the fullest exposure of their children to English-speaking environments. In our impression, the reverse is true. Parents instead tend to pay the costs of lowered earnings to assure themselves that their children get an academic foundation in Dutch, Swedish, Norwegian, or Danish; and, when their children are grown up, these parents are more willing to explore opportunities internationally. Here members of dominated languages are willing to pay a price for a linguistic strategy that would in effect reduce their children's communicative facilities in the dominant world language.

We might also consider the articulated demands for justice in multilingual societies. In the Soviet Union, educational reforms initiated by Chairman Khrushchev in the late 1950s permitted parents of all nationalities to enrol their children in Russian-language schools, allowing their children to remedy any linguistic gap between them and native Russian-speakers. In the non-Russian-speaking republics of the Soviet Union, to the extent that public opinion could be aired, parents and educators were outraged, and blamed the government, using a Leninist epithet, for its Great Russian chauvinism. Similarly in independent India, any attempt by the central government to lower the costs for non-Hindi-speakers to learn Hindi is met with political fire, especially in the south of the country. People instead continue to demand from their State governments the right to have their children educated in minority languages.

In the United States, as in the case of most industrialized countries, children of poor immigrant families are in fact getting a compensatory distribution in regard to language. Assume that tax contributions of immigrants are far less than the value of the education received by their children. They are thereby receiving subsidized public education in the dominant state language. But this isn't the justice that many politically active minority leaders are asking for, and there are few if any public demands for higher subsidies for immigrant children to learn the state language. Rather, many of their leaders claim that justice demands subsidies to provide for their children an academic foundation in the home language.

Here, then, is our question: why would so many people turn down bribes as pay-offs to learn a dominant language at the expense of their mother tongues? In fact, many minority members expend resources in order to lower the communicative range of their children. Are they happy slaves, enjoying the lowered social mobility available to their children due to their misfortune of having the wrong mother tongue? Does the compensatory perspective correctly understand the nature of the justice issue, when many spokespersons for minorities are asking for compensation not to remedy but to exacerbate the injustice? Nationalists have an answer to this, and we address their perspective below.

## The Nationalist Perspective

An alternative approach to linguistic injustice is one that emerges from the nationalist uprisings in the Austro-Hungarian and Ottoman Empires in the late nineteenth century. Czechs, Serbs, Croats, Ukrainians, and Slovaks, speaking rurally-based language forms, were migrating into the great cosmopolitan capitals of Prague, Vienna, Kiev, and Zagreb. They (as analysed by Hroch 1985) recognized that cosmopolitan elites, speaking standardized languages quite different from their own, were in power. The migrants responded to pleas of bilingual nationalists, orating in the languages of the countryside, that they mobilize for control over national states in which people who spoke their language, so marginalized under imperial rule, would be the rulers. The portrait of restoration was drawn to justify this nationalist effort, but in reality peasant speech forms were being rationalized for the first time to become the basis for national states.

The notion that each language group merited its own national state, a notion that was constructed on the collapsed foundations of two empires, became enshrined in the ideas of Woodrow Wilson and Lenin. After the Second World War, these ideas were appropriated by those seeking to undermine the Dutch, French, British, and Belgian empires. The anti-imperialist theories of the twentieth century that grew from these experiences focused attention on imperial centres and how they marginalized peripheral languages. These theories supported national independence as a mechanism to restore the health and viability of historically marginalized peoples and their languages. In the post- Second World War era, UNESCO has carried the anti-imperialist flag in regard to national languages, and many of its publications have declared education and governance in one's mother tongue to be a right of all people (UNESCO 1953). A considerable portion of UNESCO funding has gone to fulfil that dream, through the support of national literatures in marginal languages.

Developing more fully the UNESCO perspective, Stephen May in his *Language and Minority Rights* (2001) connects the protection of dominated languages with issues of justice. He makes two crucial claims that bear on issues of justice. First, May emphasizes that the switch of minority peoples from using their mother tongues to the language of the dominant group was never a free choice, but the result of ideological coercion. Borrowing from the work of R. D. Grillo (1989), May argues that the 'ideology of contempt' that is expressed by cultural leaders from the dominant language group in reference to the language of the minority group lowers the status of the dominated language. And low status for a language leads over time to language death (May 2001: 19). Justice, he argues, demands that these coercive acts against minority populations be remedied.

Second, May agrees with the 1993 Draft Declaration of Indigenous Peoples as demonstrating 'the clear desire of indigenous peoples for greater linguistic and educational control . . .' (May 2001: 284). If this is what marginalized people want, and they have been driven to marginalization by the dominant groups, the dominant groups should facilitate (but not dominate over) a remedy in which the marginalized languages are revivified. Nationalists' concerns for justice focus not on facilitating assimilation but rather on reclaiming ancestral identities and seeking state support for the effort. In this view, the value of language is much more than instrumental. As Denise Réaume (2000: 251) has put it, 'Most people value their language not only instrumentally, as a tool, but also intrinsically, as a cultural inheritance and as a marker of identity as a participant in the way of life it represents'.

The most compelling critique of this nationalist perspective on linguistic just-ice comes from within the liberal tradition (Barry 2001). Barry takes on virtually all advocates of cultural group rights. In regard to language, he does not worry much if a language, for whatever historical reason, becomes marginalized. He writes:

But it may still be that a language becomes extinct, simply because those speaking it take decisions that in aggregate result in its disappearing. Very many languages have done just that in the past and doubtless many more will do so in the future . . . A liberal society cannot adopt policies designed to keep a language in existence if those who speak it prefer to let it go. Thus, [Charles] Taylor is quite correct in saying that liberalism 'can't capture the full thrust of policies designed for cultural survival'. But why should it be expected to? (Barry 2001: 65)

With a perspective that accords no standing to public goods that are not sustained by individual contributors, Barry addresses practical questions on state language policy. He is especially bothered by the required learning of Welsh in public education in Wales. To be sure, he repudiates the nineteenth century practice of beating children for speaking Welsh. Nonetheless, he argues,

it has to be recognized that the great majority of people in Wales do not speak Welsh at home, and for them learning Welsh in school from scratch is in direct competition for time with learning a major foreign language. It is therefore scarcely surprising that com-pulsory instruction in Welsh in schools has aroused opposition from English-speaking parents; and the principles put forward here [in defence of liberalism] would lend support to their case. The labor market advantages of those with an educational qualification in the Welsh language have been boosted by policies adopted by local authorities that require knowledge of Welsh as a condition of employment. Cases have been brought under the 1976 Race Relations Act challenging such policies, though without success. Unless knowledge of Welsh can be shown to be related to the effective discharge of the duties of the job, however, requiring it is clearly unfair discrimination. Creating an artifi-cially protected labor market in order to motivate acceptance of compulsory instruction in Welsh in the schools is simply to compound one abuse of state power by another. Where language is concerned, a state cannot adopt a neutral stance: it must provide its services in one or more languages . . . At the same time, however, it can be said of lan-guage as of no other cultural trait that it is a matter of convention . . . This is one case involving cultural attributes in which 'This is how we do things here'—the appeal to local convention—is a self-sufficient response to pleas for the public recognition of diversity. (Barry 2001: 105–6)

Barry is saying in effect that a proper understanding of liberalism denies the right of local communities to exert a tax on a minority to promote a public good as defined by the majority. He is not entirely consistent here. In regard, for example, to public support of the arts, Barry (2001: 198) claims that, if art is of high excellence but not commercially viable, states that have a 'serious policy of public support for the arts' will subsidize these things. By 'serious' he means one that is not subject to the multicultural pork barrel. It follows that the state can coerce a lover of banjo music to have his taxes go to support Beethoven, but it should not coerce a native speaker of English living in Wales to have her children exposed to Welsh. Nonetheless, Barry would prefer to have Beethoven supported by universities (which support philosophers and writers) rather than by taxpayers. So Barry's overall argument that individuals should not be coerced to provide public goods for which they have no (revealed) preference is consistently upheld.

Going back to Wales, in focusing on the rights of English-speaking parents, Barry rightly zeroes in on the principal flaw of the nationalist logic. And by 'English-speaking parents' Barry surely includes people who consider themselves Welsh by nationality. Ignoring this fundamental fact, May and many nationalists err when they portray a marginalized cultural group as inevitably having an abiding interest in sustaining ancestral cultural forms. This is obviously false, as many members of marginalized groups would prefer linguistic assimilation even if it were not ideologically coerced. Worse, many nationalist commentators write despairingly of individuals who have lost 'their' language as if they had some obligation to speak the language of their ancestors. Children of Welsh parents who speak only English are speaking 'their' language, whether nationalists like it or not. Claiming that people of Maori or Welsh ancestry have an obligation to carry on the language of their ancestors is to primordialize culture, and to force people into cultural milieus from which they might want to exit. In disregarding the preferences of potential assimilators, nationalist commentators are fundamentally illiberal. Here Barry is right.

Barry's argument, however cogent, carries with it two curious moves. First, in his treatment of the Welsh language case, he rather quickly skirts around the issue of whether historical injustices towards a group require remedy. Consider again the case of Catalonia. During the Franco period, the authoritarian regime subsidized through its housing policies a massive migration of Castilian speakers into Catalonia. This strategy substantially raised the costs to a future autonomist government of Catalonia in fulfilling a programme of the restitution of Catalan as the language of everyday interchange. Who should be held responsible for the historical injustice felt by linguistic nationalists? On the face of it, coercively making the immigrants pay that cost (through demanding that their children learn Catalan whether they want to or not) is unjust. Yet this does not imply that the effort to restore Catalan is inconsistent with liberal justice. Similarly with Barry's Welsh example. To be sure, asking English-speaking migrants into Wales to pay the heaviest costs to remedy eighteenth-century injustices to the Welsh people is itself unjust. But that should not invalidate the justice claims of Welsh-speaking Welsh that they have a right to restore the Welsh language where it had been forcibly eradicated in the past. The historical coercion that led to linguistic marginalization, as emphasized by May, does not in Barry's critique cry out for remedy.

Second, in defiance of empirical reality, Barry writes that language is quintessentially conventional. But this is not precisely the case. While there is indeed no inherent value to speaking English rather than speaking Iroquois, both English-speakers and Iroquois-speakers over generations tend to place powerful normative value on the languages they transmit to their children. Nationalists are right to say that the value of one's native tongue goes beyond mere instrumentality. Language can be bound up with one's identity and with how one understands one's way of life. Thus, we would gladly take a bribe to compensate us for the costs of driving on the right side of the road, or of using euros instead of dollars. But we would be (as were Laitin's Ghanaian informants) far less willing to accept a bribe so that all Americans would speak Iroquois. This does not mean that in many situations (largely through immigration) families would not assimilate into new languages. It means that the cultural values embedded in languages, and the literatures that were written in those languages, will be lost. In a controlled comparison of Somali/English bilinguals, Laitin reports that, in role-playing sessions mandated in English, conversations systematically turned on different evaluative criteria from those mandated in Somali. For example, in a role-playing session between a headmaster and a teacher within a school, in the English-language portrayals the debate concerned which professional role (the headmaster or teacher) had the authority to decide the issue. In the same role sessions acted out by fellow secondary school students in the Somali language, the debate concerned the merits of the issue, and the professional roles of headmaster or teacher had little bearing. Authority was debated in terms of different criteria among the same students depending on the language mandated for debate (Laitin 1977: Chs 6–8; but see also Eva Hoffman 1990 for more compelling personal evidence on this factor). May's approach is sensitive to the fact that languages are not merely conventions. But Barry is deaf to the cultural nuances of linguistic difference.

Two compelling points from the nationalist perspective need to be acknowledged in any successful normative theory of linguistic injustice. First, speakers of minority languages will, at least in some circumstances, seek to remedy historical injustices through the reinvigoration of marginalized languages rather than through help in getting their children access to the dominant language. Second, because of the problem of network externalities, standard remedies to reinvigorate marginalized languages require coercive limits on the choices of those living in polities in which a marginalized language is being revived. This poses a threat to liberalism. Barry is powerful in subverting the illiberal claims of many nationalists (in the guise of multiculturalism). But he is less convincing in laying down more general liberal principles to remedy linguistic injustice.

## Liberal Culturalism

For liberal culturalists, just language policy cannot be merely a matter of deciding the fair redistributionist scheme in order to attain linguistic convergence.

Neither should it be a matter of endowing linguistic minorities with unbounded rights to recreate or revitalize their native tongues. By insisting upon the view that culture and language are not valuable *as such* but rather only in so far as they are valuable to individuals, liberal culturalism marries ethical individualism with group rights for cultural minorities. The liberal culturalist approach attempts to capture the nationalist perspective but contain it within liberal principles.

Will Kymlicka is the foremost exponent of liberal culturalism. As a liberal, Kymlicka demands that a state guarantee the basic civil and political rights of all its citizens and he defends the value of personal autonomy. As a culturalist, Kymlicka thinks that individuals exercise freedom only through their moorings to a societal culture, and that this fact should lead liberals to take a moral interest in cultures. Thus, according to Kymlicka (2001a: 42), liberal culturalism holds that 'liberal democratic states should not only uphold the familiar set of common civil and political rights of citizenship which are protected in all liberal democracies; they must also adopt various group-specific rights or policies which are intended to recognize and accommodate the distinctive identities and needs of ethnocultural groups'. Not all kinds of group rights and policies are permissible, however. A liberal state should not craft rights or policies that constitute internal restrictions on the freedoms of group members. Only external protections that protect a subgroup from the influences of a larger, more dominant culture pass liberal muster.

What does this translate to in practice? It means that liberal culturalists 'support policies which make it possible for members of ethnic and national groups to express and promote their culture and identity, but reject any policies which impose a *duty* on people to do so' (Kymlicka 2001a: 42). The policies Kymlicka has in mind cover a broad spectrum of issues, including language rights, group representation, and multicultural education. But language is central among these group rights, and Kymlicka defends language policies favourable to linguistic minorities from the schoolroom (2001a: 26–7) to the courthouse (1995a: 45) to the business office (2001a: 78–9) and beyond (2001a: 79). And, importantly, these policies are not just advisable for liberal democracies, but rather 'are often required for ethnocultural justice' (Kymlicka 2001a: 42).

This is an attractive argument in many respects. It rejects notions of cultural essentialism or purity while giving due weight to the significance of one's native tongue beyond mere communication. It avoids turning cultural minorities into the equivalent of endangered species that warrant preservation for the sake of maintaining diversity. It rightly posits membership in cultural communities as a precondition for exercising liberal freedoms. And it properly refuses to allow basic individual rights to be overridden by the interests of subgroups in coercively maintaining the loyalty of their members.

Where the liberal culturalist position falters, however, is in its tendency to view ethnocultural groups as speaking with one voice. This leads Kymlicka to an over-hasty assumption that all members of cultural minorities value membership in their own culture above all others. Moreover, the careful distinction Kymlicka makes between internal restrictions and external protections fails when we consider the problems involved with the intergenerational transmission of language. We examine each problem in turn.

Kymlicka claims that cultures matter morally only in so far as they matter to individuals. 'Liberalism', he writes, 'is committed to (perhaps even defined by) the view that individuals should have the freedom and capacity to question and possibly revise the traditional practices of their community, should they come to see them as no longer worthy of their allegiance' (Kymlicka 1995a: 152). Yet he quite often refers to groups as monolithic, having preferences of their own. Thus, in one of the central conclusions of his argument, he writes that, 'we should aim at ensuring that all national groups have the opportunity to maintain themselves as a distinct culture, if they so choose' (Kymlicka 1995a: 113). If individuals exercising their personal autonomy have the freedom to contest, reject, revise, and negotiate what is of value in their cultural heritage, it would be surprising to find ethnocultural groups without considerable intra-group tension over what makes the culture distinct and what elements are worthy of passing on to future generations. Given intra-group tension, ascribing preferences to societal cultures as such is unrealistic.

It might be objected here that adherents of cultural groups might seek to contest or revise any of a number of values, traditions, or beliefs, but that, given the central importance of a native tongue to one's identity, they are hardly likely to question the value of speaking the language of their cultural group. But some of our earlier and Barry's examples illustrate just this point. Welsh parents may wish for their children to learn English as rapidly as possible in order to give them broader economic mobility options. According to Barry, well over half of the second generation Spanish-speaking Cuban refugees in Florida, who on Kymlicka's definition appear to constitute a societal culture, speak English primarily, and likely envisage a future within the broader societal culture of the United States rather than within any Spanish-speaking enclaves, however institutionally complete, in Miami (Barry 2001: 219) or back in a post-Castro Cuba. And we can well imagine the decision of members of some small national minorities in Europe, say Italian Swiss or Hungarian Slovaks, that their lives would go better if they were to give up speaking Italian or Hungarian and seek their professional and political fortune in the German- or French- or English-speaking parts of the European Union.

It may be true, of course, that *most* members of *most* national minorities do seek to retain their mother tongue and transmit it to future generations. But the point is that we cannot assume this as a matter of course. Unfortunately, this is precisely what the liberal culturalist position does. Kymlicka argues that membership in a societal culture is a precondition of meaningful choice making. He also insists that people should have access to their *own* culture. 'The freedom which liberals demand for individuals is not primarily the freedom to go beyond one's language and history, but rather the freedom to move around one's societal culture . . .' (Kymlicka 1995*a*: 90).

In our view, theorists should not assume that access to one's own societal culture is what every individual wants. We should make no assumptions about people's preferences on this matter, for if, as Kymlicka believes, individual autonomy endows people with the capacity to revise and even reject their ancestral traditions, including their language, we can expect the preferences of individuals to vary, even within national minorities, on the subject of language policies. If people's preferences about how to lead their lives are informed at least in part by assessments of how to broaden their social and economic mobility, then it seems reasonable to assume that members of national minorities may sometimes want to integrate into the more dominant societal culture, sometimes abandon their multination state for some other political entity (for example, from one European country to another country in the European Union), or at other times pursue a life of cosmopolitan transnationalism, where there is no single societal culture circumscribing and enabling the exercise of one's freedom. In short, it may appear that justice requires a slate of minority rights for ethnocultural groups in order to improve their position vis-à-vis the broader society. But justice must also be sensitive to the fact that conferring minority rights on ethnocultural groups may worsen the position of some members of groups vis-à-vis their own group and broader society by making it far more difficult for them to realize their preferences or even to contest and negotiate their inherited traditions and beliefs.

When we realize that ethnocultural groups do not speak with one voice and that we should not assume that the preference of each group member is to maintain access to his or her societal culture, we are forced to confront the dilemmas that arise with the intergenerational transmission of language. According to Kymlicka (2001*a*: 25), societal cultures are defined by linguistic and institutional cohesion. Thus, if national minorities deserve rights as a matter of justice that will enable them to maintain their societal cultures, they deserve to maintain their languages. For Kymlicka, this implies control over the language and curriculum of schooling, language of government, and perhaps private employment. 'There is evidence', he writes, 'that language communities can only survive intergenerationally if they are numerically dominant within a particular territory, and if their language is the language of opportunity in that territory' (Kymlicka 2001*a*: 79). Thus national minorities can demand not only that schooling and the business of public institutions be conducted in their language but that private business be so as well, and that this hold for immigrants and other societal cultures living within the territory of the national minority.

Kymlicka counts these measures as external protections, for they ensure that a societal culture continues to provide sufficient venues in public and private life to maintain that culture as a vibrant context of choice. Such measures do indeed

protect the ability of adult members of national minorities to exercise their freedom within their societal culture. But they also require coercive restraints on
the children of these same adults, for their opportunities to learn the language
of some broader societal culture will be curtailed. With respect to children,
then, external protections can become internal restrictions. Or, to put the tension in more general terms, cultural rights designed to ensure the protection of
minority groups from the pressures of dominant society may seem desirable
and just in so far as they apply to adults who freely choose membership in their
group or can critically evaluate whether the freedom they wish for themselves is
really the capacity to explore and revise the ways of life made available to them
by their societal culture of birth. But since children neither choose membership
in a group nor possess sufficiently the ability to evaluate their ends, cultural
rights for adults may not respect the future autonomy of children. What passes
on Kymlicka's view as a legitimate external protection can be, from the perspective of the children within the national minority group, an internal restriction.

Now, there is no escaping the fact that all parents make consequential decisions that both open up and close off possibilities for their children. This is an
inevitable truth. Neither a parent nor a societal culture should be responsible for
maximizing the choice set of children. But as liberals we worry about
Kymlicka's assertion that the freedom we should most care about is the freedom
to move within one's own societal culture. When the political leaders of
national minorities take advantage of minority rights that in effect close off the
possibility of children learning how to participate in the dominant societal culture, or an alternative culture, this seems unduly and illiberally to constrain the
preferences of some parents and children to exercise their freedom outside of
their own societal culture, or among a variety of societal cultures, if they so
choose. That parents, and especially children, should wish sometimes to move
beyond their societal culture should not be surprising, for societal cultures
are not equally capacious. As we just argued, we think liberals should not presume that individuals prefer their own societal culture. Liberals should instead
be sure to set up institutions, first, that allow for the expression of people's
preferences, and second, that aid their realization. They should allow much wider
play for the expression of preferences within the realm of democratic politics.

## 2. The Liberal Democratic Approach to Linguistic Justice

We wish here to defend a liberal democratic approach to linguistic justice. It
views the resolution of many questions and problems of linguistic justice as the
proper subject of the messy contestation of democratic politics rather than as
the result of clean specifications from first principles. We endorse as a general
approach what Kymlicka says about so-called hard cases: '[They] must
be resolved politically, by good-faith negotiations and the give and take of

democratic politics' (Kymlicka 1995a: 131). But we go further than Kymlicka, closer to frameworks drawn by Tamir (1993) and Carens (2000), in charting a large and desirable area of indeterminacy where liberal principles offer no clear prescription in regard to language policy. In Carens's terms, liberalism permits a wide zone of policies that fall within the bounds of the morally permissible. Even more, we are untroubled by the fact that democratic procedures will yield outcomes at odds with everyday intuitions about the language interests of various groups.

A liberal democratic approach views any citizen or set of citizens in a state as possessing the right to mobilize support for a language community or language policies that it considers a collective or public good. All citizens have an equal right to exert electoral or interest-group pressure, to foster broader coalitions, and to engage the broader polity in democratic deliberation in the quest to provide this collective or public good. They are constrained in these efforts only by the liberal requirement that the fundamental rights of all citizens not be violated.

This liberal democratic approach leads us to picture (as did Tamir 1993: 54, in regard to nationalism more generally) the construction of a viable language community as a consumption item. Through the vote, all members of a community must help pay for public goods that are democratically chosen. If a political unit within a state votes to have a once marginalized language treated as an official one within the boundaries of the polity, all taxpayers assume a responsibility to provide for it. If a political unit decides through the democratic process to subsidize translation services for language minorities in public institutions, all taxpayers ought to shoulder the burden for it.

The right of a community to tax its members to create a language community as a public good implies for liberal democrats such as Tamir and Carens the right to reverse course and to let the language fall into public desuetude. Tamir raises the case of Hebrew in Israel. In the period of early Israeli statehood, it was considered betrayal by many Zionists to speak a language other than Hebrew, but in the 1970s Israelis began to feel secure enough to allow for an infusion of English into their culture (Tamir 1993: 88). Suppose Israelis, who were so adamant a half-century ago about the privileged status of Hebrew for their state, agreed to allow English, or Arabic, or Russian, or Yiddish to have co-official status? This would reflect a change in the culture of the state and the self-understanding of that culture by its citizens. Tamir would respect this changed conception, even if she prefers an Israeli society in which all future generations rely principally on Hebrew. In a similar vein, Carens raises the possibility that immigrants into Quebec, who learn French and earn citizenship, might vote to undermine the very language laws that paved the way to their cultural integration into Quebec. As citizens of Quebec, Carens argues, immigrants would have rights equal to those with deeper roots to define Quebec's future. If not, then there would be unjustifiable classes of citizenship (Carens 2000: 132–3). Unlike nationalists or even liberal culturalists, liberal democrats make no presumptions as to the language interests of the citizenry. This implies that they would be open to changes in those interests over time, and would leave ample room for democratic disagreement both between and within cultural groups concerning the best language policies.

Suppose linguistic entrepreneurs of a minority group mobilize to revive its ancestral language. Nationalists defend the resulting expenditures, but their defence is inadequate. May, for example, reiterates several times that the promotion of minority languages in schools has long-term benefits for students from minority backgrounds, both in wider educational attainment and in success in the future job market. He heaps scorn on the ideologues of the English Only Movement, which he says 'stands in sharp contrast to the bulk of academic research on the topic which points strongly to the attested social and educational merits of learning in one's first language . . .' Equally questionable, he continues, are the federally funded research studies that showed no educational gains for students enrolled in bilingual programs. He counters these results with a study that has 183 control variables and interaction terms that show admirable success of these programmes. There is, May notes, 'wide acknowledgment' of the quality of these results (May 2001: 217). This is consistent with recent research showing the limits of English immersion educational programmes in the US (Butler et al. 2000). Therefore, May argues, restoring the vitality of language communities helps make members of those communities better educated and more productive citizens.

The data, despite May's assurances, are ambiguous. Consider the problem of selection bias. Are those students enrolled in bilingual programmes more ambitious than the others, as in the case of many experimental programmes? Or are they less ambitious, thrown into these programmes by principals who want to keep the least able students out of the standard tracks? Unless we know the criteria of selection, we cannot assess the overall impact of these experimental programmes on student performance. One serious study addressing this and other methodological issues is a Ph.D. dissertation by Mark Hugo López. In his US-based national study, he finds a small but significant downward effect of exposure to bilingual schools in retention and in salary ten years after the entry into a secondary school programme. For these losses, the estimated annual cost per pupil of bilingual programmes is $1,000 (López 1996).

In this light, it is interesting to note that in May's book we learn that the popular Kura Kaupapa (the Maori language-medium primary schools), as in the case of bilingual US schools (as reported by López), do not give any added educational value over Maoris who enter directly into the English system (May 2001: 304). So, for uncertain gains at best and losses at worst, taxpayers are being asked to provide curricula that help sustain or rebuild language communities.

Our view, unlike that of the nationalists, is that the consumption of a language community as a public good requires no defence. In the abstract, we regard the construction of a new language community or the reconstruction of a formerly oppressed language community in a morally neutral way. It is like subsidizing a museum, an opera house, or a local stadium to house a professional sports team. Communities are free to provide the public goods its taxpayers demand, just so long as fundamental liberal principles are not violated.

In practice, language issues are not the moral equivalent of preferences about sports stadiums. Some theorists in the liberal tradition differentiate 'constitutive' from 'consumptive' markers of identity, with the former outside the realm of choice. Tamir (1993: 41), for instance, argues that cultural choices are constitutive and they therefore take 'priority over a choice of restaurant . . . [or] a specific make of car'. And thus, language is sometimes coded as a constitutive marker of identity, and consequently of far greater import than arts or sports promotion. We agree that language policies are not on a moral or political par with culinary, automotive, or artistic options, yet we see no need at the level of theory to give pre-eminence to constitutive identity markers. But by challenging this rigid distinction between constitutive and consumptive markers, and viewing a language community as a consumption item, we are not diminishing its value to its speakers. We hold instead that the value of one's ancestral language may be deep, but that is best revealed through cultural, social, and political action.

The revelation of preferences through action will show that different dimensions of one's identity are central for different people: for some, it may be religion, for others gender, for others nationalist allegiances, and for others perhaps a sports team. Once again, the forum of democratic politics should allow the intensity of individual preferences to be registered in a way that reflects the centrality of certain markers. If language issues register strongly, their democratic expression conveys their importance widely within the public realm. And the need for citizens to articulate the public goods implications of recreating a language community draws people into democratic politics. Our liberal democratic approach therefore provides greater space for democratic contestation than either Tamir's or Carens's.

The problem any polity faces is that, for this public good to be achieved, there needs to be a critical mass of speakers of that language within the boundaries of the community. To achieve that critical mass, it may be necessary to induce nonspeakers of the once-marginalized language to learn it, even if they prefer the status quo.

Liberals, we would think, should applaud individuals who wish to rebuild language communities lost due to historical injustices. Perhaps liberals might even feel obligated to subsidize minority organizations that have dedicated themselves to the provision of a new public good. Moreover, liberals should have no qualms about the imposition of a local tax to pay for this public good, even if some members within the taxpaying community do not want it. (We may not want a strong national defence, but we pay for it anyway, in accord with democratic principles.) And, despite Barry's refusal 'to compound one abuse of state power by another', we as liberals think it is reasonable for a community, in an attempt to create a new language regime, to demand that all public servants be able to offer public services in the once-marginalized language. This in effect creates a rent on wider society by speakers of the once-marginalized language.

Liberals should not restrict linguistic groups in seeking to gain official status for their language communities. But liberals would want to restrict what a local community can do in creating a language community. Indeed, there are limits to what falls within the bounds of morally permissible language policies adopted through democratic politics. Without doubt, it would be outrageous for a community to prohibit use of the dominant state language (or any language) in private realms, just as it was illiberal for the Franco state to prohibit the private use of Catalan among Spanish citizens or for the Turkish state to outlaw the speaking of Kurdish among its citizens. Next to clear violations of liberal principles, there are many borderline cases. Suppose an autonomous region used criteria of ancestry to determine who has a right to opt out of the local language regime. This rule would violate a fundamental liberal principle treating people as individuals and not as members of predefined categories. Quebec comes close to this in limiting citizens of some ancestries to French-medium public schools while allowing others—namely, those whose parents were educated in English in Canada—the option of attending English-language schools. However, Quebec nationalists will respond that the opt-out for those whose parents studied in English in Canada is more liberal (in the sense of enhancing choice) than a blind policy that would allow no group to opt-out. Another borderline issue concerns laws that prohibit media of instruction in the dominant language for public education while allowing it in the private realm, as does Catalonia. The law permits the rich to buy themselves out of the language regime (through private education in Spanish or English) while the poor are left with no choice (but to study in Catalan). Here is a case where the poor are paying the costs of fulfilling the national imaginings of the rich. This comes close to violating Barry's view of liberalism. However, it could well be argued that the Catalan policies are not so much a violation of liberal principles as to place it outside the realm of political (rather than judicial) decision making.

In aspects of both the Quebec and the Catalan cases, liberal commitments to equal opportunity, not limited by the fortunes or misfortunes of birth, are potentially violated by overzealous nationalists. However, as liberal *democrats*, we would expect political entrepreneurs representing minority language communities to use all available means to induce a critical mass of their communities to use and expect others to use that language in schools and workplaces. A good example of the liberal democratic approach to linguistic justice is provided by the passage by the Catalan autonomous government in Spain of the Linguistic Policy Act of 1998. Through the Spanish Constitution, autonomous governments were permitted to grant regional languages official status within their autonomies. In the Law of Linguistic Normalization in 1983, the Catalan government legislated wide-ranging programmes for the promotion of a Catalan language community within Catalonia. A series of decrees over the next 15 years deepened this programme. But, fearful of losing a subsequent election, the highly nationalist party that has led Catalonia throughout the post-Franco years (the CiU) sought to lock future governments (perhaps less committed to the nationalist programme) into the linguistic framework it had built. The 1998 Act, as analysed by Costa (2003), was an attempt by the CiU coercively to commit future legislatures to fulfil the nationalist programme of the sitting legislature. This is democratic politics with a coercive face. The debates over this act, pitting those seeking individual rights for non-Catalan speakers against those seeking remedial rights to the community for centuries of discrimination by the Spanish state, were filled with rancour. Partisans on both sides accused their opponents of bad faith. But, all told, democratic procedures were followed, and both sides to the debate were constrained by liberal principles. Eventually the CiU proposal was passed by an overwhelming majority, including many legislators whose ancestry was not Catalan. Deliberation had therefore brought something approaching a consensus. As liberal democrats, we applaud this form of politics, as it represents an appropriate political response to the fact of pluralism. Both sides presented what in Rawlsian terms would qualify as 'reasonable comprehensive doctrines' between which liberalism ought not take a side (Rawls 1993: 61).

We have emphasized here our democratic orientation. But as *liberal* democrats, we set limits to what is permissible in the public realm of democratic politics. We would surely expect the courts to set limits to the coercive aspects of those means if they violate fundamental liberal principles. Furthermore, we would place restrictions on what a local community can do in creating a language community. Our liberal commitments demand that we seek to promote individual autonomy, such that all citizens have the capacity to make critically informed choices about the lives they lead (Reich 2002). This does not imply the image, as implied by Galston (1995), of an autonomous person as a disembodied chooser of options, as if from a menu. It implies rather that autonomous persons must be capable of opting to lead lives different from those of their parents.

Our perspective on autonomy highlights two constraints on language policy, one on the state and the other on parents. First, the state should have no requirement that children develop full facility in the dominant language of social, political, and economic life. Perhaps a parent sees herself as a member of a diaspora, and seeks to prepare her child for a return to a homeland. Perhaps a parent is a regional separatist, and sees his own language as the language in which things *will* be done here once separatism succeeds. Notions of a 'dominant' language, or a language in which, as Barry puts it, this is how things are done here, are conservative, and don't give citizens the right to invest in language repertoires that they think will best further their own future interests. Thus, though a liberal state may provide heavy incentives for learning the state language or languages, it should not require that all parents have their children develop competence in the state language.

It might be objected that the future interest here belongs to the child, if we're talking about schooling. Indeed, it could well be argued, the state should prepare the child for citizenship in the political community in which the child is already a citizen. In this case, the state may have equal claim to represent the rights of its future citizens as do parents to represent the present rights of their children. It is a reasonable assumption, first made by Max Weber, that rulers seek rationalization of rule through common weights and measures, laws, and languages. From this point of view, it is in the interest of the state to promote language homogeneity through the imposition of an official language. But just as we do not assign to linguistic groups equal moral weight as we do to individuals, we see the interests of the state as secondary to the interests of individuals who live within its boundaries.

Second, parallel to those against the state, there are liberal limits to parental discretion. What if parents educate their children solely in a language spoken by only a very tiny community of speakers? We think this violates the liberal principle of autonomy, and we would therefore want to empower states to constrain parents from so limiting their children's language repertoires. We would demand that parents provide linguistic repertoires to their children that allow them a meaningful range of choices as adults, for which speaking a language that allows a broad range of mobility and vocational opportunities is a sine qua non. As liberals, we would oppose any attempt by the some 4,500 speakers of Aranese (living in the Catalan autonomy of Spain) to restrict their children's language repertoire to Aran. Nothing in liberalism would demand that these children also learn Catalan (the language of the region), or Spanish (the language of the state), or French (the language of the neighbouring state), or English (the language of the proto-European state). Liberalism and its concern for autonomy would require only that Aranese be complemented with at least one of these languages. Similarly with the Cree language community in North America. This language is spoken by about 45,000 people in Quebec, in Manitoba, and as far south as Montana. Within Canada there are some local institutions that operate in Cree. Nonetheless, the range of mobility opportunities available to monolingual Crees is exceptionally limited. Liberalism and the demand for autonomy would not help us decide whether Cree parents should have their children learn French or English or both. But it would require at least one language of wider opportunity.

How can the sometimes conflicting goals of state and parent be reconciled, especially when either or both violate liberal principles? Absent the expression of a considered preference by an autonomous child, probably a teenager, on his or her preferred language repertoire, which the liberal state would be obliged to respect, there is no tidy resolution. Our liberal democratic framework would require that the conflict between the parents and the state be resolved through the courts or alternative democratic institutions that are designed to adjudicate fundamental principles. And this implies that neither the liberal state nor parents have unconstrained rights to legislate the language repertoires of the children for whom both are responsible.

Thus, though our liberal democratic approach provides much greater space than any of the other approaches we discussed for a wide range of permissible language policies, this space is not infinitely elastic. Both the state and organized groups of linguistic minorities are capable of passing through democratic means laws and propositions that violate liberal justice. Consider Proposition 227 in California, which mandated an extremely short transitional period from bilingual to all-English education. Suppose it were proven that such a scheme provided no academic foundation in the children's ancestral language and consequently weakened their performance in the general curriculum. Is our approach too swayed by majority tyrannies? We think not. Our view here is that injured parties should have recourse—and where that recourse should be depends crucially on the institutions of the country and the administrative level at which educational decisions are made—if liberal principles are being violated. If parents can show that the equal opportunity of their children to advance in wider society is constrained by democratically chosen restrictions, those restrictions should be overturned (for example, by the courts) on liberal grounds.

But if our approach successfully escapes the problem of majoritarian politics yielding illiberal outcomes, perhaps it is vulnerable to the charge that we depend on the prior and just resolution of boundaries within the liberal state.[1] If a dominant national group is able to draw internal boundaries as it sees fit, then it will do so, frustrating always the attempts of linguistic minorities to secure a winning coalition for their political agendas. In his *Multicultural Citizenship*, Kymlicka (1995a: 112–13) insists that societal cultures each get territorial autonomy within legal boundaries. He suggests that liberal principles of justice can provide the parameters for boundary readjustment.

But there are no liberal principles of cartography. As we know from a long history of such attempts to make nations commensurate with state boundaries, going back to Wilson's Fourteen Points, there is no cultural cartography that would satisfy such an aspiration. Populations and identities are too internally varied and mixed for such romantic projects to succeed. The most impressive attempt to reset internal state boundaries so that they would be commensurate with national boundaries was performed by Stalin (Schwartz 1990). The unintended results are instructive. Once national territories were provided with resources, many groups that had previously seen themselves as united split apart, demanding separate autonomies. Meanwhile groups given their own autonomies treated internal minorities far worse than had been the case under the previous regime. The irony is that this project was fostered by an appallingly illiberal regime.

---

[1] We thank Will Kymlicka for pressing this objection.

There is a liberal democratic alternative to the allocation of boundaries. In our vision of a liberal democratic state, a set of politically determined language policy outcomes can be equally consistent with liberal principles. Thus, internal boundaries ought to be open for change through political processes, subject to liberal constraints. Consider redistricting for Congress in the United States. Within limits, state legislatures that face reductions or enhancements of congressional districts alter boundaries on largely political criteria. More relevant for our concerns has been the creation of the Basque and Catalan autonomous regions in Spain. Basque nationalists considered Navarra to be a core province of Basque Country, but a referendum within Navarra showed the population to be against incorporation into a Basque autonomy. Similarly, Catalan nationalists argued that Valencian is a dialect of Catalan, and that the province of Valencia should therefore be incorporated into the Catalan autonomous community. Valencians voted 'no'. So the boundaries of the two principal autonomies of Spain were delimited by democratic politics. While the autonomists did not get all they wanted, they each got a conjunction of willing provinces to form an autonomous government within the Spanish state. A final example is Canada, where democratic politics has determined that Quebec will remain within the boundaries of Canada. These boundary outcomes reflect the push and pull of those who want to belong versus those who don't. Liberalism should insist that boundary adjustments be among acceptable political demands, subject of course to the proviso that fundamental civil and political rights are not violated. Any group that sees an advantage from promoting its language through boundary adjustment should be given access to the variety of democratic mechanisms to press its claims in the political realm.

What belongs to the domain of 'justice' and what to 'politics' are not mutually exclusive. Liberal democrats need not decide, as a matter of justice, what the precise boundaries of internal sub-units are before democratic politics can get off the ground. Liberal principles of justice do indeed generate certain moral and legal requirements that no democratically determined outcome should undermine or compromise. But, as Carens (2000: 6 ff.) has put it, there is a difference between what liberalism morally requires and what is morally permissible under liberalism. Liberal democracy permits much more than what liberal democracy demands. Within the wide range of morally permissible policies, democratic processes are the proper institutional mechanisms for choosing among them and revisiting them over time.

More generally, liberal culturalists seek to derive substantive and detailed language policies from the liberal principles of justice. Moreover, liberal culturalists envisage the public realm as a place where citizens tie up loose ends of how best to administer policies that have been set outside democratic venues. While these citizens may have differing conceptions of what justice entails, their public role in the liberal culturalist account is to determine through debate what the best theory is and how to apply it in policy. Our position is different on two counts. First, we agree that the public realm is a place that might entertain disputes on the requirements of justice. However, we also see that realm as a place where interest-based arguments are legitimately expressed. Second, a core liberal principle is the institutionalization of a public realm in which citizens can express their interests, justify their claims to others, contest the views of their fellow citizens, and resolve differences politically. To the extent that liberal culturalists wish to constrain the range of issues that are subject to the warp and woof of debate in the public realm, they subvert a liberal aspiration.

It might be said that the liberal democratic approach to linguistic justice puts in place structural incentives toward territorial concentration of minorities. But doesn't the nurturing of such minorities lead to Balkanization and higher levels of ethnic tension? Our answer is that it is indeed true that our approach favours groups that are territorially compact, and it will, if groups organize successfully to create an administratively protected minority language community, sustain territorial concentration. While this might pose a danger, there is no liberal principle that compels national minorities to integrate socially with majorities in their nation-state. It might be pointed out that J. S. Mill (1991: Ch. 16), in recognizing the reality of state boundaries based on common culture, was inadvertently making possible inter-state wars. Our approach in a parallel way opens up the possibilities of civil wars. That liberal principles carry with them certain risks should be acknowledged. As Kymlicka has often stressed, it should be pointed out that, under conditions of modern democratic society, as in the cases of Belgium, Canada, Spain (with the partial exception of Basque Country), and Switzerland, compact settlements of linguistic groups yield political conflict but not civil war.

We have insisted that in the realm of language policy the results of democratic procedures are, with certain restrictions, legitimate. This liberal democratic approach is predicated on the view that neither theorists nor the state should make assumptions about what individuals will prefer concerning their language repertoires. But what of the claim that historical injustices to linguistic minorities, independent of the current preferences of members of linguistic groups (or perhaps *because* their preferences have been unjustly shaped by historical oppression), cry out for state remedy? In our account, this might imply that the more successful the past injustice has been in erasing minority languages by dominant groups, the less likely it is that the descendants of the oppressed group will receive a remedy. That Welsh was only partially eradicated enabled a small coterie of Welsh cultural entrepreneurs to make demands for restitution; that Highlands Gaelic fell into complete desuetude meant that there exists no credible voice to make political demands for its revival.

We do not wish to advocate a theory of language justice in which the incompletely conquered have recourse and remedies that are not available to the completely conquered. Instead, liberal justice demands that the state offer a range of policies designed to enable members of linguistic minorities to re-establish connections with the culture of their ancestors. For instance, the liberal state could provide seed money to individuals or groups to publish literature or newspapers in the native tongue of their ancestors; it could provide resources to fund historical documentation about their lost ancestral language. If such subsidies help create an interest that had previously been dormant, a step toward remedying the historical injustice would have been taken. It would then be up to those who received the seed money to parlay their new interests into a political movement. But if nearly all descendants, say of Highland Gaelic speakers, show no interest in a political movement to revitalize a minority language, the state should not, in an effort to rectify a past injustice, ignore the current preferences of these descendants.

## 3. Conclusion

The *liberal democratic* approach to linguistic justice encourages political mobilization by linguistic entrepreneurs with regard to fulfilling cultural agendas. But it puts constraints on what entrepreneurs, even if they are victorious in the democratic process in creating micro-linguistic communities, can demand of people living within those communities, especially concerning the education of children. Liberalism also puts constraints on states on the degree to which they can demand of citizens that they develop competence in the language of state business.

We find it odd that compensatory, nationalist, and liberal culturalist approaches to linguistic justice are allergic to politics. Redistributionists treat the issue of linguistic justice as if the political claims for justice were irrelevant to their philosophy. While they have concentrated their collective energies on figuring out the pay-off for minority speakers to learn the majority language, the political stage is rife with battles over the rights of minority communities to revive languages that were unjustly marginalized. Redistributionists can portray these activists only as happy slaves. But in so doing, they ignore what it is these activists are optimizing.

Meanwhile nationalists such as May rail against the opponents of bilingualism with epithets such as 'fatuous', 'nativist', and 'intellectually dishonest' (May 2001: 215). In a parallel manner, compensatory liberals such as Barry have almost nothing but contempt for those acting on the political stage with liberal culturalist agendas.[2] What is universally dismissed by those seeking compensation, by those seeking nationalist protection, and by those condemning multiculturalists of ignoring individual rights is political competition.

---

[2] We applaud Barry's preference for the remedy of economic inequality over that of linguistic marginality. But we do not endorse his view that a liberal point of view demands that we all subscribe to his preference ordering.

Why, we might ask, are 'politics' often distrusted by theorists of justice, and policy derived from principle so treasured? That theories of justice do not, and should not, generate detailed blueprints of institutional structure and policy is no indication of failure or cause for disappointment. We should not wish for signage laws in Quebec, for example, to be a deduction from political principle. Liberalism will never provide an answer to the most reasonable rule for the size of the lettering in the French and English versions of a billboard. Restraint in translating principles of justice into exact policy and practice is proper philosophical humility.

Political competition, for liberal democrats, should be considered a 'good'. It compels people to address concerns that are of great importance to them. It allows those people who think they are being hurt to be heard. It gives incentives to people to hide their bad motives and to put forward more publicly spirited ones. And it tends to give groups with intense opinions a hearing. Our liberal democratic alternative brings politics back into liberalism. It encourages groups to seek linguistic remedies through political agitation, legal confrontation, and moderate levels of coercion—limited only by fundamental liberal principles. Under liberal democratic conditions, linguistic revivals will rarely succeed, as the votes for the creation of linguistic communities are hard to harvest. But when linguistic revivals do succeed, they will be a product of democracy, properly tempered by liberal principles.

Language revival tends to be a generally peaceful form of political combat, even in non-democratic societies (Laitin 2000). So we should as liberal democrats welcome the politicization of linguistic difference rather than decry it. And we should in theorizing about linguistic justice take seriously the demands of citizens who make claims in the public realm seeking to remedy injustice or engaging in cultural entrepreneurship. Our liberal democratic approach to linguistic justice provides the widest realm for political contestation in the creation of language communities as public goods, constrained only when language laws violate fundamental liberal rights of individuals (including children), as determined by political institutions designed to protect individuals from such encroachments.

We were careful to advertise our approach at the beginning as providing only a framework to answer normative questions arising from the social fact of linguistic diversity. Our reason should now be clear. Short of guaranteeing a slate of rights concerning basic liberties, there are no clear rules embedded in liberal principles that would allow us to deduce an entire programme of language policies. But a liberal democratic framework allows us to develop a critical perspective on public claims for the achievement of linguistic justice. First, it compels liberals to listen attentively to justice claims made in the public realm. Second, it suggests limits to the claims that can be made in regard to such remedies, if they violate liberal principles such as individual liberty and autonomy. Third, it welcomes the expression of conflicting visions of liberal resolution as a healthy manifestation of democratic deliberation. Compensatory theorists tend to belittle the claims of nationalists and liberal culturalists as irrelevant to the real needs of justice. Meanwhile liberal culturalists and nationalists accuse compensatory theorists of being deaf to history and insensitive to culture. The liberal democratic approach sees these apparently incompatible doctrines not as a theoretical puzzle to solve, but as a political opportunity to grasp. From the point of view of liberal democracy, we should celebrate the large space of indeterminacy, for, as long as the differing sides refrain from fundamentally illiberal exaggerations of their approaches, their differing sensitivities add lustre and interest to the public domain. We might press this even further. Liberal justice requires a political realm and, without fights over public goods (a point made by Carens 2000: 13), our political realm would be nearly vacuous, limited to distributive issues, without any positive or substantive component.

# 4

# Accommodation Rights for Hispanics in the United States

THOMAS W. POGGE

## 1. The Questionable Relevance of History

English is the predominant language in the United States. However, Spanish is the native language of some 35 million US citizens and residents, whom, in this chapter, I will refer to as 'Hispanics'.[1] Many of them do not speak English well. Clearly, the fact that English is the predominant language brings a number of significant advantages to native speakers of English ('Anglos') and, correspondingly, a number of significant disadvantages to at least those Hispanics who do not speak English well. This suggests the question whether justice might require special measures designed to protect and/or support Hispanics and the Spanish language within the US and, if so, what specific measures might be appropriate. I refer to such special measures as 'accommodation rights'—an expression Will Kymlicka now prefers to his earlier talk of 'minority rights' as well as to the widely used 'recognition rights' (Kymlicka 1997: 73 and n. 3). My discussion of the moral plausibility of such accommodation rights for Hispanics in the US will be informed by the more general theoretical framework I have outlined earlier (Pogge 1997).

One might think that the answer to these questions depends heavily on historical facts. Opponents of accommodation rights can argue that the United States has been an English-speaking country pretty much from its beginning some 200 years ago. People who come to the United States or choose to stay here certainly have had fair warning of this fact. If they have nevertheless not learned to speak English well, or have not ensured that their children would be fluent speakers of English, then the responsibility for any resulting disadvantages is surely their own. Conversely, supporters of accommodation rights can argue that many current native speakers of Spanish are descendants of persons who were incorporated into the US without their consent with Spain's cessation of Florida to Great Britain in 1763 or later, in the 1830s and 1840s, when the lands

---

[1] 'Latinos' is also frequently used. I prefer 'Hispanics' because of its etymological connection to the Spanish language, which will be a main theme of this chapter.

of Texas, California, Nevada, Arizona, Utah, and New Mexico were ceded to the US by Mexico under circumstances that were rather less than ideal from a moral point of view.

I do not believe that such historical arguments have much weight, one way or the other. Our question concerns the plausibility of accommodations among members of the present generation; and it is unclear why the two historical arguments I have sketched should have much relevance to this question. For most of the persons presently disadvantaged by the predominance of the English language have not chosen to incorporate themselves into an English-speaking society—they were simply born here, into Spanish-speaking households and neighbourhoods. And none of those currently advantaged by the predominance of English have had anything to do with the cessation of Florida or the annexation of Texas and the Southwest (though they might perhaps be said to benefit disproportionately from the effects of these events).

My downplaying of historical arguments puts me in sharp contrast to Kymlicka, who attaches great moral significance to the distinction between *national* groups or minorities, 'i.e. groups whose homeland has been incorporated through conquest, colonization, or federation' (Kymlicka 1995a: 79), and *ethnic* groups or minorities, which formed on the present state's territory as a result of immigration.[2] The great significance Kymlicka assigns to this distinction strikes me as morally implausible, especially within the liberal outlook Kymlicka professes to share. Consider two persons, aged 18, say, who were born in the US into Spanish-speaking households and are disadvantaged by their poor English. Carmen is a member of a national minority, descendant from Chicanos who were involuntarily incorporated into the United States in 1848; Leticia is a member of an ethnic minority, descendant from more recent Latino immigrants. Other things being equal, can this difference really make a major difference to the claims these two persons (and their respective groups) have on us? Kymlicka thinks so.[3] But, as we shall see, he also takes it to be part of the very essence of the liberalism he endorses that persons should not be disadvantaged by unchosen inequalities. However, our two women, like all current members of the groups they symbolize, had no choice whatsoever about whether they belong to a national or to an ethnic minority in Kymlicka's sense. On this point, Kymlicka's position is then not only implausible but downright self-contradictory.

[2] The distinction is most fully explicated in Kymlicka (1995a: Ch. 2, §1).

[3] Witness how he conceives of Hispanics as a loose assortment of different groups (Kymlicka 1995a: 16) and recognizes Puerto Ricans (1995a: 16, 167) and Chicanos whose ancestors fell to the US together with the Southwest territory (1995a: 16, 116) as two 'Spanish-speaking national minorities' (1995a: 16). But these categorizations are mere constructs of Kymlicka's theory. In the real world, there are Tejanos (Texans with Mexican ancestry), Chicanos (other US residents with Mexican ancestry), Hispanos (New Mexicans with pretensions to Spanish ancestry), and so on, but (as far as I know) no distinction is made by Hispanics themselves between Tejanos who did and did not have ancestors in Texas before 1836, or between Chicanos who did and did not have ancestors in the Southwest before 1848.

Let me expand upon this contradiction in a little more detail. One might characterize the disadvantage suffered specifically by national minorities in Nozickean diachronic terms: Members of national minorities—unlike members of ethnic ones—continue to be deprived of something that was once taken from their ancestors by force or fraud. But Kymlicka, as a good liberal, does not do this. Rather, he characterizes this disadvantage in entirely synchronic terms: Members of national minorities—unlike members of ethnic ones—now suffer inferior access to a social primary good that others enjoy in abundance, namely, the good of cultural membership.

But why then bring in the past at all? Why not simply look at each member of society today to find who does and who does not have access to cultural membership? In a sense, this is precisely what Kymlicka does. He explicates the relevant good as follows:

> . . . cultural membership is not a means used in the pursuit of one's ends. It is rather the context within which we choose our ends, and come to see their value, and this is the precondition of self-respect, of the sense that one's ends are worth pursuing . . . When we take cultural identity seriously, we'll understand that asking someone to trade off her cultural identity for some amount of money is like expecting someone to trade off her self-respect for some amount of money. Having money for the pursuit of one's ends is of little help if the price involves giving up the context within which those ends are worth pursuing. (Kymlicka 1989: 192–3)

As minority cultures become marginalized and finally cease to be viable, their members will be forced to give up their cultural identity and context, and to adjust to the cultural identity and context of the majority (Anglo) culture. Do persons to whom this happens count as lacking access to the good of cultural membership? Or can we just tell them that they *do* have plenty of access to the majority culture?

That depends, Kymlicka answers. If they are members of a national minority, then they suffer a loss of cultural membership which the society ought to have prevented. If they are members of an ethnic minority, on the other hand, they suffer no loss of cultural membership, because such groups once immigrated voluntarily, knowing that they would be 'expected to become members of the national societies which already exist in their new country' (Kymlicka 1995a: 114).[4] Unlike national minorities, ethnic groups traded off their right to their own native cultural identity when they immigrated. It would be unreasonable for them to expect society to protect their culture—for example, unreasonable for US immigrants to Sweden to demand special efforts from the Swedes toward protecting their anglophone minority culture (Kymlicka 1995a: 96).

But what about the *descendants* of immigrants? Even if it is true that Leticia's grandparents knew when they immigrated, or should have known, that they

---

[4] Kymlicka does recognize that some 'immigrants' came involuntarily, as slaves or refugees, and he exempts them in this context.

would be expected to assimilate, how can this be held against Leticia? Why should Leticia's culture, her cultural membership and identity, not be deserving of protection while Carmen's is? Kymlicka addresses this problem in a footnote: 'Of course, the children of immigrants do not consent, and it is not clear that parents should be able to waive their children's rights. For this reason, it is important that governments should strive to make the children of immigrants feel "at home" in the mainstream culture' (Kymlicka 1995a: 215–16 and n. 19). But this will not do at all. With respect to members of national minorities, Kymlicka holds that we must not without their consent allow them to be deprived of access to the culture in which they were raised—no matter how much we may strive to make them feel at home in our majority culture. If members of national minorities have this claim on us, how can Kymlicka deny that members of ethnic minorities have it as well? Conversely, if it is permissible to allow descendants of immigrants, who have consented to nothing and whose ancestors could not have consented for them, to be deprived of access to the culture in which they were raised provided we welcome them into the majority culture, then why isn't the same permissible with regard to the members of national minorities?

To conclude this digression: The great moral weight Kymlicka places on the distinction between national and ethnic minorities is implausible and also contradicted by Kymlicka's own liberal commitment. This conclusion could be buttressed by further, more empirical arguments specific to the case of Hispanics, showing that Kymlicka's distinction is not drawn, and could not be drawn, in the real world. It is not drawn, most importantly, by Hispanics themselves,[5] who increasingly see themselves as *one* group united by (*inter alia*) their language, Catholicism, work ethic, and love of soccer, as well as by their own music and media (including the television networks *Univision* and *Telemundo*, the daily *La Opinion*, and the magazine *Hispanic*). And it could not be drawn, because there are just too many Hispanics with mixed ancestry and too many intermediate cases of other sorts.[6]

## 2. A Questionable A Priori Claim to Economic Disadvantage

If the historical arguments are largely irrelevant, then settling the issue before us would seem to turn centrally on the value of equality or, more specifically, of equal citizenship; and this is in fact the value Kymlicka primarily invokes in his

---

[5] See n. 3.

[6] Such as Puerto Ricans within the 50 States, who might count as members of a national minority in so far as ancestors of theirs were incorporated into the US together with their homeland and who might also count as members of an ethnic minority in so far as ancestors of theirs voluntarily left Puerto Rico.

discussion of the pros and cons of various kinds of accommodation rights.[7] An appeal to equality, too, can be made by both sides. Kymlicka (1997: 72) sketches the egalitarian position *against* accommodation rights as follows: 'Ethno-cultural groups, like religious groups, should be protected from discrimination, but the maintenance and reproduction of these groups should be left to the free choices of individuals in the private sphere, neither helped nor hindered by the state.' Or, one might rather substitute, 'equally helped or hindered by the state'. Here, the basic idea is that, if the state were to help or hinder such groups differentially, it would thereby implicitly make a judgement on the relative worth of these groups—a judgement of precisely the kind that a liberal theory and a liberal state should scrupulously avoid. But if this is the main idea behind this egalitarian argument, then Kymlicka is wrong to associate its conclusion (opposing accommodation rights for minorities in favour of 'benign neglect') with the claim: 'If a societal culture is worth saving . . . the members of the culture will sustain it through their own choices. If a culture is decaying, it must be because some people no longer find it worthy of their allegiance' (Kymlicka 1995a: 107–8). A good liberal will avoid making any judgements about the relative value of different cultures and hence, a fortiori, will make no judgements about how the value of a culture correlates with the willingness of its members to sustain it through their choices.

Kymlicka argues that liberalism so understood delivers a kind of formal equality, but one that in fact amounts to substantive *inequality*. An early version of this argument involves a modification of a thought experiment initially introduced by Ronald Dworkin.[8] This thought experiment involves an island about to be settled by newcomers. Since no newcomer has a better claim to the island's natural resources than any other, Dworkin suggests an original auction in which the newcomers, each equipped with an equal number of clamshells, can enter bids for particular island resources. These bids may be indefinitely revised in light of the bids entered by others until at long last a stable distribution of resources emerges. In this final distribution, each item goes to the highest bidder, who pays at least as much for it as any other person was prepared to bid. Because this is so, Dworkin reasons, the emerging personal bundles of resources necessarily pass a no-envy test: Immediately after the auction is completed, none of the newcomers will prefer any other newcomer's bundle to his or her own.[9]

Kymlicka's modification involves the assumption that the newcomers arrive simultaneously on two vessels of very different sizes, on which different

[7] He considers various additional and complementary arguments for accommodation rights in Kymlicka (1995a: Ch. 6).

[8] Dworkin (1981). See also Ackerman (1980), featuring denizens of a spacecraft about to touch down upon a virgin planet.

[9] If any newcomer did prefer another's bundle to her own, she would rationally have asked for another round of bidding in which she would then have bid for some or all of the resources in the other bundle. Some complication is required to cope with ties (two or more exactly equal bids for the same item).

languages are spoken. We may stipulate that the vast majority of the newcomers, arriving on the larger vessel, speak English, while the remaining new-comers, arriving on the smaller vessel, speak Spanish. If this fact is known, the Hispanics are likely to want to live near one another and their bids will reflect this preference. Kymlicka concludes:

> In order to ensure that they can also live and work in their own culture, the minority members may decide, prior to the rerun of the auction, to buy resources in one area of the island, which would involve outbidding the present majority owners for resources which *qua* resources are less useful to their chosen way of life. They must incur this addi-tional cost in order to secure the existence of their cultural community. This is a cost which the members of the majority culture do not incur, but which in no way reflects different choices about the good life (or about the importance of cultural membership within it). (Kymlicka 1989: 188–9)

This argument does not go through. Suppose that, in early runs of the auction, the northern part of the island happens to receive a disproportionate number of Hispanic bids. This fact may indeed incline other Hispanics to shift their bids toward the north. But any resulting increase in the price of northern resources would be negated by Anglos shifting their bids southward. Anglos have no rea-son to pay a premium for northern real estate (on the contrary, many of them may prefer to avoid the more heavily Hispanic north). As the auction is run over and over again, the geographical preference may well strengthen, so that Hispanics will in the end be prepared to pay a considerable premium for north-ern resources over southern ones, even if the latter are, qua resources, no less useful to their chosen way of life. But no such premium will actually emerge so long as the Anglos don't share the same preference. To see this clearly, consider an analogous scenario in which phone numbers are auctioned off in a large city. One tenth of available numbers begin with a 6 and a superstitious 10 per cent of the city's population are prepared to pay a fat premium for such a 'lucky' num-ber while the remaining 90 per cent don't care about the first digit. In this sce-nario, the superstitious would get their 'lucky' numbers for free, because the slightest premium would induce those who do not care about the first digit to switch their bids to a number that does not begin with a 6.[10]

The point Kymlicka seeks to establish through his thought experiment is not borne out in the real world either. Resources located in predominantly Hispanic

[10] All this is not to say that Kymlicka's modification of Dworkin's thought experiment will make no difference to individuals. Clearly, some Hispanics will be hurt by their linguistic preference in conjunction with their other preferences. A hilltop lover may face a hard choice between living in the north, where hilltops are scarce or highly coveted and therefore expensive, and living among Anglos in the south, where hilltops are more plentiful or less coveted and therefore cheaper. But then, indi-vidual Anglos may face similar hard choices, for example, between a cheaper beachfront site among Hispanics and a more expensive one in the south. Moreover, the prevailing linguistic preferences may also *benefit* individuals: if hilltops are coveted mainly by Hispanics, Anglo hilltop lovers will benefit from Hispanic bids shifting north. And if beachfront is coveted mainly by Anglos, Hispanic beachfront lovers will benefit from Anglo bids shifting south.

THE RIGHTS OF HISPANICS IN THE US 111

areas are actually, if anything, cheaper than intrinsically similar resources located in predominantly Anglo areas. This is no doubt due in part to the fact that Anglos are, on the whole, more affluent than Hispanics. Still, this inequality in affluence is to some extent mitigated by the fact that Hispanics find it cheaper than Anglos do to live among their own.

## 3. A Questionable Plea to Even Out Unchosen Inequalities

Even if it is no more expensive for Hispanics to avoid living in Anglo areas than it is for Anglos to avoid living in Hispanic areas, it is still undeniable that, ordinarily, 'the members of minority cultures [do] not have the same ability to live and work in their own language and culture that the members of majority cultures take for granted' (Kymlicka 1995a: 107). Kymlicka can then argue that, if the distribution of resources is fair in abstraction from this 'morally arbitrary disadvantage' (1995a: 107), then it is unfair when this disadvantage is taken into account. And from this he can conclude that, in order to rectify this situation, in order to ensure a fair distribution all things considered, Hispanics must receive some accommodation that evens out their disadvantage.

The problem with this reasoning is that, if fully generalized, it proves far too much. The problem is neatly shown through a famous argument that John Roemer has presented against Dworkin's original proposal of an equality-of-resources view (Roemer 1986). Roemer demonstrates how this proposal is in danger of collapsing into its main competitor, an equality-of-welfare view, as follows. Suppose two persons have equal resources as assessed by the criterion Dworkin proposes. And suppose they nevertheless have unequal welfare. Then there must be some difference between the two persons that explains the divergence. Now Roemer assumes, without loss of generality, that the persons differ in their capacity to generate welfare out of resources, that the person with greater welfare has more endorphins which, Roemer stipulates, facilitate the 'conversion' of resources into welfare. Once we become aware of this differential endorphin endowment, it seems only fair to take endorphins into account as yet another resource. This has the consequence that equality-of-resources now favours an equal distribution of resources broadly conceived (endorphins included) which presumably entails that the distribution of non-endorphin resources should be *unequal* and negatively correlated with the natural distribution of endorphins so as to approximate equal welfare.

Kymlicka himself rejects such an equality-of-welfare position, specifically exempting inequalities that are due to persons' own free choices. Still, he does emphasize again and again throughout his work 'the importance of rectifying unchosen inequalities' (Kymlicka 1995a: 109)—always appealing to Rawls and Dworkin in support of this view. In his earlier book, we find the same distinction, albeit expressed as a distinction between differential choices and unequal circumstances. Kymlicka (1989: 186) writes there:

No one chooses to be born into a disadvantaged social group, or with natural disabilities, and so no one should have to pay for the costs imposed by those disadvantageous circumstances. Hence liberals favour compensating people who suffer from disadvantages in social environment or natural endowment . . . Someone who cultivates a taste for expensive wine has no legitimate claim to special public subsidy, since she is responsible for the cost of her choice. Someone who needs expensive medicine due to a natural disability has a legitimate claim to special public subsidy, since she is not responsible for the costs of her disadvantageous circumstances.

The distinction between chosen and unchosen inequalities Kymlicka invokes does prevent his view from collapsing into an equality-of-welfare position. But it nevertheless entails many of the same counter-intuitive results. Do we really believe that unchosen natural differentials—in looks, height, talents, or cheerfulness, for example—ought to be 'rectified' through state compensation? This is certainly not a position widely endorsed among liberals, not even among the two Kymlicka cites so frequently. Through his device of a hypothetical insurance market, Dworkin (1981: 297–9) does provide a general approach for dealing with this issue: if persons would, if they could, buy pre-birth insurance against homely looks or a melancholy temperament, then he would want the state to mandate compensatory side payments in the amount of the hypothetical insurance premiums and benefits. Rawls, on the other hand, explicitly rejects any such compensation, insisting that 'the natural distribution is neither just nor unjust' and that social positions should thus be defined in terms of social primary goods alone, without regard to the distribution of natural primary goods (such as 'health and vigor, intelligence and imagination'). 'A hypothetical initial arrangement in which all the social primary goods are equally distributed . . . provides a benchmark for judging improvements.'[11] Note also that Rawls's difference principle *permits* (unchosen) inequalities in income and wealth due to differential talents, in so far as they raise the lowest socioeconomic position. Rawls specifically allows then that the more demanding leadership positions be better paid even though they will typically also require special talents and thus be closed to those who, through no choice of their own, lack these gifts. He specifically allows, that is, unchosen inequalities.

The discussion has shown, I believe, that Kymlicka's strategy of defending accommodation rights for Hispanics as one instance under a general principle of rectifying unchosen inequalities is not promising. The latter principle does support the desired conclusion; but it supports a lot of other demands

---

[11] Rawls (1971: 62, 102). See also Pogge (1989: §§ 3.5, 4.4, 10.4), where I argue at some length that Rawls's criterion of justice does not take account of natural inequalities and is therefore a 'semiconsequentialist' criterion. Kymlicka overlooks this important departure by Rawls from the more Dworkinian liberalism he himself takes for granted.

a well—demands that for most of his readers (liberals and non-liberals alike) constitute a *reductio ad absurdum* of the principle.[12]

## 4. A Plausible Demand for Equal Treatment

In his later book, Kymlicka also presents a quite different, far more plausible argument in favour of rectification (though he does not distinguish the two arguments clearly from each other). This argument turns, not on the contingent distribution of language skills (and cultural affiliations) in the society, but on the way its government—funded by and responsible to all citizens—treats various linguistic groups:

Many liberals say that just as the state should not recognize, endorse, or support any particular church, so it should not recognize, endorse, or support any particular cultural group or identity . . . But the analogy does not work. It is quite possible for a state not to have an established church. But the state cannot help but give at least partial establishment to a culture when it decides which language is to be used in public schooling, or in the provision of state services. The state can (and should) replace religious oaths in courts with secular oaths, but it cannot replace the use of English in courts with no language. (Kymlicka 1995a: 111)[13]

Government decisions on languages, internal boundaries, public holidays, and state symbols unavoidably involve recognizing, accommodating, and supporting the needs and identities of particular ethnic and national groups. The state unavoidably promotes certain cultural identities, and thereby disadvantages others (Kymlicka 1995a: 108)

[12] Is there perhaps an even narrower principle that would be more plausible and still entail Kymlicka's desired conclusion? One may think that what entitles those disadvantaged by an inequality to compensation (or 'rectification') is not the mere fact that their disadvantage is due to no choice of their own, but rather this fact in conjunction with the further fact that this disadvantage *is* due to the choices of others: it is unchosen *social* inequalities that call for compensation, unchosen *natural* inequalities do not. This proposal runs into two difficulties. First, the boundary between these two inequalities is often unclear, as when both natural and social factors are necessary to explain why someone has a melancholy temperament or is considered homely looking. Second, the proposal does not fully capture common intuitions, as it is generally believed that serious natural handicaps (such as blindness) should be compensated and that certain social disadvantages (unpopularity) should not be. Kymlicka's view is, basically, that Hispanics should be compensated for the bad luck they encounter with regard to the distribution of language skills in the society into which they were born. It is unfortunate for them that their native language is spoken only by a minority while almost everyone speaks English. But life is full of bad luck of this kind. I have unchosen talents whose market value greatly depends on what capacities are in demand in my society—for example, on the kind of music, sports, and other entertainment cherished by my compatriots. I have unchosen desires for things whose market price depends heavily on how strongly they are desired by others. And I have unchosen desires for social activities whose possibility depends importantly on whether others have similar or complementary interests and preferences. I may find myself strongly drawn to a certain research topic, for example, only to discover that this topic is of interest to barely a dozen people or so. In all these cases, demands for compensation or rectification would be laughed out of public debate. So why should we take seriously the demand, so justified, to compensate native speakers of minority languages?

[13] For extensive discussion and refinement of this argument, see also Lagerspetz (1998).

—at least the state cannot help doing so, one should say more precisely, in certain particular respects. If this is so, and if the state ought to treat all of its citizens with their diverse cultural identities equally, then it is incumbent upon it to rectify the unequal treatment it unavoidably metes out in some respects through inversely unequal treatment in others. If the state gives preference to the Anglos by maintaining English as the official public language, then it must somehow make it up to those of its citizens who are native speakers of any other language.

This line of argument is far more convincing than its predecessor, and has been invoked in many other contexts, often to widespread acclaim. Thus, it has been argued that it is unjust for the state to subsidize some kinds of art (opera) but not others (rock and roll), to recognize some kinds of domestic partnership but not others, to construct public facilities without compensating those who cannot use them—for example, because of handicap, obesity, or claustrophobia—and so forth.

Before we can determine which arguments of this sort work, and what rectificatory measures they might then justify, we must first distinguish two different ways in which a government might support cultural groups. First, a government might merely act as a facilitator, allowing any subset of the citizenry to agree to finance some jointly desired good on mutually acceptable terms. Here the government's task is that of finding a distribution of the good's cost which can win unanimous approval: each citizen either contributes nothing or else is willing to contribute his or her assigned share for the sake of securing the good in question.[14] This idea is, of course, vulnerable to free-rider problems, as persons may have an incentive to understate what a particular good is worth to them in order to reduce the contribution assigned to them. Still, this problem can generally be solved for 'excludable' goods: when the cost of a music hall is covered through ticket sales or the cost of a highway through road tolls, potential users have no incentive to dissimulate. In these cases, the government ideally incurs no cost at all, as it can, for instance, issue construction bonds and then finance its interest outlays out of project revenues. The government may nevertheless play an indispensable catalyst role if the project is too large or too risky or too long-term to be undertaken by the corporate sector. And the government may then rightly be accused of injustice when it is willing to play this facilitating role for some groups and projects but not for others.

Second, a government may, with the support of a mere majority (if that), impose itself on all citizens by subjecting them to rules and procedures, and by forcing them to contribute to projects, irrespective of their individual consent. Government measures of this sort must pass a stringent dual test: they must promote justice or another important good, and the burdens they require must

---

[14] Rawls (1971: 282–4) suggests the idea of a branch of government, the exchange branch, which is devoted to all and only projects of this sort. He borrows the general idea from Wicksell (1958).

be shared equitably.[15] These two requirements—purpose and equity—may conflict with each other, in which case a plausible balance may have to be found. An example of such balancing occurs when a society is defending itself from an armed attack. Here the purpose (effective defence) would suggest that combat roles be concentrated on citizens likely to do well in them, while equity would suggest that the risk of death in combat be equally shared by all.

## 5. A Concrete Example: How to Decide on the Language(s) of School Instruction

These considerations are perhaps best brought to life through the discussion of a concrete issue concerning language rights with regard to public schools. The government finances a public school system, and it also requires that children attend school—either a public school free of charge or else a private school. I assume that there is a plausible justification for requiring all children to attend school and for requiring all taxpayers to contribute to the public school system: the maintenance of just institutions operated by equal citizens requires that all have a basic education, that all can, at minimum, read and write as well as understand the history and structure of the institutional scheme in whose operation they are to participate. Moreover, an educated workforce is necessary for the operation of a modern economy, from which all citizens benefit in a non-excludable way. If we take all this for granted, the difficult question is what the language(s) of instruction ought to be.

Let us, once more, start out with Kymlicka (1989: 194–5):

> In a society where the members of minority cultures (e.g. Indians, francophones) could get their fair share of resources within their own cultural community, it's not clear what would justify denying people access to publicly funded education in English. If some of the members of a minority culture choose to learn in that language, the notion of protecting the cultural context provides no ground for denying them that opportunity. On the other hand it's not clear why there should be rights to publicly funded education in any given language other than that of the community. Why should the members of minority cultures have a right to a public education in English, but not, say, in Greek? They should of course be free to run a school system in whatever language they choose at their own expense, but why a right to it at public expense?

This passage is not entirely transparent, so let me highlight the three main points Kymlicka is making, as I see them. One quite radical claim is not made explicit, but only suggested in the first two sentences of the passage.

*Claim 1. In a society where the members of a minority culture cannot get their fair share of resources within their own cultural community, denying the members of this*

---

[15] My formulation of the two requirements is intentionally left somewhat vague as there is some disagreement about how they should be specified exactly.

*community access to publicly funded education in English is justifiable by the purpose of protecting the cultural context of this community.*

I cannot be sure that Kymlicka would in fact endorse Claim 1. In any case, it would be a very surprising one for an avowed liberal to make. Claim 1 denies minority families—and only them—the right to avail themselves of an opportunity for their children on the grounds that this restriction on their liberty helps protect an endangered minority culture. It allows the state coercively to press minority children into the service of perpetuating a cultural community irrespective of whether this benefits the children concerned and irrespective also of whether the children themselves, or their parents, support this purpose.[16] This is a clear violation of Kymlicka's own liberal principle, because it would introduce an unchosen inequality: Anglo children are offered public schooling in English, minority children are not. One might respond here with a separate-but-equal argument: both groups *are* treated equally, as all children receive a public education in their respective native language. But this argument holds little promise: a public education in a minority language—and one that, by assumption, is endangered in the US—is not equal, because it does not give children the same opportunities to participate in the social, economic, and political life of this country.

Another radical claim, again not clearly endorsed in the passage, is put forward in its third and fourth sentences:

**Claim 2.** *There is no more reason to entitle the members of a minority culture to a public education in English than there is to entitle them to a public education in any other (for them) foreign language, such as Greek.*

This claim, too, is highly problematic. Hispanic or Chinese or Navajo children derive very much more benefit from receiving an education in English than they would derive from an (otherwise equivalent) education in Greek. Does Kymlicka propose to count the greater benefit to these children as no reason at all? Moreover, offering Navajos a (less useful) public education in Greek and Anglos a (more useful) public education in English would discriminate against the former on the basis of their national origin. Offering both Navajos and Anglos a public education in English would at least greatly reduce, if not eliminate, this unchosen inequality.[17]

I conclude that Claims 1 and 2 must be rejected. They give entirely unacceptable reasons for denying members of minority cultures access to a publicly funded education in English on a par with the education available to members of the dominant Anglo culture. More acceptable reasons for such a denial will be considered below.

---

[16] The word 'coercively' is not out of place. Most minority families cannot legally avoid sending their children to public school. Only the affluent families can, by enrolling their children in private schools—an option Kymlicka graciously concedes in the final sentence of the passage quoted.

[17] I use 'Navajo' here as a stand-in for all minorities. I do so because I am not sure how broadly Kymlicka intends his term 'minority culture' here. We can be sure, however, that this term covers the *national*-minority Navajo culture, so I use this culture to illustrate how Claim 2 is untenable.

A less radical claim, which Kymlicka is clearly endorsing, is this:

**Claim 3.** *Members of minority cultures should have the right to send their children to a public school where their instruction is entirely in the minority language.*

Kymlicka does little to support this claim, simply writing that 'people should have, as part of the respect owed them as members of a cultural community, the opportunity to have a public education in the language of their community' (Kymlicka 1989: 195). But this appeal to respect is somewhat problematic. It is certainly desirable to show persons respect by allowing them to make decisions about their own lives. But in the case at hand, we would be showing parents respect by allowing them to make decisions about how *their children* will be educated at public expense. In this case, there could be a countervailing reason—a reason against allowing parents to make decisions that would be worse for their children.[18] To see whether and how this countervailing reason might come into play, let us examine Claim 3 against its most prominent alternative, the thesis that it is permissible for a government in the US to run its public education system in English. (California voters, by passing Proposition 227 with a 61 per cent to 39 per cent margin, have obliged their government to do just that.) How might we settle the conflict between such an English public education system and a multilingual one in which parents are entitled to choose the language in which their children will be instructed?

I propose that we resolve this conflict in three steps. First, Kymlicka is right to stress that a government has a fundamental duty of equal treatment. Within a liberal outlook, this duty is understood, however, as a government's duty to its individual citizens and residents rather than as a duty to various groups and cultures. Thus, it is by reference to the interests of individual citizens and residents that the conflict is to be resolved.

Second, among the individual interests bearing on the question of how to design a public education system for our children, the interests *of these children* are to be of paramount importance. Many other individual interests may bear on the question: the interest of adult minority members that their language should continue to be spoken in the US (or perhaps even, in the case of Spanish, that their language should one day become co-equal with English in the US); the interest of adult minority members to communicate easily with their children and grandchildren; the interest of some corporations and government agencies in prospective employees with native foreign-language skills; and so forth. I am not suggesting that all these interest are minor and should be ignored—only that they should not be allowed to outweigh the best interests of the children.

---

[18] This reason is recognized in many other contexts. Parents' choices are constrained by child labour laws, for example, and parents are required to send their children to school up to a certain age and forbidden to withhold modern medical care from their children. In all these cases, we do not allow parents to make certain choices for their children—even when we recognize that such choices would be conscientiously based on deeply held (for example, religious) values that deserve recognition and respect.

The other interests can be brought in, then, only in so far as the interests of the children themselves do not clearly settle the matter.

To summarize after two steps: I have proposed a Fundamental Principle of Public Education, holding, roughly, that the best education for each child is the education that is best for this child. Of course, our public education system does not have the resources to provide each child with the best possible education for him or her. But, within the limits of its resources, it should provide our children with whatever education is best for them. My hope is that, if this fundamental principle can be agreed upon, the remaining differences will be much less divisive and probably resolvable through empirical research, on whose design experts now in conflict can agree in advance.

Given the principle I have proposed, the fundamental duty of a just public education system is to promote the best interests of each and every child and to do so equally. This duty must trump any desire to increase or decrease the prominence of this or that language or culture in the US.[19] It is in light of this duty that the legislature must decide whether (A) to mandate that minority children be offered a public education in their native language only, (B) to mandate that all children be offered a public education only in English, or (C) to make available an education in various languages from among which parents can choose for their children.

This brings us to the third and most difficult step, which consists in deciding which of these options is, under given empirical circumstances, favoured by the test I have proposed. My discussion of this step is meant to be illustrative only because much depends on complex empirical assessments with regard to which I have no expertise. We should also keep in mind that these empirical assessments may well turn out differently in different contexts (California vs Florida) and differently also for different languages in the same context (Navajo vs Spanish in New Mexico). My objective here is not then to propose any particular settlement, but merely to sketch what the debate leading up to such a settlement might look like.

Given the constraints I have imposed, each option would have to be defended by appeal primarily to the best interests of the children whom the public education system in question is supposed to educate. Thus one might argue for Option B (California Proposition 227), for example, by claiming that it best serves the goal of enabling all students to participate fully in US society— socially, economically, and politically. Here is a straightforward way of filling in this kind of argument: One postulates a principle of English First: *the most important linguistic competence for children now growing up in the US is the ability to communicate in English; and the language of instruction in public schools in the US should therefore be chosen by reference to the goal of effectively helping pupils develop*

---

[19] It is frustratingly unclear whether Kymlicka agrees on this point or whether he would think it permissible, under certain circumstances, to sacrifice the best interests of children to the political goal of preserving an existing culture for the benefit of those for whom it provides their context of choice.

*fluency in English*. And one tries then to support the empirical claim that choosing English as the universal language of instruction is part of the most effective method for helping students develop fluency in English.

Let us consider two ways in which this argument could be attacked.[20] One line of attack would deny the empirical claim, asserting that Option B does not provide the most effective method for helping students develop fluency in English, that minority students will reach higher levels of English proficiency if they are first helped to develop full literacy in their native language. This line of attack is exemplified by Kymlicka (1995a: 97) when he writes that 'people learn English best when they view it as supplementing, rather than displacing, their mother tongue'. If this line of attack were fully successful, it might provide an acceptable argument for Option A, in contrast to the unacceptable arguments suggested by Claims 1 and 2 discussed above. The other line of attack would appeal to *other* interests of minority children (besides their interest to develop fluency in English), arguing that, once their bearing on the question before us is considered, Option B will not come out ahead.

Though formally distinct, both lines of attack are likely to appeal to similar empirical considerations. They would seek to show that being abruptly exposed to a foreign-language environment for several hours per day would constitute a significant shock for many young children—a shock that would make it difficult for them to relate well to their teachers and fellow pupils,[21] and—partly for this reason—difficult also to make good progress in English as well as in other subjects.

Now, one might argue in response that these problems, however real, do not alter the fact that children's important long-term interest in being fully literate in English is best served by early immersion and that this interest is stronger than the interest in avoiding those temporary problems. But one might also think of various ways in which Option B might be revised to accommodate the stated concerns. Thus one might support programmes that make it easier for minority parents to afford pre-school exposure to English for their children, and programmes that would make it easier for such parents to achieve fluency in

[20] I will not consider a third kind of attack which would deny that the ability to communicate in English is the most important linguistic competence for children now growing up in the US. This denial can be made plausible by emphasizing that what matters here is the importance of English proficiency in the future, for which our public education system is supposed to prepare the children in its care. But then the *future* importance of English and Spanish proficiencies cannot straightforwardly inform the design of the present education system, because it also depends on this very design: The more children now receive their education in Spanish, the more important Spanish proficiency will be during their adult lives (Linda Alcoff forcefully made this point in discussion). And yet it remains true, nevertheless, under any foreseeable realistic scenario, that during the lifespan of the children we raise today, English proficiency will continue to be more important than Spanish proficiency for almost all residents of the US (most Puerto Ricans excepted).

[21] And even to their parents, who, if they have little command of the universal language of public education, may come to be seen by their own children as existing at the margins of society.

English themselves. One might further support the availability of special foreign-language tutors whom pupils could turn to outside regular hours if they find it difficult to follow lessons in English during their first few school years. In addition, one might also support the early (elementary-school) introduction of sufficiently prominent minority languages as academic subjects in order to give students the opportunity to develop full literacy also in their native language, and in order also to give them a manifest indication that their native language is being valued rather than displaced. Such instruction should be continued through all grades so that native speakers of Spanish, say, as well as other students after they have learned basic Spanish in more elementary courses, have an opportunity to study the literature and culture of the Spanish-speaking world and to perfect their competence in this language. Such course offerings would make clear that the public school system is endeavouring not merely to give every student full competence in English, but also to give students the opportunity to develop an equally full competence in the native languages of any minorities that (locally) are numerically significant.[22]

Enriched by complementary programmes of these four kinds, Option B may well become widely accepted among those willing to put the interests of the children before all else. To be sure, acceptance of the English First principle would tend to reduce the prominence of other languages in the US below what it would be if they were also used, alongside English, as languages of school instruction. In this sense, English First privileges English at the expense of these other languages. But this unfairness toward the various languages[23] does not here reflect an unfairness toward the various speakers of different languages. The choice of English as the universal language of instruction is justified by reference to the best interests of children with other native languages, for whom speaking good English (in addition to their native language) will be an enormous advantage in their future social and professional lives. As supplemented, English First could not then, I believe, be charged with disadvantaging children who are native speakers of other languages vis-à-vis Anglo children. Such children are, in a sense, initially disadvantaged by getting a somewhat later start toward English competence (though they also have a significant and permanent advantage through the head start they enjoy in their native language). But this disadvantage exists before these children enter the public education system and it is one that this system is designed to erase.

Let me end my illustrative discussion of the third step by emphasizing that the English First principle I have canvassed is not of a piece with the English

---

[22] I would like to express this point as a demand for (the availability of) *bilingual education*. But this expression is now often used not for an education system under which students can become bilingual, but rather for one under which some students are taught in one language and others in another.

[23] Which cannot be completely avoided in any case, assuming we reject the goal of making all languages equally prominent in the US and lack the resources to provide even the sole Kazakh child in Putnam County with a public education in her native language.

Only initiatives that have been cropping up in the last 20 years in the federal and many State legislatures. Endorsement of English First is fully consistent with the view that it is highly desirable that Spanish and other minority languages should survive as native languages in the US.[24] This goal is well served by giving native speakers of Spanish, and other children as well, the opportunity to develop full competence in Spanish through the public school system.

While I share the commitment to this goal, I have argued that its pursuit must be constrained by an overriding commitment to the interests of the children that our schools are supposed to educate—an overriding commitment to the principle that the best education for each child is the education that is best for this child. It is this Fundamental Principle of Public Education (which emerged from the second step, and whose application my discussion of the third step was intended to illustrate) that deserves our most basic allegiance, or so I believe. This principle has the potential to bring together all those who genuinely care about the children whose lives our education system will shape so profoundly, guiding us toward a shared assessment of the English First principle as well as of the more specific institutional options that have been in dispute.

## 6.  The Costs of Accommodation Rights and Their Universalizability

I am well aware that this chapter is a disappointment to many readers in the US who are proud of their Hispanic heritage and inclined to favour more extensive accommodation rights than could be supported by the general ideas and principles I have here proposed and defended.[25]

Let me emphasize once more, in conclusion, that my rather cautious stance is motivated by a concern for the moral costs of accommodation rights. Moral costs we should be mindful of include, in particular, 'liberal' costs in terms of freedom and equality, which arise when individuals are used to promote some

[24] As far as Spanish is concerned, there is little doubt that it will survive and even thrive as a native language. Through high birth rates as well as legal and illegal immigration, Hispanics are the fastest-growing group in the US, expected to reach 100 million around the year 2015. It is not inconceivable that the Spanish language will in fact one day become co-equal with English in the US. There are many obvious reasons to welcome such a development, but also reasons to regret it: if it were as important for persons living in the US to know both Spanish and English as it now is to know English, then it would most likely become even harder for other languages to survive in this country.

[25] Such readers may also view the accommodation rights I *have* supported (in connection with Options B and C) as entrenching, rather than overcoming, the current dominance of the English language and may thus be distinctly unenthusiastic about programmes that make it easier for minority parents to afford pre-school exposure to English for their children, programmes that would make it easier for such parents to achieve fluency in English themselves, availability of special foreign-language tutors for minority pupils, and early introduction of prominent minority languages as academic subjects.

group interest. We should be especially alert to such costs when they would be imposed on children, who have so very little influence on the social environment that will shape them so profoundly. An important example of this kind was Claim 1, discussed in Section 5 above, which asserted that access to publicly funded education in English may be withheld from minority children if this helps to protect the cultural context of their community whose other members cannot get their fair share of resources within it. Moral costs we should be mindful of also include the costs to other ethnic, linguistic, religious, or lifestyle groups. These costs are especially obvious in the case of language: Even if we agree that residents of the US should speak more languages than they now do, the number of languages each of us might speak fluently is quite limited. And the promotion of one language through the public education system will thus inevitably come at the expense of other languages, some of which may then not survive at all (at least in the US). To be sensitive to such potential costs, those who demand accommodation rights for some group(s) should take care to base these demands on principles by which they would be prepared to judge the demands of any other groups as well.

What I have written is not meant as the last word, not even as *my* last word, on these issues. If future discussions of them pay somewhat more attention to the concerns I have stressed, this essay will have been worthwhile.

# 5

# Misconceiving Minority Language Rights: Implications for Liberal Political Theory

STEPHEN MAY

> . . . leaving one's culture, while possible, is best seen as renouncing something to which one is reasonably entitled.
>
> (Kymlicka 1995a: 90)

I do not claim to be a political theorist—my academic background is in sociology, education, and linguistics—and so it is with some trepidation that I venture directly onto this terrain here. But I do so because of the ongoing misconceptions—and, in some cases, blatant misrepresentations—evident in political theory debates around minority language rights; misconceptions and misrepresentations, moreover, that are still apparent at times in this present collection.

Accordingly, in what follows, I want to respond directly to two other contributions to this collection—those of David Laitin and Rob Reich (Chapter 3) and Thomas Pogge (Chapter 4)—which, at least to my mind, clearly continue to rehearse some of these misconceptions and misrepresentations. However, along with a critique of their respective positions, I will also offer possible alternative conceptions or solutions to the issues and concerns raised by these commentators. This is important because, however misinformed the particular responses in question might be, the actual issues and concerns raised about the potential problematics and limitations of minority language rights must be seriously addressed if we are to make any further progress on them, in political theory as elsewhere.

## 1. Political Theory and Language Rights

A significant part of the problem with respect to minority language rights is simply that they have not been much discussed within political theory, at least until recently. Indeed, the extent to which the relationship between language and politics has been overlooked in much political analysis is surprising. After all, language is a contributing feature in many political conflicts in the world today, including those in the Baltics, Belgium, Canada, Spain, Sri Lanka, and Turkey, to name but a few (see Horowitz 1985; Safran 1999; May 2001). Yet, as Weinstein (1983) observes, while commentators have had much to say about 'the language of politics', very few have had anything to say about 'the politics of language' (for similar observations, see also Grillo 1989; Kymlicka 1995a; Blommaert 1996; Holborow 1999).[1]

Why is this? Part of the reason can be located in the general antipathy in both political theory and political practice towards group-based rights per se in the 50-year period following the Second World War, along with the concomitant valorization of individual rights (see Kymlicka 1989; 1995a). In contrast, the right to the maintenance of a minority language has generally been articulated in the political arena—both well before the Second World War and since (see Thornberry 1991; de Varennes 1996)—on the basis that the particular language in question constitutes a collective or communally shared good of a particular linguistic community.[2] Little wonder then that such claims have received little sympathy and made even less progress in a political environment largely opposed to group-based rights claims. Recent debates within political theory, not least as a result of Will Kymlicka's prominent interventions, suggest that this may be changing, or at the very least that the possibility of group-based rights can no longer be ruled immediately out of court. That said, it is clear that, 'on the ground', opposition to group-based rights remains firmly entrenched.[3]

But there is another reason for the peripheral place of minority language rights in political theory and practice—a reason that has to do with the perception of minority languages themselves. I have written at length about this elsewhere (see May 2001), but briefly it can be said to relate to the almost de rigueur distinction made between majority languages as vehicles of modernity (and mobility, of which more later) and minority languages as carriers of culture and tradition. I use the terms 'vehicles' and 'carriers' advisedly here, since the former is clearly associated with progress and the expansion of opportunity,

---

[1] The few notable exceptions, at least to date, have been French Canadian political theorists discussing the issue of Quebec; see, for example, Coulombe (1995; 1999) and Réaume (2000). Of course, one might add Charles Taylor's (1994) seminal contribution on the 'politics of recognition' here as well, although language forms only a part of his wider discussion and, when it does, tends also to be framed primarily in relation to Quebec.

[2] After all, if a language is to continue to be spoken it requires, by definition, someone else to talk *with*. On this basis, when a language ceases to be spoken by a *community* of speakers, it has already effectively perished.

[3] A representative but by no means exhaustive list with respect to minority language rights includes the English Only movement in the United States, ongoing opposition in Canada to Quebec language laws, ongoing opposition in Spain to Catalunyan language laws, and ongoing opposition in Wales to Welsh language laws (for further discussion of Catalunya and Wales, see 2.3). I have charted these various language controversies, and many others, in May (2001). See also May (2000; 2002a), Blommaert (1999), and Wright (2000).

while the latter is most often equated with regression and the active foreclosing of opportunities, an irremediably antediluvian tendency to hold on to a past that is clearly long past its useful sell-by date. Or so the story goes.

Closely allied with this position is a deeply held liberal tendency to regard the ongoing promotion of ethnocultural and/or ethnolinguistic difference as problematic in and of itself. This general view, one that is by no means confined to political theorists, is ably summarized by the prominent sociolinguist Joshua Fishman (1991: 72):

Unlike 'human rights' which strike Western and Westernized intellectuals as fostering wider participation in general societal benefits and interactions, 'language rights' still are widely interpreted as 'regressive' since they would, most probably, prolong the existence of ethnolinguistic differences. The value of such differences and the right to value such differences have not yet generally been recognised by the modern Western sense of justice . . .

But staying at this general level of debate about language rights can get us only so far—not very far, in fact. So what of the specific arguments within political theory that are employed by liberal sceptics of minority language rights claims? To what extent are their arguments concerning language rights informed, valid, and/or reasonable? I want to suggest that they are often still not as sufficiently well informed as they should be, and that they contain many errors of fact as well as presumption. Let me attempt to defend this rather perilous claim in more detail.

## 2.  Misconceiving Minority Language Rights

In this section, I will highlight a few key misconceptions about minority language rights, as rehearsed by language rights' sceptics, and will do so, by way of example, with particular reference to the arguments developed in this present collection by Pogge, and Laitin and Reich. In the following discussion, there will inevitably be some crossover with debates on minority language rights in particular and more generalized minority rights claims. Where possible, however, I will avoid the latter, given that these broader discussions are already well rehearsed elsewhere.

### 2.1  Language and History

There are three features with respect to the use of history that are often evident in political theory discussions that dismiss the validity of minority language rights' claims: (1) historical disavowal, or the problem of 'presentism', (2) historical simplification and/or misrepresentation, or the problem of sanitization, and (3) historical inevitability, or the problem of the linguistic fait accompli. As we shall see, each understates the historical injustices invariably attendant upon the social and political minoritization of languages, while also often wilfully ignoring alternative possibilities that countenance a greater accommodation of minority language rights.

### 2.1.1 The Problem of 'Presentism'

Pierre Bourdieu, the French sociologist and social anthropologist, has often criticized the discipline of linguistics for its tendency towards a synchronic or 'presentist' approach to the study of language, of examining language in isolation from the social and political conditions in which it is used. As Bourdieu (1991: 34) comments ironically of this process: 'bracketing out the social . . . allows language or any other symbolic object to be treated like an end in itself, [this] contributed considerably to the success of structural linguistics, for it endowed the "pure" exercises that characterise a purely internal and formal analysis with the charm of a game devoid of consequences'.

Much the same can be said about the ahistorical, apolitical approach to language too often adopted in political theory by opponents of language rights. This is particularly evident in the almost unquestioned legitimacy ascribed to national languages in such discussions (see, for example, Barry 2001) and the similarly unquestioned acceptance of their dominant social and political position and function—their normative ascendancy—within modern nation-states. One can see both aspects clearly exemplified, for example, in Pogge's discussion of English in the United States. I will return to the details of Pogge's analysis of the historical language context in the USA, such as it is, in the following section when I examine the process of historical sanitization. However, suffice it to say at this point that adopting a presentist approach—exemplified again by Pogge in his subsequent disavowal of the relevance of history to questions of language rights—inevitably entails ignoring, or at best underemphasizing, the specific socio-historical and socio-political processes by which particular national languages have come to be created, and accepted as dominant and legitimate, in the first place. As Bourdieu again observes of this process:

To speak of *the* language, without further specification, as linguists [or political theorists] do, is tacitly to accept the *official* definition of the *official* language of a political unit. This language is the one which, within the territorial limits of that unit, imposes itself on the whole population as the only legitimate language . . . The official language is bound up with the state, both in its genesis and its social uses . . . this state language becomes the theoretical norm against which all linguistic practices are objectively measured. (Bourdieu 1991: 45; emphases in original)

A synchronic or presentist approach to the question of language rights within political theory is particularly problematic because it fails to address adequately, if at all, the unavoidable historical and contemporary fact that the establishment of state-mandated or national languages is, in almost all cases, an inherently deliberate (and deliberative) political act and one, moreover, that clearly advantages some individuals and groups at the expense of others. Fernand de Varennes summarizes the processes and its implications thus:

By imposing a language requirement, the state shows a definite preference towards some individuals on the basis of language . . . In other words, the imposition of a single language for use in state activities and services is by no means a neutral act, since:

1) The state's chosen language becomes a condition for the full access to a number of services, resources and privileges, such as education or public employment . . .
2) Those for whom the chosen state speech is not the primary language are thus treated differently from those for whom it is: the latter have the advantage or benefit of receiving the state's largesse in their primary tongue, whereas the former do not and find themselves in a more or less disadvantaged position . . . Whether it is for employment in state institutions . . . or the need to translate or obtain assistance . . . a person faced with not being able to use his primary language *assumes a heavier burden*. (de Varennes 1996: 86–7; my emphasis)

In effect, speakers of the dominant language variety are immediately placed at an advantage in both accessing and benefiting from the civic culture of the nation-state. A dominant language group usually controls the crucial authority in the areas of administration, politics, education, and the economy, and gives preference to those with a command of that language. Concomitantly, other language groups are limited in their language use to specific domains, usually solely private and/or low-status, and are thus left with the choice of renouncing their social ambitions, assimilating, or resisting in order to gain greater access to the public realm (Nelde 1997). Indeed, the whole tenor of the critiques of minority language rights with respect to greater access to social mobility (see 2.2) presupposes this position.

Given this, I do not think it unreasonable to interrogate critically the historical processes that have seen particular language varieties accorded the status and prestige of 'national' languages, while other languages have been 'minoritized' and, most often, stigmatized. As I have argued elsewhere (May 2001; see also Blommaert 1999; Wright 2000), this is, in turn, the specific result of the formation of modern nation-states and the key organizational principle underpinning their formation: that of linguistic and cultural homogeneity via the establishment of a common, usually singular, 'national' language.

The requirement of speaking a common language is unique to nation-states, and a relatively recent historical phenomenon. It is unique because previous forms of political organization did not require this degree of linguistic uniformity. For example, empires were quite happy for the most part to leave unmolested the plethora of cultures and languages subsumed within them: as long as taxes were paid, all was well. It is historically recent because nation-states are themselves the product of the nationalisms of the last few centuries, beginning most notably with the French Revolution.

That the subsequent establishment of so-called national languages was inevitably an arbitrary and artificial process, driven by the politics of state making, is also worthy of critical historical interrogation. This is clearly illustrated by the fact that the same language may be regarded as both a majority *and* a minority language, depending on the national context. Thus Spanish is a majority language in Spain and many Latin American states, but a minority language in the USA. Likewise, the distinction often drawn between a 'language' and a 'dialect' cannot be easily made on linguistic grounds, since some languages are mutually intelligible, while some dialects of the same language are not. The example often employed here is that of Norwegian, since it was regarded as a dialect of Danish until the end of Danish rule in 1814. But it was only with the advent of Norwegian independence from Sweden in 1905 that Norwegian actually acquired the status of a separate language, albeit one that has since remained mutually intelligible with both Danish and Swedish. Contemporary examples can be seen in the re-emergence in the early 1990s of distinct Czech and Slovak varieties in place of the previously prescribed 'common' language of Czechoslovakia; while in the former Yugoslavia we are currently seeing the broadly comparable redevelopment of separate Serbian and Croatian language varieties in place of Serbo-Croat, the artificial language product of the former Communist Yugoslav Federation. As Nash (1989: 6), observes, 'It has been said that "language is a dialect with an army and a navy". And what official or recognised languages are in any given instance is often the result of politics and power interplays'.

In short, the politics of state making has largely determined the politics of language, not the other way around, as any historical account of national language formation will demonstrate. Thus, the attempt by political theorists such as Pogge to dismiss a diachronic analysis of language rights in favour of a solely synchronic one is fundamentally misplaced, since it is only via the former that we can come to a critical understanding of how particular language ideologies are created in the first place and subsequently legitimated politically (Blommaert 1999). As Blommaert argues, a synchronic analysis takes no account of human agency, political intervention, power, or authority in the formation of particular (national) language ideologies. Nor, by definition, is it able to identify the establishment and maintenance of a national language as a specific 'form of practice, historically contingent and socially embedded' (1999: 7). Historical arguments are clearly irrelevant only to those who have benefited from the particular history concerned. This perhaps explains why it is speakers of dominant languages who most often dismiss the relevance of history and historical injustice as usefully informing the question of minority language rights.

### 2.1.2 The Problem of Sanitization

Where language histories are actually discussed by language rights sceptics, there is a tendency to both simplify and sanitize them. Again, Pogge's brief discussion of the historical US language context is indicative of this more general trend.

Pogge begins his essay on the linguistic rights of Hispanics in the USA by asserting that English is the predominant language in the USA. This is not in doubt; it is clearly the accepted language in the public domain, the language of the state, the language of power, and the language of social mobility (although with respect to the last, see 2.2). What is interesting here, though, is that Pogge then elides the current hegemony of English with a view of its historical ascendancy as inevitable, unproblematic, and, crucially, uncontested—as, in effect, a natural, evolutionary, and seamless march to linguistic victory. He does this first by vicariously providing us with two exemplary claims made by opponents and proponents of minority language accommodation respectively. In relation to the former, he employs the well-trailed claim of the likes of the English Only movement that the USA has always been an English-speaking (and the implication here is *monolingual* English-speaking) country. For the latter, he invokes the distinction made between national minorities and migrants as a basis for according greater linguistic rights to national minorities—many of them Hispanic—given that their incorporation into the USA was involuntary.

Pogge points out, in response to the latter, the problem of disentangling involuntary from voluntary minorities in relation to the heterogeneous Hispanic populations in the USA. This is an important limitation, although his claim that an obviously complex case such as this therefore somehow invalidates the national minority/migrant distinction per se is neither warranted nor supported, not least because there are clearly a host of other national contexts, and other groups, where these distinctions can be clearly made. Indigenous peoples present perhaps the clearest example of distinct national minorities here (see Kymlicka 1999; Ivison, Sanders, and Patton 2000; Feldman 2001; May 2002c) and, in what follows, I will illustrate this point in more detail via the specific case of Native Americans in the USA.

If Pogge's caveat with respect to the proponents of language accommodation is nonetheless made, no comparable caveat is forthcoming for the central claim of language accommodation opponents on the monolingual English-speaking history of the USA. Coupled with Pogge's initial assertion regarding the pre-eminence of English, this might lead some to assume that the public recognition and representation of languages other than English has *never* been countenanced in the USA. This is simply wrong (see Dicker 1996; Crawford 2001; May 2001). While English *is* clearly pre-eminent, it was not inevitably so, particularly in the early colonial period when a number of languages—notably German, French, and Spanish—competed with English in the public domain. The deliberate reluctance of the drafters of the Declaration of Independence and the Constitution to formalize English, or any language for that matter, as the official language of the United States suggests as much (Shell 1993). Underpinning this decision of the Founding Fathers was the centrality of the principle of individual choice. This was exemplified in the notion of free speech and the related adoption of a laissez-faire language policy, deriving from the British model, which eschewed the legislative formality of granting 'official status' to English (see Marshall 1986). Coupled with the widespread multilingualism evident at the time,[4] 'the intellectual climate of the times, which depended upon communication across language groups . . . supported maximum flexibility in language use' (Heath 1977: 270).

This 'flexibility in language use' was also reflected in the well-established practice of granting limited minority language rights to (some) minority language speakers in the USA, albeit mostly at local and regional levels. This formal accommodation of minority language rights extended to both private and publicly funded bilingual schools and continued into the early part of the twentieth century, until the combination of the nativism of the Americanization movement and the anti-foreigner sentiments generated by the First World War put paid to it since it was, most often, German-speaking minorities who laid claim to such bilingual education provisions.[5]

Pogge's discussion of US language history thus ignores its multilingualism and its historical accommodation, albeit clearly limited, of some minority language rights. Even more problematically, it ignores its more punitive, proscriptive aspects as well. To take just one obvious example here, one only has to look to the case of Native American languages. When the Spanish first arrived on the North American continent in the early sixteenth century, it is estimated that at least 500 Native American languages were spoken (Leap 1981). The subsequent impact of European colonization on Native Americans—along with its usual corollaries of introduced diseases, land dispossession, and genocide—were to change all that. By 1920, the Native American population reached a nadir of 400,000, having fallen from an estimated 30–40 million at time of contact (see McKay and Wong 1988). An educational policy over this period

---

[4] In American colonies between 1750 and 1850, non-English-speaking European settlers made up one-quarter of the white population and Dutch (New York), Swedish (Delaware), and German (Pennsylvania) were widely spoken. Indeed, in 1790 German speakers comprised 8.7 per cent of the total US population (Zentella 1997). Meanwhile, Black Americans—mostly slaves, and with their many African languages—numbered more than one-fifth of the total population (Shell 1993). Outside of the early colonies, Spanish- and French-language speakers predominated. Many of these language speakers were eventually incorporated into the United States as it expanded. For example, the (1803) Louisiana Purchase saw this territory, which included a majority of French speakers, acquired from France. Likewise, the (1848) Treaty of Guadalupe Hidalgo saw Mexico cede nearly half of its predominantly Spanish-speaking territory to the US, including areas of present day New Mexico, Texas, Arizona, Colorado, and California (see Menchaca 2001: Ch. 8).

[5] The right to bilingual schooling, for example, survived in Louisiana law until 1921 (Crawford 1992a), while the German-speaking minority in the USA were accorded a wide range of accommodative language rights. Official proclamations were published in German until 1794 and at least 32 German language newspapers were published between 1732 and 1800 (Crawford 1992b). Beginning in 1839, a number of States passed laws allowing German as the language of instruction in public schools, where numbers warranted (Dicker 1996; see also 2.6).

of actively repressing Native American languages and replacing them with English also contributed significantly to the related decline and extinction of many Native American languages.

One notable example of this assimilationist and also clearly racialized approach can be seen in the US Congress's passing in 1887 of the General Allotment and Compulsory Education Acts. This amounted to a two-fisted policy of forced assimilation, aimed at transforming Native Americans into yeoman farmers by dividing their lands, while schooling their children in English *specifically* for the trades and domestic service (McCarty 2002; for comparable examples elsewhere, see May 2001: Ch. 8). As a federal commissioner of Indian Affairs, J. D. C. Atkins, observed in his annual report at the time: 'schools should be established, which [Native American] children should be required to attend, [and where] their barbarous *dialects* should be blotted out and the English *language* substituted' (1887; reprinted in Crawford 1992b: 48; my emphases).[6] So much for English as a language of educational opportunity and wider social mobility (see 2.2). Although the Bureau of Indian Affairs formally rescinded this assimilationist education policy in 1934, punishment for native language use in schools continued through to the 1950s (Crawford 1989). Notwithstanding this sorry history, Native American languages are still spoken today in the USA, although they are seldom commented upon,[7] and include numerous examples that have undergone more recent language revitalization efforts (May 1999a; McCarty 2002).

To reiterate, then, my point in this section is not to deny the current or even the historical ascendancy of English in the USA. Rather, it is to highlight that the USA, as with most modern nation-states, has had a much more *diverse, punitive*, and *contested* language history than bald assertions of English language dominance might suggest. To return to the question of Hispanic minorities, even the ongoing public discussions of Spanish–English bilingualism and bilingual education in the USA, usually in apocalyptic terms (see Schlesinger 1992; Barry 2001), indicate as much, albeit perhaps unwittingly.

Furthermore, the example of Native Americans highlights clearly—if there was ever any doubt about this—the *selective* nature of state-mandated language proscription. Such proscription is almost always situated within a wider racialized policy directed at marginalized and disadvantaged groups—with indigenous peoples being perhaps the most marginalized of all people groups (Tully 1995). As Crawford (1994) notes, such practices seldom occur among communities of wealth and privilege, but frequently among the dispossessed and disempowered.

---

[6] Note here the deliberate relegation of Native American language varieties to mere 'dialects' in contradistinction to the English 'language', along with all this implies about language hierarchy (see the earlier discussion in 2.1.1 on language and dialects).

[7] In the 1990 census, 1,878,275 people identified as Native Americans, of whom 331,600 over the age of five years reported speaking a Native American language. Altogether, 26 such languages were identified in the 1990 census as having at least 1,000 speakers (Ricento 1996).

Moreover, linguistic dislocation for a particular community of speakers seldom, if ever, occurs in isolation from socio-cultural and socio-economic dislocation as well. The proscription of a minority language almost always forms part of a wider process of social, cultural, and political displacement. In terms of developing a normative political theory on language rights that takes seriously questions of justice/injustice, this often inconvenient historical feature and its ongoing consequences in the present in many instances cannot simply be rationalized or overlooked.

### 2.1.3 The Problem of the Linguistic Fait Accompli

Even if we recognize and accept the often brutalizing language practices of the past—almost always instigated by the state, and invoked on the principle of cultural and linguistic homogeneity—there is still the problem of the historical fait accompli. We may well regret the past, but there is nothing we can now do about it, so it should not, nor can it, usefully inform our present. What is done is done.

The problem with this position is that it attenuates, and in most instances forecloses, the possibility of considering alternative conceptions—of rethinking the nation-state in more culturally and linguistically plural ways, not least via the application of minority language rights (see also 3). It also understates, and often overlooks, the many counter-examples evident, not only historically but also contemporaneously, where minority language rights have been considered and in some cases successfully implemented. The historical accommodation of limited minority language rights in the US historical context is one example here that I have already discussed and, as we shall see, there are many others.

The accommodation of minority language rights within nation-states is usually based on one of two organizing principles. The first is the 'territorial language principle' which grants language rights that are limited to a particular territory in order to ensure the maintenance of a particular language in that area. The most prominent examples of this principle can be found in Quebec, Catalonia, Wales, Belgium, and Switzerland. Quebec has already been much discussed elsewhere (see, for example, Coulombe 1995; Carens 2000: Ch. 5; May 2001: Ch. 6), and I will return to the examples of Catalonia and Wales in 2.3, so let me highlight briefly here the examples of Belgium and Switzerland.

In Belgium, there had been linguistic conflict between its two principal language groups—the French and Flemish—since the inception of the Belgian state in 1830. However, much of this had to do with the de facto supremacy of French and the concomitant marginalizing of Flemish throughout its history, despite the fact that Flemish speakers were a numerical majority. This ongoing conflict led eventually to the adoption of linguistic legislation in 1962–3 which enshrined the territorial language principle in Belgium, thus ensuring equal linguistic status for Flemish-speakers. This legislation divided the country into three administrative regions: Flanders and Wallonia, which are subject to strict monolingualism (Flemish to the north and French to the south), and the capital,

Brussels, which is officially bilingual. However, even in Brussels the French/Flemish linguistic infrastructure is quite separate, extending to the workplace as well as to the more common domains of administration and education. In short, this means that in the whole country there are only mono-lingual educational institutions, while administration is also monolingual, even in multilingual regions. That said, it is also clear that the territorial principle adopted in Belgium has contributed significantly to its socio-political and economic stability by ensuring the maintenance of group language rights (Blommaert 1996; Nelde 1997).

A similar pattern pertains in Switzerland where the Swiss nation-state is offi-cially multilingual in German, French, Italian, and Romansch and, as in Belgium, this formal multilingualism is achieved via the enforcement of regional monolingualism. That said, there are also significant infrastructural differences between the four official languages, with German being spoken by 63.6 per cent of the Swiss population, while Romansch is spoken by only 0.6 per cent. The consequent difficulties of status and use for Romansch have led to a recent overhaul of Swiss language policy to provide more support for that language (Grin 1994; 1999b).

The second approach is predicated on the 'personality language principle' which attaches language rights to individuals, irrespective of their geographical position. This provides greater flexibility than the territorial language principle in the apportionment of group-based language rights, although it also has its strictures. The most notable of these is the criterion 'where numbers warrant'—that is, language rights may be granted only when there are a *sufficient* number of particular language speakers to warrant language protection—a key criterion to which I will return in 2.6, along with related examples of this approach adopted in Canada, Finland, India, and South Africa.

But it is not only national minorities to which policies of minority linguistic accommodation can and do apply. Australia and Canada, for example, have since the 1970s both pursued a policy of official multiculturalism, recognizing in so doing the rights of migrant minority groups to retain their first languages, alongside that of the majority language(s), if they so choose. The (1978) Galbally Report, which introduced multiculturalism as public policy into Australia, clearly reflects this emphasis when it states: 'We are convinced that migrants have the right to maintain their cultural and racial [*sic*] identity and that it is clearly in the best interests of our nation that they should be encour-aged and assisted to do so if they wish' (cited in Kane 1997: 550).[8]

---

[8] I cannot discuss here the many limitations and anomalies attendant on the actual policy and practice of multiculturalism, although for further discussion see May (1999b; 2002a). For analyses of Australia's official policy of multiculturalism, see Ozolins (1993), Kane (1997), and Clyne (1998). For analyses of Canada's official multiculturalism, see Fleras and Elliot (1991), Fleras (1994), Berry (1998), and Kymlicka (1998).

These national examples are also supplemented by a plethora of local and regional initiatives with respect to minority language accommodation within nation-states. The recognition of indigenous language and education initiatives, often as part of a wider recognition of indigenous self-determination, is a clear example here. I have written at length elsewhere about prominent recent developments in the New Zealand context with respect to the recognition of indigenous Maori rights to land, language, and education. These developments have resulted in a substantial realignment of public policy there in favour of group-based rights for Maori (see May 1999a; 2002c). Other examples include Norway's recent abandonment of its stringent 'Norwegianization' (read assimilationist) policy towards the indigenous Sámi, their languages, and their culture, resulting in 1988 in a revision of its constitution in order to grant greater autonomy for Sámi. As the amendment to the constitution stated: 'It is incumbent on the governmental authorities to take the necessary steps to enable the Sámi population to safeguard and develop their language, their culture and their social life' (cited in Magga 1996: 76). The effects of this new amendment are most apparent in the regional area of Finnmark, in the northernmost part of Norway, where the largest percentage of Sámi live. The formal recognition accorded to Sámi has led to the subsequent establishment of a Sámi parliament in Finnmark (in 1989), while the Sámi Language Act, passed in 1992, recognized Northern Sámi as its official regional language. The latter act saw the formal promotion of the language within the Sámi parliament, the courts of law, and all levels of education (see Corson 1995; Todal 1999).

The precedent of regional autonomy for indigenous peoples set by Finnmark has been built upon considerably in more recent times in Canada. Most notable here, at least thus far, is the formal establishment of the new Arctic province of Nunavut. The establishment of Nunavut, the first formal subdivision of territory in Canada for 50 years, is the end result of a 20-year negotiation process with the 22,000 Inuit of the region (out of a total regional population of 25,000). The new Provincial administration is dominated by Inuit and it is proposed that the local Inuit language, Inuktitut, be made co-official with English and French in the region, as well as being the first working language of the Provincial government (Purvis 1999; Corson 2001).

Suffice it to say, these examples indicate that minority language accommodation—while clearly not easily achieved, or necessarily without its tensions—can nonetheless be successfully implemented when there is sufficient political will to do so. The absolutist approach to language policy (see Carens 2000: 79) need not be inevitable, and to suggest otherwise amounts to little more than a *post hoc* rationalization of social and political inaction and the related acceptance of the linguistic status quo. In the process, the legitimacy of minority language rights claims—in relation to both addressing and redressing historical linguistic injustice and, often, contemporary circumstances of ongoing disadvantage and discrimination as well (see 2.1.2)—are not given their due weight.

## 2.2 Language and Mobility

If the area of language and history is problematic in dismissals within political theory of minority language rights, an equally problematic area of analysis centres on the apparent link between majority, or dominant, languages and subsequent social mobility. Specifically, there are an implicit, and often explicit, number of erroneous and contradictory assumptions made in arguments opposing the accommodation of minority language rights with respect to the issue of mobility:

- majority languages are lauded for their 'instrumental' value, while minority languages are accorded 'sentimental' value but are broadly constructed as obstacles to social mobility and progress;
- learning a majority language will thus provide individuals with greater economic and social mobility;
- learning a minority language, while (possibly) important for reasons of cultural continuity, delimits an individual's mobility; in its strongest terms, this might amount to actual 'ghettoization';
- if minority language speakers are 'sensible' they will apply a version of rational choice theory and opt for mobility and modernity via the majority language; and
- whatever decision is made, the choice between opting for a majority or minority language is constructed as oppositional, even mutually exclusive.

This general line of thinking is clearly apparent in both Pogge's and Laitin and Reich's contributions. Pogge adopts this stance overtly, for example in his discussion of the potential for minority parents to opt for an education for their children in a minority language. He suggests that those parents who opt in favour of such schooling may be 'perpetuating a cultural community irrespective of whether this benefits the children concerned . . . ', and that this may amount to an illiberal 'unchosen inequality' for their children (p. 116). In other words, it is illiberal and injurious for parents to 'consign' their children to a minority language education, a position made even more stark by Pogge's intimation that such a choice could possibly warrant the same constraints applied to parents as other child protection laws.[9]

This position is also clearly endorsed by Laitin and Reich, who worry that 'individuals have no influence over the language of their parents, yet their parents' language, if it is a minority one . . . constrains social mobility'. As a result,

---

[9] The logic of Pogge's position is strikingly similar to that of a judge in Amarillo, Texas, who, in a 1995 court case, ordered a mother not to speak Spanish to her child at home on the grounds that this was equivalent to a form of 'child abuse': 'If she starts [school] with the other children and cannot even speak the language that the teachers and others speak, and she's a full-blooded American citizen, you're abusing that child . . . Now get this straight: you start speaking English to that child, because if she doesn't do good in school, then I can remove her because it's not in her best interests to be ignorant' (cited in de Varennes 1996: 165–6).

'those who speak a minority (or dominated) language are more likely to stand *permanently* on the lower-rungs of the socio-economic ladder' (p. 82, my emphasis). Laitin and Reich return to this concern in their later discussions of bilingual education (see also 2.5) to make much the same point, citing one study which found that those who attended bilingual schools did less well in the workplace over a subsequent ten-year period. Thus, if minority individuals are foolish enough to perpetuate the speaking of a minority language, then they can simply be regarded as 'happy slaves', having no one else to blame but themselves for their subsequent limited social mobility.[10]

If we leave aside the rather patronizing and paternalistic tone of their discussions, the principal problem with the construction of this general argument is that it confuses cause and effect. It is clear that a lack of knowledge of a dominant language will limit the options for those who do not speak that language variety, for reasons already outlined. But that is not the *only* reason why such individuals might find themselves 'permanently on the lower-rungs of the socio-economic ladder'. This is because arguments asserting that English is the key to social mobility, and conversely that its lack is the principal cause of social and economic marginalization, conveniently overlook the central question of the wider structural disadvantages facing minority language speakers, not least racism and discrimination. After all, African Americans have been speaking English for 200 years and yet many still find themselves relegated to urban ghettos (Macedo 1994). Likewise, English is almost as inoperative with respect to Hispanic social mobility in the USA as it is with respect to black social mobility. Twenty-five per cent of Hispanics currently live at or below the poverty line, a rate that is at least twice as high as the proportion of Hispanics who are not English-speaking (Garcia 1995; San Miguel and Valencia 1998).

Even when language *is* a factor, it may have as much or more to do with the linguistic intolerance of the state, judiciary, or workplace than with the individuals concerned. Thus, we cannot tell from the study cited by Laitin and Reich what factors contributed to the subsequent (marginally) reduced mobility in the workplace of students who had undertaken bilingual education. However, it is surely not beyond the realms of possibility to suggest that at least some of them

---

[10] These arguments, dressed up as political theory, are broadly comparable to those of the English Only movement in the US (despite Pogge's own attempt to distance himself from them). In both cases, English is viewed as essential for social mobility in US society, or, rather, a lack of English is seen to *consign* one inevitably to the social and economic margins. As Linda Chávez, a former President of US English, has argued: 'Hispanics who learn English will be able to avail themselves of opportunities. Those who do not will be relegated to second class citizenship' (cited in Crawford 1992b: 172). Guy Wright, a prominent media supporter of English Only policies, takes a similar line in a 1983 editorial in the *San Francisco Examiner*, asserting that 'the individual who fails to learn English is condemned to semi-citizenship, condemned to low pay, condemned to remain in the ghetto' (cited in Secada and Lightfoot 1993: 47). A more recent example can be found in US English advertising in 1998: 'Deprive a child of an education. Handicap a young life outside the classroom. Restrict social mobility. If it came at the hand of a parent it would be called child abuse. At the hand of our schools . . . it's called "bilingual education" ' (see Dicker 2000: 53; see also 2.5).

might have faced discrimination on the grounds of continuing to be overtly Spanish-speaking. This is demonstrated clearly, for example, in the legal issue of the right to speak Spanish in the workplace, as highlighted in *Garcia v. Spun Steak* (1993).[11]

But there is a second problem here, and that is one of consistency. On the one hand, we have the construction of minority languages in these accounts as essentially anti-instrumental, as merely 'carriers' of 'identity', and yet, on the other, when such languages do become useful instrumentally in the public realm, this is held against them as well! This overt double standard clearly applies to the Welsh language case discussed by Barry (2001) and referred to by Laitin and Reich (for a fuller discussion, see May 2000). Thus we get Barry bemoaning the labour market advantages of those with an educational qualification in the Welsh language because local authorities increasingly require knowledge of Welsh as a condition of employment. This is rich indeed, given that these exact same arguments are made without apology by Barry and other 'egalitarian liberals' of his kind[12] on behalf of majority languages. They simply can't have it both ways: deriding minority languages for their lack of utility, and then opposing their utility when it proves to be politically inconvenient.

Cries of discrimination on this basis by majority-language speakers are also largely spurious, since in almost all cases (the Baltic states being a possible exception) the formalization of a minority language in the public realm does not preclude the ongoing use of the majority language which, by definition, remains dominant in most language domains anyway. Indeed, opposition to minority languages in the public domain, usually couched in the rhetoric of individual language rights, is based primarily upon the implicit, sometimes explicit, wish of majority-language speakers to remain monolingual. Levelling charges of 'abuse of state power' (as do Laitin and Reich) or 'racism' with regard to language requirements for education or employment can be seen in this light, rather than as a legitimate or a sustainable argument. Likewise, to return to the argument of utility, being able to speak Welsh within Wales (whether as a first- or second-language speaker) is surely more immediately useful than speaking another language, particularly if Welsh is already established in the public domain. If it is deemed not to be useful (as in Barry's case), this is a question of perceived

[11] In *Garcia v. Spun Steak* (United States Court of Appeals for the Ninth Circuit 1993), Spanish-speaking workers lodged a claim of language discrimination, under the Fourteenth Amendment, on the grounds that their employer prohibited them from speaking privately in Spanish to each other while at work. This claim was eventually unsuccessful because the Court declined to examine the principal point raised by the Spanish-speaking workers: that is, if some employees have the privilege of conversing with others privately at work in their primary language, Spanish-speakers should not be denied the same privilege (de Varennes 1996).

[12] In reading Barry's polemic against multiculturalism and in defence (and praise) of orthodox or 'egalitarian' liberalism, one almost gets the feeling that the only person who still qualifies as a 'true' liberal is Barry himself. Indeed, as David Miller (2002: 256) observes, 'Barry at times seems to want to invert the old Groucho Marx joke by refusing to join any club that would let anyone besides himself in as a member'.

language status, itself the product of wider power relations, not an argument for or in defence of civic neutrality—that is, the supposedly 'disinterested' and 'depoliticized' acceptance of the linguistic status quo (see 2.1).

## 2.3 Language and Nationalism

And this brings me to the third key problematic in liberal dismissals of minority language rights. Arguments for civic neutrality with respect to language and language rights *equate* and *elide* civic culture with what is, in effect, no more than a *majoritarian* form of linguistic nationalism (Taylor 1994). If I am a 'linguistic nationalist', as Laitin and Reich erroneously suggest (see 2.4), I am one only to the extent that we are *all* linguistic nationalists. It is just that minority language claims become 'marked' as 'nationalist' while majoritarian linguistic claims, as the unmarked category, do not. The latter process has been usefully described by the sociologist Michael Billig (1995) as 'banal nationalism' and it is demonstrated in countless historical and contemporary language-based debates and conflicts the world over. To take just one, since it is a case that Laitin and Reich also discuss, let us look briefly at Catalunya (see also May 2002b).

In their discussion, Laitin and Reich accept the eventual ratification of the 1998 Catalan Linguistic Policy Act on the basis that it was subject to a full process of democratic contestability, which they clearly see as the benchmark for any acceptance of accommodative language rights. Apart from the inherent limits of a thin version of electoral democracy in relation to minority rights more generally (see Pettit 2000), there are two key difficulties here. The first has to do with the substance and tenor of the debates on language and language rights in Catalunya; the second with the historical background to them (see 2.1).

The campaign mounted against the Act, and against Catalan language laws more generally, was played out prominently in the Spanish media and in the Spanish courts over the course of the 1990s (DiGiacomo 1999). The general tenor of this campaign is captured well by the following banner headline in a national Spanish paper in 1993: 'como Franco pero al revés: Persecución del castellano en Cataluña' (The same as Franco but the other way round: Persecution of Spanish in Catalonia) (quoted in Costa and Wynants 1999). The inference here is abundantly clear: minority language rights constitute 'special treatment' and may well be illiberal. Consequently, much of the subsequent vocal and often vituperative debates on Catalan language laws have focused on the supposed threat they pose to the right to speak the majority language, (Castilian) Spanish, and, even more seriously for opponents, to the unity of the Spanish state.

With respect to the perceived threat to Castilian Spanish, oppositionists termed themselves, without any degree of irony it seems, 'bilingüistas' (see Strubell 1998). I say 'without any degree of irony' because, while opponents of Catalan language laws ostensibly couch their arguments on the basis of wanting to ensure some form of institutional bilingualism, they are more often than not simply arguing for the right of majority (Spanish) language speakers to remain monolingual (see also my discussion on Wales in 2.2). With respect to the perceived threat to the unity of the Spanish state, what we see here are simply two versions of nationalism, a majoritarian Spanish one and a minority Catalan one (although only the latter is termed as such). This leads Susan DiGiacomo to observe, in similar vein to Billig's conception of 'banal nationalism', that while both nationalisms may exhibit a degree of essentialism (see 2.4), 'some essentialisms are more essentialized than others—more naturalized and thus less "marked" and problematic—and this is the case with Spanish nationalism, because it possesses the state'. From this, DiGiacomo also usefully critiques the apportionment of differential status and value accorded to Catalan and Castilian—as provincial and 'modern', respectively—a process clearly reflected in both the academic and the media debates at the time. As she concludes: 'It is the ironic condition of stateless nations like Catalonia that the "imagined community" . . . is always challenged, by putatively objective scholarship as well as by the state and those who share its interests, as merely imaginary, while the imagined community of state nationalism is treated as objectively real, part of the natural order' (1999: 131).

Notwithstanding these concerns, the eventual acceptance of the Linguistic Policy Act poses another problem for the democratic litmus test advocated by Laitin and Reich, since the acceptance of the Act in the face of such trenchant and powerful opposition could have been achieved only in the light of historical circumstances that had *already* significantly changed the position of the minority language (Catalan) within the state. In other words, the more gradual but nonetheless deliberate process of 'linguistic normalization' pursued in Catalunya since the death of Franco (Woolard 1989; Hoffmann 1999) was an essential prerequisite for the subsequent acceptance of its higher legal status and institutional reach via the Linguistic Policy Act. In short, informed debate on and acceptance of accommodative language rights is likely to occur only in a political context already conducive to it. And yet, in their arguments elsewhere—and particularly in relation to the United States—Laitin and Reich and Pogge, simply don't, or won't, entertain such a possibility.

## 2.4 *Language and Identity*

Another misconstruction that regularly occurs in liberal critiques of minority language rights is to equate/elide any advocacy of group-based language rights with the politics of primordialism. In this view, all such forms of linguistic advocacy can be dismissed on the basis that they simply amount to, or result in the reification of, language and culture and a related essentializing and homogenizing of language groups. Laitin and Reich clearly suggest as much of my own work when they term me, wrongly, as a 'linguistic nationalist', with all the pejorative Herderian associations of linguistic determinism that this phrase implies (see below).[13]

There is, of course, an obvious inconsistency here that seems to escape these commentators: they dismiss such group-based language claims for their supposed homogenizing tendencies, while in turn advocating an apparently inviolate conception of the nation-state as linguistically uniform and homogeneous—as, in effect, a given, objective, and fixed social entity (see also 3). But, even more problematically, the ineluctable linking of minority language rights with primordialism and essentialism is simply wrong. While some proponents of minority language rights may well present us with a culturally and linguistically determined basis for their rights claims, not all do, nor do they need to. This is certainly the case in my own work, not least because I reject unequivocally any conception of language as a 'primordial' feature of identity, along with any related essentialist notions of the language–identity link. In fact, my own position is clearly situated within the 'liberal culturalist' position rather than the 'nationalist', as Laitin and Reich would have it, since it specifically follows on from, and attempts to build upon, the work of Will Kymlicka and others.

Given that I have clearly been misinterpreted here, let me outline my position in more detail. As we know, the eighteenth century German romantics, Herder and von Humboldt and Fichte, advocated an 'organic' or 'linguistic' nationalism where culture, and particularly language, were viewed as central to the essence or character (*Volksgeist*) of the nation. In this perspective, language came to be constructed as the *most* important distinguishing characteristic of nationhood—indeed, its very soul. The interrelationship between language and the soul or spirit of the nation is most clearly stated by von Humboldt: '[the nation's] language is its spirit and its spirit is its language' (see Cowan 1963: 277). Or, as he observes elsewhere: 'From every language we can infer backwards to the national character' (von Humboldt 1988: 154). Put another way, the continuing existence of a nation was inconceivable without its own language. Without a language, Herder argued, a *Volk* is an absurdity (*Unding*), a contradiction in terms (see Barnard 1965: 57).

These arguments for linguistic nationalism have long since been dismissed as both essentialist and determinist, and rightly so. In their place, we have seen the rise of constructivist accounts of nationalism (within sociology and politics) and ethnicity (within anthropology and sociology) that argue, for the most part convincingly, that language, or any specific cultural aspect of ethnic and/or

---

[13] Of course, this claim is often made about the advocacy of minority group-based rights more generally. Thus, Barry (2001: 11) dismisses the work of James Tully and Iris Marion Young on the basis of the latter's supposed views of cultural groups as 'quasi-biological collectives'; 'internally homogenous, clearly bounded, mutually exclusive and maintaining specific determinate interests'. As Tully (2002) observes, this amounts to a deliberate misreading and misrepresentation of both his and Young's work, given that both specifically reject this 'billiard ball concept of culture' in favour of a dialogic concept of culture. As we shall see, much the same may be said about my own work with respect to language rights.

national identity for that matter, *must* be recognized as a contingent factor in that identity (see May 2001: Chs 1–2); to suggest otherwise is to reinforce an essentialist conception of groupness. This general position first began to be articulated in the late nineteenth century by sociological commentators on nationalism such as Ernest Renan and Max Weber. Renan, for example, in his lecture 'Qu'est ce qu'une nation?' delivered at the Sorbonne on 11 March 1882, argued that various objective criteria—language, religion, material interest, geography, and 'race'—were all insufficient delimiters of the nation. In relation to language, for example, and in direct contravention to the German romantics, he states: 'Language may invite us to unite but it does not compel us to do so' (Renan 1990: 16). This leads him to conclude that the nation is, in essence, 'a soul, a spiritual principle' (1990: 19) that is not directly linked to any particular objective marker(s).

Subsequent academic commentary on ethnicity and nationalism has broadly followed this course ever since. Language clearly does *not* define us, and may not be a necessary feature, or even an important one, in the construction of our identities, whether at the individual or the collective level. I agree broadly with this constructivist analysis—indeed, who could not? Where I beg to differ is in refusing to take the next step that is often then taken by constructivists: that is, to assume that, if language is merely a contingent factor of identity, it cannot therefore (ever) be a *significant* or *constitutive* factor of identity. In other words, contingency is elided with unimportance or peripheralism.

This position is extremely problematic, not least because it simply does not reflect adequately, let alone explain, the heightened saliency of language issues in many historical and contemporary political conflicts. This is particularly apparent at the intrastate level where 'minority' languages have been most often proscribed or at least vitiated as a result of the nationalist principle of cultural and linguistic homogeneity (see 2.1.1). In the subsequent conflicts which have arisen, particular languages clearly *are* for many people an important and constitutive factor of their individual and, at times, collective identities. Moreover, the issue of experience and commitment to a particular language applies in both directions, so that we are not talking just about the emotional attachments underpinning minority language claims, as is often assumed, but also those underpinning majority language (counter-) claims as well. How else can we explain the vociferousness of those, political theorists among them, who argue for the ongoing retention of a singular national language? There is clearly something more than questions of utility, mobility, and political expediency going on here.

In theory then, language may well be just one of many markers of identity. In practice, it is often much more than that. Indeed, this should not surprise us since the link between language and identity encompasses both significant cultural and political dimensions. The former is demonstrated by the fact that one's individual and social identities and their complex interconnections are inevitably mediated in and through particular languages. The latter is significant to the extent that those languages come to be formally (and informally) associated with particular ethnic and national identities. These interconnections also help to explain why a 'detached' scientific view of the link between language and identity may fail to capture the degree to which language is *experienced* as vital by those who speak it. It may also significantly understate the role that language plays in social and political organization and mobilization. The 'shibboleth of language', as Toynbee (1953) coined it, still holds much sway.

Taking this more even-handed approach also helps us to reconnect the instrumental and identity aspects of language. This is important because, as we saw in 2.2, majority and/or national languages are often dichotomized with minority languages on an instrumental–identity basis; majority languages fulfil the former function, minority languages the latter. What I want to suggest is that *all* languages—whether minority or majority—accomplish *both* for those who speak them, albeit to varying degrees, depending on the social and political constraints in which they operate (see also Carens 2000: 128). Thus, in the case of minority languages, their instrumental value is often constrained, as we have seen, by wider social and political processes that have resulted in the privileging of another language variety as the language of the nation-state.[14] Meanwhile, for majority languages, the identity characteristics of the language are clearly important for their speakers, but often become subsumed within and normalized by the civic, instrumental functions that these languages fulfil.

To pursue this latter point further, one can argue that, if majority languages do provide their speakers with particular and often significant individual and collective forms of linguistic identity, it seems unjust to deny these same benefits, out of court, to minority language speakers. Paraphrasing Habermas, a correctly understood theory of citizenship rights requires a politics of recognition that protects the individual in the life contexts in which his or her cultural and linguistic identity is formed (see 1994: 113).

This does not preclude cultural and linguistic change and adaptation—all languages and cultures are subject to such processes. But what it does immediately bring into question is the necessity/validity of the unidirectional movement of cultural and linguistic adaptation and change *from* a minority language/culture *to* a majority one. This is where Kymlicka's notion of 'external protections' is particularly useful and important, as Laitin and Reich, though not Pogge, acknowledge. What external protections presuppose is the opportunity and right of ethnic or national minority groups to seek to protect their distinct identities by limiting the impact of the decisions of the larger society. External protections are thus intended to ensure that individual members are able to maintain a distinctive way of life *if they so choose* and are not prevented from doing so by the decisions of members outside of their community (see Kymlicka 1995*a*: 204. n. 11).

---

[14] The same may be said currently for many national languages in relation to international languages such as English.

Nor do external protections necessarily result in new forms of illiberalism (see also 2.2 on language and employment rights). As Kymlicka (1995a: 36–7) is at pains to point out, external protections need not result in injustice: 'Granting special representation rights, land claims, *or language rights* to a minority need not, and often does not, put it in a position to dominate other groups. On the contrary . . . such rights can be seen as putting the various groups on a more equal footing, by reducing the extent to which the smaller group is vulnerable to the larger'. What we see here then is the opportunity or potential for holding multiple, complementary cultural and linguistic identities at both individual and collective levels. On this view, maintaining one's minority ethnically affiliated language—or one's national majority language, for that matter—avoids 'freezing' the development of particular languages in the roles that they currently occupy. Equally importantly, it questions and discards the requirement of a singular and/or replacement approach to the issue of other linguistic identities which, as we have seen, arises specifically from the nationalist principle of linguistic and cultural homogeneity. Linguistic identities, and social and cultural identities more broadly, need not be constructed as irredeemably oppositional. Narrower identities do not necessarily need to be traded in for broader ones— one can clearly remain both Spanish-speaking and American, Catalan-speaking and Spanish, or Welsh-speaking and British. The same process applies to national and international language identities, where these differ. To insist otherwise—as do Pogge and Laitin and Reich at times—betrays, ironically, both a reductionist and an essentialist approach to language and identity.

## 2.5 Language and Education

The problems of reductionism and essentialism are also clearly evident in the position that liberal critiques of minority rights adopt on the issue of bilingual education. What we see constructed here is a bipolar approach to language education, in line with the previous idea of incommensurable linguistic identities: *either* learn the dominant language through submersion in that language *or* choose to exit from this opportunity via bilingual education. This position relates closely to the concerns already discussed around education and mobility (2.2), but it is recast here via the external protection/internal restriction dialectic. Thus Laitin and Reich observe that 'forcing' bilingual education on children might amount to an internal restriction on the grounds that 'their opportunities to learn the language of some broader societal culture will be curtailed' (p. 92). Pogge does not address the notion of internal restrictions directly. However, in his discussion of the merits of a public education *in* English versus a more multilingual approach, he clearly equates the former with the 'best interests of the child' in relation both to developing 'fluency in English' and in 'enabling all students to participate fully in US society' (p. 118). The problem with these arguments is that the educational and linguistic premises upon which they are based are nonsense.

The arguments of both commentators reveal a deeply uncritical and highly normative view of English monolingualism, and a related and deeply flawed understanding of bilingualism and bilingual education. For a start, we do not see such commentators arguing that 'elite' bilingualism—say, learning English and French—is injurious to one's involvement in and grasp of 'broader societal culture'. Quite the reverse, in fact. So why should it be different for any other language? Why should bilingualism be good for the rich but not for the poor (Cummins 2001)? What we need to separate here then are on the one hand the educational and linguistic factors in learning other languages (including learning *in* other languages), and on the other the broader social and political issues concerning the perceived status of the particular languages involved. In so doing, we can begin to deconstruct and critique the rhetorical move often employed by sceptics of minority language rights in this instance—that is, to attempt to discredit the educational and linguistic merits of bilingual education on the basis of the *political* challenge it presents for a monolingual conception of the nation-state.

In the process, what is conveniently overlooked is that educational and linguistic research over the last 40 years has demonstrated unequivocally that bilingualism is a cognitive advantage rather than a deficit[15] and that being educated in one's first language provides the *most* effective means of subsequently transferring those first-language skills to those of a second language (see Romaine 1995, Baker and Prys Jones 1998 for useful overviews). Conversely, being submerged too early in a second language, such as the English-submersion educational approaches advocated for Spanish speakers in the US, has been found to be the *least* effective educational approach for achieving first-to-second language transfer, something that even Laitin and Reich concede (see also Cummins 1996; 1999; Corson 1998; Baker 2001).[16] I clearly cannot go into the particularities of this research here (see May 2001: Ch. 6; for further discussion, also Crawford 2001; Cummins 2001), but suffice it to say that it stands in direct contrast to the public and policy *perception*, particularly in the USA, of bilingual education as a cognitive and educational (as well as social) *disadvantage*. How can this be explained?

Partly, at least, by the effective political mobilization by minority language rights' opponents of two deeply flawed US government-sponsored research studies which cast (some) doubt on bilingual education. The first of these, the

---

[15] There are now close to 150 major research studies, carried out since the early 1960s, that consistently report significant advantages for bilingual students on a range of metalinguistic and cognitive tasks. As a result, it is now widely recognized that bilinguals mature earlier than monolinguals in acquiring skills for linguistic abstraction, are superior to monolinguals on divergent thinking tasks and in their analytical orientation to language, and demonstrate greater social sensitivity than monolinguals in situations requiring verbal communication. See Romaine (1995), Cummins (1996; 2001), Corson (1998), and Baker (2001).

[16] This is in direct contradistinction to Pogge's assertion at one point that 'children's important long-term interest in being fully literate in English is best served by early immersion [in English]' (p. 119).

American Institutes for Research's (AIR) evaluation of bilingual education programmes, was commissioned in the 1970s by the United States Office of Education (Danoff *et al.* 1978). It provided an overview of federally funded bilingual programmes operating at the time and found that such programmes had no significant impact on educational achievement in English, although they did enhance native-like proficiency. It furthermore suggested that pupils were being kept in bilingual programmes longer than necessary, thus contributing to the segregation of such students from 'mainstream' classes (Moran 1990).

Despite concerns about its methodology (see below), the conclusions of the AIR study were seemingly replicated by a second piece of federally commissioned research by Baker and de Kanter (1981; 1983; see also Rossell and Baker 1996). They reviewed the literature and likewise concluded that bilingual education was not advancing the English language skills and academic achievements of minority language students. In short, Baker and de Kanter argued that students had no clear advantage over those in English-only programmes. Given the increasingly sceptical political climate of the time, this research generated enormous publicity and exerted even more influence on subsequent federal policy. However, as Crawford (1989) observes, while the Baker and de Kanter (1983) report is easily the most quoted federal pronouncement on bilingual education, it is probably the most criticized as well. As with its predecessor, much of this criticism had to do with the methodology that was employed. For example, as with the AIR study, Baker and de Kanter specifically rejected the use of data gathered through students' first languages. They also failed to account for the fact that two-thirds of the comparison group in English-only education programmes *had previously been in bilingual programmes* where, presumably, they had benefited from first-language instruction (Crawford 1992a). Moreover, neither report distinguished between the wide variety of educational approaches to bilingual education, particularly in relation to the degree to which the first language (L1) was used as the medium of instruction. This is a crucial omission since the least effective bilingual education programmes are those which are bilingual in name only, with minimal presence and use of L1 in the classroom—that is, those which are most like English-submersion programmes—while the most effective bilingual education programmes are those where the presence and instructional use of L1 is prominent. Relatedly, since both reports failed to differentiate between early- and late-exit bilingual programmes[17] in their analyses, the somewhat lesser educational effectiveness of the former, which constituted the majority of the programmes under review, inevitably subsumed the better educational results of the latter (Cummins 1996). Overall, the inadequacy of Baker and de Kanter's

[17] As their names suggest, the former begin by teaching in the minority language but aim specifically to transfer students to the majority language as soon as possible. The latter maintain education in the minority language either throughout schooling or for significantly longer periods. The latter approach thus ensures that first-language literacy skills are well established, facilitating and enhancing, in turn, first-to-second language transfer.

findings has been confirmed by Willig's (1985; 1987) subsequent meta-analyses of their data. Willig controlled for 183 variables that they had failed to take into account. She found, as a result, small to moderate differences in favour of bilingual education, even when these were predominantly early-exit programmes (see also Thomas and Collier 1997).

Willig's conclusions, which confirm what is elsewhere widely acknowledged, are also replicated in more recent federally funded bilingual research. For example, Ramírez, Yuen, and Ramey (1991) compared English-only programmes with early- and late-exit bilingual programmes, following 2,300 Spanish-speaking students over four years. The findings clearly supported bilingual education and found that the greatest growth in mathematics, English language skills, and English reading was particularly evident among students in late-exit bilingual programmes where students had been taught predominantly in Spanish. By implication, the Ramírez study also confirmed another feature which is widely corroborated by other research on bilingual education: minority language students who receive most of their education in English rather than their first language are *more* likely to fall behind and drop out of school.[18] What is so interesting here is that this research has generated far less interest and had far less impact on subsequent federal policy than its two predecessors (see Krashen 1999). As Ricento (1996: 142) observes of this, in spite of an impressive amount of both qualitative and quantitative research now available on the merits of bilingual education, 'the public debate (to the extent that there is one) [in the USA] tends to focus on perceptions and not on facts'. Suffice it to say, this public perception rests on a resolutely monolingual and largely ill-informed view of language and language education policy.

Even when we take into account variations in the overall efficacy of individual bilingual education programmes, what remains undisputed is that bilingual education is, at the very least, not injurious to the acquisition of a second language and, in fact, when managed effectively results in significant educational gains *in both languages* for the students concerned. In other words, bilingual education facilitates not only the maintenance of a minority language but also the effective acquisition of a majority language as well. When this becomes clear, the claim that 'English-First' educational approaches are justified because the public importance of non-English speakers acquiring English outweighs any private claim to maintaining a first language can be seen for what it is: a proposition based on a false and unnecessary dichotomy. In this light, the crucial normative work being undertaken by the public good/private choice distinction also no longer holds. Bilingual education (as with English-medium education for first

---

[18] In fact, it is important to note here that the English-only programmes used for comparison in the Ramírez study were not typical to the extent that, while the teachers taught in English, they nonetheless understood Spanish. This suggests that, in the far more common situation where the teacher does not understand the students' first language, the trends described here are likely to be further accentuated.

language speakers) can be both a private good in relation to the maintenance of a first language and a public good in effectively learning the majority language.

What are the consequences of this critique? If, as the linguistic and educational research suggests, the acquisition of the dominant societal language is not curtailed (and may in fact be enhanced) by bilingual education, then the state has no legitimate business in curtailing or proscribing such programmes. This is important, not least given recent developments in the USA with respect to just these proscriptions being applied to bilingual education, most prominently via the adoption of Proposition 227 in California in June 1998.[19] Under these circumstances, as Joseph Carens (2000: 83) observes, 'to require the minority group to have its public services delivered and its children educated in the language of the majority would be rightly perceived as a form of majority tyranny, a blatant disregard for the interests of the minority in a context where those interests could be taken into account with comparatively little cost to the majority'.

But recognizing and accepting this position, important though this is, still amounts to little more than a negative right. How can a more positive right to bilingual education be formulated? Simply, on the basis that, if the issues of potential educational harm and wider public participation have already been effectively addressed, the state should be obliged to allow minority language students to maintain their first languages via state-funded education in the same way as it allows majority students to do the same. This approach is actually closer, to my mind, to the 'neutral' approach to language education that egalitarian liberals in particular appear to hold so dear, since it does not confuse neutrality of educational treatment with uniformity of educational delivery.

## 2.6 Language and Equivalence

The acceptance of minority language education as a public good and its state-funded provision as a public right is an important and necessary first step if minority language rights are ever to be established more fully in modern nation-states. And, as we have seen, the establishment of this initial premise is by no means easily achieved. But, even if this step is taken, it does not provide us with an answer to a question that is often raised at this point by critics of accommodative language rights, and at earlier points also: the question of equivalence. The argument, which is usually dressed up in the guise of practicality, invariably goes something like this. If we allow for state-funded bilingual education, or any other state-funded minority language provision for that matter, for one linguistic

[19] Proposition 227, titled 'The English Language Education for Children in Public Schools Initiative', characterized California's previous record on educating immigrant children (by which was meant bilingual education) as a failure. In its place, it required that all children for whom English is not a first language be educated in 'sheltered' English-only programmes, for one year only, after which they would be transferred into mainstream classes. Limited exceptions to this model are allowed, but only by parental request and on being granted written waivers (Dicker 2000). Similar measures have subsequently been widely adopted in other US States (Crawford 2001).

minority, where might it all end? Thus, even if we are sympathetic to the justice and equity principles underlying the public funding of minority language education, it is still far easier simply to allow for private education in minority languages rather than to open a Pandora's box of an ever-increasing range of minority language education claimants at the expense of the public purse.

There are two responses that can be made to this assertion. The first is that international law provides us with clear parameters for the potential provision of minority language education. While there are still no watertight legal guarantees to state-funded minority language education (see May 2001: Ch. 5), not least because of the ongoing jurisdiction accorded to nation-states with respect to these issues, there *is* an increasing recognition within international and national law that significant minorities within the nation-state have a *reasonable* expectation to some form of state support (de Varennes 1996). In other words, while it would be unreasonable for nation-states to be required to fund language and education services for all minorities (see Carens 2000: Ch. 3; Grin, this volume), it is increasingly accepted that; where a language is spoken by a significant number within the nation-state, it would also be unreasonable not to provide some level of state services and activity in that language.

This position allows minority language speakers to use their language(s) in the public domain as part of the exercise of their individual rights as citizens, if they so choose to exercise that right. As Fernand de Varennes (1996: 117) argues, 'the respect of the language principles of individuals, where appropriate and reasonable, flows from a fundamental right and is not some special concession or privileged treatment. Simply put, it is the right to be treated equally without discrimination, to which everyone is entitled'. As to what determines what is 'appropriate and reasonable', the key principle that can be applied here, again from international law, is that of 'where numbers warrant'. Canada adopts this criterion in relation to French speakers outside Quebec, via the 1982 Canadian Charter of Rights and Freedoms, while a similar approach is adopted in Finland with respect to first-language Swedish speakers living there. India provides perhaps the best example of this principle in operation since the Constitution of India (art. 350A) directs every State, and every local authority within that State, to provide 'adequate' educational facilities for instruction in the first language of linguistic minorities where such numbers warrant, at least at primary (elementary) school level. This is in addition to the 18 official languages recognized in India and the division of India's States along largely linguistic lines. These political divisions result in local linguistic communities having control over their public schools and other educational institutions. This, in turn, ensures that the primary language of the area is used as a medium of instruction in state schools (see Pattanayak 1990; Schiffman 1996). South Africa's establishment in 1994 of formal multilingualism in eleven State languages also has the potential to follow the Indian model in the provision of minority language education along these lines (see Heugh, Siegrühn, and Plüddermann 1995; Langtag 1996).

There is also a second response that can be made to the concern over equivalence, and it relates to the differing language rights potentially attributable to
national minority and migrant minority groups (see Kymlicka 1995a). The criterion of 'where numbers warrant' can apply to all minority groups, irrespective
of their social and political status. But there are strong arguments for extending
this numerical test to include the particular language claims of national minorities *irrespective* of their number. This can be argued on the basis of their greater
historical and political entitlement and on a corresponding obligation or duty of
the state to recognize that entitlement (see Kymlicka 1999; Carens 2000; Ivison,
Sanders, and Patton 2000). As de Varennes observes of indigenous peoples,
although his argument can be extended here to all national minorities:

Indigenous peoples, in particular, may have a strong argument that they should receive
state services such as education in their primary language, beyond what a strictly
'numerical' criterion would perhaps normally warrant. In the case of indigenous
peoples [and national minorities more generally], the state may have a *greater* duty to
respect their wishes in view of the nature of the relationship between the two, and of the
duties and obligations involved. (1996: 97–8; my emphasis)

To return to what might be 'appropriate and reasonable' under these circumstances, it could be argued that a duly appropriate and reasonable response
would be to recognize publicly *all* the 'national' languages of a given nation-
state, irrespective of their current majority/minority status, on the basis that
national minorities and their languages should be accorded at least some of the
linguistic privileges that majority language speakers currently enjoy. To do so
only for majority national languages, particularly given the arbitrary and con-
trived nature of their historical ascendancy via the nation-state (see 2.1), is both
inconsistent and unjust. Rather, a process of mutual accommodation is
required (Carens 2000; May 2001).

This position, broadly defined, amounts to an argument for greater ethnolinguistic democracy for linguistic minorities in modern nation-states. This is *not* a call
for ethnolinguistic equality or equivalence. Dominant languages will continue to
dominate in most, if not all, language domains; that is the nature of their privileged
position. Nor does ethnolinguistic democracy necessarily imply a lack of friction
between the language groups involved. Nonetheless, when minority language
rights are formally recognized and employed in state and civil society, at least to
some degree, greater autonomy can usually be accorded to minority groups in
relation to the actual control, organization, and delivery of minority language education, along with a potentially wide range of other social and political activities.

## 3. Some Caveats and Conclusions

One issue I have addressed only in passing in the preceding discussion is the
question of exit—that is, the ability of minority language speakers to exit their

linguistic group, if they so wish, by 'shifting' to the speaking of another (usually more dominant) language. Pogge and Laitin and Reich argue that the ongoing maintenance of a minority language, particularly via education, delimits this possibility. I disagree.

The availability of exit is an important concern for any liberal defence of minority language rights, but it should not be over-elaborated. Children are constrained by many aspects of compulsory education without these being deemed to be 'illiberal', so why should the maintenance of a minority language via schooling not also be included here, particularly when, as I have argued, such a process is not at the expense of acquiring a majority language? Moreover, being required to learn in a minority language at school can be seen not only as a constraint but as an opportunity—providing the individual with the opportunity to be bilingual. Whether individuals subsequently pursue or capitalize upon this opportunity after compulsory education is obviously their choice, but, given the dominance of majority languages in most if not all language domains, without a compulsory language element at some point, no such choice would be available in the first place (May 2000).

From another direction, we can also question and critique the 'voluntary' nature of much of the minority–majority language shift occurring in the world today. The voluntary nature of language shift is invariably canvassed in arguments that deride the attempts of so called minority language 'elites'[20] to maintain a language in the face of a linguistic community that is already dispensing with it (see Edwards 1994; Barry 2001). Nathan Glazer argues, in the US context for example, that most immigrants wanted 'to become Americanised as fast as possible, and this [means appropriating] English language and culture . . . while they often found, as time went on, that they regretted what they and their children had lost, this was *their* choice rather than an imposed choice' (Glazer 1983: 149; see also Levy 2000: 108). However, it can equally be argued that the degree to which *voluntary* shift actually occurs is extremely problematic. After all, if minority languages are consistently viewed as low-status, socially and culturally restrictive, and an obstacle to social mobility, is it any wonder that such patterns of language shift exist?

On this basis, one can legitimately assert that so-called 'individual choice' is neither as unconstrained nor as neutral as proponents of language shift suggest. Rather it is at best a 'forced choice', propelled by wider forces of social, political,

---

[20] The question of an 'unrepresentative' minority leadership is largely a red herring—merely a useful stick, in effect, with which to beat proponents of minority language rights. After all, the charges of self-interest and distinction from the 'rank and file' can be invoked against any leadership, including those advocating a majority language (for a critique of the 'self-interested elite' position with respect to nationalist movements generally, see Brubaker 1998: 289–92). Similarly, all groups speak with more than 'one voice', not just minority ones. As such, it is a *reductio ad absurdum* to imply, as do Laitin and Reich for example, that the presence of internal differences within minority groups over the question of language somehow negates the legitimacy of minority language claims.

economic, and *linguistic* inequality and discrimination. The question one might then begin to explore from a normative liberal perspective concerns the extent to which individuals should be allowed to benefit from the currency of a dominant language while also, at the same time, being allowed to 'stay put' with respect to their own first language(s). In other words, we can legitimately ask to what extent the 'language replacement' ideology underlying the nationalist principle of cultural and linguistic homogeneity is actually *illiberal*. After all, to return to Will Kymlicka's (1995a: 90) observation which began this chapter, 'leaving one's culture, while possible, is best seen as renouncing something to which one is reasonably entitled'.

To turn finally to potential political consequences, the issue of minority language rights clearly poses significant moral and political choices for nation-states in the immediate future, since the long-held practice of making no accommodations to such demands is not so readily defensible in today's social and political climate. Ignoring demands for minority language rights is unlikely to quell or abate the questions and concerns of minority linguistic groups underlying them, as it might once have done. Indeed, it is much more likely to intensify and escalate them. Under these circumstances, 'any policy favouring a single language to the exclusion of all others can be extremely risky . . . because it is then a factor promoting division rather than unification. Instead of integration, an ill-advised and inappropriate state language policy may have the opposite effect and cause a *levée de bouclier*' (de Varennes 1996: 91).

This, in turn, poses a central challenge for normative political theory: how to rethink nation-states, and the national identities therein, in more linguistically plural and inclusive ways, in order to better represent the various and varied cultural and linguistic communities situated within them (Parekh 2000). This issue takes us right to the heart of the question of political legitimacy. As Jeremy Waldron (1993: 50) observes, it is fundamental to liberalism that 'a social and political order is illegitimate unless it is rooted in the consent of all those who have to live under it'. On this basis, one can argue that changing the language preferences of the state and civil society, or at least broadening them, would better reflect the diverse and legitimate linguistic interests of *all* those within them. Not only this, it could significantly improve the life chances of those minority individuals and groups who are presently disadvantaged in their access to and participation in public services, employment, and education as a result of restrictive majoritarian language policies.

And yet what is equally clear is the basic unwillingness in many liberal accounts of political theory to countenance this possibility—to continue to view the historical and ongoing minoritization of languages as, in Bourdieu's words, a 'game devoid of consequences' (see 2.1.1). This is unfortunate, not least because such a position equates normative political theory ineluctably with a static, closed, and essentialist view of the nation-state, as for ever culturally and linguistically homogenous. Barry's (2001) defence of egalitarian liberalism, for example, is most notable for the almost quasi-ontological status attributed to the traditional organization of modern nation-states in this respect (Schmidtke 2002). In the process, no account is taken of the historical conting-ency, arbitrariness, and recency of this particular form of social and political organization. Nation-states, as we know them today, are themselves the product only of the last few centuries of nationalism, and their current organization, particularly in relation to the public principle of cultural and linguistic homo-geneity, is neither inevitable nor inviolate. If justice and fairness are to remain central concerns of normative political theory, they demand that we adopt a more situated, critical, and diachronic analysis of this organizational principle of cultural and linguistic homogeneity. In so doing, we need also to address directly, and remedy, the linguistic and wider social harm that this principle has inflicted on minority language groups. Only then will a more dialogic, inclusive, and (truly) egalitarian response to the question of minority language rights, and their accommodation in modern nation-states, be achieved.

# 6

# Linguistic Justice

PHILIPPE VAN PARIJS

## 1. The Issue

Al and Bo grew up learning different mother tongues. At some later stage, Bo learns Al's, while Al does not learn Bo's. They can now communicate with one another. Not quite on an equal footing, of course—Al tends to have the upper hand in any argument they might have with one another and in any competition in which they might have to take part using the shared language—but nonetheless with significant benefits, both material and non-material, accruing to both.

So far, therefore, so good enough—except perhaps that the cost of producing this benefit, though enjoyed by Al with greater comfort and with the bonus of some pleasing by-products, is borne entirely by Bo. Is this nothing to worry about, as Bo freely chose to learn Al's language? Or is it fair, on the contrary, that Al should make a substantial contribution towards this cost and, if so, at what level?

This chapter aims to spell out and assess alternative answers to this question. Which answer is chosen has no implications whatever in the context of the homogeneous nation-state tacitly taken for granted in most thinking about social justice. But it may have momentous implications for the question of the fair distribution of resources in the Indian Union, in the South African Federation, in the European Union, indeed in most countries of the old continents, and even more so at the level of the world as a whole, as economic globalization irresistibly and irreversibly snowballs into existence the first worldwide lingua franca.

A slightly different version of this chapter was published in the first issue of the new journal *Politics, Philosophy and Economics* (Spring 2002, edited by Jerry Gaus), whose permission to reprint is gratefully acknowledged. Earlier drafts had been discussed at the founding conference of the journal (Tulane University, New Orleans, 9–10 March 2001), at the Chaire Hoover's doctoral seminar in social and political philosophy (Université catholique de Louvain, 16 March 2001), and, under the title 'If you're an egalitarian, how come you speak English?', at the Festconference celebrating G. A. Cohen's 60th birthday. I am particularly grateful to Bruce Ackerman, Brian Barry, Idil Boran, Paula Casal, Jerry Gaus, François Grin, Alan Patten, Tim Scanlon, Hillel Steiner, Andrew Williams, and above all Laurent de Briey, with whom I published a generalization to the case of *n* linguistic groups of the approach defended here in the most elementary case of two groups (de Briey and Van Parijs 2002).

## 2. Cooperative Justice versus Distributive Justice

The way I shall phrase the central question of this chapter rests on two crucial assumptions, both debatable but, I believe, defensible. The first is that it makes sense to think of linguistic justice as a form of inter-community cooperative justice, and not only as an aspect of inter-personal distributive justice.

A person's linguistic competence can of course be regarded as a complex skill which significantly affects her life chances, including her earning power, and is itself the product of a combination of effort and circumstance—in particular, of a human environment which can make the learning of one or more languages in one or more variants either so easy that it is hardly noticeable or prohibitively difficult. Unequal linguistic endowment can be the source of major inter-personal injustice. To determine whether, how, and to what extent it needs to be corrected, we can appeal to the usual set of principles of distributive justice.

For example, from a Rawlsian perspective, in so far as a person's mother tongue—or one's 'accent' when speaking the standard idiom—is an economically irrelevant characteristic, the principle of fair equality of opportunity will require that it should not influence in any way that person's access to valued social positions. Mother tongue, in this perspective, is as illegitimate a basis for discrimination as race, gender, or faith. But there are of course many contexts in which linguistic competence operates as a productive skill. To this extent, the linguistic equipment one owes to one's childhood environment can be regarded as a talent, and the principle of fair equality of opportunity, that is, of equal opportunities with given talents, is irrelevant. But the difference principle is not. Among those who occupy the worst social position (in terms of lifetime expectations of social and economic advantages), those with the misfortune of speaking the wrong language, or of speaking the right language with the wrong accent, are bound to be over-represented. Rawlsian justice does not let them down. The difference principle requires that the expectations of the incumbents of this position be maximized, that they be higher than those associated with the worst position under any alternative arrangement. Under neither principle, however, does the rent associated with having one type of linguistic competence rather than another, or having inherited one mother tongue rather than another, require separate treatment. It is possible and instructive to provide estimates of the lifetime earnings differential associated, in a particular country at a particular time, with having one mother tongue rather than another.[1] But there is no reason to single out linguistic assets for special treatment: they can be safely lumped together with other personal assets.[2]

---

[1] See, for example, Grin and Vaillancourt (1997) and Grin (1999a).

[2] The same holds, *mutatis mutandis*, within the framework of the 'real-libertarian' conception of justice presented and defended in Van Parijs (1995; 2001). The fact that possessing a mother tongue different from the dominant one may constitute a handicap makes undominated diversity less likely to obtain spontaneously (thus justifying that some resources be specifically targeted at dominated

There is, however, a distinct perspective from which it makes sense to discuss linguistic justice independently of other dimensions of justice. To characterize it, think of the following analogy. Some years ago, I spent a number of months, together with my family, living with my father-in-law. After a while, one feature of our common life started bothering me: as soon as any amount of dust or crumbs became visible, my father-in-law got the vacuum-cleaner out of the cupboard to get rid of them. As a result, all the cleaning was done long before we reached the threshold which would have triggered me into doing the cleaning myself, and my standards of cleanliness were more than met without my ever doing any work for it. No power relationship or altruism was involved, or at least needed to be. Yet the structure of the situation was such that I systematically benefited from my father-in-law's toil without contributing myself in any way to the public good he produced. Even on the generous assumption that I was not responsible for any of the crumbs, this seemed unfair to me, and to restore my peace of mind (and enhance the probability of remaining welcome?) we soon struck an explicit deal involving some compensatory performance—toilet cleaning, if I can trust my memory.[3]

What connection does this have with linguistic justice? Quite simple. In the example of the opening paragraph, Bo is in a situation analogous to my father-in-law's. By learning a second language in her own best interest, she is producing a public good which Al is enjoying at no cost, just as my father-in-law is doing by cleaning the floor. Now, if Al and Bo are just individuals who differ in many respects and among whom justice needs to be done, the disadvantage to Bo arising from the opportunity cost of having to learn the majority language and from the lesser comfort in using it is just one dimension in a set of advantages and disadvantages which may make her condition, on the whole, better or worse than Al's. But now think of Al and Bo as two non-overlapping linguistic communities who have to live together in a country or on a planet, in the same way as my father-in-law and I had to live, albeit for a short while, in the same house. Laissez-faire would lead to 'free riding', here simply defined by the fact that two people (or categories of people) enjoy some benefit while the work required to produce it is (self-interestedly) performed by only one of them. Under such conditions, if only to avoid embarrassment or resentment, or to make our interaction smoother, more relaxed, and thereby, conceivably, more profitable, all things considered, for both, it makes sense to think together about what could count as a fair arrangement.[4] The latter need not entail equal contributions to

linguistic communities), while employment rents will be more than proportionally appropriated by people with more valuable linguistic assets (and their maximin redistribution through the highest sustainable basic income will therefore benefit more than proportionally those with less valuable linguistic assets). In neither case does linguistic justice need to be treated separately.

[3] I used this story in Van Parijs (1996) to illustrate and motivate one potential application of David Gauthier's principle of maximin relative benefit, to which I return shortly.

[4] I do not need to assume that, whenever anyone is producing a positive externality, she can legitimately turn to whoever benefits from it in order to collect a fee (that would not exceed the value

the cost of producing the joint benefit. It may even allow free riding to continue in one domain of interaction, providing it is offset by compensatory free riding in another. But to assess the fairness of the pattern of interaction that generates the benefit of communication between linguistic communities, one needs an appropriate criterion of fairness. This is precisely how I shall understand the subject of linguistic justice.

## 3.  Permanent Commuting versus One-Off Move

There is a second basic assumption which further specifies this understanding and which I shall briefly motivate, again by using an analogy. Suppose the dwellers of both a city and its surrounding countryside all greatly benefit from spending most of their days side by side, for example by working together. It therefore makes sense for the country dwellers, spread all around the city, to do the commuting. It also makes sense to ask how fair it would be for city dwellers to contribute to the cost of the commuting, at least if we suppose that country dwellers did not deliberately choose to settle in the country, but happened to live there at the time the potential benefit from spending days side by side arose. However, beyond the short term, the acknowledgement of this joint benefit and of the legitimacy of co-financing it unavoidably prompt the question of whether the right thing to do is to subsidize permanent commuting or to subsidize a one-off move. The former is bound to prove more expensive in the long run, and the only way of justifying it is by invoking, in addition to the collective good of spending days close to each other, the collective good of spending nights and weekends spread over a broader space. In the absence of a further collective benefit of this sort (maintenance of the rural landscape, better social control in smaller towns?), it seems fair that the share of the cost of indefinite commuting that exceeds the cost of moving once and for all should be entirely borne by those with an expensive taste for living far from the centre.

Justice between linguistic communities could analogously be conceived either as a fair sharing of the cost of permanent commuting—the learning of the 'dominant' language by the present and all subsequent generations of speakers of the 'dominated' languages—or as a fair sharing of the cost of a one-off move—the replacement of the 'dominated' languages by the 'dominant' language as a common mother tongue. If the permanence of linguistic diversity is a general nuisance rather than a general benefit, those who are asked to support it by funding the asymmetric bilingualism of many generations rather than the conversion process of one or two could legitimately complain. Against the background of this sort of assumption, perhaps the Bretons were inadequately

of the benefit), but only that she can do so in a subset of cases (long-term interaction, voluntary contribution by the beneficiary to the creation of situations in which the externality is being enjoyed?) to which my two examples belong.

compensated for being toughly turned into unilingual French citizens, but they could not expect the rest of the French population to subsidize for ever their learning of French as a second language. Similarly, if the world were to be turned, linguistically speaking, into a Republic of Ireland writ large, its linguistic communities might be entitled to a far more generous compensation from today's anglophone countries than the Irish people got from the United Kingdom, as Irish was driven out by English even as a mother tongue, but this would be far less, in the long run, than what would be required by the cost sharing of permanent second language learning. My second assumption will simply be that the collective value of undoing the multilingual outcome of the Babel fiasco is significantly less than that of maintaining a significant degree of linguistic diversity. I gladly concede that there is nothing self-evident about this assumption—except for those who have language(s) as their subject matter. A pretty strong argument is needed to vindicate it in the face of the tremendous efficiency gains that would follow from having all six or ten billion of us share the same mother tongue. I am not making the slightest attempt to provide such an argument here, but I believe it can be made.[5]

## 4. The Bare Bones of the Problem

Against the background of these two key assumptions, the problem of linguistic justice can be formulated in its barest form as follows. There are two linguistic communities, respectively called $D$(ominant) and $d$(ominated), with respectively $N$ and $n$ native speakers ($N > n$). The per capita (gross) cost $c$ of learning a second language is the same for both communities. The learning of the other language by either of the two communities generates a per capita (gross) benefit $B$ for members of $D$, and $b$ for members of $d$. In both cases, the benefit is given by the number of speakers this learning enables them to communicate with, lifted upward or downward by a comfort coefficient $s$ that reflects superiority or inferiority in the interaction: the per capita benefit is higher if communication occurs in one's own mother tongue, it is lower if it takes place in an idiom learned later in which one never feels quite as comfortable. Hence, supposing that $d$-speakers learn the other language while $D$-speakers don't, the per capita gross benefit to $d$-speakers is $b = N(1 - s)$ and the per capita gross benefit to $D$-speakers is $B = n(1 + s)$.

The learning is worth doing in the aggregate if and only if the total benefit of one of the two communities learning the other community's language exceeds the total cost. The total benefit $\beta$ is given by $NB + nb$. Under the simplifying assumptions just made, this is equal—irrespective of whether the learning is done by $d$ or $D$—to $2Nn$, or twice the number of pairs of people who become able to communicate with one another as a result of one of the communities

---

[5] I sketch two families of possible arguments of this type in Van Parijs (2000b).

learning the language of the other. The total cost is $nc$ if $d$ does the learning and $Nc$ ($>nc$) if D does it. The necessary and sufficient condition for the overall net benefit to be positive is therefore $2Nn > nc$, or $2N > c$.

It is of crucial importance to note that the necessary and sufficient condition for either of the two communities to derive a positive net benefit from learning the other language is unavoidably more demanding. $D$ will benefit if and only if $B = n(1 - s) > c$, while $d$ will benefit if and only if $b = N(1 - s) > c$. It is of course arithmetically possible for the per capita cost $c$ to fall short of $2N$, while exceeding $N(1 - s)$ and a fortiori $n(1 - s)$, thus making room for a discrepancy between laissez-faire and efficiency in the minimal sense of Pareto optimality: the individual cost of learning exceeds the benefit from learning for every potential learner, even though the overall potential gain from learning is such that everyone could be made better off without anyone needing to become worse off.

To illustrate this possibility in the framework of our initial example, let us assume that Al has a sister, An, with identical language skills, to mirror the assumption that the dominant community $D$ they form is twice the size of the dominated community $d$, with Bo as its sole member. Let us further assume that costs and benefits can be estimated, using the same one-dimensional metric, as follows. While the gross benefit (that is, abstracting from the cost, if any) to a person of the learning of a second language (by herself or with someone else) is posited to be 1 for each of the speakers with whom this learning enables her to communicate (thus disregarding for the moment the complexity arising from the comfort coefficient $s$), its *gross cost* (that is, abstracting from the benefit, if any) is posited to be 3 for the person who does the learning. The net benefit is then given by the difference between gross benefit and gross cost. (See rows i–x in Table 6.1.)

## 5. Reconciling Freedom and Efficiency: Church and King

What would happen, in this simple example, under laissez-faire, that is, in the absence of any transfer targeted at language learners? Al and An will not learn Bo's language, since the net benefit of doing so would be negative for each of them ($1 - 3 = -2$). Nor will Bo learn language A, for the same reason ($2 \times 1 - 3 = -1$). But this outcome is clearly inefficient if one takes account of communication externalities, that is, the benefits for some from the language-learning of others. True, if Al and An were learning Bo's language, the overall net benefit would remain negative, as the free benefit for Bo ($2 \times 1 = 2$) would not offset the net cost to Al and An ($2 \times (-2) = -4$). But if Bo were learning the language of the majority, the free benefit for Al and An ($2 \times 1 = 2$) would exceed the net cost to Bo ($2 \times 1 - 3 = -1$).

Under such circumstances, there is an obvious case for intervention, and a no less obvious suggestion as to its level. Efficiency can be reconciled with freedom—everyone can be made better off without anyone needing to be

TABLE 6.1  Al, An, and Bo under four compensation regimes

|  | Al & An | Bo | Total |
|---|---|---|---|
| *Basic facts* | | | |
| i. Gross benefits if the *As* learn | 1 ($\times$ 2) | 2 | 4 |
| ii. Gross benefits if Bo learns | 1 ($\times$ 2) | 2 | 4 |
| iii. Gross benefits if all learn | 1 ($\times$ 2) | 2 | 4 |
| iv. Gross costs if the *As* learn | 3 ($\times$ 2) | 0 | 6 |
| v. Gross costs if Bo learns | 0 | 3 | 3 |
| vi. Gross costs if all learn (= iv + v) | 3 ($\times$ 2) | 3 | 9 |
| *In the absence of any transfer* | | | |
| vii. Net benefits if the *As* learn (= i − iv) | −2 ($\times$ 2) | 2 | −2 |
| viii. Net benefits if Bo learns (= ii − v) | 1 ($\times$ 2) | −1 | 1 |
| ix. Net benefits if all learn (= iii − vi) | −2 ($\times$ 2) | −1 | −5 |
| x. Net benefits if no one learns | 0 | 0 | 0 |
| *Under a Church and King regime* | | | |
| xi. Subsidies if Bo learns | −0.5 ($\times$ 2) − $\epsilon$ | 1 + $\epsilon$ | 0 |
| xii. Net benefits if Bo learns (= viii + xi) | 0.5 ($\times$ 2) − $\epsilon$ | $\epsilon$ | 1 |
| xiii. Contributions to the cost of learning (= v − xi) | 0.5 ($\times$ 2) + $\epsilon$ | 2 − $\epsilon$ | 3 |
| *Under a Pool regime* | | | |
| xiv. Proportionally shared learning costs | 1 ($\times$ 2) | 1 | 3 |
| xv. Subsidies if Bo learns (v − xiv) | −1 ($\times$ 2) | 2 | 0 |
| xvi. Net benefits if Bo learns (viii + xv) | 0 ($\times$ 2) | 1 | 1 |
| *Under a Gauthier regime* | | | |
| xvii. Maximum net benefits (= total net benefit) | 1 | 1 | 1 |
| xviii. Equal (or maximin) net benefits | 1/3 ($\times$ 2) | 1/3 | 1 |
| xix. Subsidies if Bo learns (xviii − viii) | −2/3 ($\times$ 2) | 4/3 | 0 |
| xx. Shares in the cost of learning (= v − xix) | 2/3 ($\times$ 2) | 5/3 | 3 |
| *Under the proposed regime* | | | |
| xxi. Equal benefit/cost ratio | 4/3 | 4/3 | 4/3 |
| xxii. Subsidies if Bo learns (v − ii/xxi) | (−3/4) ($\times$ 2) | 3/2 | 0 |
| xxiii. Post-subsidy gross costs if Bo learns (v − xxii) | 3/4 ($\times$ 2) | 3/2 | 3 |
| xxiv. Net benefits if Bo learns (ii − xxiii) | 1/4 ($\times$ 2) | 1/2 | 1 |

coerced into learning another language—if Bo's willingness to learn the *As*' language earns her a subsidy at a level just sufficient to induce her to do so. In our example, this sharing of the cost of learning will need to take the form of a tax of slightly more than 0.5 on both Al and An and a subsidy of slightly more than 1 to Bo that will, jointly with the direct benefit of being able to communicate with the As (=2), more than offset her gross cost (=3). Relative to the no-learning situation, the total net benefit is then 1, and everyone is better off. (See rows xi–xiii in Table 6.1.) This corresponds exactly to the cost-sharing rule proposed, on grounds of sheer efficiency, by economists Jeffrey Church and Ian King (1993) as an appropriate way of internalizing the 'network externalities' of language learning, that is, the benefits generated for any user of the network by the fact that one more user joins it.

From such a standpoint, it is crucial to note, there are many situations in which communication externalities do not need to be compensated. Suppose, for example, that there are four As instead of just two. It now makes sense for Bo to learn the As' language even if she has to bear the entire cost. For her gross cost remains the same (3), while her gross benefit doubles (4 × 1), thus yielding a positive net benefit for her (4 − 3 = 1), even in the absence of any cost-sharing by the As. No Pareto-improvement is then achievable through the introduction of a subsidy, and the latter, therefore, could not be justified on efficiency grounds.

Our problem, however, is not linguistic efficiency but linguistic justice. And the distribution of costs and benefits that emerges from the previous criterion is, to put it mildly, not self-evidently fair. In the original version of our example (with only two As), Bo ends up (after subsidies) paying two-thirds of the cost of producing a net benefit nearly 100 per cent of which is enjoyed by Al and An. In the expanded version (with four As), Bo's net benefit (=1) is the same as for each of the As, but she bears alone 100 per cent of the cost. In this linguistic example, just as in the case of my father-in-law's cleaning, this is surely not good enough. Is there any criterion around that could make a more credible claim to express- ing what is required by justice, which may diverge significantly from what is required by efficiency?

## 6. Reconciling Justice and Efficiency: Pool

Reconciling linguistic justice and linguistic efficiency is precisely the chief object- ive of an essay on 'the official language' by political scientist Jonathan Pool (1991a). His point of departure can be presented as follows. In a situation in which there are two or more mother tongues, it is easy enough to identify a solu- tion that would be fair: for example, no one learning any other language, or everyone learning all other languages, or everyone learning another language, either natural or artificial, equidistant from all the mother tongues involved. It is also easy to identify a solution that would be efficient: everyone whose mother tongue is not the most widespread learning the one that is most widespread—at least if it does not happen to be exceptionally difficult to learn. But the fair solu- tions seem bound to be inefficient, and the efficient solution is clearly unfair. Is there an inescapable dilemma between fairness and efficiency?

Pool thinks not, providing one selects the most widespread language as the common language and organizes transfers to those who learn it as a second language for everyone's benefit, whether or not the personal benefit they derive from learning it is sufficient to motivate this learning. What is the criterion that determines the fair level of transfers? Necessarily one that is more demanding than Church and King's efficiency-driven rule: Pool's criterion requires the cost of learning to be shared by the various linguistic groups in proportion to their sizes. In the original version of our example (with two As only), this amounts to requiring Bo to do the learning, while dividing the cost of this learning (=3) equally among Al, An, and Bo (1 each). (See rows xiv–xvi in Table 6.1.)

This rule certainly looks far more appealing than Church and King's as a proposal for a fair sharing of the burden of producing a good that benefits everyone; or at least it does so as long as one does not scrutinize the way in which the total net benefit of the learning is distributed among the three speakers. As it happens, Bo appropriates 100 per cent of this benefit, since Al's or An's contribution (=1) to the cost of Bo's learning is exactly equal to the benefit each derives from being able to communicate with her. Indeed, had Bo's learning cost been even very slightly higher (say, 3.3 instead of 3), the total net benefit would have remained positive (4 − 3.3 = 0.7), and hence the learning would still have been worth doing, but Al and An's net benefit would have become negative (1 − 1.1 = −0.1), as the cost sharing required of them by Pool's rule would have made them worse off than if Bo had not bothered to learn their language.

Consequently, if Pool's rule is meant to govern—without the supplementation of an ad hoc restriction—the distribution of the benefits of a cooperative venture to which people can be assumed to consent voluntarily, it looks as if it is overshooting the mark. It does reconcile efficiency (the overall-net-benefit-maximizing learning pattern) with some attractive egalitarian conception of fair burden sharing (a proportional contribution to learning costs by each linguistic group), but at the cost of having to coerce A-speakers into joining the deal or, for short, at the cost of giving up freedom.

## 7. Reconciling Justice, Efficiency, and Freedom: Gauthier

To solve this difficulty, a third formula may be available in the literature. After the economics of networks and the politics of language policy, let us now turn to moral philosophy. As a general criterion for fairly distributing the benefits from voluntary cooperation, David Gauthier (1986: 271–2) proposes maximin relative benefit. If one assumes away any indivisibility in the range of contributions to the cost of learning, maximin relative benefit is not distinct from equal relative benefit, that is, the equalization of the ratio of each cooperator's actual benefit from the cooperative venture (relative to what her fate would have been in the absence of cooperation) to the maximum benefit she could have derived from it.

To determine this maximum benefit for one of the cooperators, one must select the level of production of the good (in this case, a pattern of competence in the mother tongue of the other group) that maximizes the net benefit for that cooperator, under the constraint that the net benefit of none of the other cooperators can be negative. What this 'maximum benefit' of each of our three cooperators amounts to can be conveniently read from the table of net benefits in the absence of any transfer (rows vii–x). The level of production chosen, in the calculation of each of the cooperators' maximum benefit, is necessarily the one that maximizes the total net benefit, namely Bo learning the As' language and the As learning nothing (1 compared with $-2$ if the As learned, or even $-5$ if all learned). Bo's maximum benefit then consists in her appropriating 100 per cent of this total net benefit ($1 = 2 \times 1 - 3 + 2 \times 1$), thanks to a transfer of 1 from both Al and An, which leaves the latter indifferent between cooperation and the status quo. Symmetrically, Al's (or An's) maximum benefit is achieved when he (or she) appropriates 100 per cent of the total net benefit, by letting An (Al) alone contribute a transfer of 1 towards Bo's learning costs, thus leaving both An (Al) and Bo indifferent between cooperation and the status quo. (See rows xvii–xx in Table 6.1.)

Given that the maximum benefit is the same for all three, equalizing their relative benefits will obviously require that each should achieve the same absolute net benefit level of 1/3. This requires, in our example, a pattern of transfers to the language learner less stingy than under the Church and King regime, but less generous than under the Pool regime. To lift Bo's net benefit to the level of their own, Al and An will both have to pay her 2/3, so that Bo ends up with a total subsidy of 4/3 towards her learning effort. The risk of overshooting inherent in Pool's criterion has now vanished. For, as the cost of learning increases, the subsidy by non-learners will increase (as long as the learning is worthwhile), but it will never make them worse off than in the absence of cooperation. Suppose, for example, that the cost of learning increases from 3 to 3.7. Learning is still efficient, as its cost falls short of its total gross benefit ($=4$). With a surplus now shrunk to 0.3, Gauthier's criterion entails a shrinking of each cooperator's absolute level of net benefit from 1/3 to 1/10 (which still corresponds to one-third of the surplus for each). This is achieved through a subsidy of 1.8 to Bo (which grants her a net benefit of $2 \times 1 - 3.7 + 1.8 = 0.1$) funded equally by Al and An (which shrinks the net benefit of each to $1 - 0.9 = 0.1$). But the very fact that transfers are calibrated to equalize (positive) net benefits protects this upward adjustment of the As' contribution from overshooting in the way it did under Pool's regime.

Note, however, that even after the transfer, Bo is still bearing a disproportionate share of the learning costs. Not only is she contributing more (5/3) towards the cost of the good enjoyed by all three than either Al or An taken separately ($=2/3$), but also more than the two of them together ($=4/3$), despite the fact that the two linguistic groups derive the same gross benefit ($=2$) from the good produced. Indeed, this imbalance is getting worse as the inequality in the sizes of the two linguistic groups increases. (See rows viii–xiii in Table 6.2.)

TABLE 6.2  Variable number of speakers of the dominant language

| | | | |
|---|---|---|---|
| i. Number of $As$ | 2 | 4 | 9 |
| ii. Total gross benefit of Bo's learning (i $\times$ 2) | 4 | 8 | 18 |
| iii. Total gross cost of Bo's learning | 3 | 3 | 3 |
| iv. Total net benefit of Bo's learning (ii $-$ iii) | 1 | 5 | 15 |
| v. Pre-transfer net benefit for Bo (i $-$ iii) | $-1$ | 1 | 6 |
| vi. Pre-transfer net benefit for each $A$ | 1 | 1 | 1 |
| vii. Pre-transfer net benefit for all $As$ (vi $\times$ i) | 2 | 4 | 9 |

*Under a Gauthier regime*

| | | | |
|---|---|---|---|
| viii. Equal individual net benefit ($=$ iv/(i + 1)) | 1/3 | 1 | 3/2 |
| ix. Subsidy to Bo (viii $-$ v) | 4/3 | 0 | 9/2 |
| x. Transfer to each $A$ ($-$ ix/i) | $-2/3$ | 0 | 1/2 |
| xi. Bo's share in the cost of learning (iii $-$ ix) | 5/3 | 3 | 15/2 |
| xii. $As$' total share in the cost ($=$ ix $= -x . i$) | 4/3 | 0 | $-9/2$ |
| xiii. $As$' total net benefit (viii . i) | 2/3 | 4 | 27/2 |

*Under the proposed regime*

| | | | |
|---|---|---|---|
| xiv. Equal benefit/cost ratio (i $\times$ 2)/iii | 4/3 | 8/3 | 18/3 |
| xv. Subsidy to Bo (iii $-$ i/xiv) | 3/2 | 3/2 | 3/2 |
| xvi. Transfer from each $A$ (xv/i) | 3/4 | 3/8 | 1/6 |
| xvii. Bo's share in the cost of learning (iii $-$ xv) | 3/2 | 3/2 | 3/2 |
| xviii. $As$' total share in the cost ($=$ xv $=$ xvi . i) | 3/2 | 3/2 | 3/2 |
| xix. Net benefit for each $A$ (vi $-$ xvi) | 1/4 | 5/8 | 5/6 |

*Under a Church and King regime*

| | | | |
|---|---|---|---|
| xx. Subsidy to Bo | $1 + \epsilon$ | 0 | 0 |
| xxi. Bo's implied share in the cost (iii $-$ xx) | $2 - \epsilon$ | 3 | 3 |
| xxii. Each $A$'s share in the cost (xx/i) | $1 + \epsilon./2$ | 0 | 0 |
| xxiii. Net benefit for Bo (v $+$ xx) | $\epsilon$ | 1 | 6 |
| xxiv. $As$' total net benefit (vii $-$ xx) | $1 - \epsilon$ | 4 | 9 |
| xxv. Net benefit for each $A$ (xxiv/i) | $(1 - \epsilon)/2$ | 1 | 1 |

*Under a Pool regime*

| | | | |
|---|---|---|---|
| xxvi. Bo's proportional share in the cost (iii/(i + 1)) | 1 | 0.6 | 0.3 |
| xxvii. Subsidy to Bo (iii $-$ xxvi) | 2 | 2.4 | 2.7 |
| xxviii. Each $A$'s share of the cost (xxvii/i) | 1 | 0.6 | 0.3 |
| xxix. Net benefit for Bo (v $+$ xxvii) | 1 | 3.4 | 8.7 |
| xxx. $As$' total benefit (vii $-$ xxvii) | 0 | 1.6 | 6.3 |
| xxxi. Net benefit for each $A$ (xxv/i) | 0 | 0.4 | 0.7 |

For example, if the number of As is doubled, the total gross benefit of Bo's learning A swells from 4 to 8 (4 for each group), while the gross cost remains
unchanged ($=3$). The equal division of the total net benefit ($=5$) attributes 1 to
each of the five speakers, and, since this is what emerges in this case in the
absence of any transfer, Bo can be left to bear the whole of the learning cost by
herself. If the number of As further swells from 4 to 9, the total gross benefit
becomes 18, the total net benefit 15, and its per-capita equal share 1.5. Since Bo's
pre-transfer net benefit (given by the number of speakers she gets access to
minus the learning cost) far exceeds this level ($9 - 3 = 6$), she must now not only
pick up the full bill of the learning but in addition finance an aggregate subsidy
larger than this cost, so that each of the nine (non-learning) As can enjoy, in addition to costless access to a new speech partner, a transfer of 0.5, presumably as a
reward for the large communication potential As jointly offer so cheaply to Bo.

## 8. An Alternative: Equal Ratios of Benefit to Cost

As in the case of Pool's criterion, it would be possible to get rid of the most
extreme counter-intuitive implications by adding an ad hoc stipulation, in this
case the condition that the learners must not be worse off under the deal than
they would be under laissez-faire. Gauthier himself would certainly subscribe to
such a stipulation, as he meant his criterion to apply exclusively to the sharing of
the benefits that flow from a cooperative improvement upon the laissez-faire
outcome. However, it is also possible to formulate a distinct criterion, which
avoids at one swoop the undershooting of Church and King and the overshooting of both Gauthier and Pool, while also getting rid of the less extreme
counter-intuitive implications. Here it is: simply equalize the ratio of (gross)
benefit to (gross) cost.[6]

Of course, the learning is worth doing only if the total (gross) benefit exceeds
the total (gross) cost, which entails that the ratio between them will be strictly
larger than 1. What the criterion requires is that this overall ratio should apply to
each speaker involved, whether a member of the learning or non-learning
group, and hence also to each of the two groups as a whole. Its implications in
our three-person example are illustrated in rows xxi–xxiv of Table 6.1. Contrary

---

[6] A very different criterion, which also avoids in one fell swoop the various difficulties mentioned
so far, consists in applying Gauthier's criterion to whole linguistic groups rather than individual
speakers. In the case of two groups, the total cooperative surplus is then divided equally among
them—rather than distributed between them in proportion to their sizes—which yields, given our
simplifying assumptions, precisely the same cost-sharing formula as the equal-ratios-of-benefit-to-
cost criterion which I am about to present and defend: each of the two groups needs to pay half the
cost. In the general case of n linguistic groups, however, this 'global Gauthier criterion' generates
wildly counter-intuitive implications (for example, a high sensitivity of the fair distribution of costs
to how finely linguistic groups are subdivided), which the equal-ratios criterion avoids. See de Briey
and Van Parijs (2002) for a detailed discussion of this further criterion.

to the Church and King regime, it follows that as soon as there is some cost to be borne by someone, no one can fairly derive a benefit without contributing to that cost. Contrary to the Pool regime, it follows that the cost can never exceed the benefit for some without exceeding it for all (and hence making the learning pointless). And, contrary to the Gauthier regime, it follows that no one will ever be required to pay more than the full cost of the learning. In our example, as the number of speakers in the majority group increases—and hence also the potential net benefit from the minority group's learning—the size of subsidy to the learners remains fixed at half the cost (see rows xiv–xix in Table 6.2). This simply reflects the fact that the aggregate gross benefit grows equally for the learning group and the non-learning group. Under our simple assumptions, therefore, the equal benefit/cost ratio criterion generates a simple 50/50 cost-sharing rule between the two linguistic groups.

## 9. Four Formulas

By using the abbreviations and assumptions made at the start, each of the four criteria thus briefly discussed can be compactly restated as a formula for the size of the subsidy to each of the $D$-learning $d$-speakers. Let us remember that, abstracting from the comfort coefficient $s$, the per capita gross benefits of there being a shared language, respectively for each of the $N$ $D$-speakers (Al and An in our example) and for each of the $n$ $d$-speakers (Bo in our example), are given by $B = n$ and $b = N$. The per capita cost of the $d$-speakers learning the $D$-language is given by $c$, the per capita subsidy (to the $d$-speakers) by $t$, and the per capita tax (on the $D$-speakers) by $T = (n/N) \cdot t$.

According to Church and King's efficiency-driven criterion, the transfer must very slightly exceed the difference between the per capita cost and the per capita benefit for $d$-speakers, subject to this difference being positive and to learning generating an overall surplus. The conjunction of these two conditions simplifies into requiring $c$ to be larger than $N$ but smaller than $2N$. Hence:

$$Church\ and\ King: t = c - b + \epsilon = c - N + \epsilon, subject\ to\ N < c < 2N.$$

Pool's criterion of proportional cost sharing demands that the tax paid by each (non-learning) $D$-speaker be equal to the gross cost of learning borne by each $d$-speaker minus the subsidy each of them receives. Given the budget constraint ($N \cdot T = n \cdot t$), this amounts to subsidizing a proportion of the cost of learning equal to the share of $D$-speakers in the total population. Hence:

$$Pool: t = c - T = c - (n \cdot t/N) = c \cdot N/(N + n).$$

Gauthier's criterion of maximin relative benefit simplifies, in the case of our problem, to the equalization of net benefits. The subsidy to each $d$-speaker must therefore be equal to the difference between the cost of learning and the gross benefit of each $d$-speaker (essentially as in Church and King) plus the net benefit (after tax) of each $D$-speaker. Bearing in mind again the budget constraint, this amounts to demanding that one subsidize the cost of learning in the same proportion as under Pool's criterion, but only after deduction of difference between the (higher) per capita gross benefit of the minority group and that of the majority group. Hence:

$$Gauthier: t = (c - b) + (B - T) = (c - (N - n)) \cdot N/N + n.$$

Lastly, my own preferred criterion of equal benefit/cost ratios requires the gross benefits derived from the learning by each person (and hence by each group) to be proportional to her contribution to its cost, namely, the gross cost of learning minus the subsidy for $d$-speakers and the tax for $D$-speakers. Whereas Church and King subsidies cover only the gap between gross cost and gross benefit, the subsidy implied by the alternative proposal covers the gap between gross cost and a proportion (smaller than 1) of the $d$-speakers' gross benefit corresponding to $D$-speakers' ratio of contributions to benefits ($T/B$). Whereas Pool subsidies cover the whole of the gap between the $d$-speakers' per capita learning cost and the $D$-speakers' per capita tax, the subsidy implied by the alternative proposal covers only the gap between the learning cost and a proportion (higher than 1) of the per capita tax given by the ratio of the $d$-speakers' to the $D$-speaker's per capita gross benefits ($b/B$). Bearing in mind again the budget constraint ($n \cdot t = N \cdot T$) and the simple assumptions about gross benefits ($b = N$ and $B = n$), this reduces to requiring a per capita subsidy corresponding to half the cost of learning. In brief:

$$Alternative: t = c - (T/B) \cdot b = c - (b/B) \cdot T = c - (b/B) \cdot (n \cdot t/N) = c/2.$$

The key factual assumption that generates this simple result is that the communication links opened up through a language learner's toil are symmetrically valued, and hence that proportionality to benefit requires the set of all those who become able to communicate with the learner to jointly foot half the bill. If our comfort factor $s$ had been introduced to reflect superiority/inferiority in competition and other interaction, the subsidy would have needed to be higher than $c/2$. If one had heeded the differential importance attached to communication, for example, owing to inequalities in wealth or power, the subsidy, in most circumstances, would have needed to be lower.

## 10. Policy Implications

My aim, here, has not been to provide a fully-fledged rigorous formulation of a precise and general criterion of linguistic justice, let alone to present a comprehensive case for its validity. I have examined four possible criteria, each with at least some prima facie plausibility, but with widely diverging implications, as illustrated for example by the very different profiles of subsidies they justify as the size of the majority linguistic group expands (see rows xx, xxvii, ix, and xv in Table 6.2). Through sketching what I regard as decisive objections to the first three criteria, I have indicated why I believed the fourth criterion to make most sense, at least against the background of the two fundamental assumptions spelt out at the start. I shall say no more in its defence.[7] To conclude, I shall simply outline the sort of policy implication such a criterion, or related ones, would have in the real world.

Whether coerced or, more often, uncoerced, asymmetric bilingualism has been a frequent phenomenon in many places for a long time. But as schooling, mobility, and communication expand and intensify, it is becoming more ubiquitous and more massive than ever. As Abram de Swaan (1993; 2001) has elegantly put it, mankind as a speaking species forms a worldwide language system firmly held together by asymmetric plurilingualism: natives of peripheral languages learn the central language of their area; natives of central (or lesser) languages learn one of 13 or so supercentral languages, or regional lingua francas; and natives of supercentral (or lesser) languages learn the one emerging hypercentral language.

This ubiquitous asymmetric bilingualism is arguably very efficient. But nothing guarantees that it be fair. To make it fair, a simple rule of thumb emerges from the above discussion: whenever a language is the object of asymmetric bilingualism, the linguistic group whose mother tongue it is must pay half the cost of this learning, in a comprehensive sense that should cover both the explicit cost of language tuition and the huge implicit opportunity cost of having to learn a language rather than devoting one's (children's and own) time to other activities. Exact assessments are of course out of reach, but a cost sharing that would charge the wages of language teachers and all the teaching material used to the linguistic group whose language is being learned, while leaving the opportunity cost altogether uncompensated, would seem to be a minimum demand—especially as equal cost sharing between the two linguistic groups takes no account of the inequality in interaction and of the other incidental advantages of the free-riding linguistic group hinted at the beginning.

Quibbling about exact amounts can go on for ever. But there is no need to wait for it to die out before the Castilian natives should start preparing the cash they owe to the Catalans, or the Hindi natives what they owe to the Santals, or the French natives what they owe to the Congolese, or indeed the English natives the huge and ever growing amount they owe to much of the rest of the world—unless they find it more convenient for them, possibly even mutually beneficial, to replace cash transfers by tolerance for, indeed promotion of, free-riding in other dimensions, for example by making an electronic version of all

---

[7] See the final sections of de Briey and Van Parijs (2002) for a generalization of the criterion to the case of *n* language groups and a discussion of its acceptability.

English-language scientific journals available free of charge to all academics outside the English-speaking world, or by waiving intellectual property rights on the reproduction of English publications in any country in which English is not the mother tongue of the majority. However, as such measures would in all likelihood further deepen the asymmetric bilingualism which called for compensation in the first place,[8] it is very doubtful that they could go a long way towards extinguishing the *D*-natives' debts, and generous direct cash subsidies to the teaching of English (and supercentral languages) seem inescapable, not as a matter of charity, nor merely as a tool of cultural imperialism, but as a duty of justice.

I can already think of more than a handful of objections, more or less self-serving, which worried natives of supercentral and hypercentral languages will no doubt be keen to raise. As this contribution is meant for an audience consisting mainly of English natives, who stand to lose most (at least in an immediate, zero-sum sense) from bringing fairness to the world language system, I am sure there is no need for me to get the discussion off the ground by spelling out some of these objections myself.[9] They can be trusted to take care of that. If it makes them more comfortable, they can even do it in English. I won't charge.

[8] Indeed, for this very reason, members of other linguistic communities have expressed fierce opposition to my proposal, which would, in their view, amplify the problem rather than cure it.

[9] In fairness, however, I should refer the reader to de Briey and Van Parijs (2002), which generalizes the criterion of linguistic justice proposed here to the case of *n* linguistic groups. One (no so obvious) implication is that, in case the mandarinophones join the global crowd and seriously start learning English in turn, it is not just the anglophones but also the francophones (and even more all smaller linguistic groups) who will have, out of justice, to subsidize China's huge learning effort— even irrespective of the fact that learning English is much harder against a Chinese background than with an Indo-European mother tongue.

# 7

# Diversity as Paradigm, Analytical Device, and Policy Goal

FRANÇOIS GRIN

## 1. Introduction

Recent years, most visibly since the fall of the Berlin Wall in November 1989, have witnessed a marked increase in scholars' interest in minority issues, in particular minority rights and linguistic rights. One striking aspect of this interest is the fact that it has emerged, more or less simultaneously, in different quarters, and now finds expression in very different families of discourse. However, these families of discourse have remained, for the most part, quite insulated from one another, and this fragmentation, which is only just beginning to make way for a higher degree of interconnection, can seriously hamper not only analytical accuracy but also the relevance of policy proposals concerning language rights.

This chapter discusses the links between these families of discourse and argues that 'diversity' has a useful role to play as a federating concept. The function of such a federating concept is not only to combine these discourses into a consistent, more general discourse, but also to help account more accurately for the social and political reality that they all describe—albeit from different standpoints—and to clarify some of the more delicate policy choices that have to be made in this area.

The argument pursued in this paper attempts to tie together ideas proposed in earlier contributions (Grin 1994; 1996a; 2000a). It does not, however, attempt to make the case that 'diversity is good' (or bad), and largely sidesteps the normative debate which inspires many of the contributions in this volume. Instead, I explore some of the questions that arise under a twin set of related assumptions. The first assumption is that diversity is generally seen as an issue that requires

The author is former Deputy Director of the European Centre for Minority Issues (ECMI) in Flensburg, Germany. He is currently Senior Lecturer, University of Geneva, and Adjunct Director, Education Research Unit (SRED). This chapter builds on comments on Stephen May's book *Language and Minority Rights* (2001) drafted for the language rights workshop at Queen's University (Kingston) in March 2001. The author expresses his gratitude to the participants at the workshop for stimulating discussions, as well as to Jean-Jacques Ducret, Will Kymlicka, Alan Patten, and Robert Phillipson for insightful comments on an earlier version of this text. The usual disclaimer applies.

social intervention. The relevance of this assumption is evident from the fact that advocates and adversaries of diversity alike constantly call upon the authorities to either protect and promote diversity or, on the contrary, to keep it in check. In other words, diversity seems to be a feature that cannot just be left alone. The other, yet related, assumption under which my argument is developed is that there is a degree of social consensus over the notion that diversity is, by and large, a 'good thing', albeit perhaps a costly one. This is borne out by frequent examples of official discourse and international treaties extolling the virtues of diversity, or by the fact that the preservation of linguistic diversity is sometimes presented as a policy objective in its own right—for example, by the European Parliament. Hence, the notion that 'diversity is good' seems to guide (together with other, possibly conflicting motivations) the action of important political entities. It is therefore worth exploring some of the corresponding logical implications, and investigating the set of concepts needed to devise appropriate policy responses to the challenges posed by diversity.

The chapter is organized as follows. In section 2, I briefly comment on the relevance of the assumption that 'diversity is good' and then move on to the claims that make up the core of my argument, and which can be summarized as follows:

1. Spelling out the logical implications of minority rights and language rights reveals the need to situate them in a broader, more integrative framework, in which diversity is a key concept. The fragmentation and parallelism between different discourses on minorities can be illustrated by the image of the 'diversity clover' (section 3).
2. Such an integrative framework should, in particular, allow for the interconnection of different types of discourse whose common theme is ethnic, linguistic, and cultural diversity, as well as the challenges to which such diversity gives rise. The selection, design, and implementation of appropriate policy responses to these challenges can be characterized as 'diversity management'. Explicit reference to diversity as an object of public policy can serve to operationalize interdisciplinarity in research (section 4).
3. The coalescence into diversity management of the concerns voiced by, and of the analytical tools used in, different types of discourse is not a purely abstract exercise. It has practical consequences, and can for example help to formulate principled policy responses to traditional dilemmas in the area of language rights, such as the apparent contradiction between 'autochthonous' and 'immigrant' language rights (section 5).

Before we embark on this discussion, a few words of definition are in order. First, the manifestations of social diversity referred to in this chapter belong to the language sphere. However, I believe that, for the most part, the points made here carry over to other manifestations of diversity. These may be cultural or ethnic in a non-linguistic sense; they may be embodied, for example, in religious practice.

Second, it may be useful, despite this chapter's focus on language, to say what is meant here by ethnicity. I view ethnicity as the result of subjective assignation or self-assignation to a non-elective group perceived as distinct. The contradiction between the possibility of self-assignation and the non-elective character of the group is only apparent, as a comparison with the concepts of 'sex' and 'gender' will show. Sex is a non-elective—in this case biological—category, but gender is an assignation, socially constructed by oneself and by others. Although we have to make do with the sole word 'ethnicity', a similar distinction can be made here, and ethnicity can be defined as a two-tier social construction in which one tier is non-elective (particularly one's ancestry, mother tongue, and cultural models internalized during childhood), and the other results from assignation, by oneself or by others. This simple representation is fully compatible with Fishman's (1989) definition of ethnicity as made up of three elements: paternity (the perception of intergenerational continuity), patrimony (the linguistic and cultural substance of what is passed on and gives material expression to this continuity), and phenomenology (the 'self-perceived or attributed' character of ethnicity).

## 2. On the 'Value' of Diversity

The argument proposed in this chapter is not concerned with establishing the claim that 'diversity is a good'. Many people, including this author, certainly share this conviction, but for our purposes it is enough to consider it as just that—a personal conviction, or a preference, just as one may have a preference for more or less environmental quality, more or less socio-economic equality, and so forth. From a public policy standpoint, a considerable amount of progress, both theoretical and empirical, remains necessary before we can confidently conclude that diversity is, indeed, a social good. Often-heard claims to the effect that languages constitute a 'treasure' or a form of 'wealth' play on economic metaphors, but metaphor is not sufficient to establish the 'value' of any individual language or of the diversity that results from the presence of a variety of languages.

When something is valuable, actors reveal their valuation of it through their behaviour. Observable behavioural patterns regarding linguistic diversity, however, are ambiguous in that not all manifestations of diversity appear to be valued equally, while some may be actively opposed—as evidenced by expressions of racism. Actors appear to favour manifestations of diversity that directly or indirectly benefit them, yet see others as useless. They appear to reject uniformity, possibly because more diverse societies are often claimed to be more lively, more interesting, more adaptable, and hence potentially more prosperous; another reason for people to endorse diversity (as a matter of *principle*) to a certain degree may be the realization that, if they were to support the opposite view, they might unwittingly be undermining the legitimacy and standing of components of diversity particularly dear to them, namely, their own language or culture. At the same time, people appear to be less willing to countenance diversity beyond a certain point, often on the grounds that certain forms of legitimacy in the public space are not divisible. Another common argument is that diversity is too costly, despite the fact that reliable information on this question is remarkably rare, and that very little is actually known on the subject; this attitude may be an illustration of the fact that language is an area in which people, as Pool (1991b: 7) observes, 'seem to hold extraordinarily stubborn beliefs'.

In the above respects as in many others, linguistic diversity bears striking resemblance to environmental quality, suggesting that the type of policy issues that arise in language and in environmental matters are analytically related; some of the corresponding concepts are presented in the Appendix. This parallel is borne out by research in the economic analysis of language policy (Grin 2002b); from a language economics standpoint, there are solid theoretical and empirical grounds to support the notion (which cannot, at this time, be considered an established result) that diversity is a social 'good'—but that, just like environmental quality, a certain cost attaches to it, and that a balance between benefits and costs must be struck.[1]

This set of issues, however, is not my concern here, and I shall keep well away from the associated normative questions in order to focus on a logically distinct topic: if diversity is seen as an issue that requires social intervention through policy, doing so efficiently requires a proper understanding of diversity as the concept that underpins (or 'federates') various manifestations of diversity that are all too often considered in isolation.

## 3. The Diversity Clover

The rising interest in minorities, minority rights, and their realization in the sphere of language is apparent in the work of scholars from disciplines spanning the entire range of the social and human sciences, from psychology to political science and anthropology to economics.

[1] On the value of language and diversity from an economic perspective, see for example Grin (1996b); Grin and Vaillancourt (1997); Grin (2000a,b). The policy problems arise with respect less to *private* value than to *social* value, which results from the aggregation of private valuations. However, not all the elements to be combined in the aggregation are appropriately identified and measured. Furthermore, the conceptual and technical difficulties posed by the aggregation procedure are, at this time, only partly solved—particularly if non-market forms of value are taken into account along with the more standard market values. Available empirical results indicate that the market costs of diversity-maintenance policies are much lower than is commonly believed, and that there is no correlation between indicators of linguistic diversity (or uniformity) and indicators of economic prosperity. Even if solutions can be found to these allocative questions, the associated distributive issues require further examination as a prerequisite for formulating policy recommendations.

Such issues are, of course, a long-standing interest of disciplines like sociolin-guistics, applied linguistics, and language planning (for a recent assessment of the field, see Jernudd 2001); many language scholars can legitimately claim to have been pioneers in identifying questions and developing concepts to address them. However, scholars from other disciplines, who until recent years had paid scant attention to language matters, are now turning to them. This flurry of activity results in the production of richly varied but also, quite frequently, self-referential families of discourse. The degree of interconnection between them, despite an a priori community of interests, remains limited. Examples of this problem are quoted in May (2001: 52), who notes that 'discussions of ethnicity and nationalism have until recently been conducted largely in isolation from one another'. Yet 'ethnicity' and 'nationalism' are only two of the terms that need to be embraced in a more integrative discussion.

In practice, this situation means that discussions on language and minority rights often take place in discrete spheres, in which authors may be tempted to reinvent the wheel, at great cost in terms of time—and corresponding limita-tions to the relevance of some of their results. The problem is compounded by confusion that may arise from the fact that terminology is not stable—to wit, the rather different meaning of the very word 'minority' in contexts such as those of the United States, Canada, Switzerland, or Hungary. Acknowledging these *glissements de sens* requires us first to take stock of the joint presence of dif-ferent manifestations of diversity and different discourses about them. Explicit awareness of the joint existence of different manifestations of diversity is not very frequent in the literature, but it can be found for example in Eriksen (1993; discussed in May 2001: 83–8) who distinguishes the following 'cases': 'indigen-ous peoples', 'proto-nations', 'urban ethnic minorities', and 'ethnic groups in plural societies'. Although this typology may be convenient for many purposes of applied research, it seems not to do full justice to the nature of diversity, if only because it makes a number of implicit assumptions.

For one, it appears to endorse the concept of 'nation' as a matter of course by defining as 'proto-nations' groups for whom this characterization, upon closer examination, is inappropriate. The use of the qualifying 'proto' is telling in itself, because it characterizes its object as a deviation from the 'nation', which is therefore implicitly taken as a norm. In fact, the applicability of the concept of nation is probably less, in empirical terms, than is often assumed (Grin 2002a); moreover, it frequently carries essentialist assumptions which should not go unquestioned. Likewise, the expression 'urban ethnic minorities' is apparently nothing but an elaborate or euphemistic way of referring to immigrants who may have retained, deliberately or not, a greater or lesser range of linguistic and cultural traits associated with the part of the world that they or their parents (sometimes their grandparents) have migrated from. However, apart from the restriction to 'urban' groups (an empirically understandable but analytically ad hoc one), the reference to ethnicity seems to assume that the content of this term is unambiguous, and that processes of assignment and self-assignment are unproblematic.[2]

In the same way, the appropriateness of the fourth label—that is, 'ethnic groups in plural societies'—is not obvious. Since none of the other labels appears to fit groups such as linguistic minorities in Switzerland, users of Friulian in north-eastern Italy, or users of Flemish in the very northernmost corner of France, one is led to suppose that these groups should fall under this fourth category; yet anyone familiar with those cases will observe that, in the absence of a number of caveats and qualifications (which automatically detract from the generality of the analysis), the adjective 'ethnic' is awkward or even irrelevant there.

Hence, instead of adopting categories like the above as part of a typology of cases that would be supposed to accurately account for reality, let us start from the observation of academic and terrain practice, which will enable us to identify genres characterized by the presence of a certain number of traits. This practice can be symbolized by the figure of the four-leafed clover. Each of the four leaves of the clover corresponds to the 'complexus' that characterizes it. I do not apply any formal method to identify each complexus, although I submit that a good discourse analysis would be well-suited to this purpose, if only because the primary clue revealing its existence is the presence of a coordinated (and self-referential) type of discourse.[3]

Each complexus is defined by a set of three elements. The first contains the leading topic or set of topics addressed within it, without assuming any intrinsic validity to attach to the demarcation of these topics. The second element denotes, through examples, the practical cases and geographic areas that are most actively studied by scholars from a given leaf of this clover. The third element identifies the dominant or at least centrally positioned academic disciplines in which the type of discourse is produced (see Fig. 7.1).

The clover is, of course, a very simplified depiction of the research practice, and the complexes are not as sharply demarcated; yet they may be seen as archetypes. What needs to be underlined—and does not appear explicitly in the figure—is the fact that each complexus has its associated professional

[2] The notion of ethnicity has been eloquently deconstructed by May (2001), who shows that it applies to dominant majority groups no less than to minority groups.

[3] This representation of research (taken in a broad sense to include academic research conducted at universities, as well as applied research taking place in specialized research centres or units in international organizations and NGOs), is largely based on what might be called participant observation accumulated in the course of my work as Deputy or Acting Director of the European Centre for Minority Issues (ECMI) from 1998 to 2001. I readily acknowledge the limitations of this characterization. However, it has often proved useful in such contexts, and it appears to resonate with the experience of many researchers. The 'clover' is therefore offered here with no ambition other than that of serving as a stepping-stone towards epistemologically more sophisticated representations of research activity on ethnic, linguistic, and cultural diversity.

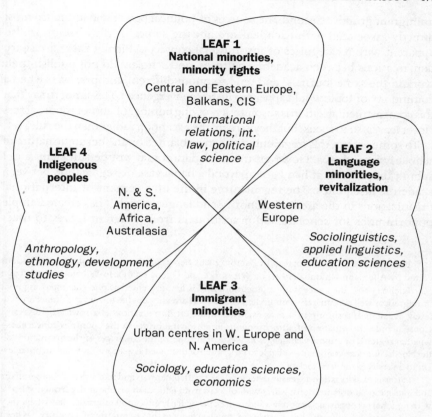

FIGURE 7.1 The diversity clover

culture, crystallizing around its conference circuits, scholarly journals, and, of course, academic and non-academic networks. For the most part, researchers from a particular leaf of the clover have few opportunities to meet researchers from another leaf. This is even more true of practitioners (as distinct from academics) of the issues concerned—for example, government officials, diplomats, civil servants, officers from international organizations, representatives of local or international non-governmental organisations, and so on. This fragmentation finds illustration at different levels.

First, to the extent that diversity is acknowledged as the higher-order, more general issue raised by a specific concern, there is a tendency to equate one specific type of issue with diversity as a whole. For example, many of the commentators concerned with immigrant minorities apparently consider that diversity in modern societies is mostly coterminous with the presence of immigrant groups.[4] Second, the sources of political power and influence most directly associated with each leaf are not the same.[5] A distribution is also apparent within categories of institutional contacts.[6] Finally, there are sharp demarcations between academic cultures, and scholars do not publish their work in the same journals[7] and tend to quote different authors, even when a community of topic would appear to justify convergence.[8] This is not to say that this compartmentalization is absolute; a growing number of authors quote across clover leaves, so to speak, but they remain the exception rather than the rule.

To some extent, this fragmentation can be blamed on the hermetic nature of scholarly boundaries. However, this explanation may not be sufficient, and I submit that what is at hand goes beyond a banal case of segregation between academic disciplines. The recent surge in the involvement of international organizations in the areas of minority and language rights has created ample opportunities for scholars and practitioners from different leaves to meet

[4] This equation is apparent in texts by Banton (2000), Berry (2000), or in most of the contributions edited by Allemann-Ghionda (1994) or Wieviorka and Ohana (2001). In Wieviorka (1998) and Martiniello (1998), the concept of 'multiculturalism' is first presented as one encompassing non-immigrant as well as immigrant components of cultural diversity, but the former are almost immediately evacuated, resulting in a near-exclusive focus on immigration as a source of diversity. Consequently, the situation of autochthonous linguistic minorities in the countries concerned—whether regional or minority languages in Western Europe, or the languages of the first nations on the North American continent—is liable to be ignored or dismissed as a secondary problem not relevant to diversity in modern society.

[5] Patterns of association are easily detected: leaf 1 with diplomats and ministries of foreign affairs and international organizations; leaf 3 with officials from education or labour departments; leaf 2 with regional (as opposed to national) authorities, particularly education ministries or—where they exist—language planning bodies. As to leaf 4, much activity in the last quarter of a century has been devoted to raising its political and media profile through contacts with international organizations.

[6] Let us for example consider international organizations. The Organization for Security and Cooperation in Europe (OSCE) is a quintessentially leaf 1 institution, operating within a frame of reference appropriate to leaf 1 issues, but inadequate for leaf 2 issues, about which the Council of Europe, while also active in leaf 1 issues, deploys considerably more targeted action. Interpersonal networks develop accordingly.

[7] This text being written in English, let us take examples from the scholarly literature published in this language: quite predictably, researchers from leaf 1 tend to publish their work in journals like *Nations and Nationalism*; leaf 2 scholars may choose to target the *Journal of Multilingual and Multicultural Development*; in leaf 3, authors are likely to prefer, say, the *Journal of Migration Studies*, and in leaf 4, the *Annual Review of Anthropology*.

[8] For example, when an analyst of nationalism or ethnic conflict is quoted, leaf 1 scholars will frequently mention books by Horowitz (1985), Brubaker (1996), or Gellner (1997); those from leaf 2, however, typically ignore these authors, but quote Anderson (1991). Reciprocally, when scholars primarily interested in national minorities (leaf 1) need to write about language and ethnicity (which is, a priori, an area in which what is quoted by leaf 2 authors might serve as a useful guide), they almost always overlook Fishman, although his work on language shift and reverse language shift (for example, Fishman 1991) remains a key reference for almost everyone working on language and language policy. This echoes another observation by May (2001: 7) to the effect that 'little [has] actually been written on the interrelationship between nationalism and language'.

and start learning about one another's work.[9] What may be lacking, rather, is adequate awareness of the fact that it is hardly possible to formulate very much in the way of policy-relevant discourse regarding any of these components of diversity without taking other components of diversity into account.

This brings us to the policy side of the argument. The limitations of a 'one-leaf approach' can be illustrated with reference to the apparent competition between immigrant and autochthonous language rights. These rights (quite tellingly) were for a long time not considered jointly in the literature. Advocating the recognition of (minority) autochthonous languages as, say, official languages raises the question of whether the same status ought to be accorded to immigrant languages, and if not—or not to the same extent—in application of what criteria. Reciprocally, calls for some degree of recognition of immigrant languages raise the question of the treatment accorded to local, traditional minorities, whose languages may be considerably more threatened in their existence than the immigrant languages. In the same way, a professed concern for the rights of 'national minorities' or 'indigenous peoples' raises the question of the rights of other groups which, though autochthonous and different from the majority because of language, do not define themselves as 'nations', 'proto-nations', or 'nations without states', even less as 'indigenous peoples', and whose concerns crystallize around issues of language policy or cultural policy. Hence, it is difficult to formulate propositions concerning one component of diversity without having some vision of what such propositions entail for other components.

The need for the joint consideration of the presence of different minority situations is further exemplified by the logical and empirical limitations of discrete and static categories. Defining a group as a minority requires an identification of the majority, making it immediately clear that the issues at hand are not 'minority problems' but actually pertain to the relative position of the minority with respect to the majority or, putting it differently, to minority–majority relations. Yet this notion can, in turn, be generalized, because minority and majority can be, depending on context, rather fluid notions. Most would probably agree with May (2001) that the postmodernist argument of purely contingent identities is overstated, and that identity—including as a member of a minority or a majority—is more deeply anchored. This is evidenced by, among other things, the strength of emotional attachments to identity markers like language. Yet the

---

[9] Cases in point include, among others, the adoption and implementation of international legal instruments such as the Framework Convention for the Protection of National Minorities (adopted by the Council of Europe in 1995) and the European Charter for Regional or Minority Languages (adopted by the Council of Europe in 1992). The development of a set of recommendations by the OSCE's Office of the High Commissioner for National Minorities, in particular the 'Oslo Recommendations' (drafted for the High Commissioner by the Foundation on Inter-Ethnic Relations in 1998), has created another set of opportunities for exchange 'across clover leaves'. An extensive range of international legal documents pertaining to minority languages in Europe can be found in Ó Riagáin (1998).

assumption that a person is at all times and unequivocally a member of a minority or a majority is empirically fragile. Therefore, the issue with which society is confronted is not one of handling relations between a static majority and an equally static minority, but one of diversity management, where social actors' involvement in the creation and re-creation of manifestations of diversity results in constantly evolving patterns.

More generally, any proposals made regarding the relative position of minority groups, particularly the languages that they speak, amount to recommendations to amend the *linguistic environment* as a whole—or the linguistic dimensions of the surroundings in which people live. A linguistic environment is defined by the sum total of demolinguistic and sociolinguistic features, including, for example, the relative visibility and legal status of the various languages in society (Grin 1997). Hence, issuing proposals pertaining to one component of diversity presupposes that one advocates a certain linguistic environment, which also affects the role and standing of other components of diversity. The need to offer responses to the many challenges brought on by diversity, as well as the fact that a linguistic environment, by definition, is not confined to the traits specific to any given leaf, is what the four leaves have in common. Diversity therefore emerges as a unifying paradigm—the stem of the clover, as it were—within which the interrelations between the lines of work pursued in these four leaves can best be clarified.

Let us conclude this section on a brief semantic note. A deliberate choice is made here to talk about 'diversity' rather than 'difference', since 'difference' presupposes a reference *from which* a person or group differs, raising, in turn, the question of the possibly privileged or somehow more legitimate status of the persons or group taken as a reference. Diversity can therefore serve as a more neutral term containing fewer implicit assumptions.

## 4. 'Subjective Diversity' and the Operationalization of Rights

I now turn to the second claim made in this chapter, namely, that diversity is a concept that can be useful in clarifying the notion of rights (particularly language rights) and operationalizing them in public policy. In order to see why, let us first return to the notion of diversity management. The need for diversity to be 'managed' through policy arises from the fact that diversity is simultaneously conflictual and threatened. Commentators often focus on one or the other aspect, but little attention is devoted to the fact that both are present at the same time.[10]

The *conflictual* nature of ethnic, linguistic, and cultural diversity (most present in the minds of representatives of leaves 1 and 3 of the clover) arises

---

[10] One exception is Patten (2001).

from the fact that distinct groups defined or self-defined as such through language, ethnicity, or culture often are in competition over economic, political, and symbolic resources. Arbitrating between conflicting claims prompts the formulation, by scholars, practitioners, and activists, of normative arguments in favour of one or another settlement of conflicting claims; it also requires the development of analytical concepts in terms of which such arbitration can occur.

The *threatened* character of diversity is usually most evident to representatives of leaves 2 and 4. They are particularly concerned with the rapid disappearance of the traditional environment, both natural and cultural, in which indigenous people live, as well as with the predicted demise, over the twenty-first century, of about half of the approximately 6,000 languages used in the world today (Grimes 1998; Crystal 2000).

It may seem paradoxical that diversity should be simultaneously threatened and conflictual: if diversity is threatened, it must be because it is eroding, and with this erosion sources of conflict would be expected to fade away. Prima facie, if diversity is threatened, it will soon cease to be conflictual—in fact, there is no lack of voices calling, more or less openly, if not for the elimination of diversity, at least for the elimination of measures which prevent uniformity;[11] and if diversity is seriously conflictual, it must be because it is not seriously threatened. This apparent paradox, however, is easily resolved once a distinction is made between objective and subjective diversity.

Many components of *objective* linguistic diversity—as measured, for example, by the number of languages in use at a given point in time—are obviously under threat. This threat is evidenced not only by the demise of small languages (with the passing away of their last remaining speakers), but also by the worldwide spread of specific cultural contents in forms of entertainment, types of consumer goods, and socio-political models of society. The spread is not strictly unidirectional, and processes of cultural creolization and *métissage* certainly occur, but such re-creations of cultural diversity appear rather like outgrowths from a common substratum, of which a growing proportion is found everywhere in the world. For all these reasons, the notion that objective diversity is seriously threatened is one not easily dismissed.

At the same time, *perceived* or *subjective* diversity is an increasingly prevalent feature of modern societies. Several trends coincide in this evolution, in particular the reassertion of long-suppressed manifestations of ethnic identity (including language) after the fall of the Berlin Wall; large-scale migration flows, with a much more varied range of combinations of country of origin and country of

---

[11] This is particularly evident in the current debate over the position of English vis-à-vis other languages in the world, with some authors criticizing policy measures that might curb the spread of English. In this context, the frequently used term 'spread' should be taken with a pinch of salt, to keep clear from any implicit assumption that the influence of this or any language is a natural or agentless process (on this question, see Phillipson 2001 or Durand 2001).

destination;[12] the deepening and broadening of supra-national organizations such as the European Union; and the advance of what is usually referred to as 'globalization', and attendant processes such as the intensification of international trade. All four trends put people from different linguistic and cultural backgrounds in increasingly normal and frequent contact with one another, both in private and in working life; hence, the degree of diversity to which younger generations are exposed is significantly greater than that which characterized the everyday life of their grandparents. In short, objective diversity is declining, but subjective (or 'perceived') diversity is on the rise, and these twin trends are particularly manifest in the case of languages.

Owing to its conflictual and threatened character, ethnic, linguistic, and cultural diversity cannot simply be left to itself, and emerges as a necessary area of policy intervention for modern societies. Such policy intervention is not structurally different from public policy in the fields of education, health, transport, or the environment. In practice, however, it is usually not identified as such, and instead of viewing their work as discourse about or intervention on 'diversity' as an object of policy in its own right, most scholars and practitioners still focus on specific manifestations of diversity, as featured in the clover.

This somewhat piecemeal approach is reaching its limits. Some analytical issues have been discussed in the preceding section. However, limits are also apparent on the operational plane. It is convenient to discuss them with reference to the discourse of rights, because the upsurge of interest in minority issues in recent years has largely found expression in this type of discourse. For the purposes of this chapter, I shall characterize the latter, somewhat summarily, as a family of discourse primarily resting on legal and institutional expertise and concepts. It is made up of (1) a set of legal texts in which certain rights are explicitly or implicitly accorded to certain categories of persons; (2) a body of (mostly legal) commentary pertaining to these texts and their application in different polities; (3) a strand of literature, often rooted in sociolinguistics, which seeks to formulate a minimal set of universal linguistic rights to be included in the list of universal human rights;[13] and (4) political and institutional claims made on behalf of specific groups in terms of rights-based arguments.

I shall leave aside the classical problem of the possibly contradictory relationship between 'human rights' and 'minority rights', as well as the no less complex question of whether language rights should be seen as individual or collective rights.[14] What matters here is that the discourse of rights can only ever make up

---

[12]  A process Hollinger (1995) calls the 'diversification of diversity'.

[13]  This strand of literature is often referred to as the 'linguistic human rights approach'. See Kontra *et al.* (1999); Skutnabb-Kangas (2000).

[14]  However, I concur with de Varennes (1999: 131) that 'European and international documents agree as to the individual nature of those rights [that is, the rights of linguistic minorities]' (my translation). It is important to note that what some scholars describe as 'collective rights' are seen by others, including de Varennes, as the logical consequence of individual rights, and therefore contained in the latter.

but a small part of diversity management. The discourse of rights, particularly in its expressly legal form, remains an exercise in commentary or exegesis on normative texts—whether analysing the true extent of the rights recognized in some international legal instrument, or evaluating the conformity of some national constitutional provisions with international standards regarding minority rights. Despite the high visibility of legal considerations and their prominence in the range of expertise marshalled by governments and international organizations, the analytical issues crucial to diversity management are elsewhere—upstream and downstream from the discourse of rights.

Upstream from it, we find the analysis of the criteria that should govern our choices regarding alternatives in diversity management. In the academic world, this task, for the most part, has been taken up by political science, particularly normative political science leaning towards political philosophy (for example, Kymlicka 1995b; Shapiro and Kymlicka 1997; Patten 2001). These issues are sometimes formalized in models of policy analysis (Pool 1991a; see also Van Parijs, this volume), in which the emphasis is placed on conjugating efficiency and fairness, defined as decisive evaluation criteria. The function of both types of analysis is to clarify the choices open to democratic debate, checking in particular if the alternatives contemplated meet certain requirements—whether these concern their compatibility with the principles of liberalism or the relative 'fairness' of the distributive effects associated with all policy choices. These questions, however, are usually given short shrift in the discourse of rights as characterized above, owing to the latter's emphasis on the commentary of subjective norms[15] rather than on the logic of the principles and criteria inspiring them.

Downstream from the discourse of rights, once *political* principles and choices are embodied in legislation, the question arises of whether the *policy* measures adopted to give them substance are effective or not. Alternatively, we may define the issue as one of assessing whether, given a set of constitutional and legal norms, the policy measures actually selected, designed, and implemented successfully achieve—or at least approach—the goals put forward as a result of democratic political debate. This requires a shift of emphasis away from the intrinsically normative discourse of rights to the positive approach of policy analysis and policy evaluation.[16] What matters then is not just whether a constitutional provision meets international human rights standards or accords with principles of liberal political theory, but what the results of the measures adopted are: Are these measures effective in terms of diversity management?

[15] Although lawyers talk of 'objective rights', this notion makes little sense in the social sciences, and is almost oxymoronic in economic theory where, as Simonnot (1998) observes, there are no such things as rights—other than those which it is in the interest of the powerful to grant and respect.

[16] This contrast between positive and normative discourse is a standard one, presented for example in any economic theory textbook. The fact that a positive approach is assumed to eschew normative judgements should not, however, be interpreted as a belief that the analytical concepts used are value-free, but that a constant and deliberate effort is made to keep them at bay, and that all assumptions are (or at least ought to be) explicitly stated. See Mayer (1993).

Are the benefits derived from them commensurate with their costs? And are their distributive implications fair? This opens up a new range of questions about diversity, which are perhaps formulated most articulately, at this time, in the field of language policy.[17]

I have so far tried to show that the management of diversity is the true nature of the research and terrain work represented by the four leaves of the clover. If so, then not only should each component of diversity be explicitly understood as one aspect only of overall ethnic, linguistic, and cultural diversity, but the academic disciplines that respectively play a leading role in each leaf should be combined in an integrative perspective. The latter ought to encompass the three levels just described, namely, philosophical criteria of choice, legislative development, and policy design, implementation, and evaluation. The recognition of diversity as the fundamental social issue to be addressed therefore generates a rationale for combining the inputs from different disciplines into a general framework for diversity management—a *transdisciplinary* approach, as it were, to the management of diversity. The articulation of the concepts privileged in various leaves is an exciting task, to which recent work, for example by May (2001), is making highly valuable contributions.

Interestingly, contemporary developments in the field of minority rights and language rights are indicative of a move in the same direction (Dunbar 2001). This is evidenced by the evolution of international legal instruments which formulate the obligations that states may enter regarding minorities. A shift from states' duty to 'protect' to a duty to 'promote' can increasingly be detected in such texts. What is more, this latter obligation reaches much further than may appear at first. It requires states not only to take steps to guarantee certain rights (such as freedom from discrimination) but to guarantee certain results, for which the granting of certain rights is a necessary, but not a sufficient, condition. Accordingly, the object of protection is not so much the rights themselves as that through which rights are manifested and exercised.

The most achieved example of this evolution, at this time, is the European Charter for Regional or Minority Languages. The Charter is *not* about rights, as Council of Europe officials and experts tirelessly explain; in fact, the term 'right' turns up only once, in the Preamble to the Charter.[18] By contrast, the Charter proposes a whole range of practical measures for the protection and promotion of regional and minority languages in the fields of education (art. 8), judicial authorities (art. 9), administrative authorities and public services (art. 10),

---

[17] Readers may note that the adjective 'effective' is used here whereas the adjective 'efficient' has been avoided. The reason is that 'efficiency', as distinct from 'effectiveness', harks back to a very specific set of three conditions derived in economics—more specifically, in general equilibrium theory. These three conditions are rather abstract and practically nowhere present but in textbook expositions. Using the term 'effectiveness' is intended to indicate that the policy evaluation criteria referred to here are the formally less demanding ones of effectiveness and cost-effectiveness (Grin 2000b).

[18] On this point, see Council of Europe (1998a,b) or Blair (2000).

media (art. 11), cultural activities and facilities (art. 12), economic and social life (art. 13), and trans-frontier exchanges (art. 14). Signatories are expected to choose a minimum of 35 paragraphs, corresponding to so many concrete undertakings, out of a total of 68. Precise specifications regarding groups of paragraphs that may not be passed over entirely are mentioned in art. 2. The Charter, therefore, goes well beyond the principles laid out in other international instruments such as the Framework Convention for the Protection of National Minorities, or recommendations of the Organization for Security and Cooperation in Europe in this area. The modernity of the Charter is also in evidence in the ideology underpinning it, namely, the maintenance of regional and minority languages as components of diversity.

This brings us to the third issue of this chapter, namely, the implications that can be derived when diversity itself is recognized not just as the object of policy intervention but as an appropriate policy goal.

## 5.  Diversity and the Differentiation of Language Rights

One of the most delicate issues in the debate on language rights is whether it is acceptable, from the standpoint of liberal political theory, to accord different formal rights to users of different languages. Following Habermas (1994), commentators generally agree that the 'politics of recognition' can require, for users of minority languages, the enforcement of rules that give them special protection. Consequently, such rules, which aim at preserving a 'context of choice', should not be interpreted as special rights but, rather, as conditions for equal rights, in application of the principle that persons in the same situation should be treated equally, and persons in different situations should be treated differently. Hence, the application of this general principle provides an answer to the problems posed by *some* language laws, particularly those that appear to offer privileged treatment to one language group, by showing that such legislation actually restores a level playing field and guarantees equality of opportunity. The idea, quite simply, is that individuals should enjoy the same range of opportunities.[19]

This principle is not always sufficient, however, as a logical basis for establishing or maintaining distinctions between different types of minorities. The well-known case in point is that of the respective status of immigrant and autochthonous language rights. The problem arises if we assume that immigrant

---

[19] Pending closer examination, I submit that this principle can be seen as an interpretation of Dworkin's (1981) principle of 'equality of opportunity'—as distinct from his other principle of 'equality of resources', which requires individuals to enjoy not only the same opportunity set but also the same degree of satisfaction from life. If the analogy is valid, many of Dworkin's analytical results, initially developed with respect to socio-economic inequality, may be applicable to language policy development.

groups living in democratic states want or expect the language of their country of origin to receive formal recognition in their new country of residence. Whether such an expectation generally exists is an empirical question rather than a fore-gone conclusion; and whether it should be encouraged to exist is a question that will not be addressed in this chapter—although the considerations below would suggest that the answer to this question must be: 'it depends'. For our purposes, we shall assume, as do many scholars and practitioners hailing from leaf 3 of the clover, that this expectation does exist.

In theory, the nature and degree of the recognition expected could vary from a general, non-committal endorsement to the granting of full-fledged official language status along with the setting up of a complete education system oper-ating through the medium of the language concerned. What matters here, however, is not so much the extent of such recognition as a possible inequality of treatment arising between resident users of immigrant languages and users of traditional autochthonous languages—whether or not these users identify as part of an indigenous people.

In practice, this inequality of treatment exists in *all* multilingual states, because the extent of recognition granted to autochthonous languages, limited as it often is, is greater than that accorded to the languages of immigration. For example, minority languages such as Sorbian, Danish, and two varieties of Frisian enjoy more official recognition and support in Germany than does Turkish, the country's main immigrant language. South Africa recognizes eleven official languages, but they do not include the Lingala spoken by numer-ous (illegal) immigrants from the centre of the African continent. Scottish Gaelic and Welsh benefit from varying degrees of official recognition or pro-motion in parts of Britain (namely, Scotland and Wales), but Bihari does not. As it turns out, the only states where immigrants' languages and autochthonous minority languages are treated equally are those where neither are given any status whatsoever.

Some advocates of immigrant minorities often criticize the absence or feebleness of support for immigrant languages as bordering on a violation of immigrants' human rights (for example, Skutnabb-Kangas 2000). The extent of the improvements called for in the 'linguistic human rights' literature, as well as the criteria invoked for demanding some improvements (but not others), are not altogether clear. However, these typically concern the education system and the provision of some health and social services. From a legal perspective, how-ever, such claims may be rejected by invoking existing constitutional texts and international legal instruments.[20] Yet, as we have seen above, the analytical

---

[20] Legal commentary is unambiguous; for example; de Varennes (1999: 136), who notes that 'A State could never be expected to carry out the entirety of its activities in all the languages spoken by persons residing on its territory' (my translation). Some documents like the Proposal for an Additional Protocol to the Convention for the Protection of Human Rights and Fundamental Freedoms Concerning Persons Belonging to National Minorities insist on the maintenance of

function of legal discourse is limited because it is centred around the codification of norms. It is probably more relevant to turn to political philosophy or normative political theory for guidance.

These disciplines, however, appear to be grappling with the same question. If the manifestation of difference is a legitimate part of social life and its recognition a condition for democracy (Taylor 1992), then there may not exist any criterion justifying a different treatment of different forms of difference. Immigrants are taxpayers, no less than users of autochthonous minority languages; and if the latter have access to an education system operating in their language, on what grounds should this be denied to users of immigrant languages? The invocation of time as a source of superior legitimacy ('the Filipinos/Moroccans/Vietnamese are newcomers to the United States/Spain/France, whereas the Navajo/Basque/Bretons have been there for hundreds or thousands of years, even before the establishment of the current nation-state') may sound grudging or even jingoistic, and its power of conviction erodes with, precisely, the passage of time. Yet not everyone would acclaim the implied notion that the severely threatened Amerindian languages deserve no particular protection.

From the broader perspective of diversity management, the issue looks quite different. Assuming, as I do in this chapter, that diversity is perceived as a good (though possibly a costly one), a general principle for choosing between alternatives is the following: *all other things being equal* (or—more loosely—'within a certain range of financial and symbolic costs'), a policy that promises to deliver more diversity should be preferred over one that promises to deliver less. By the same token, choices that would result in diversity loss, or imply measures that would fail to prevent such loss, should be rejected. A rule flowing from this principle is that choices that favour relatively threatened components of diversity should take precedence over choices that favour less threatened components of diversity. Hence, priority should be given to some languages vis-à-vis others not so much on grounds of antiquity or the long-standing presence of the groups that speak them, but in proportion to the opportunity cost of the diversity that would be lost if these languages were to die. This rule can be interpreted as an absolute priority of the weakest.[21]

It is well-known that special protection is often necessary for the survival of severely threatened languages; an appropriate goal for special protection,

'longstanding, firm and lasting ties with that State' for a person to be recognized as a subject of those rights (see Thornberry 1994: 19).

[21] This decision rule can be seen as reminiscent of Rawls's third principle of justice, according to which any deviation from equality of treatment, *given equality of opportunity resulting from his first two principles of justice*, is justified by a resulting improvement of the position of the most disadvantaged in society (Rawls 1971; Van Parijs 1999). This parallel needs to be examined at closer range to assess whether elements of Rawlsian theory can be profitably incorporated into the emerging theory of language policy.

materialized in a set of language policy measures, is the 'recreation of a self-priming mechanism of language reproduction' (Fishman 1991). In cases where the maintenance of diversity does require such protection, non-threatened languages would not be treated on the same footing. It follows from the above that it is logical for North Frisian to be given priority over Turkish in the northern German *Land* of Schleswig-Holstein, as it would be for Breton to be given priority over Arabic in Brittany, or for aboriginal languages to have precedence over Greek in Australia.[22]

Adequate support to small languages—particularly to 'unique' languages, as distinct from languages spoken by national minorities with a kin state across the border—is not incompatible with the recognition of immigrant languages. In the perspective of the rule just outlined, restrictions on non-threatened languages—that is, curbs on diversity in a given area—are justified only to the extent that their very presence worsens the position of a small language (and would therefore pose a much greater threat to diversity). In this case, however, restrictions would apply to an autochthonous majority language as much as to non-threatened immigrant languages.

More generally, this diversity argument opens the door to the recognition of immigrant languages and the granting of language rights to their speakers. However, the respective treatment of different minority languages would still be different and result in the deliberate maintenance of privileges for the most threatened of those minority languages, for as long as this is necessary to ensure their survival. In that it combines the goal of the effective protection of diversity with the principle (usually considered a morally sound one) of the defence of the weakest—from which even some immigrant languages could benefit—this rule may be considered a more principled justification for the granting of different rights to different minorities than the currently dominant one, which predicates recognition on history and long-standing tradition.

The diversity-based argument can be taken a few steps further in order to test its robustness and confront its general, abstract principles with real-world constraints that impose asymmetries to the basic decision rule. The general assumption that linguistic diversity positively influences welfare can be used to design a system for the allocation of language rights in a multilingual, decentralized polity with three levels of government (national, regional, and local). In this polity with three languages—majority; autochthonous minority; immigrant minority—each demolinguistic configuration, jointly defined by the local

---

[22] By the same token, immigrant speakers of relatively threatened languages may be given priority over speakers of a vigorous autochthonous minority language. Examples, however, are more difficult to find. For the sake of the argument, consider the case of Binukid, spoken by approximately 50,000 speakers in the Philippines (figures vary depending on source) despite the widespread adoption of Cebuano as a vehicular. A group of Filipino immigrants working in Barcelona and having Binukid as their first language would then, under the 'territorial multilingualism model' described later on in this chapter, be entitled to no less protection and promotion than Catalan.

and regional degree of linguistic diversity, is associated with a more or less pluralist or *diversitist* language regime.[23] This 'territorial multilingualism model' (Grin 1996a) can then be augmented to allow for inequalities in power and in the extent of legitimacy recognized to any given group by the more powerful one, as well as issues of tolerability of minority rights by the majority. Owing to limitations of space, the territorial multilingualism model will not be presented here. Still, its results suggest that recognizing linguistic diversity as a relevant policy goal helps to formulate solutions to difficult problems involving language rights.

In this chapter, I have tried to show that diversity should be recognized as a federating paradigm, as a tool for operationalizing interdisciplinarity in research, and as an appropriate criterion for policy decisions. In conclusion, I wish to return briefly to this third point.

The diversity-based argument is not meant to replace other decision rules. However, it can serve as a complement to them by offering principled decision criteria when difficult policy choices have to be made. In particular, though not antithetic to a rights-based argument, it makes it clear that, as soon as linguistic diversity is considered as a 'good' (in the same way as environmental quality), 'rights', though still necessary, no longer represent a sufficient guiding principle. Fundamentally, the ideology of rights and the ideology of diversity are not at variance with one another. Authors like Gobard (1966), Phillipson (1992), Durand (2001), or May (2001) usefully remind us that macro-level language dynamics are not agentless processes, and that the invocation of 'structural forces' should not be allowed to conceal the power issues at hand. If understood in this light, a defence of linguistic diversity will generally coincide with a defence of human rights.

## Appendix: Diversity, 'Diversitism', and Welfare

Policy choices affecting ethnic, linguistic, and cultural diversity do not directly determine diversity itself. Rather, these policies may be more or less favourable to the maintenance and expression of diversity—let us say that they display a greater or lesser degree of 'diversitism'. We have assumed (see section 2 of this chapter) that diversity is by and large considered 'good'; yet it also carries costs. We may logically expect more 'diversitist' policies, if they are effective at all, to be conducive to a higher degree of diversity; hence, there also exists a positive relationship between the degree of diversitism of a policy and the benefits that flow from the policy. At the same time, diversitist policies carry a cost. Existing work (Vaillancourt 1978; Vaillancourt and Grin 2000; Grin 2002b) indicates that such costs are moderate (at least much more so than is commonly believed); nonetheless, we may assume that policy costs are a rising function of a policy's

[23] See the Appendix for a definition of 'diversitism'.

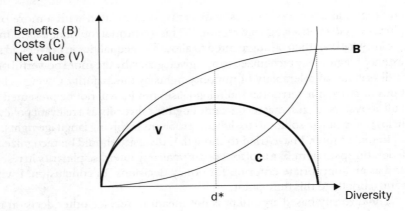

FIGURE 7.2 Diversity: benefits and costs

degree of diversitism. However, a very fundamental rule of economic theory reminds us that the marginal utility of goods is decreasing, while the production of most goods is characterized by decreasing returns. Hence, benefits rise at a decreasing rate and costs rise at an increasing rate. The assumptions made so far can be combined into the representation of benefit (B) and cost (C) curves proposed in Fig. 7.2.

What this simple diagram suggests is that, to the extent that preferences can be expressed at all regarding the degree of diversity in society, and if a link with costs can be established through the relative diversitism of policy responses, then certain degrees of diversitism in policy are likely to deliver more welfare than others. Given the smooth, monotonous curves assumed here, there exists an 'optimal' degree of diversitism associated with the level of diversity $d^*$ where the net difference between benefits and costs—that is, the net value ($V$) of diversity, represented by the thick curve in Fig. 7.2—is largest. Though seemingly innocuous, this result indicates that very general assumptions can be enough to dismiss the notion, put forward by advocates of uniformity, that diversity is a burden to be minimized, as well as the notion, put forward by advocates of boundless multiculturalism, that no limits should be set when embracing diversity. If a preferable level of diversity exists, it is likely to be neither zero nor infinite, but an unambiguously positive interior solution. Given the public good character of linguistic diversity, the cost curve is likely to be comparatively lower than depicted here, because it would be less steep or even downward-sloping over certain ranges; this would move the optimal level of diversity $d^*$ further to the right.

# 8

# Global Linguistic Diversity, Public Goods, and the Principle of Fairness

IDIL BORAN

The world's languages are dying. We hear this lament from many anthropologists, sociologists, and linguists searching theoretical grounds for better preserving the world's languages for a world with less injustice and more diversity. Of course, language death is not a new phenomenon. The Etruscan and Sumerian languages, for example, died centuries ago for reasons, obviously, other than the rise of modern nationalism. About half of the known languages of the world have died in the last five centuries. But what worries linguists is that, whereas language death was not uncommon in the past, the rate of extinction increased dramatically in the twentieth century, and has reached alarming levels. Scholars disagree on the reasons why small languages face the threat of extinction in such increasing numbers. For many, the massive linguistic decline around the world has been prompted by the rise of the nation-state and modern nationalism. Others argue that it was in fact the rise of the industrial society, related to the nation-state with its need for centralized economy and mobile citizenry, that brought about linguistic homogeneity, threatening many small languages. Some hold that most languages were doing well once, but things were never the same after the rise of 'modernity', and became even worse with the Enlightenment. Yet others argue that languages were still holding on until 'globalization' became a feature of the era in which we live. Regardless of their accounts of the social and political causes of language loss, these scholars share the view that language loss is a major concern and that something ought to be done about it, not just for reasons that concern linguists in particular, but for moral reasons as well.

Preliminary ideas developed in this chapter began to take shape at the Language Rights Workshop, Queen's University (Canada), March 2001. Earlier versions of the chapter were presented at the Doctoral Seminar of the Hoover Chair in Economic and Social Ethics, Université catholique de Louvain (Louvain-la-Neuve), The Nuffield Political Theory Workshop (Oxford), and the University of Pompeu Fabra (Barcelona). For helpful discussions, I am thankful to participants on these occasions. For comments and suggestions, I am particularly grateful to Will Kymlicka, Alan Patten, Philippe Van Parijs, Kok-Chor Tan, Neus Torbisco, Paula Casal, David Miller, Patti Lenard, Alain Maskens, and Dan McArthur. When working on this chapter, I was a holder of a postdoctoral fellowship at the Hoover Chair in Economic and Social Ethics, which I gratefully acknowledge.

For many theorists, therefore, the concern about the loss of languages has been the starting point of normative reflection about justice and language.[1] One type of reasoning views the decline of linguistic diversity as akin to the decline of biodiversity and argues that the protection of threatened languages is important for reasons not dissimilar to those that justify the conservation of threatened species. In this chapter, I enquire whether a case for linguistic justice can be convincingly made on these grounds, and evaluate the merits and limitations of this way of conceiving of linguistic justice.

I will proceed as follows. The first section explains how some of the existing studies of language rights find a correlation between linguistic diversity and biodiversity. In arguing for environmental protection, many invoke the concept of public goods, a concept used by both political philosophers and economists. The second section discusses whether linguistic diversity can reasonably be viewed as a public good. I argue that this is possible and outline what I call a 'public good argument' for linguistic diversity. Section 3 argues that if the public good argument is acceptable, then the principle of fairness can be applied to establish the fair terms of the distribution of costs and benefits. Section 4 deepens the public good argument by identifying three objections which place limitations on the principle of fairness and which a defender would have to address: the voluntary acceptance condition, the intentional production condition, and the free-rider problem. Throughout, the question I will be concerned with is this: Assuming that the maintenance of linguistic diversity produces a public good, if we accept a public good argument regarding biodiversity can we accept a similar argument regarding linguistic diversity? My answer will be 'yes': an argument for the protection of linguistic diversity can be informed by environmental arguments. Yet, as I will then argue in section 5, this way of conceptualizing linguistic justice has serious limitations for reasons other than environmental concerns. I will show this by raising further objections that are not easily answerable from any perspective that takes language loss as the primary concern, and will conclude that the politics of linguistic diversity as a public good would have intolerable implications. My aim is to find a balanced assessment of the conception of justice based on a concern about language loss. If I am right, my analyses will also shed some new light, in the context of linguistic diversity, on ideals of fairness that have been central to many debates in political philosophy.

---

[1] Stephen May (2001), for example, is a representative supporter of this standpoint regarding language rights. Other theorists who adopt this approach include Tove Skutnabb-Kangas (1999; 2000). Not everyone who is concerned with language loss adopts a biodiversity approach to the issue of linguistic justice, but many do. May, for instance, does not develop a distinctly ecological argument for linguistic protection but, as someone concerned with the loss of languages, acknowledges the literature on biodiversity as relevant.

# 1. Patterns of Language Loss and Environmentalism

One way of approaching the issue of linguistic justice is to track the processes of language loss that occur around the world and make recommendations on what ought to be done about them in light of principles of justice. The concern about language loss around the world is emphasized and discussed extensively in a range of disciplines including sociolinguistics, sociology, and interdisciplinary work (for example, May 2001; Skutnabb-Kangas 2000). Some scholars (for example, May 2001) have argued that language loss occurs as a result of pro- grammes of assimilation that have been, and continue to be, pursued by nation- states. The result of this process is that small languages face the danger of losing the critical mass of speakers that a language needs in order to live, and thus enter the category of 'threatened languages'.

This process is supported by powerful empirical evidence: there are approx- imately 6 billion people on the planet and approximately 6,000 languages. However, the 6,000 languages are very unequally distributed globally. While a handful of powerful languages are secured with millions of speakers, a dramati- cally larger number of languages are spoken by small numbers of people and many are shrinking at such a fast rate that they face the serious danger of being lost in the next few generations. According to linguists, 90 per cent of the world's population speaks the 100 most used languages and the rest of the approximately 6,000 languages of the world are spoken by about 10 per cent of the world's population (Nettle and Romaine 2000: 8). According to some measurements, languages with fewer than 100,000 speakers enter the category of 'languages at risk of extinction'. On this categorization, then, only a few of the some 6,000 lan- guages can be regarded as being secure, and the overwhelming majority of the world's linguistic communities face the danger of losing their language due to increasing pressures to shift to more powerful languages. This is at the core of the concept of 'language loss', also referred to as 'language death'.

Theorists concerned with language loss aim to formulate a scheme of lin- guistic rights (as rights to linguistic protection or protection of small languages) specially construed to reverse this process of linguistic decline.[2] For those who

---

[2] This approach has also been described by some commentators as the 'nationalist perspective' to language rights (for example, Laitin and Reich, this volume). This is not surprising because patterns of language loss are directly linked to the programmes of linguistic assimilation and unification conducted by modern nation-states. And, conversely, demands for the protection of small languages stem from the notion that a language can meaningfully survive only if it is an official language with a given territory. The flip side of linguistic assimilation based on the view that national groups deserve their own states, then, is linguistic protection to be granted to small language communities. If nation-states promote and secure a national language through policies of official language, this causes small language commun- ities to remain increasingly marginalized. If every linguistic/national group deserves its own national state, or a facsimile of it, then so too does every small language group. What is needed, then, if full sovereignty is not possible, is a system of language rights that allows the minority language to be used in public institutions, becoming the language of, for example, education, courts, bureaucracy, and the like.

are primarily concerned with language loss, environmental ethics offers a useful theoretical resource.

Interestingly, patterns of language loss bear some similarities, many sociologists of language have remarked, with patterns of decline in biodiversity due to environmental threats. There is a substantial literature in the social sciences that defends the view that there is a correlation between linguistic diversity and biodiversity, both being subject to analogous kinds of threats. A recent publication that represents this approach is Nettle and Romaine (2000).[3] According to Nettle and Romaine, there is an important correlation between linguistic loss and the extinction of endangered species that allows them to talk about a common repository which they call 'bio-linguistic diversity'.

Those sympathetic with this position, which I will refer to as the 'ecology of language', give several reasons in support of their claims, some of which Nettle and Romaine outline. I will mention here three of them. One similarity concerns geographical patterns. Comparing two different world maps, one showing patterns of biodiversity and the other patterns of linguistic diversity, we see that 'those areas which are rich in languages also tend to be rich in biodiversity value' (Nettle and Romaine 2000: 43). Biodiversity is concentrated through the tropics and tails off toward the poles; so is linguistic diversity. Moreover, most of the endangered species are in the tropics and the same applies to languages. Another similarity concerns the patterns of vulnerability. A large number of species are vulnerable to the destabilizing activities of a small number of large and powerful groups. Similarly, an overwhelmingly large number of small languages are vulnerable to the assimilating forces of powerful languages. A third similarity emphasized in the literature is that we would benefit from a better preservation of linguistic diversity and biodiversity in comparable ways (Nettle and Romaine 2000: Ch. 3), a point I will return to in following sections. The literature identifies other forms of convergence, but for present purposes the above three are sufficiently representative features of the dominant position regarding the importance of global 'bio-linguistic diversity'.

Nor are these similarities presented merely as analogies, that is, as tools of reasoning to help us better understand the dynamics of language loss, but as an indication of an inherent correlation between languages and the environment (see also Edwards 2001). Those who make moral prescriptions regarding the preservation of language along lines similar to arguments for the preservation of biodiversity assume that such a correlation ought to be made, to support these kinds of prescriptions. This is partially why the inherent correlation theory is heavily emphasized in support of prescriptive claims. For Nettle and Romaine, for example, global linguistic diversity does not just display an apparent resemblance to biodiversity. It is for them an integral part of the larger fragile ecosystem we inhabit. By extension, the various threats to small languages should be counted among the larger threats to the environment.

---

[3] Other representatives of this approach are Skutnabb-Kangas (1999; 2000) and Mülhäusler (2000).

Philosophers might (rightly) look at these generalizations with a jaundiced eye. For one thing, the assumption about linguistic diversity being part of the larger ecosystem is an ambitious statement about the nature of our complex relationship with the environment. Like most statements of this nature, it is subject to reasonable disagreement mainly because the central (descriptive) claim—that there is a thick correlation between linguistic and biological diversity on the planet—is a controversial claim still subject to debate, not a settled assumption. It is one thing to find a neat similarity between two things and quite another to demonstrate that the similarity is indicative of an inherent correlation. Similarities in (unequal) geographic distribution around the globe between endangered species and languages themselves are no proof that there is an inherent correlation. Nor can the matter be settled easily through debate. Those who assume an inherent correlation postulate a common cause for both phenomena (biodiversity and linguistic diversity). However, neither phenomenon is likely to result from a single cause as opposed to a complex set of factors. To postulate a common cause is probably to overstate the genuine relation that may or may not exist.

But this is not the point I want to emphasize here; my purpose is not to engage in a discussion to prove that the descriptive statement regarding the relation between biodiversity and linguistic diversity is true or false. Although I believe that there are problems with associating linguistic diversity with biodiversity for reasons I have just mentioned, I also think that we do not need to engage in a controversial discussion about whether linguistic diversity is in fact a subset of the larger biodiversity in the world to examine the applicability of some environmental arguments to issues of linguistic protection. If concepts of environmental ethics can shed light on issues of language rights, we have reason to consider them, although the conclusions may turn out to be unfavourable. I will therefore examine in greater detail, in the following sections, the third claim of the ecologists of language, that we would benefit from the protection of biodiversity and linguistic diversity in similar ways.

## 2. Linguistic Diversity as a Public Good

The concept that I want to consider here is the notion of 'public goods', a concept that has been developed by political philosophers and economists and that has seen ample use in environmental ethics. As I will explain below, I believe the arguments in favour of the protection of small languages can be matched by a public good argument specially tailored to capture the value of global linguistic diversity. I will argue, however, that although this kind of argument can be made, we have reasons to remain reluctant to embrace it as a basis for a theory of language rights.

Let me explain first how I understand the concept of public goods. As is also recognized by some authors (for example, Cullity 1995), many definitions of 'public goods' have been put forward and they vary widely.[4] Here, I intend to arrive at a narrow conception of public good by identifying some features that are sufficient conditions for a good to count as a public good for the purposes of this analysis.[5] The conception of public good that I identify here is not meant to be an exhaustive definition but an analytic tool instrumental to the argument to follow.

In general terms, I will assume that a good that has at least the following features can qualify as a public good: (1) *jointness* (in supply and consumption): if a good is available for one person, it is available for others; its consumption by one does not diminish the consumption by others; (2) *non-excludability*: if a good benefits anyone, no one else can be prevented from doing so; and (3) *indivisibility*: the good cannot be divided into private goods. Examples are clean air, an unspoiled environment, or street lights, although these examples are by no means exhaustive.

A sub-class of public goods of relevance to the analysis to follow includes what some authors have called *compulsoriness*: if the good benefits anyone, it is unfeasible (that is, either impossible or prohibitively costly) to avoid benefiting. Compulsoriness rules out the possibility of opting out. Compulsoriness does not apply to all public goods but only to some. For expository purposes, I will refer to those public goods that include, in addition to the three features mentioned above, the compulsoriness feature *compulsory public goods*, and I will assume that they are a subset of the larger concept of public goods.

In principle, some public goods, to be produced, need the efforts of only a single individual. For example, an individual who carefully maintains the beautiful façade of a heritage house she owns may well be producing a public good that passers-by can enjoy at no cost. However, not every good that counts as a public good can be produced by a single individual. Some public goods need the combined efforts of a collectivity to be secured. Call this the 'collectivity requirement'. Those philosophers who appeal to the collectivity requirement have in mind cases like a group of environmentalists combining their efforts for the preservation of a wilderness area (for example, Casal 1999: 365). Because languages need a number of people to be spoken, maintained, and passed on to further generations, any argument that appeals to public goods to make a case for the preservation of languages would have to assume the collectivity requirement. Therefore, in the analysis that follows I will assume an understanding of public goods that meets the collectivity requirement and I will call this sub-class

[4] For a larger list of characteristics see Cullity (1995), who includes jointness in supply, non-excludability, jointness in consumption, non-rivalness, compulsoriness, equality, indivisibility. Philosophers are far from being unanimous about which of these properties are definitive of publicness. Some have also derived sub-categories, and distinguish 'collective goods' from public goods (for example, Miller 1999; Beckerman and Pasek 2001); others refer to those public goods that have the compulsoriness feature as 'pure public goods' (for example, Arneson 1982). A useful guide on the public goods literature is found in the appendix of Cullity (1995).

[5] For a thorough review of the literature of definitions of 'public goods' and a comprehensive set of features that is arrived at by combining all the definitions, see Cullity (1995: 32–4).

of public goods *collectively produced public goods*. Combining the two additional features, I will work in what follows with a conception of public good that could be called, for ease of exposition, *collectively produced compulsory public goods*.

It is possible to see single languages as public goods, each varying in the benefits they provide in terms of the communication potential they offer to their speakers. Abram de Swaan (2001) develops one such conception of single languages as public goods, which has been of particular interest to political philosophers. Philippe Van Parijs (2002), for example, makes a similar argument about how an international lingua franca like English can be viewed as a public good and then discusses different models for the fair distribution of costs and benefits regarding this type of public good. But it is also possible to regard the diversity of languages itself as a public good, an asset in the sense that biodiversity is often presented as one. When ecologists of language, such as Nettle and Romaine, stress the importance of the protection of world languages, the underlying assumption is that there is something globally beneficial in the preservation of linguistic diversity, something that adds a positive value to human lives. This assumption and its moral implications are what I wish to consider here.

There are several ways in which one can view the preservation of linguistic diversity around the world as being beneficial to the larger world community of human beings. One such benefit is *aesthetic appreciation*, which gives rise to what I will call an *argument from aesthetic value*. There are many different languages and, as a result, many different ways of expressing views or emotions, or even of producing art. Consider different ways of creating art or engaging in artistic performance, such as writing and/or reading poetry. Indeed, some forms of poetry are associated with particular languages. Haiku is a particular form of poetry that we associate with Japanese culture. It is a kind of poetry that is written in Japanese. Although Haiku is now produced in other languages, we wouldn't have known about it if the Japanese language were dead before the West made contact with Japanese culture. We can therefore imagine a world in which we would have never known some of the cultural and artistic elements if some languages had been lost before we came into contact with them. And these may be features of our lives that we have aesthetic reasons to appreciate, but that we often take for granted. When we factor in all the things we value aesthetically, this kind of world, although imaginable, would be much less preferable, for purely aesthetic reasons, to the world that offers all the aesthetic enjoyments.

But, one may object, aesthetic needs that give meaning to our lives are not strong or urgent enough to make a moral claim for their protection. It would be implausible, for example, to expect public funds to be used to protect only those goods that have a merely aesthetic value for those who benefit from them. A purely aesthetic appreciation may have an urgency for the art enthusiast who has the means to visit the Van Gogh Museum in Amsterdam one day and attend a concert in Salzburg the next. But does this type of aesthetic value generate obligations? Surely, aesthetic needs rank lower than more urgent needs, such as those of people who do not enjoy protection of their basic liberties, or the poorest members of society, or those who have to work under unacceptable conditions.

For these and other reasons, philosophers have been reluctant to derive moral obligations from mere aesthetic appreciation, and this applies to the concept of public goods. Consider the following example. An amateur botanist puts a strikingly beautiful orchid display on his window. In so doing, he produces a public good that people walking down the street can enjoy at no cost. It would be an odd request, however, to ask pedestrians to contribute to the production of this good, as public as the good in question may be. As Richard Arneson (1982: 621) puts it, in another similar example, fashionable pedestrians may well be producing a public good that others can enjoy but 'cooperatively organized fashionable dressers cannot claim the right to enforce a charge against ogling pedestrians'. For Arneson, this is so because 'the value supplied is less than the disvalue of enforced collection of costs'. The example of the enthusiastic botanist is an analogous one, and therefore is vulnerable to the critique phrased by Arneson. The underlying rationale, in both cases, relies not only on the small change the benefit supplies but also on the diversity of people's preferences. Some people would not be willing to contribute even a very small sum due to personal preferences, and given that the benefit is so small an enforced collection of costs would be hard to justify.

So, for a public good argument to be viable, the good identified, and the benefit it provides, has to be substantial enough to justify obligations. In other words, the value for each individual should be greater than their fair share of the cost they might have to pay for securing it. Purely aesthetic values simply make little change to justify obligations. They are also an object of (reasonable) disagreement, due to different private preferences. Now environmental goods have a purely aesthetic dimension too, and they are also subject to varying preferences. Some may like the experience of idyllic scenery in the countryside, others may find seeing a Woody Allen film in a downtown cinema more rewarding and worthwhile. It is difficult, at least for those steeped in the liberal tradition, to make moral prescriptions based on things people can reasonably differ over due to their personal preferences. But arguments for the protection of environmental goods are not based merely on aesthetic value. They are justified precisely because they do not just have aesthetic value, although they have that too, but because they have, in addition, a more vital function in the well-being of humans as well as of the world in which we live.

Similarly, the ecological position regarding linguistic diversity leaves room for an appeal to *scientific value*, which can be shown to have more urgency for the well-being of the whole of humanity than purely aesthetic appreciation. The *argument from scientific value*, as I will call it for ease of exposition, is often invoked by supporters of biolinguistic diversity. Nettle and Romaine, for example, give a specific account of how indigenous languages can contribute to scientific advancement. The vocabulary of a language, they argue, is an inventory of items a culture talks about, categorized 'to make sense of the world and to survive in a local ecosystem' (2000: 60). Science is, partly, about categorizing objects in the world and developing taxonomies. Different classificatory systems in specific languages not yet well known to us may represent different ways of organizing local knowledge, which then can give useful clues about the world (Nettle and Romaine 2000: 69–70).

Knowledge about small languages that are not yet well known to us, ecologists of language insist, is scientifically valuable. For example, if a plant that is not yet known to us and is already known by a culture that has a name for the plant, then that information can be used to learn about that particular plant, which in turn can potentially be used to cure a disease that is not yet well understood. The preservation of languages on the planet can be beneficial in the long run, the argument goes, because they can give information that can be scientifically useful for the whole of humanity. This information can be (1) about the language or the people who are speaking it, useful to linguists or anthropologists, or (2) about something other than the speakers of that language, useful to researchers in other fields, and perhaps beneficial for the whole of humanity, as in the example of the plant that can potentially help find a cure for a disease.

We need to be cautious, however, in making this claim regarding scientific value, for it can easily be overstated. That is, it is important not to conflate (a) a *probable* loss of useful scientific knowledge and ( b) an *actual* loss of the same order. To say that small languages of which we have little knowledge may prove useful for scientific reasons in the long run is not tantamount to concluding that they are actually useful or that we actually lose specific knowledge if small languages are lost. We may, or we may not. Neil Levy (2001: 377) stresses this characteristic of the scientific value argument and holds that, as an argument from probability, it gives us only weak reasons for their protection. Though there may be a high probability, Levy argues, 'that one of the many thousands of languages will turn out to be useful in the manner envisaged, there is a much lower chance that any particular language will have this property' (2001: 377). If the value we place on languages is proportional to the probability of the epistemic value they present us, then it gives us only a weak reason, Levy concludes, to regret their passing.

Although I ultimately remain sympathetic with Levy's scepticism about the concern with language loss, his reasons for being sceptical here are not sound. His criticism of this argument is based on a misunderstanding of the nature of our values regarding languages and cultures. I don't think it is desirable to hold that languages (and cultures) are valuable if they are useful and less valuable if they are less useful. If this is what Levy implies, it's misleading, for it encourages us to rank languages in terms of utility considerations. If he is in fact not implying this but offering a *reductio ad absurdum*, then his reasoning is muddled. The scientific value argument is not an argument from probability in the way Levy describes; he misrepresents the role probability plays in the reasoning. Although probability factors in, it does so only to highlight lack of knowledge, not to rank the value of languages (or cultures) by reference to utility measurements. As a result, it is simply a prudential argument that suggests the following: since we do not know whether small languages will bring new knowledge that could be beneficial to the larger world community, we have prudential reasons to make an effort not to lose them. By treating probability as a means of ranking languages, Levy's analysis pushes the argument to an extreme that forces us to admit that we have weak reasons to regret the loss of languages. It would have been an apt *reductio* if he were correct about the role of probability in the argument. There may be other reasons to remain sceptical about the value of global linguistic diversity, but in so far as defenders of diversity make a prudential argument of this sort, then their reasoning up to this point is fair. But we need to be careful not to lose sight of the fact that it is a prudential argument.[6]

The benefits of linguistic diversity described thus far are of course controversial. Many will not be convinced that the (prudential) argument from scientific value is strong enough to convincingly supplement the already weak argument from aesthetic value. Others will think that these benefits are too speculative. But the argument from scientific value is the strongest case an ecological position can make, and its defenders put a great deal of emphasis on it (for example, Nettle and Romaine 2000: Ch. 3). Another reason to value diversity can be offered from a liberal perspective, which could potentially supplement the ecological reasons. We have reason to care about languages of the world, the liberal can say, because some people (for example, users of the languages) take them to be worthy, and a non-threatened multiplicity of languages gives people the choice of using them and passing them on to further generations. Surely it is preferable for pretty much everyone to live in a world that offers choices to people rather than in one that does not. The (liberal) reason to care about linguistic diversity, then, would be about respecting what other individuals take to be meaningful to them. These considerations indicate that, although controversial (that is, debatable), there are reasons to care about global linguistic diversity.

To sum up, I have sketched two ways in which global linguistic diversity can be valued, and both appeal to the ecologists of language: *aesthetic appreciation* and *scientific value*. I have also identified a third reason, *respect for individual choice*, that might come from a liberal to potentially supplement the concerns of the ecologists. In light of these reasons, it may be possible to qualify diversity of languages as a public good. It may well be possible to come up with other types of reasons, but for present purposes these suffice to show why some people argue that linguistic diversity around the world should be valued. Global linguistic diversity as a public good would meet the four criteria as follows:

(1) *jointness (of supply and consumption)*: the supply and consumption of the benefits that may come from the protection of small languages would not

---

[6] I am in full agreement with Levy, however, that the use of the language of genocide to characterize language loss is an overstatement.

diminish the availability for others, nor would it diminish its consumption by others;

(2) *non-excludability*: if the protection of linguistic diversity benefits anyone, no one else can be prevented from being benefited;

(3) *indivisibility*: the benefits that may come from linguistic diversity cannot be divided up into private goods to be privately owned; and

(4) *compulsoriness*: it would be unfeasible to avoid benefiting from linguistic diversity.

If the reasons to view global linguistic diversity as a public good are sound, then this leads us to consider the fair distribution of the costs and benefits regarding its production and consumption. The sceptic might still insist that these reasons are too speculative. There are many ways of spending public money to encourage, for example, scientific discovery; is protection of small languages a strong candidate for the optimal use of scarce resources? But a clarification needs to be made here. Of course, some ecologists of language simply claim that the languages of the world should be saved at all costs; like some of their environmentalist counterparts, they make cataclysmic predictions about the consequences of environmental decline. But the jump from the reasons to care about linguistic diversity to the blunt statement 'diversity ought to be protected' is not a safe move. It is too vulnerable to the reasonable objections of the sceptic. A safer, and more sophisticated, alternative for the ecologist of language is to make a fairness argument. If there is a public good that is being produced, then it makes sense to think about the fair terms of distributing costs and benefits. I will now turn my attention to a principle—the *principle of fairness*—that is often invoked as a principle to guide such distribution. I will assume that, if we can plausibly apply this principle, then this can be a basis for defenders of global linguistic diversity to talk about linguistic justice.

## 3. The Principle of Fairness

The principle of fairness can be summarized as follows. If some people are contributing to the production of a public good, one should not simply enjoy the benefits without contributing one's share of the cost of the production of that good. The intuitive rationale of the principle, in Rawls's words (1972: 112), is that:

when a number of persons engage in a mutually advantageous cooperative venture according to rules, and thus restrict their liberty in ways necessary to yield to advantages for all, those who have submitted to these restrictions have a right to a similar acquiescence on the part of those who have benefited from their submission. We do not gain from the cooperative labours of others without doing our fair share.

The principle of fairness is often invoked in arguments in support of unspoiled environment and the protection of biodiversity (Casal 1999). Imagine that there is a spectacular waterfall near a town. At the weekends the inhabitants of the town go to the waterfall to picnic, swim, and enjoy the natural beauty of the area, but as a result pollute it. Imagine now that a group of environmentalists clean the area, thereby producing a public good. But the next weekend the picnickers come back and pollute again. It is not fair, the environmentalists could argue, that they are making efforts to maintain the beauty of the waterfall, which is something everyone benefits from, if those people who benefit from it do not contribute to its production, and in fact threaten it by polluting. Is it morally acceptable to free-ride on other people's cooperative efforts? A possible solution would be to make the waterfall and its environs a regulated and publicly owned park, which relies on public funds (not the charitable efforts of a group of environmentalists) for the maintenance and preservation of its natural beauty. In that case, Rawls's requirement of cooperative effort based on the principle of fairness would be met.[7]

It is not implausible to appeal to the principle of fairness for the preservation of linguistic diversity around the world in a way akin to its use in environmental arguments. I have tried to show that global linguistic diversity can be viewed as an asset that the whole of humanity does benefit from, and have done so by focusing on the benefits that it is thought to bring. Now, this conception of linguistic diversity as a public good can be further developed by focusing on how it is produced.

Linguistic minorities and speakers of small languages around the globe, by making efforts to maintain their language, by speaking it and passing it on to further generations, are contributing to the production of the public good that linguistic diversity is. They play a part in the maintenance of linguistic diversity on the planet. Most of us enjoy the short- and long-term benefits of this public good. For example, we benefit from this by living in a multilingual world that (1) provides us with the aesthetic and scientific values praised by defenders of the ecological position and (2) respects what other people take to be meaningful to them. But by being speakers of already secure languages, we do not participate in the production of this public good—we do not make any efforts to learn these languages and pass them on to further generations, nor is there a system of linguistic taxation that allows a transfer of funds to distribute the costs fairly[8]—despite the fact that we enjoy its benefits. In fact, speakers of stronger languages do not just fail to contribute to the production of this public good. They threaten it. When small languages are increasingly marginalized in the face of stronger, more widely spoken languages, it becomes more and more costly and more difficult for its speakers to maintain them: hence the threat of language death. If nothing is done, they would either have to give up their language or shoulder the extra efforts that are required to maintain the increasingly marginalized language. Since the defenders of the ecology of language position do not want

---

[7] For Rawls (1972: 267), financing public goods must be taken over by the state and some binding rule requiring payment must be enforced.

[8] For a proposed linguistic tax scheme, see Philippe Van Parijs (2002).

languages to be lost, it is reasonable for them to look for ways to make the maintenance of those languages at risk more equitable, that is, for better, fairer terms of securing the public good in question.

For the production of the public good to be secured in fair terms, the principle of fairness would impose some obligations on those who are not contributing directly to its production, such as speakers of secure, dominant languages. I shall not discuss here what exactly those obligations might be, for I am mainly interested at this stage in the structure and validity of the arguments. They could be policy measures to give greater language rights or protections to smaller (minority) languages applicable locally, or a system of transfer of funds to provide minority language education, and so forth. Whatever those specific measures may be, implicit in the principle of fairness is that public goods entail moral obligations. The underlying idea is that it is simply not fair to free-ride on other people's efforts to produce a public good that everyone enjoys, and speakers of dominant languages owe to small-language communities some forms of language rights on those grounds.

## 4. How Acceptable is the Application of the Principle of Fairness to Global Linguistic Diversity?

A number of questions could be raised against the application of the principle of fairness to the issue of global linguistic diversity. I will consider here three objections that a full defence of a public good argument would have to address, and will indicate how a defender could meet them.

### Voluntary Acceptance Condition

One of the most debated aspects of the principle of fairness is the moral relevance of people's acceptance of the benefits that a public good offers. In Rawls's formulation, one of the requirements of the principle of fairness is that it is unfair to *willingly* enjoy the benefits of a public good without contributing one's share in its production. What counts as willing receipt of the benefits, and how relevant it is morally, have been a matter of debate amongst philosophers. The most well-known objection to the principle of fairness is Robert Nozick's. One cannot, Nozick argues, 'whatever one's purposes, just act so as to give people benefits and then demand (or seize) payments' (Nozick 1974: 95). The voluntary acceptance condition is broadly defined as follows: it is not enough that a public good is produced, to justify obligations; those who benefit from it should willingly accept it.

How, then, could a public-good argument for linguistic diversity respond to the voluntary acceptance condition? In the waterfall example, the inhabitants of the town have a habit of going out of their way to receive the benefits of the public good that the group of environmentalists produce by keeping it clean.

It is fair to assume that they willingly accept the benefits. But it is one thing to go out your way to receive (or enjoy) a good, the sceptic would point out, and quite another if someone forcibly gives it to you and then asks for a contribution. Even then, a hard-nosed sceptic would insist, there will be people who simply never go to the waterfall, due to other preferences, or go there so seldom that the cost they would have to pay to the cooperative scheme would be higher than the benefit they receive (unlike in the case of avid consumers of the waterfall area).

The objection would apply to the case of global linguistic diversity as follows. It is not clear how anyone does (or could) show their voluntary acceptance of either aesthetic or scientific benefits of global linguistic diversity that would jus- tify the application of the principle of fairness. There are two ways of address- ing this type of objection. One would be to argue, through a complicated and controversial empirical discussion, that people do (or could) in fact show their voluntary acceptance of the benefits. But that would be a daunting task to undertake in this context. Another way of addressing the challenge of voluntary acceptance would be to engage in a schematic analysis of the principle of fair- ness and argue, through a reformulation of the principle if necessary, that some public goods cannot be voluntarily accepted or rejected, but they nevertheless generate obligations (for example, Arneson 1982).

In order to show this, it may be useful to look at the features of the public good more closely. Many definitions of public goods include non-excludability and compulsoriness, which I too have included. Every public good meets the non-excludability criterion. In the waterfall example, the good is there and it is unfeasible to prevent people from enjoying it as long as they want to do so; they can go there and spend time or look at it from a distance. But not every public good meets the compulsoriness criterion. The waterfall example doesn't. I may choose to stay home and read books, maybe because I don't like the noisy crowds, or may divert my eyes from the waterfall each time I am at a visible dis- tance. I may not be excluded from enjoying it, but my enjoyment is not com- pulsory. But there are public goods, like clean air or safety from infectious diseases, that cannot avoid the compulsoriness criterion (the avid environ- mentalist may even be able to argue that this applies to the waterfall too but this is beside the point). In those cases, the public good is there and you cannot avoid benefiting from it. By being born at a certain time rather than earlier, you bene- fit from the existence of penicillin even if you never had any serious infection that required the use of it, as in the case of pneumonia, which used to be a com- mon cause of death in pre-penicillin times. This is a feature that comes from the compulsoriness criterion. Some (for example, Arneson 1982) have argued that compulsoriness generates obligations.

The way we benefit from global linguistic diversity, the defender of the public- good approach can respond, meets the compulsoriness criterion. We just benefit from the existence of different languages, their existence gives us a safety we have reasons to protect. We don't even need to know, or be in contact with, any of these languages to benefit from them, just as we don't need to know, or actually use, all of the species of plants and animals to be the beneficiaries of their safe existence in our ecosystem. We may benefit from them without realizing that we do. I get through every day without thinking that I live in a place and a time safe from infectious disease, being in good health; I don't realize that I in fact do benefit from it, but the truth is I do. We can therefore safely conclude that the aesthetic and scientific benefits of global linguistic diversity can be shown to meet the compulsoriness criterion, and as a result generate obligations. This is one way a defender of the public good argument may try to meet the voluntary acceptance condition.

## Intentional Production Condition

Although many discussions of the principle of fairness focus on the terms of the consumption of a public good to determine which ones are morally relevant, few of them focus on the moral relevance of the terms of their production (Casal 1999: 368). However, it is possible to argue that the conditions under which a good is produced can put constraints on public good arguments. For example, one could raise the question whether it meets what I will call the *intentional production condition*.

The intentional production condition, as I see it, takes the following schematic form: the production of a public good generates obligations only if it is produced intentionally and with considerable costs to those who are producing it. Suppose that a good meets the publicness criteria. But it happens to be the by-product of activities that some people engage in because they simply enjoy them. These people may have reasons to value these activities, but the reasons are independent of the production of the public good. This puts restrictions, some have remarked, on the application of the principle of fairness.

Paula Casal gives a succinct summary of such constraints in her argument against the extension of the public good argument to procreation. Against the claim that the whole society should contribute to the cost of having and raising children on the grounds that procreation produces a public good that we all benefit from, Casal focuses on intentions and costs. Regarding intentions, she argues that parents do not normally decide to have children to produce a public good; these beneficial effects are unintended consequences of their decision. As for costs, she argues that parents do not regard having children as a cost, since they attach a positive value to having children. By contrast, when environmentalists fit a catalytic converter, they do not attach a positive value to the fitting of the converter. She then asks:

If they wanted converters anyway—say, because they developed a converter fetish—and converters happen to have the unintended beneficial effect of reducing pollution, should we think that the principle of fairness applies? (Casal 1999: 367)

The intuitive idea behind this is that we do not usually think that we are under an obligation to reward people for a benefit they produced unintentionally, when doing something they already prefer, and that is not a costly, burdensome activity for them, but an enjoyable experience. If the good is something that people already prefer doing and do not view it as a costly thing to do (or the enjoyment overrides the cost), though the general benefit is the by-product, this fact would put constraints on obligations generated by that good.

The intentional production condition could apply to linguistic diversity as follows. It is not clear that speakers of small languages are producing the good intentionally. We do not usually regard, the sceptic could remark, learning and speaking one's own language, and passing it to further generations, as an activity intentionally pursued to produce a public good. Moreover, speaking one's language, or a language one is comfortable with, is an enjoyable activity to which people attribute a positive value. It is not comparable to the activity of, say, fitting a converter for environmental purposes. It is not clear, the sceptic would conclude, why speakers of dominant languages owe something to speakers of small languages on the moral grounds laid out by the principle of fairness.

Again, there are two ways to respond to this challenge. One is to question the degree of constraint this condition puts on obligations. The other is to engage in a discussion to show that members of small linguistic communities do in fact meet this condition, perhaps by showing that there is considerable cost involved in their efforts to maintain their language, and it is not something done effortlessly. I think both forms of reasoning are promising here.

I don't think it is easy to establish how much restriction, if at all, the intentional production condition is supposed to put on obligations. Certain activities meet the condition. Recall the orchid display as an example of accidental public good. If we follow the intentional production condition, pedestrians are under no obligation to contribute to costs of the production of the public good, not just because of the small change it makes in their lives. Even if it made a more substantial change, it would still not impose obligations because it is the result of a gratifying activity the amateur botanist already loves doing and is not costly. I recognize this is a difficult question that would require a lengthier discussion. But I believe it suffices for present purposes to mention that our intuitions tell us that there are activities, provided that the benefit they offer is substantial enough, that would nevertheless put obligations on others even if they are pursued for their own sake.

Moreover, and this leads to the second way of addressing the challenge, people may produce some goods which might involve considerable effort or costs even though those who produce it were not doing so with the intention of producing a public good. With regard to language, even if one supposes that speaking one's language, or a language one is comfortable with, is an enjoyable and rewarding activity for many, it involves no effort or costs to its speakers in so far as the language spoken is secure, powerful, and under no major competitive pressure. However, for speakers of small languages under the competitive pressure of more powerful languages, maintaining the small, less-used language is seldom effortless or costless.

## The Free-Rider Problem

Another problem that arises in public good arguments that appeal to the principle of fairness is the 'free-rider' problem. When the public is large there is a temptation for each individual to try to avoid contributing his or her share. Whatever one person does, the action will not significantly affect the amount produced (Rawls 1972: 267). The free-rider problem arises from a dilemma that Parfit has called *contributor's dilemma*. In Parfit's words,

It can be true for each person that, if he helps, he will add to the sum of benefits, or expected benefits. But only a very small portion of the benefit he adds will come back to *him*. Since his share of what he adds will be very small, it may not repay his contribution. It may thus be better for each if he does not contribute. This can be so whatever others do. But it would be worse for each if fewer others contribute. And if none contribute this would be worse for each than if all do. (Parfit 1986: 61, emphasis in original) [9]

As a result, those who benefit from a public good (or a cooperative scheme) are likely to reason as follows: either other persons will contribute sufficient amounts to assure continued provision of the good, or they will not. In either case the individual is better off if she does not contribute. If the individual does not contribute as a result of this kind of reasoning, she counts as a free rider (Arneson 1982: 622).

The free-rider problem has concerned many philosophers interested in public goods. For some the free-rider problem is raised as a challenge to public good arguments that invoke the principle of fairness. It is viewed as a problem that potentially weakens the appeal of the argument or sets limits to its application. For others, it is invoked as a problem to justify the application of the principle of fairness. Note that the free-rider problem plays a pivotal role in the formulation of the principle of fairness. Richard Arneson, for example, uses the potential of free-rider conduct to show that obligations arise under the principle of fairness when he says 'where free-rider conduct is possible, there obligations arise, under the principle on fairness, prohibiting such conduct' (1982: 623). It is an interesting feature of the free-rider problem that it has, almost paradoxically, this double function in public good arguments.

The public good argument about linguistic diversity as I have described it thus far is vulnerable to the challenge that arises from the free-rider problem. But it is

[9] Rawls suggests that the financing of public goods, then, must be taken over by the state. But there are problems with crudely applying the model of a liberal egalitarian society to the international community. A full rehearsal of these problems is not within the scope of this paper, but suffice it to mention here that we do not yet have the rudiments of a world state.

not less vulnerable than analogous arguments for the preservation of environmental public goods. The same problem arises with environmental public goods. However, this does not make the public good argument about linguistic diversity a bad one. My purpose was to show that, if we accept a public good argument about biodiversity defended by environmentalists, we could also make a similar argument without incoherence about linguistic diversity. The free-rider problem would have a similar role in a conception of linguistic justice based on public goods and the principle of fairness.

I have raised three possible objections that a defender of a public good argument for global linguistic diversity needs to address. There may be reasonable disagreement over how these objections are to be addressed. I tried to suggest possible ways out that a full defence of this position would need to develop. Ultimately, I believe these challenges are surmountable. I will now turn my attention to what the politics of global linguistic diversity as a public good would look like; this will raise two further objections that are more difficult to answer, as will become clear, than the objections thus far considered.

## 5.  The Politics of Linguistic Diversity as a Public Good

The analysis so far has shown that a defence of linguistic justice can be made by an appeal to concepts and arguments developed in environmental ethics. A public good argument can plausibly be formulated in order to justify obligations to contribute to the maintenance of linguistic diversity conceived of as a global asset analogous to global environmental assets, and it is coherent, as I tried to show, in its schematic form.

Despite its appeal, however, I believe the general approach has limitations when political implications are considered. I see at least two weaknesses that emerge from the public good approach, and by extension from the worry about language loss, to linguistic justice. One concerns the inadequacy of the approach as a conception of justice due to its limited scope. The other concerns the illiberal implications that would make a politics of linguistic diversity as a public good potentially intolerable.

First, a theory construed on the value of global linguistic diversity rests on empirically misleading assumptions and does not adequately capture many forms of what one might intuitively call 'linguistic injustice'. If we want to attend to those forms of injustice, we need to distinguish between 'language loss' on the one hand and 'linguistic injustice' on the other, for there is no inherent correlation between the two concepts. Although language loss in the world is often related to the unjust internal institutional structures of countries, there are cases of linguistic injustice without language loss (for example, cases where members of a linguistic minority claim recognition even though their language isn't threatened).

Although many small languages are declining, it is not the case that all minority languages are threatened languages. Although some minority languages also happen to be 'threatened languages', there are many contexts in which the language of a minority group is not threatened in the larger context of world languages. Consider the Canadian context. French is in no danger of dying as a language in a global context, but it is a minority language in Canada. Spanish, to give another example, is by no means under any threat of decline, but Spanish-speakers in the United States form a linguistic minority. And these are not just obscure examples but representative cases of linguistic diversity. This alone indicates that there is no inherent correlation between minority languages and language decline, loss, or death. Even if all languages in the world were secured and a fair distribution of burdens and benefits applied, there could still be inequalities between linguistic groups, and language politics would still be a relevant topic worth discussing. If we rely solely on the public good argument, the theory will run the risk of remaining silent about some important categories of linguistic issues. This is one way in which the argument from public goods in support of diversity is inadequate.[10]

There are also cases of language loss without injustice (for example, cases of very small linguistic groups whose members voluntarily choose to integrate into the dominant linguistic group), which brings me to the other limitation that concerns the potential implications that would be unacceptable under a liberal programme. It is important to note that the argument I have sketched is really a *fairness* argument in that it ascribes and justifies moral obligations with regard to the distribution of costs and benefits. It is not, for instance, an incentive argument that would aim to encourage, through incentives, the maximization of the number of languages on the planet. So it is primarily concerned with obligations on those who benefit from the public good, in this case the speakers of powerful, secure languages. It does not, itself, extend obligations to small language communities to maintain their language. But although it does not extend such obligations, it may nevertheless have those implications.

It is possible to imagine, once responsibilities are distributed, speakers of secure languages addressing the small language communities as follows: 'Look, we agreed to contribute to the costs of maintaining your language, now you must continue to maintain it.' There may be (and are) cases in which a language is too small or dispersed to provide adequate opportunities for its speakers, or those speakers may reasonably decide to raise their children in another language that gives more opportunities to its speakers. Unlike in the case of endangered species, it is possible to imagine a situation in which a language at

---

[10] One could try to respond to this by saying that minority languages, even if they are not at risk globally, are endangered locally. But that would be a bad response, for there are many cases in which that is not even true. The number of Spanish speakers is growing in the United States, not shrinking, and the Spanish language is under no risk of declining locally in, say, California. The issue in those contexts is not one of language loss but one of social marginalization.

risk becomes extinct but its individual speakers are doing well, perhaps even better than when they were speaking the now moribund language. But it is not possible to think, or even say, 'the species of lions has become extinct but the individual lions are doing well'(!). The bio-linguistic diversity position does not allow us to make this kind of distinction[11] and forces us to think that, unless we do everything we can to save endangered languages, something will seriously go wrong. But it is an important distinction liberals would want to make when drawing a line between what is and isn't permissible with respect to protecting languages. A possible implication of a politics of linguistic diversity as a public good might be, especially if people are very keen on saving languages, what some theorists have called 'ethnic incarceration', which is intolerable under a liberal programme. It would be a questionable practice, for example, if small language communities are pressured to preserve languages they no longer wish to use so as to preserve a 'global public good'. For it would be odd to think that the aesthetic and scientific benefits to people in Europe and North America could justify policies that maintained the marginalization of small linguistic groups in Papua New Guinea against their will or interests. Let me emphasize again that the principle of fairness that guides the public good argument as I have described it does not prescribe this. But I remain reluctant to embrace a purely environmentalist approach to linguistic justice in the face of these possible illiberal implications.

Moreover, by worrying about what obligations should be ascribed in order to save endangered languages, environmental approaches overlook what might be going on within linguistic groups. Whether the group puts pressure on its own members to maintain the language, what those pressures are, and whether they contradict principles of liberty, are invisible when a theory of linguistic justice is primarily and only concerned with the well-being of languages or the benefits to others. A politics of global linguistic diversity, by itself, would remain 'toothless', as it were, against possible conservative or illiberal ramifications.

What I tried to show in this chapter is that a coherent basis for linguistic justice that stems from a concern with language loss can be developed using some tools of environmental ethics and social justice. To show this, I laid out the basic elements of what I have called a public good argument for linguistic diversity, and showed the possible ways in which it may try to respond to some of the standard questions that arise in debates regarding public goods. Then, I raised two further questions about possible political implications, which I find are much less easily answered, without questioning the general approach. These considerations do not necessarily delegitimize the general ecological approach to linguistic rights (and obligations), but they justify a certain unease one might have about embracing a theory of linguistic justice based on a worry about

---

[11] This may be evidence that the very idea of trying to equate biodiversity and linguistic diversity is itself not sound.

language loss and the preservation of linguistic diversity akin to biodiversity. It may be possible to further analyse the public good argument and to see if it can be applied locally before constructing a full-fledged theory to be applied globally. But it follows from my analysis that any theory that appeals to those values has to take extra care to address the worries that I have highlighted. And if they cannot be addressed in a satisfactory way, then this would be good enough reason to seek alternative perspectives, regardless of how coherent or logically flawless the schematic form of an environmentalist theory of linguistic justice is.

# 9

# Language Death and Liberal Politics

MICHAEL BLAKE

Consider two stories of linguistic change:

1. The members of a given linguistic community are free to modify and supplement the syntax and vocabulary of the language they have inherited. Over generations, this change becomes quite far-reaching. In the limit case, at time *t*, the language has become such that it could be neither spoken nor understood by a fluent speaker of the original language. (We may posit rapid technological change, encounter with foreign linguistic traditions, and so on as the reasons for this transformation.) The linguistic community, however, continues to exist as a distinct entity. While the language spoken at *t* is not the same language spoken at the start of the tale, it is nonetheless best described *as* a language—rather than as a dialect of some other linguistic tradition.[1]

2. The members of a given linguistic community are similarly free to modify and supplement the syntax and vocabulary of the language they have inherited. Over generations, this change becomes as far-reaching as the change in the story above. The linguistic change, however, involves more and more the adoption of the norms of a foreign linguistic community. Over time, the same results occur; a fluent speaker of the original language could neither understand nor be understood by a fluent speaker at time *t*. In this tale, however, the language spoken at time *t* no longer represents a distinct language. It represents, at best, a dialect of some other language; while minor differences in pronunciation and vocabulary may persist, speakers of the foreign language in question can easily understand and be understood by the descendants of what was originally a distinct linguistic community.

How ought liberal political philosophy understand the political morality of these forms of linguistic change? Our first response, I think, might be to press for more information. The moral quality of such large-scale demographic change always demands an attention to context and detail, and the stories given above abstract from such concerns.

---

[1] The distinction between dialect and language is famously difficult to make; it represents an attempt to differentiate between variations within a linguistic community and distinct linguistic communities themselves. It is open to dispute whether this distinction can be used in any way not involving significant normative and political choices on the part of the user. See Chambers and Trudgill (1980).

Nevertheless, I think it is possible to use these two stories to tease out some intuitions about the morality of linguistic destruction. We have, I think, distinct reactions to the two stories given above. The first story—which we may call *radical alteration without assimilation*—seems to involve certain forms of loss; a certain way of looking at the world, a means of analysing and communicating experience, is lost for ever. Intergenerational communication is made vastly more difficult. Central historical texts can now be understood only in translation. Despite these costs, however, I suspect few of us would regard this pattern of linguistic change as one demanding intervention from the standpoint of liberal politics. A representative of the linguistic community insisting that this process is pernicious and that it ought to be halted by political means before time *t* arrives would likely face a fairly high hurdle before her argument could be accepted.

The second story—which we may call *radical alteration with assimilation*—strikes many of us as morally more problematic. The threat of a given language being at risk of assimilation seems to many thinkers a matter of moral gravity. Linguistic commentators have been most forceful on this subject; David Crystal (2000: vii), for instance, suggests that indigenous language disappearance, if it continues at its present pace, will represent 'the greatest intellectual disaster the planet has ever known'. Political commentators, especially those attempting to articulate a vision of multicultural community, have tended to agree that the threat of assimilation is one demanding political attention (Taylor 1994; Kymlicka 1995a; Patten 2001). If a representative of a linguistic community were to push for political measures designed to slow or halt the process of assimilation, she would likely face a more sympathetic audience than her counterpart above.

The divergence of these two reactions, however, seems somewhat odd. After all, the two cases above seem to share many central elements. In neither case does the *content* of the language at the start of the tale survive. Just as much seems lost when the content is lost by internal revision as when the content is lost by assimilation. A native speaker of the language at the start of the process might have good reason to resent and object to either form of linguistic alteration. After all, from the standpoint of a partisan of the language, it seems hardly relevant whether the language goes out of the world by means of assimilation or by means of some other pattern of linguistic change. In either case, the language itself is gone; if languages can die, then surely either pattern of change counts as language death.[2]

---

[2] The usual definition of 'language death' makes reference to the death of the last speaker for whom a given language is the native tongue. Since my analysis asks about the identity of language over time, it does not easily mesh with this definition; there is no single person who represents 'the last speaker' of a language in any non-problematic way. Nevertheless, I believe it is appropriate to regard radical linguistic alteration as equivalent to language death. If no one exists who presently employs the vocabulary and syntax of a given language as a native tongue, I believe it is appropriate to understand that language as dead, regardless of whether or not some set of people now speak some other language descended from the original one. For discussion of the more orthodox analysis, see Crystal (2000) and Nettle and Romaine (2000).

What I want to defend in the present context, however, is the idea that we are *right* to distinguish between these two cases. The reasons *why* we are right, however, will point the way to a new understanding of how and why liberals ought to be concerned with linguistic preservation. Specifically, I want to establish the following two related theses:

1. The focus of liberal attention should be not on linguistic change itself, but on the causal story explaining the linguistic change; we differentiate the above two cases not because they involve different costs, but because we presume different reasons for the linguistic change which has occurred.
2. The threat of linguistic destruction becomes problematic when this threat exists as a result of domination and discrimination; not all cases of linguistic endangerment, however, can be understood in such a way. The threat of linguistic endangerment is not itself sufficient to trigger any claims from the standpoint of liberal justice.

In defending these two theses, I will limit myself to arguments which are distinctly liberal in character—by which I mean arguments making reference to the interests, goods, and rights of individual persons. Appeals to linguistic communities as rights-bearing entities are ruled out at the outset. I hope, by this limitation, to determine what liberals have reason to believe about linguistic destruction. Liberalism, I believe, can make sense of our intuitions about language death; we have no need to alter our moral ontology in order to answer the questions this topic poses.

I will make my argument in two parts. The first will defend the thesis that we cannot distinguish between the above two cases based upon different costs to individuals. This section will also defend the idea that the difference between these two cases is to be found in the causal story we can infer giving rise to the linguistic vulnerability in question. The final section will introduce, more tentatively, the thesis that not all forms of linguistic vulnerability give rise to a liberal demand for linguistic protection.

## 1. Linguistic Vulnerability: The Costs of Language Death

We might begin our inquiry by examining what other liberal theorists have had to say about the importance of linguistic preservation. What reasons do we have for thinking that the preservation of any given linguistic tradition is important? One simple way of beginning is by examining how language death affects individuals: what the costs are, that is, of the destruction of any given linguistic tradition. Here, three distinct forms of cost might be identified: costs understood in terms of identity and self-description; costs deriving from communicative interests; and costs to the world as a whole deriving from the loss of diversity and knowledge.

## Language and Identity

Language is not simply a neutral means of communication; it forms, for many people, a crucial aspect of self-understanding and social self-description. Linguistic membership, like cultural membership, provides individuals with a means by which they can understand their place in the social world; it provides the possibility of social solidarity based upon shared linguistic traditions. As such, it is natural to think that individuals will find their own goods tied up with the fates of their linguistic community. Charles Taylor (1994), for one, urges that this fact is significant enough to demand a revision of liberal thinking. Individuals are rightly concerned with the fates of their languages, and a liberal theory which cannot account for the moral importance of linguistic survival is a theory we have reason to reject. Thus, liberal theory has a reason to condemn the possibility of language death simply by virtue of the relationship between language and social identity. If this means that liberalism has to alter its self-understanding—if it means, for instance, that liberalism can no longer remain 'neutral' between competing versions of the good—then so much the worse for our earlier, flawed vision of liberal thought.

This analysis, however, fails to make sense of the different forms of radical linguistic alteration discussed above. Radical alteration with assimilation seems to be a chief case in which analyses such as Taylor's are plausible; as Taylor notes, if any goal is axiomatic among a linguistic minority, it is that linguistic assimilation is to be avoided. Radical alteration without assimilation, however, seems harder to understand. What are we to make of analyses such as Taylor's in view of the possibility of internal linguistic reformation? We face, I think, an odd sort of dilemma. To argue that liberalism has reason to respect the desire of the present generation that its language not be altered in the ways described here seems to represent an odd privileging of the present. The current content of any language represents the end result of a historical process of human interaction; there is no such thing as a pure language, unsullied by human choices and historical contingency. Each past generation has left its mark on the content of the language, altering its content from what has come before. To deny the same privilege to any future generation seems to represent a sort of narcissism. It is to take a very natural human desire—that the world we know never change in ways we cannot understand—and transform it into a very flawed political ideal.

The alternative position, however—that partisans of linguistic survival have no reason to reject radical alteration without assimilation—seems similarly difficult to endorse. It would hardly please an advocate of *la survivance* in Quebec to be told that his descendants will speak a language utterly unlike his own, one he could neither speak nor understand; the fact that this language will not be English would represent, at best, cold comfort. Indeed, to the degree that such an advocate were to be comforted by the fact that this future language is not English, we might surmise that his desire for *survivance* begins to resemble resentment rather than linguistic self-identification. Such an advocate says: I do not care what language my descendants speak, so long as it is not English. This position, however, seems very poorly described in terms of linguistic self-identification. It is difficult, at least, to derive support for such a position from the premises of liberal thought.

What all this suggests, I think, is that the two cases we have seen above are not easily distinguished in terms of considerations of identity. If we do have different reactions to the two cases, we must look elsewhere for the reasons why.

## Communicative Interests

Language, as noted above, is more than a mere means for communication; but we should not overlook the fact that it is also a means by which people communicate. As such, individuals have interests in linguistic security which liberals have reason to value. The process of linguistic destruction may have negative effects upon individuals by virtue of their interests in being able to communicate their experiences and being able to understand the communications of others. Will Kymlicka's (1995a) notion of a secure cultural framework as a precondition for autonomy may be employed to buttress this conclusion; if individuals face the prospect of linguistic decay so that they have no community within which to discuss and formulate options, they are not able to act as liberal agents in the manner Kymlicka's theory defends. James Nickel (1995) emphasizes the intergenerational costs from linguistic assimilation; if descendants are not able to discuss ideas and experiences with their elders, an important deliberative arena is lost. Alan Patten (2001), finally, emphasizes the political importance of shared language. Deliberation requires a shared vocabulary and a shared linguistic tradition; rapid linguistic change can undermine the possibilities of democratic self-rule.

These considerations, however, fail to distinguish between the cases presently at issue. Kymlicka's notion of a secure cultural framework depends upon an individual having enough cultural and linguistic materials at her disposal to make informed decisions about the trajectory of her life; this can be provided, it seems, under conditions of gradual linguistic change, so long as every generation has an adequate linguistic framework within which to operate. Indeed, it seems that both of our stories above provide what Kymlicka's theory demands—members of each generation have access to a language sufficient to provide the goods of self-development and autonomous choice. The linguistic alteration in question is slow enough so that no individual member faces a deprivation of needed linguistic tools. Whether the process of change ends in assimilation or internal revision seems quite irrelevant from the standpoint of Kymlicka's theory.

Similar considerations seem to apply to the interests identified by Nickel and Patten. Patten's analysis demands that there be a language with which political self-government can take place; but this is perfectly compatible with gradual linguistic change, and so both with gradual assimilation and with radical internal change. Nickel's analysis, similarly, cannot provide the tools needed to distinguish between the cases. It is, undoubtedly, one of the costs associated with linguistic change that intergenerational communication is made more difficult. This cost, however, seems to exist in both of the cases described above. We cannot explain our divergent reactions based upon such communicative interests.

I should note, here, that Kymlicka, unlike Taylor, can welcome this fact. Kymlicka, more than Taylor, is acutely aware of the possibility that languages can go out of the world in a manner not invoking any moral or political concern. Kymlicka's analysis defends a right, not a duty, of linguistic self-preservation. While members of national minorities have the right to those (liberal) policy tools which are needed to defend their linguistic traditions against the national majority, there is no duty incumbent upon them to make use of these tools. If such individuals choose assimilation, nothing morally problematic has occurred. Indeed, it is precisely on this point that Taylor (1994) accuses Kymlicka of an inability to account for the true moral importance of linguistic survival.

These cases, however, can push us to re-examine the justification given by Kymlicka for some of his political conclusions. The forms of linguistic change involved in these two cases of assimilation may make it more difficult for us to accept Kymlicka's conclusions that distinct linguistic rights are due the members of minority societal cultures. Kymlicka (1995a: 84–93) argues that such rights must be granted to members of distinct societal cultures, based upon the value of cultural membership to those who belong to the culture in question. It is not enough, that is, that individuals be granted adequate cultural and linguistic tools to develop a plan of life; they are entitled to the preservation of the specific cultural context in which they are presently situated—to, that is, their *own* culture, rather than just *a* culture. Kymlicka's full argument, that is, has both an identity component and a communicative component. Kymlicka needs both aspects of his argument to defend the proposition that national minorities are entitled to such policy tools as are needed to allow the preservation of their language and culture. If the members of that culture choose to assimilate, that is their right; but the choice must be made from an antecedent position in which that culture exists as a stable and workable backdrop for deliberation.

These conclusions, however, rest uneasily with the forms of linguistic change described above. Kymlicka's political analysis works well so long as we imagine linguistic conflict as a conflict between societal cultures. In such a conflict, insiders battle outsiders for the right to preserve their linguistic tradition. Assimilation might still result after the gaining of such rights, but we can now be confident that such assimilation would be the result of free decision making against an acceptable range of alternatives. The forms of linguistic change above, however, seem much more complex; there is no *decision* to assimilate—assimilation would be the result of a multitude of smaller linguistic decisions, none of which itself counts as a decision to abandon the linguistic tradition. This pattern of linguistic change makes the analysis of linguistic conflict similarly complex. Linguistic conflict is no longer between insiders and outsiders but between rival views of what being an 'insider' really means. Some individuals identified with the culture will see such small linguistic changes as beneficial, even necessary; other individuals will see such changes as disloyal, unauthentic, or in some other way morally pernicious. Although I cannot defend this conclusion here, it is my belief that linguistic conflict inevitably involves such an internal dimension, in which advocacy is aimed as much at rival views of what the language might become as it is at any competing linguistic tradition. If this is true, and it is this sort of conflict which gives rise to radical linguistic alteration of the sort presented at the beginning, then I think we have some reason to believe that this pattern of linguistic change will not easily fit within Kymlicka's analysis. Kymlicka's argument defends the legitimacy of, for example, official linguistic status for national minorities, based upon the desire of such minorities to preserve their cultures' status as live contexts of choice. It works very well in cases in which linguistic conflict occurs between minority language cultures and the dominant majority culture. The examples I am examining here, however, suggest that in many cases Kymlicka's method will be unable to adjudicate the legitimacy of the demands made by advocates of linguistic protection. Kymlicka's moral analysis of linguistic change is powerful, and I find it much more congenial than the analysis of Taylor; it will not, I think, be sufficient to get us answers in many of the most pressing cases of political reality.

The above conclusions are compressed and tentative; and I should emphasize that Kymlicka, more than most other liberal theorists, is well aware of the complex nature of cultural change. All I suggest at present is that he has not yet dealt with the full implications of these facts for a liberal theory of language. The two cases given here of linguistic change can help us see that more clearly. Kymlicka is well aware that languages must change and develop in order to live. What I suggest here is that these facts may make our defence of linguistic preservation more problematic than Kymlicka allows; how languages live is, frequently, also how languages die.

## Diversity and Knowledge

A final attempt to distinguish between these cases might rely upon the interests, not of the participants in the linguistic tradition, but of the inhabitants of the world as a whole. Each language represents a way of viewing the world as well as a unique human achievement; when any language is destroyed, something of great beauty has gone out of the world. It might be thought, therefore, that the interests of all human persons are at stake in the preservation of endangered languages. The human community as a whole is made vastly more impoverished whenever a distinct linguistic tradition is destroyed (Crystal 2000; Nettle and Romaine 2000).

This sort of analysis seems able to distinguish between the cases given above. After all, in the case of radical alteration with assimilation, a divergent linguistic tradition has gone out of the world: what were originally two languages have now become one. In the case of radical alteration without assimilation, diversity is maintained: what were originally two languages persist as two languages, regardless of how much their contents have been altered. If diversity is a value, it seems that we have reason to distinguish these cases based upon that value.

It is unclear, however, that such diversity is properly understood as a politically relevant form of value (Blake 2000). Diversity, before it can be of use to individuals, must be understood as diversity of available options; diversity has to be a diversity *within* a culture before it can be understood as having a political value. Only when options become realistically available to individuals can a liberal defend diversity as being of political importance.

We often ignore this fact in political argument; we slip between diversity *of* cultures and diversity *in* culture, as if they were equivalent. Thus Philippe Van Parijs (2000*b*) argues for linguistic survival based upon the increased options made open to everyone based upon a diversity of linguistic traditions. The two are not the same, however; we may imagine the distinction between a single diverse culture and a diverse set of constraining, monolithic cultures to make that clear. One involves a diversity of cultures but provides none of the goods by means of which diversity is to be justified as a political value. The other involves diversity within culture—the single culture provides a wide variety of choices and plans for life—but does not provide the diversity of cultures that advocates of linguistic preservation often celebrate. The two forms of diversity are not equivalent. Indeed, efforts to provide the one will often work against the other; to defend a diversity *of* cultures often involves the effort to constrain the influx of foreign cultural materials into any one given culture, and so represents an attempt to preclude a certain form of diversity *in* culture. At the very least, we can say that the justification of linguistic and cultural diversity does not provide us with a simple way of condemning linguistic destruction from within liberal theory.

I do not think, therefore, that the value of diversity is sufficient to explain our divergent reactions to the above cases. While there may be more diversity *of* language in the one case than in the other, this does not seem sufficient to justify any great distinction between the cases from the standpoint of liberal politics. This form of diversity seems to represent, at best, an aesthetic value, not by itself sufficient to explain our differing intuitions. Nor, I think, can the human interest in human knowledge be invoked to explain the difference between the two cases. While one case ends with two languages and the other ends with only one, it should be remembered that in both cases the very same thing is lost—the language spoken by the community in question at the start of our story. There are no longer any individuals for whom that language is the first language; whatever knowledge we have of that language is the sort of knowledge we have of other 'dead' languages. In both cases, something important is lost; but in neither case, I think, does that loss by itself suffice to justify a liberal concern with linguistic preservation. If we are going to justify that concern—and thereby differentiate between the two cases given above—we will have to look elsewhere.

## Causation and Language Death

None of the above considerations, I think, is sufficient to explain our divergent reactions to the two cases. We might, therefore, start again, and examine the problem from another angle: this time by looking not at the costs of language death but at the reasons why such costs have come into the world. What I propose is that we understand the liberal concern with language death not in terms of the costs of language death itself but as an extension of a liberal concern with discrimination and humiliation. Linguistic destruction, on this analysis, does not always represent an evil with which a liberal has reason to be concerned; it will, however, frequently represent an extension and compounding of a previously existing injustice, and as such liberals have good reasons to condemn language death under such circumstances. Identifying such circumstances, however, is not an easy task.

We may begin, however, by looking at this methodology as a means of explaining our divergent reactions to the two cases given above. Assimilation, in our collective experience, is frequently the result of violence, domination, and oppression. Recent history is replete with examples of the deliberate destruction of one linguistic community by another. Radical linguistic alteration ending in assimilation tends, we think, to occur not as a result of individual linguistic choice, but when one more powerful linguistic community has robbed the members of a minority community of all other options. Such a process of injustice can occur as a result of direct political action or as a result of more social and inchoate forms of social pressure and humiliation. It can include forms of discrimination based upon ethnic status, with accompanying pressure for linguistic assimilation, and forms of discrimination based more directly upon linguistic affiliation. What is important to note here is that we have good reason, when faced with a case of assimilation, to be suspicious. Assimilation generally represents a signal that one community is exerting oppressive force over another.

This implication, of course, is defeasible; there is no inherent link between assimilation and injustice. It is simply that our recent history gives us reason to assume the worst until more information is provided. The alternative discussed above, however—radical linguistic change without assimilation—is less familiar to us. We face fewer cases of such linguistic change, and I suspect we have fewer intuitions about how such cases ought to be understood. We are, however, less confident that such cases ought to be understood as morally problematic from a liberal point of view. My contention, then, is that our divergent reactions to such cases stem, not from a difference inherent in the cases themselves, but from our different assumptions about the causal pathways giving rise to such forms of linguistic change. In the case of assimilation, we assume that the process giving rise to assimilation is one which begins with some objectionable form of oppression. This assumption, I think, is not one we have strong reason to make when presented with the alternative case.

What this means, then, is that the difference between such cases has very little to do with the distinct costs to human interests the two cases involve. We are more suspicious of the second case than the first simply because, in our world, cases of assimilation tend to reflect political evils. We ought, however, to regard these reactions not as settled intuitions about the moral distinction between the cases, but as good prima facie assumptions until further evidence can be gathered. As I noted above, our best reaction to such cases might be to press for more information. It is entirely possible for there to be assimilation without injustice; we might take the fate of the Jewish community in China, which responded to political equality by intermarriage and assimilation, as instructive. It is also possible, I think, to imagine a case in which political injustice resulted in radical linguistic change without assimilation. It is, however, reasonable to make the assumptions we do, and ask our opponents to provide us with evidence to the contrary.

This, however, should transform the way in which liberals think about linguistic survival. Language death, we can acknowledge, is always tragic; so, however, is rapid linguistic change of the sort discussed above. Both involve the destruction of a unique way of looking at the world, and both involve significant costs in terms of knowledge, identity, and communication. It is deeply disturbing to think that our descendants will not be able to read our letters except in translation; this fate, however, seems to be one that few of us can avoid, given the rapidity of change within even such 'successful' languages as English (Blake 2002). What I think we have reason to defend is the idea that such costs can result either from the free exercise of reason or from oppression. When these costs arise from the free exercise of the human imagination, as each generation remakes and rethinks the linguistic tools of its parents, then these costs represent an inevitable corollary of the goods of free agency. They represent, I think, a way in which we cannot have all human goods at the same time; the good of freedom brings with it certain necessary tragedies. When these same costs arise from oppression, however, they represent something altogether different. They represent a continuation and amplification of an original social evil. If a linguistic community undergoes assimilation as a result of ethnic prejudice and discrimination, then the world has lost something important; but what matters for our purposes is that it lost it for no good reason: this loss reflects not freedom but oppression. The original wrong is compounded by the irreversible loss to the world.

What all this suggests, however, is that liberal analyses of language preservation have been looking in the wrong place. We cannot read out anything important from the fact of linguistic endangerment itself. Before we can analyse the moral status of such endangerment, we need to look at the reasons for the endangerment. A liberal theory of language death needs to look not simply at the fact of language death but at the causal story explaining such linguistic destruction. What we need, therefore, is some approach helping us to understand what causal pathways properly invoke a liberal concern and what pathways do not. The next section of this paper will attempt a brief and inadequate answer to this appallingly huge question.

## 2. Language Death and Liberal Equality

We may begin, I think, by taking as our premise the simple liberal idea that persons have a moral title to treatment *as* equals—which, we may remember, is not always the same thing as a right to equal treatment in any particular sphere of egalitarian concern. What I want to introduce, that is, is the idea that all the individuals within a political community have a right to be treated as equal participants within that community. This right is highly abstract. It can be made more concrete in political dimensions, as involving a right to certain forms of political participation; it can also be made more concrete with regard to more purely social entitlements, such as the right to show one's face in public without shame (Sen 1992). This latter form of right, I think, is of particular importance to language policy, given the relationship noted above between language and social identity. What I propose to do in the present section, however, is not to attempt a full explication of what liberals have reason to defend in the area of linguistic preservation. What I want to do is examine four ways in which linguistic minorities might experience pressure towards assimilation. If we can analyse these from the standpoint of liberal equality, and ask ourselves which of these causal pathways necessarily involves injustice towards members of linguistic minorities, then we have some preliminary answers about the relationship between linguistic destruction and liberal politics.

The four causal pathways I want to examine are as follows: (1) present discrimination based upon linguistic status; (2) past discrimination based upon linguistic status; (3) refusal to grant official language status within the political sphere; and (4) unequal advantages stemming from minority linguistic status.

### Present Discrimination based upon Linguistic Status

This is, as may be expected, perhaps the easiest case to analyse. The importance of this case, I think, lies primarily in its use in explaining how the evil of language death is to be understood by liberal politics. Take a case in which a linguistic minority faces a hostile political government, eager to unify the members of the political community into a single linguistic entity. As a means to this end, it engages in actions designed to mock and silence those who refuse to speak the majority language. Posters are placed in public squares designed to make the populace see those who speak the minority language as inferior—and, of course, to make the minority-language speakers see themselves as similarly tainted and unequal. Children from the minority linguistic community are urged to see their linguistic heritage as backward and to reject their linguistic pasts as unworthy of a modern citizen. Any number of similar methods might be imagined as tools whereby the minority language might be destroyed; indeed, any number of similar methods have been employed in recent history.

What is instructive here is that these methods fail a simple test of liberal political morality. The state in question is using its political power to say to some members of the political community: you are not worthy of participation as you are. You must change, be transformed, before you can see yourself as equally worthy participants in the joint project of self-rule. Those members of the political community who speak the language in question are given reasons to see themselves as inferior. This, of course, creates pressure towards assimilation. If, over time, the linguistic community disappears as a distinct entity, then the assimilation results from an unjust differentiation within the political community. We may understand our sadness at this assimilation as the sadness experienced in light of a successful injustice; the world has lost something interesting and unique as a result of an illegitimate attempt to divide the populace into more and less worthy members. If the world had experienced the same loss as a result of voluntary interactions—if the minority language went out of the world as a result of intermarriage and voluntary choices—I suspect our reactions would be quite different. Once again, the liberal interest in linguistic preservation looks not simply to the fact of linguistic vulnerability, but to the causal pathway by which such vulnerability is to be explained.

This case, then, is fairly simple; understanding how such a case is to extended, however, is much more complex. It is not always clear what counts as an illegitimate form of discrimination; for every clear example, there are any number of cases whose status is more difficult to determine. There are two things which might be noted to introduce this complexity. The first is that there does not seem to be any need for state discrimination for the causal pathway to be one liberals have reason to reject. Social structures such as caste systems can, in and of themselves, prevent political equality by giving people reasons to see themselves as less than full participants in the political community. Such structures can be condemned by a liberal theory even if the political state does nothing to perpetuate or defend such structures. The second thing to note is that injustice cannot be read off from the simple perception of injustice. It is not enough that the members of a given community feel themselves to be the victims of oppression; some more intersubjective justification must be given before the oppression is determined to be real (Margalit 1997). The deterioration of social dominance, for example, is frequently felt as a threat—as when anglophone Californians complain that their language is under assault by the increased use of Spanish in Californian businesses and neighbourhoods. This complaint, however sincerely made, seems more a reflection of privilege lost than of injustice imposed. Similar considerations can be introduced more generally; we need a theory by which we might understand what counts as an illegitimate form of linguistic oppression. We cannot take any linguistic group's claim that it is under assault from external forces as sufficient.

Articulating such a theory, of course, is beyond the scope of the present chapter. I will be happy if I am able here to articulate some conclusions I believe such a theory would have to accept. As such, we can now proceed to examine some more complex situations in which linguistic communities might experience pressure towards assimilation.

## Past Discrimination

I think it is plausible that the vulnerability of most endangered languages stems ultimately from some form of injustice; I think it is also plausible that the form of injustice most explanatory of such endangerment is historical rather than present. This is not to deny the continued existence of discrimination towards linguistic minorities such as, say, aboriginal communities in Canada. It is to say, rather, that the chief injustice giving rise to the weakened nature of aboriginal linguistic communities is the historical injustice of colonization rather than currently occurring acts of prejudice and discrimination. There are multiple explanations for the imminent death of many indigenous languages; the most important, I think, is the historical fact of empire, without which the distinction between indigenous and colonizer could have no meaning.

The question thus arises: can we employ such historical injustice as a means by which we can understand current linguistic endangerment as problematic? The answer, I think, is a qualified 'yes'. It is extraordinarily difficult to articulate the precise means in which historical injustice is to be understood (Waldron 1992). Nevertheless, we can easily explain the plight of many aboriginal communities with reference to patterns of exploitation and theft originating many centuries ago. Despite the difficulties involved in counterfactual analyses, it is possible for us to say that this historical injustice is at least partly causally responsible for the current underdevelopment of groups such as Aboriginal Canadians. Linguistic destruction resulting from such a process might be understood as the culmination of a historical evil; a loss to the world ultimately traced to an illegitimate act of domination and colonization. We may, therefore, understand our condemnation of such linguistic endangerment as a corollary to our condemnation of colonization itself.

There are, however, a few things which this analysis forces upon us. One is that the survival of the aboriginal language is not the chief evil with which we are concerned; this evil, rather, represents the culmination of a larger historical evil—a loss to the world brought about by a larger process of social marginalization and oppression. What this suggests, I think, is that we can legitimately focus on the preservation of aboriginal languages only as part of a package of responses designed to counter and repair the damages of colonization. The lingering evils of colonization include the continued underdevelopment and immiseration of aboriginal communities. We have, I think, a duty to focus on these evils as much as on the preservation of linguistic traditions. Linguistic endangerment is a problem for liberals only when it is brought about as a result of other evils, whether historical or current; we have a duty, I think, to remedy the underdevelopment of aboriginal communities. If this is accomplished, and the members of a given aboriginal community choose to abandon their linguistic traditions for English, I think the rest of us have no right to complain. Most of us expect, however, that there is no reason to expect that such an abandonment would occur except under conditions of lingering inequality and injustice—and there is no reason to infer from the present endangerment of aboriginal languages that their users have no desire to see them preserved.

What this means, I think, is that successful arguments to the conclusion that linguistic preservation is demanded will have to appeal to some injustice as the causal origin of the endangerment; while this injustice can take both present and historical forms, the latter will likely predominate. This should not, I think, take us too much by surprise. Indeed, I think the continued influence of historical injustice runs through much of our current thinking about multicultural politics. Will Kymlicka's distinction between societal cultures and immigrant groups, for instance, seems arbitrary until it is re-described in terms of historical injustice. Kymlicka (1995a) argues that groups which once had a defined territory and a complete culture, but which were overcome by colonial force, have strong entitlements to linguistic rights; groups which cross the border voluntarily, however, are given a much less substantive package of linguistic guarantees. In Kymlicka's own analysis, it is not clear why these two groups should receive such distinct packages; Kymlicka's own premises, that all individuals need a secure cultural context, seems to argue for strong rights for members of both categories. Kymlicka's empirical generalization that immigrant groups generally do not want such rights does not seem sufficient to defeat this conclusion. Instead, I think Kymlicka's distinction can be justified in terms of the causal relationship between linguistic vulnerability and historical injustice. The members of a societal culture are vulnerable precisely because their ancestors were treated unjustly by the members of the majority expansionist culture. It is only with reference to this historical evil that the justification of distinct packages of rights can be made.

All this, however, still abstracts from some key questions. If it is true that present and past discrimination are the only legitimate bases for a claim to linguistic preservation, then we need a more complete analysis of what counts as discrimination. One possibility frequently discussed by theorists of language

is the language of political life itself. Is it always an illegitimate form of discrimination to refuse official language status to a linguistic minority within a given
territory?

## Official Linguistic Status and Liberal Justice

The claim has sometimes been made that the refusal to grant official linguistic
status to a linguistic minority constitutes an objectionable form of linguistic discrimination. Related to this claim is Kymlicka's idea that there can be no such
thing as 'benign neglect' of linguistic politics; given that political deliberation
and political institutions require the use of some language or other, it seems
impossible for the government to act in any neutral manner as regards the official status of linguistic communities (Kymlicka 1995a: 108–14). Alan Patten
(2001) makes a similar claim. On his view, a refusal to recognize a linguistic
group with official linguistic status marks the group out as being at a comparative disadvantage in public life; and, in the absence of any strong reason to the
contrary, public institutions ought to treat speakers of different languages as
equal by devoting the same space and capacity to each of their languages.

In view of these arguments, can we conclude that a refusal to recognize a
linguistic minority with official linguistic status is, in itself, a form of discrimination sufficient to justify regarding linguistic vulnerability as problematic? The
answer is, I think, not always. There are undoubtedly some cases in which such a
status is not required—as Kymlicka implicitly admits by refusing to grant immigrant groups the same linguistic rights as societal cultures. The mere existence of
any linguistic minority within the territorial borders of a state always gives rise to
certain requirements: translation in the judicial system, for example, and the
availability of certain social services in the minority language. But neither
Kymlicka nor, I believe, Patten would demand official status for all minority
languages. Whether the absence of such a status counts as an illegitimate form
of discrimination depends upon context; we need to know more facts before we
can conclude that an illegitimate form of discrimination exists.

What considerations can be introduced to determine when such an illegitimate form of discrimination can be adduced? There are, I think, a multiplicity of
such considerations, of which I will mention here only two: demography and
history. Demography is relevant inasmuch as the language of political life must
follow, to some degree, the language of the political community. The refusal to
grant official status to a minority language under some circumstances—such as
when the minority language is the first language of a large part of the political
community, or when the minority language forms a majority within a territorial
sub-unit—can represent in itself an illegitimate privileging of the majority.
Sometimes, a refusal to acknowledge very mundane facts of demography must
count as a form of political discrimination. More importantly, however, considerations of history can be introduced to determine when official language

status is a demand of justice. When the linguistic minority in question once constituted a sovereign nation, and was illegitimately colonized by a linguistic majority, it seems to represent a form of status insult to refuse official language status to the language in question. In this, as above, I agree with the conclusions reached by Kymlicka, but would amplify his analysis with a justification stemming from historical injustice. In light of some patterns of history, the refusal to grant such status is illegitimate. The refusal is not, in and of itself, an injustice; and we cannot conclude from the absence of official language status that the vulnerability of a minority language is something with which liberals have reason to be concerned.

## Unequal Advantage

The final consideration to be discussed is, perhaps, the most pressing. Does the simple fact of unequal opportunity stemming from linguistic status itself count as a form of injustice? If so, then we could say that any case of linguistic endangerment was something with which liberals ought to be concerned. Cases of linguistic endangerment tend to involve differential life chances for members of the minority and majority linguistic communities; were these chances equal, after all, the pressure towards linguistic assimilation would not exist.

What can be said in defence of the idea that such unequal opportunities are necessarily inimical to liberalism? One argument, I think, might be derived from Phillippe Van Parijs (2000b), who argues that the increasing global importance of English means that native English-speakers face a comparative advantage which represents an unjustified benefit. On Van Parijs's analysis, anyone concerned with global justice ought to be concerned with the unequal advantages given fluent speakers of English—especially given that educated members of impoverished nations, who are more likely than their co-nationals to speak English, will often leave these nations and not return. On this analysis, the continued advantages of English-language knowledge amplify and exacerbate the illegitimate global distribution of wealth.

This argument links the unequal opportunities of English speakers with global inequality, so that anyone concerned about the latter ought to be concerned about the former as well. It does not, I think, succeed in demonstrating that any advantage based upon linguistic membership is unjustified. We may note, in the first place, that the linguistic advantage Van Parijs here discusses is one stemming from an admittedly unjust global distribution of wealth; very few of us, regardless of how we might conceptualize the nature of global justice, would defend the current distribution of wealth as legitimate. If we remove this injustice, and imagine a situation in which the advantages of one language stem not from injustice but from sheer size, the situation seems to become somewhat different. How could we defend the idea the greater opportunities available to a native speaker of English relative to (say) a native speaker of Welsh are illegitimate?

The English-speaker can, for example, write books that can be understood by more individuals than the Welsh-speaker, simply by virtue of the greater population of English-speakers in the world. Such advantages seem to be a function simply of linguistic size, and would persist even under conditions of global economic justice: there are simply more people who speak English than Welsh, and that fact would be unlikely to become false even in a wholly just world. To say that this form of advantage is illegitimate, however, should strike us as an implausible interpretation of liberalism. Not all forms of inequality are, or should be, the legitimate focus of a liberal theory; liberals have no reason, even in principle, to compensate the sexually unattractive, however much such inequalities can affect life chances (Anderson 1999). Neither, I think, are liberals compelled to give cash payments to Welsh authors to compensate for their reduced readership.[3]

A second attempt to justify this conclusion might stem from Kymlicka's work. Kymlicka suggests that members of the minority culture face a disadvantage relative to members of the majority culture—specifically, a disadvantage in terms of the important good of a secure cultural and linguistic framework. Members of the majority do not have to worry about the gradual erosion of their cultural traditions; members of the minority, on the other hand, do have such worries and, given the central importance of a secure cultural framework, have a claim based upon equal treatment to political support for their communities. We might, therefore, argue from such an analysis that any case of linguistic endangerment represents an injustice. The injustice, in this instance, is the unequal access to the liberal good of cultural security.

There is much to admire in this analysis—in particular, the manner in which individualistic and liberal premises are employed to defend the moral relevance of cultural preservation. I think, however, that these liberal premises are unable to perform the services into which they have been pressed. Kymlicka's vision of assimilation, I think, involves what we might call 'disculturation'—the radical and complete absence of cultural materials. Such a process may be seen to arise under certain cases, such as some cases of aboriginal contact with European culture; under such circumstances, aboriginal individuals are left bereft of any culture, lost between their own culture and the European culture in question, robbed of the basic tools needed to make autonomous decisions. It is not clear, however, that all cases of linguistic vulnerability involve such a process. We can see this, I think, if we add two plausible premises to Kymlicka's story. The first is that multilingualism is increasing in the modern world (Edwards 1994). Once the province exclusively of the wealthy or the highly educated, fluency in more than one language is a much more common phenomenon in recent decades.

---

[3] Liberal political communities might decide, of course, to support such authors. As I will explain in the conclusion, much space remains in the area of deliberative politics for such measures. Welsh authors, however, do not have any just claim to compensation stemming from their unequal readership with English authors.

The second premise is that much linguistic change occurs not suddenly, but gradually, as individuals take more and more cultural materials from a foreign culture, until in the end distinctiveness itself is lost. These two premises together indicate that assimilation can occur gradually, so that at any given point all individuals have access to adequate cultural materials needed to act as autonomous agents (Blake, 2002).

If this process is possible, then what can we say about the legitimacy of unequal options in different linguistic communities? Kymlicka's argument, I take it, is that all individuals have a need to maintain their cultural and linguistic communities, and that this good is provided free of charge to the majority but not to the minority. Members of the linguistic majority thus face a comparative advantage over the minority with regard to a universally desired good. This may be true; however, if the above analysis is true, it is not clear that Kymlicka's individualistic premises can defend the idea that this is always an injustice. If, at no point in the process, any individual is left without adequate cultural materials, it is hard to see that we are entitled to argue that the process of linguistic change itself involves any injustice with which a liberal ought to be concerned.

To see this, we may examine once again the two cases with which we began. No individual in either case faces an absence of cultural materials; no individual faces an inability to act as an autonomous agent at any point in either story. The cultural change in both cases occurs slowly enough so that no individual faces disculturation. It seems, then, that Kymlicka cannot distinguish between these cases on the basis of the good of a secure cultural framework; for all given agents, the cultural framework is secure. If such a process is the means by which we imagine the linguistic community ceasing to exist, then Kymlicka will be unable to adduce an inequality between the minority and majority linguistic communities. His premises will defend the idea that members of both linguistic communities are provided with adequate frameworks for deliberation; any inequality is illusory.

We might, however, look to another form of inequality—an inequality in the likely satisfaction of our desires that our language survive into the indefinite future. In this, the members of the linguistic communities do face an inequality. The members of the linguistic minority face a threat of gradual assimilation whereas the members of the majority do not. It is not clear, however, that this inequality is one that can be condemned on liberal grounds. It has been taken for granted throughout this exercise that an individual's wishes for the fate of her language after death cannot be taken as sufficient to ground political action. The simple desire that one's descendants will use the same linguistic tools employed at present is not enough to justify any political conclusions. Kymlicka would agree with this, I think, in the case of radical alteration without assimilation; the desire that one's language survive unchanged is hardly sufficient to justify political action. It seems, however, that similar considerations would hold true in the case of radical alteration with assimilation—barring some additional consideration of present or historical injustice. We cannot take any individual's desire about the fate of his or her culture as sufficient here. It seems to follow that an inequality in the likelihood of the satisfaction of our desires is similarly insufficient. We do not think that such desires are politically relevant; if the inequality Kymlicka finds is in the space of these desires, then this inequality is similarly irrelevant.

I would note, finally, that Kymlicka's practical political conclusions are not radically affected by what I have said here; his analysis of the needs of certain linguistic minorities, especially aboriginal minorities, seems to me quite accurate. His conclusions, however, must be reached with a due recognition of history and causality. We cannot read off from the fact of linguistic endangerment any interesting conclusions of liberal political thought.

## 3. Conclusions

I will end by trying, however briefly, to give some indication of the practical effects of what I have said here. I cannot, I think, give a full account of what it would imply regarding the rights of specific linguistic minorities. I will, however, try to explain more fully what the approach I recommend here would demand in the evaluation of a given claim to protected linguistic status. In this, I think, a comparison with Kymlicka's approach in perhaps fruitful.

We might begin by noting that my approach would mandate that slightly different things be shown before a claim for linguistic minority rights could be defended. Kymlicka's approach demands primarily a showing of historical fact: namely, that the national group in question has (or recently had) a societal culture of the relevant form, and had possession of a determinate area of territory, and so forth. My own approach would supplement these requirements with a more explicitly normative inquiry. It is not enough to show that the culture in question could and did thrive in a given area; it must be shown that some form of discrimination or domination is at the root of the subsequent failure to thrive. It is not enough, that is, that a given activist party demonstrate that a cultural and linguistic tradition meets Kymlicka's historical tests. It must be demonstrated that the explanation for this fact lies in some act, whether current or historical, which itself represents a form of political injustice. This requirement, I think, will have two effects. It will, first, place a sterner restriction than Kymlicka would allow on the forms of argument that can be allowed to establish the conclusion that official linguistic status is warranted. The fact of historical prominence in a given area, for example, might bring a national minority some considerable way in Kymlicka's methodology to the conclusion that official linguistic status is warranted. In my analysis, this form of analysis does not do nearly so much work. The justification of such status must relate to the historical reason for the endangered nature of the community; some further injustice must be adduced before we can conclude that group rights are warranted. The second effect, which follows from the first, is that my approach would be more restrictive than Kymlicka's regarding which claims are those that a liberal government is obliged to accept.

A final thing to note by way of differentiation is that the analysis I give here will end up regarding all official linguistic status as being a remedial response to a past injustice. As such, I think the way such status ought to be understood differs considerably from how it is understood by Kymlicka. On Kymlicka's analysis, such status represents not a principled deviation from liberalism but the form liberalism takes under conditions of cultural diversity. My own analysis, I believe, makes things considerably messier. If, as I think is likely, linguistic communities can rarely be rendered more secure except by policies of 'linguistic normalization'—by, that is, the attempt to establish a single language as dominant within a territorial community—then a deeply troubling choice seems to exist. We may face the following dilemma: engage in what most of us see as illiberal political actions, or allow what seems to be a gross historical injustice to continue. My own belief is that in many situations we face moral hazard no matter which horn of this dilemma we choose. How worrying this dilemma becomes will depend, in part, upon what sort of policies are used to normalize the use of the given language within the given territory. It is possible to imagine, after all, more and less defensible policies by which a given language would become universal within a society. What all such policies would share, I think, is an implied public statement by the state that speakers of other languages ought to abandon their languages or emigrate; there may be, I think, always something deeply suspect about a government agency making such a proclamation. What all this means, I think, is that my analysis is likely to be both considerably more restrictive and considerably less neat than that of Kymlicka. In my defence, I can only say that there are occasions in which a messy theory better represents reality than any cleaner alternative.

The final thing I would note is that demands for such linguistic policies need not always take the form of claims of right. Even if everything I have said here is correct, there will still be tremendous scope for democratic deliberation about linguistic preservation. In the absence of some injustice, however, the form of such arguments must be different; they must argue for linguistic preservation as one good to be pursued through political means rather than as claims based directly upon liberal justice. Many policy measures designed to defend linguistic minorities are defensible on such lines—although I do not believe that all such policy tools are compatible with liberalism. Consideration of this topic, however, I gladly leave for another occasion.

# 10

# Language Rights, Literacy, and the Modern State

JACOB T. LEVY

## 1. Introduction

In this chapter I am concerned with arguments for language rights and (which is different) language preservation. In particular I am concerned with the ways in which they sometimes proceed as if language consolidation arises in a vacuum, as if it's simply a bad idea on the part of malicious majority-language policy makers. I will argue that questions of language policy and language rights cannot be understood in isolation from the social and political changes that have created such strong trends toward monolingualism at the state level. That is not to say that these trends should not be resisted; it is to say that they cannot be ignored.

In section 2, I argue, first, that there are substantial pressures toward linguistic consolidation that arise spontaneously, especially at the time when literacy becomes a widely available option; second, that this transition toward literacy and linguistic consolidation forms part of the background for the emergence of the modern state, with its interrelated tendencies toward nationalism and democracy; third, that the modern state in turn hastens and often forces linguistic consolidation. In section 3, I examine the consequences of this for the idea that the imminent desuetude[1] of many languages poses a moral problem that demands

I am grateful to the participants at the seminar out of which this volume grew for the stimulating discussion that helped me shape these arguments, and in particular to Will Kymlicka and Alan Patten for detailed and very helpful comments. Moreover, the footnotes herein inadequately convey my indebtedness to the many writings of two other participants: John Edwards, especially *Multilingualism* (1994), and David Laitin, especially *Language Repertoires and State Construction in Africa* (1992) and *Identity in Formation* (1998). Some of the work on this chapter was done while I was a visiting fellow at the Social Philosophy and Policy Center, Bowling Green State University, Ohio.

[1] I will in general refer to language 'desuetude' and 'disuse', rather than using the more common, more vivid and poetic images of 'death', 'extinction', 'genocide', and so on. I think that the latter have a generally pernicious influence on debates about language policy. They stack the deck in favour of preservationism; who, after all, is in favour of genocide? See for example George Fletcher (1997), who uses the moral weight attached to concepts associated with violence and resisting violence to reach the conclusion that there is a right to preserve languages in the face of their erosion. Moreover, such

political solutions. In section 4, I outline three arguments in favour of (some) language rights that do not rest on the idea that language preservation is a good in its own right, and so can come to terms with the reality of language consolidation.

## 2. Literacy, the State, and Language Consolidation

Even independent of any injustices in the world, there are real pressures toward linguistic homogenization in a modern world made up of modern states. These pressures are intensified by the spread of mass literacy and printing; and literacy and printing in turn intensified and even made possible some of the social trends that pointed toward homogenization.

Literacy itself, it seems to me, is under-noticed in discussions of language and multilingualism.[2] In laments for the lost world of casual polyglottism, or enthusiastic reports of that world's persistence in parts of Africa and Asia, one fails to see acknowledgment that it is much harder to be literate in several languages than it is to be conversant in them. Once 'knowing a language' comes to include the ability to read and write in it, each language (including the native language) requires a much greater investment of time, energy, and education to acquire. This of course does not force anyone into monolingualism. But it does put downward pressure on how many languages any one person is likely to know.[3]

Moreover, *any* downward pressure on the number of languages any person is likely to know also places downward pressure on the number of languages that can sustainably be spoken in any given region. A pre-literate linguistic equilibrium might include several languages, including one or two with very small numbers of native speakers. The latter are not (very) disadvantaged, and so do not face pressure to linguistically assimilate, so long as their neighbours are willing and able to learn to converse in their language(s). But that equilibrium is upset by literacy. Once language acquisition has become more costly, members of the larger groups reduce the number of languages they are willing and able to learn, and so cease acquiring the languages spoken by smaller groups.[4]

images make it too easy to blur the difference between language shift and violence. This either makes the former seem worse than it is, or cheapens our moral language for talking about the latter. There have been enough examples of states killing minority language-*speakers* that talk about 'killing a language' seems to me a dangerous dilution of important moral concepts.

[2] For important exceptions, see Edwards (2001) and Laitin (1998).

[3] It is no doubt true that literacy in a second language is easier to acquire than literacy in a first, and that it also (often, depending on the languages involved) improves one's literacy in the first. For a while, at least, there are increasing returns to marginal investments of time in learning languages. But that does *not* change the fact that learning additional languages does require an additional investment in time; the need to become literate in one language may still displace a preceding tendency to be conversant in two or three.

[4] I will sometimes say 'larger/smaller language' as shorthand for 'the language spoken by more/fewer persons' or 'the larger/smaller group of co-linguists'. That is all I shall mean by larger/smaller

This in turn makes life more difficult for members of each smaller group. They must either (1) invest time in language acquisition that members of the larger groups do not have to invest (in the simplest case, members of a minority have to learn the majority language while the reverse is not true); (2) limit interactions to members of their own linguistic community; (3) depend on interpreters and translators, who then form a bottleneck and may gain unfair power over members of the smaller group; (4) give up their ancestral language and assimilate; or (5) migrate out of the area. As some members opt for (4) or (5), (2) becomes progressively more difficult and less appealing.

Sometimes two or more of the smaller language communities might converge on a single language, in the hope of making (2) a more credible choice, of staunching the flow of members to (4) and (5), and of providing members of the larger group(s) with more incentive to learn the language. German may pose less of a threat when the local Slavic dialects have coalesced into a single written language. The same may be true of the languages of European conquerors and colonists relative to the languages of those conquered and colonized. This common strategy will be discussed below when we turn to nationalist movements; for now the interesting thing to note is that even this option results in a decline in linguistic diversity. It is a special case of linguistic assimilation—a defensive or pre-emptive or competitive case—not an alternative to it.

This set of choices is, of course, faced by members of any small linguistic minority surrounded by larger language groups. Even in the absence of literacy, there's an upper limit to how many languages can be sustained in a given area and population. But any change that makes members of the larger group(s) less willing to learn additional languages—such as the spread of literacy—makes the dilemma of members of the smaller group(s) more acute. The level of multilingualism that was sustainable before literacy is probably not thereafter.

I have been discussing 'languages' as if they were wholly discrete; but another part of what literacy does is to force a spectrum of dialects into the form of a small number of discrete languages. Linguistic frontiers turn into linguistic boundaries. Before literacy, there is little advantage to millions of persons who will never meet each other all using a common form of a language. Literacy— perhaps even more than the migration and labour mobility that is of such interest to Ernest Gellner, though the two are not independent—changes that decisively.

And all of that is true even if there is no difference in how quickly literacy spreads in the various communities and languages, how many speakers of each there are elsewhere, how much (and what) there is to read in the languages, and how strong a market there is for new written work. It is also true even if there is no difference in the political power of the groups involved. (Perhaps all the local groups are subject to an imperial state foreign to them all.) If, however, literacy spreads in the languages spoken by larger groups while the others still lack

language'; the phrasing should not be read to refer to the range of vocabularies or concepts in the languages themselves.

written forms altogether, then the smaller linguistic communities face still greater difficulties.[5]

The account so far has lacked any reference to politics; the spread of literacy by itself decreases the number of languages any given person is likely to learn and, therefore, the number of languages that can likely be sustained in a given area. But the spread of mass literacy is also tied up with the development of nationalism and of democracy, which are in turn tied up with each other. And nationalism and democracy accelerate the trend toward local linguistic homogeneity.

This part of the story has been told by many others, with varying emphases. Some version of it is common to all the theorists and historians who understand nationalism to be a distinctively modern phenomenon (see for example, Gellner 1983; Anderson 1983; Taylor 1993; 1997; 1998). Here is one version: the spread of mass literacy makes possible the growth of a national consciousness spread in part through newspapers, in part through a shared awareness of the new linguistic boundaries being formed by the crystallization of discrete languages. But nationalism is a project, not only (not even primarily) a sentiment. It is the project of forging a multitude of persons and groups into a self-conscious collective. Though modern nationalism could not get off the ground before linguistic consolidation began, it did not wait for that consolidation to reach an end-point by itself. One of the most universal components of nationalist projects is the attempt to speed linguistic consolidation along to a particular conclusion. If the nationalists—and, which is the same in this context, the nationalizers—do not control a state, then they use whatever tools are at hand to propagate the now-standardized and now-written language. They exhort, write dictionaries, found schools, link the language to the churches, translate well-known works including the locally appropriate scripture, publish newspapers, and so on. If they do control a state, the means at their disposal multiply. The state may create or subsidize schools that teach the standardized language, curtail or prohibit schools that do not, conduct official business only in the official language, instruct conscripted soldiers in it, ban publication (and, later, broadcasting) in other languages and dialects, require personal names to take forms particular to the official language, and much more. This list mixes means foul with ones relatively fair; I will turn to the question of distinguishing between the two in section 4.

Literacy makes information about official business much more accessible to the populace; the shared awareness of being part of a(n increasingly) unified linguistic community contributes to a feeling that the populace is becoming a people. Both of these trends contribute to the spread of democratic ideas. In turn, democratic states enthusiastically engage in the kinds of nationalizing

---

[5] If the language spoken by a local minority is stronger along these dimensions—literacy spreads more quickly, there is more written and more of a market for written material, and so on—then that helps to counterbalance the disadvantages of being a local minority.

234 JACOB T. LEVY

projects described above. They attempt to cement and perpetuate the feeling of being a people; they seek to create and maintain the possibility of communication among citizens and between citizens and officials; they are thought to function more smoothly and legitimately if majorities and minorities are temporary and shifting rather than permanent and entrenched; and so on. Moreover, the existence of democratic politics increases the attraction of speaking the language of state and of political discourse, even in the absence of deliberate assimilationist policies. Democracy creates yet another arena to which access can be gained by learning the dominant language. Both the animating principles and the practical demands of a democratic state call forth more nationalizing projects in general, and more linguistic homogenization in particular, than may be the case in multi-ethnic empires. The decline of polyglottism contributes to, but is also speeded by, the replacement of such polities with national democracies.

As the wars of the French revolutionary and imperial eras showed so vividly, a nationalist democratic state—even one that was then far from linguistically unified—could marshal military power unavailable to older kinds of polities. And so the events of 1789–1815 inspired competitive nationalizing projects throughout Europe. Military necessity, both real and imagined, contributed still more to the pressures to shape each populace into a people and to make each people legible to its state for purposes of taxation and conscription.[6] At best, linguistic minorities created administrative difficulties for the bureaucratic apparatus of the emerging modern state and drew attention to the untruth involved in claiming that a state's people made up a nation. At worst, they were potentially disloyal; if they perceived themselves to be members of a nation that was not the nation of the state, then they might secede or provide the pretext for revanchism. Even in the absence of such a conscious link between security and homogeneity, a security competition among modern states may hasten assimilation. Shared service in the sort of mass armed forces created during the revolutionary conflicts has been one of the most powerful forces for language consolidation and for the creation of national sentiment. In other words, the army helps to create nations directly, above and beyond the impetus given to nationalizing projects from security concerns.

It is important to remember that this drive toward uniformity and language consolidation was (and is) characteristic of *both* categories of nationalists: those who wanted to make extant states into nations, and those who wanted to make ostensibly extant nations into states.[7] The two types competed over which community was to claim the status of nation, which language would become 'the' language of the people, which group it was that would become a homogeneous unit. But they did not disagree about the need to speed along the process of language consolidation in the interest of national and popular unity. And so,

---

[6] See Scott (1998) for the idea of a state rendering its population legible.

[7] For the distinction between nationalizing states and state-seeking nations, see Brubaker (1996).

while the French Third Republic worked to replace regional languages with French, activists in the provinces tried to shore up their languages' fortunes by standardizing them, committing them to print, and smoothing out the variation in local dialects (Weber 1976: Ch. 6).

Like most other versions of the story of the nation, the modern state, and democracy, this one is drawn in the first instance from the European experience. But the interaction of literacy, nationalism, and linguistic standardization and homogenization is not uniquely European or uniquely early-modern. It was evident in the nationalist movements that challenged European empires in the twentieth centuries; Tagalog and Bahasa Indonesian have political biographies similar in kind to those of Czech and Serbo-Croatian. It remains evident in indigenous-nationalist political movements today. Pan-Mayan nationalists in Guatemala are pushing for language consolidation as part of the process of creating a Mayan nation that can credibly challenge the Ladino state, both politically and in the opportunities it can offer to its members. Dozens of languages are, on this agenda, to be replaced by one that can have a standard written form, can be taught in bilingual schools, and can unite the Mayan majority in a single alternative society. There are real advantages to fluency in a language that is written and shared by a large number of people, in addition to the advantages of fluency in the language of state. In order to balance out those advantages, nationalists pursue homogenization and literacy among the groups that they hope to make into a nation.[8]

Thus there are spontaneous trends toward linguistic consolidation—not 'natural' in that they are the results of human action, but spontaneous in that they are not the result of deliberate design—and there is also linguistic consolidation brought about, often coercively and unjustly, by deliberate political action. But the line between the two is blurred, because the same social changes that contribute to spontaneous consolidation also contribute to the political action in favour of consolidation. The widespread tendency of states to suppress minority languages is not due only to malicious intent on the part of state actors, though there has been no shortage of such intent.

None of this requires us to think that the post-literacy, or even the post-literacy-and-democracy-and-nationalism, equilibrium will be monolingualism, either at the individual level or at the state level.[9] But it does mean that the equilibrium number of languages (at both levels) will be much smaller than was its pre-modern counterpart. The idea that the world will become monolingual is a red herring in debates over multilingualism, and is in no way predicted by the analysis here. But a universal embrace of English is hardly necessary for many thousands of languages to fall into desuetude; neither is it necessary for monolingualism to reign within each region. It is only necessary that, for their second

---

[8] In addition to Brubaker, see Will Kymlicka's discussion of the 'dialectic' of nation-building at the state and minority-nation level in Kymlicka (2001b: 50–3).

[9] See Laitin (1993) for an argument that the equilibrium will not be monolingualism.

or third languages, most people prefer to learn written languages of wide currency—the language of the central state if that is not their own, the language of their province if *that* is not their own, the language of a neighbouring state, one of the languages of global business or diplomacy—instead of the language of a small local minority. First, non-native speakers of the minority language stop learning it; then, as its usefulness contracts, so do the children of native speakers.

There is something pernicious in the frequent invocation of benign pre-literate polyglottism in contemporary debates about language policy. That invocation makes multilingualism seem easier than it really is today. The acquisition of multiple languages is more difficult, both because many children now live in linguistically homogeneous areas and so are not immersed in a multilingual environment, and—more simply—because it is more difficult to become fully literate than to become fully conversant. Poorly designed bilingual education programmes, for instance, rather than recreating an idyllic Hapsburg or Baltic mosaic, can now result in large numbers of students who are illiterate in two languages.

## 3. Linguistic Preservationism

The foregoing is relevant, I think, to the normative case for language preservation.[10] The figures are by now familiar: out of some 6,000 or so languages currently existing, half are in imminent danger of ceasing to be used or spoken. Roughly 1,500 languages have fewer than 1,000 speakers each; as many more have fewer than 10,000 speakers. The endangered languages are most concentrated in India, the Pacific islands (especially New Guinea), and among the indigenous peoples of Australia and the Americas. The list of vulnerable tongues also includes many from sub-Saharan Africa and from South-east Asia, and some of those spoken by the indigenous peoples of Siberia and Scandinavia.

It is evident at a glance that this list includes many of the poorest and least powerful groups in the world. The relationships among that poverty, that lack of power, and that linguistic vulnerability are complicated, run in each of the possible directions, and tend to reinforce one another in spiralling ways. When Stephen May (2001: 4) observes that 'the vast majority of today's threatened languages are spoken by socially and politically marginalised and/or subordinated national-minority and ethnic groups . . . [L]anguage death seldom occurs in communities of wealth and privilege, but rather to [*sic*] the dispossessed and

---

[10] Language preservationism is a position that can be held with greater or lesser degrees of moderation and sophistication. I will often refer to Stephen May's work in this section; it is perhaps the most philosophically persuasive statement of the position. More widely known and influential statements have come from many linguists, sociolinguists, and anthropologists, from UNESCO, from NGOs like Terralingua, and of course from activists on behalf of particular languages. UNESCO has been particularly influential in promoting and legitimizing particularly simplistic versions of the position. See, for example, Bjeljec-Babic (2000: 18–19), Ortiz de Urbina (2000: 29), and Wurm (2001).

disempowered', the observation is right but the implication is wrong.[11] Language vulnerability has sometimes been a condition that the powerful violently inflicted on the powerless—all too often by killing the language's speakers. But most of the languages that are most vulnerable today are *not* vulnerable as a result of their speakers' subordinated status. The causation runs in nearly the opposite direction.

Nearly all of the languages likely to fall into desuetude are unwritten or have adopted written forms only very recently. While a few have large numbers of speakers, vanishingly few are widely read and written. As we saw in section 2, it should not surprise us that unwritten languages are vulnerable. But there was nothing in the analysis of section 2 to predict that *all* written languages would continue to be used. Language consolidation might well continue after the unwritten languages are swept away. But literacy appears to increase the durability of languages a great deal. Once there are a few hundred thousand readers and writers of a language geographically concentrated, once books and newspapers are widely commercially published in it—published by people trying to sell books and newspapers, not by those who give them away as part of a language plan—then its likelihood of fading away seems to fall dramatically. This is of a piece with the durability of ethnic, cultural, and national identities more broadly. While all of these do change over generations, and while there is a great deal of fluidity in each at the individual level, as a rule people shed them neither quickly nor lightly.

But a language in which there is *not* widespread literacy, a language for which there does not exist mass publishing or mass readership, has a much more difficult time persisting, despite its speakers' predictable attachment to it, and regardless of the attitudes or actions of outsiders. The opportunity cost of leading one's life primarily in that language are simply too high once movement into a larger and literate language-group becomes feasible. Language activists and outside preservationists may race to create a written form and to spread knowledge of it. Their race against the speed of language shift is quite difficult to win. By the time dictionaries are standardized, the most important local stories have been committed to print, and a few major books in outside languages have been translated, a generation of children may have grown up reading another language. The revivalists' attempts to create a social world based on the new written form are badly behind from the outset. The urge to maintain an ethnic and cultural identity and tradition remains strong; but the odds are against that identity being expressed in the traditional language.

While this situation is less common, even a literate language faces similar difficulty if its number of speakers (and readers and writers) falls or begins below some critical level. The horizon of options of lives lived in the language is

---

[11] This is a point he reiterates and makes a great deal of, usually treating it as obvious that the subordination causes the language death.

too constrained. A successful shift from non-literacy to literacy will probably not save a language of 500 speakers. In section 2, I described the process of language consolidation as the reduction of the number of languages that could continue to be spoken by a person or within a territory. It might equally be described as an increase in the minimum number of speakers required for a language to be viable. An increase in the number of speakers of a neighbouring language—like the spread of literacy among its members, or economic development, or social differentiation and modernization within its society—increases the opportunity costs of remaining in our own language community, and so leads to a marginal increase in the number of our co-linguists shifting to the other language. That further exacerbates the shift difference in the two languages' number of speakers, encouraging a further marginal shift, and so on. The durability of cultural and linguistic identities provides some push in the other direction; but when the differential between the two language communities grows too great, that push will not be enough. The range of options available to a speaker of a language spoken by half a billion persons is too much greater than the range available to the member of a 500-person language group.

May (2001: 148–9) complains that arguments of the sort I am making here 'simply represent a particular *value judgement*—a judgement that equates minority-language loss, and language shift to a majority language, with progress and modernity . . . [I]f minority languages are consistently viewed as low status, socially and culturally restrictive, and an obstacle to social mobility, is it little wonder that such patterns of language shift exist?'. He further maintains that 'the notions of "communicative currency" or "languages of wider communication" come to serve as linguistic proxies for the legitimation of the greater sociopolitical status of the majority-language group' (May 2001: 147). In general he argues that we should view the differences in the ranges of opportunities available to speakers of minority and majority languages as constructed (often maliciously) and subject to deliberate change.

In the world as it is, with all the unfairnesses and injustices that went into its creation as well as all the inequalities that just happened, it's not prejudiced or stigmatizing or arrogant to say that here and now the life chances of a monolingual speaker of an unwritten tribal language in the far north-east of India spoken by a thousand people are horribly constrained, and that no amount of state support or egalitarian rhetoric can change that fact. That is not, of course, due to any intrinsic characteristic of the language; it's not because the language is inferior or incapable of incorporating the concepts that are available in other languages. Neither is it because of any injustice in the allocation of resources or occupational roles. It's not that the high-status positions have been constructed so as to exclude speakers of the tribal language. Rather, the social world that includes high-status positions developed and evolved in isolation from that of speakers of the tribal language, and vice versa. The same is true of speakers of tribal languages in Papua New Guinea. Some of the world's poorest people and many of the most endangered languages are in places that weren't ravaged by colonialism but were rather isolated from it.[12] But even when the current language vulnerability *is* (at least in part) a result of serious past injustices, as is the case for indigenous languages in the Americas and Australia, it's still true that a massive disparity exists between the options made available by teaching a child the vulnerable language and those made available by teaching some other language (again, whether the vulnerable language is being taught as a primary or auxiliary language). Even if the state that has committed the injustices bears the entire *financial* cost of the minority language revival programme, it is still the children of the victimized group who will bear the greatest costs. There's no need to think that communicative range is the *only* value served by the ability to speak a language; I do not mean to deny the communal, aesthetic, and symbolic values associated with language preservation. But to deny that there are differences in the communicative ranges, or to think that these are exclusively the result of unjust power relations, seems to me a serious mistake. And if communicative range matters *at all* in our evaluations of what languages it is in children's interest to learn—as surely it must—then we must often admit that language preservation policies are not in children's interests.

This means that language is an unusually difficult case for compensatory or remedial justifications for cultural rights. When vast areas of land have been expropriated from a minority in the past, there is no apparent difficulty with restitution *in terms of the interests of the members of the minority*. (There are considerable difficulties that have to do with the interests of third parties who many have innocently come to possess the stolen land in the interim.) Histories of discrimination, coercion, expulsion, violence, and enslavement can justify a wide range of current policies of cultural rights and special protections, both as compensation and as protection against future abuses. And these are generally taken to be less problematic, more clearly justified cases of cultural rights than are non-remedial examples.

But if the history of injustice has driven a critical mass of a language's speakers away from it, or has prevented it from evolving and taking on modern and written forms that it otherwise might have, or has interrupted its transmission for a generation or two, then the attempt to make up for past wrongs can be quite problematic. In the world that we have, complete with its unjust history, the interests of the children and grandchildren of the language's speakers may have to be overridden in order to pursue language revival. A revival project that

[12]  No doubt, this relationship between language vulnerability and isolation is in part an artefact of selection bias. That is, the most vulnerable languages *that are still in use* are in areas that were isolated from colonialism; comparably vulnerable languages in the regions most affected by colonialism have long since disappeared. I do not mean to suggest that colonialism was somehow good for the preservation of the languages of the colonized. I do mean to suggest that the conjunction of poverty, nonliteracy, powerlessness, small language communities, and (in some global sense) low status is not a creation of colonialism or of oppression.

tries to minimize the burden on children—say, by continuing to encourage fluency and literacy in the language(s) that drove out the ancestral language, as in the case of Ireland's policy of trying to revive Irish while still encouraging knowledge of English—may not do much reviving. The opportunity costs of such a policy are low; few options are foreclosed for the children involved. But the extent of language revival is low as well. A revival policy could instead give primacy to the ancestral language, or discourage the acquisition of the rival language(s). As the policy moves farther along this dimension—as it approaches encouraging monolingualism in the ancestral language—the likelihood of success rises, but so does the opportunity cost for children. Whether the opportunity cost of years of education in the ancestral language is improved literacy in the local majority language or acquisition of a more widely used second or third language, it is likely to be high.

This is not to say there is a blanket moral prohibition on revival policies. Shoring up a language that is declining is markedly different from trying to revive one that is past its tipping point and is falling into general disuse. And there is no general obligation on the part of parents, educators, or the state to simply maximize the range of communication that an education makes possible. A native French-speaker who learns Breton instead of German as a second language trades more options (people to talk with, books to read, job opportunities, and so on) for fewer, but 'more' and 'fewer' are not the only relevant considerations. Parents who chose such a course of education for a child would not do their child an injustice. But our intuition that this is so comes from the sense that knowledge of French already provides the child with 'enough' options. I will not try to operationalize 'enough' here. Sufficiency requires a complex balance of local, statewide, and global options—and the appropriate balance will vary dramatically from case to case. But if there is an obligation to provide something like sufficiency as part of an education, then we must be willing to ask of language revival policies whether they provide it. A monolingual education in a language that is rapidly falling into disuse does not. Even if the language being revived is taught as a second language, the revival policy may well violate the requirement of sufficiency—depending on the options made available by the first.[13]

The argument that we should not, on balance, try to prevent thousands of languages from falling into disuse is an uncomfortable one. It entails allowing many past injustices to go unrectified. It requires drawing distinctions between viable and unviable languages, a process that feels all too much like distinguishing between worthy and unworthy ones. But there is no real alternative other than

---

[13] Note that the concern about opportunity costs can be sidestepped by calling attention to the decreasing marginal costs of acquiring languages after the second. The native English-speaker who learns Gaelic might then have an easier time learning French. But this would presumably be just as true for the native English-speaker who learned Hindi before learning French. If knowing Hindi would open more opportunities than knowing Gaelic, then a price has been paid. Even if sufficiency is not violated, we should not lose track of this fact entirely.

to rail against the world created by literacy and the modern state (and the modern economy and . . .). If we do not allow ourselves to draw such distinctions, if we're unable to recognize the difference between a viable literate language of a national minority that has come under some pressure and a non-literate language spoken by a few hundred people in New Guinea, then we lose the ability to say anything coherent about protecting the former. In the next section, I will consider possible defences of minority language rights that do not rest on the general preservationism criticized in this section.

One final note about language preservation. So far the discussion has proceeded mainly in terms of protecting minority languages against incursions from the local majority language or the local language of state. But many policies of language preservation—here we might call them linguistic protectionism—aim to preserve the latter kind of language against incursions by a global one. The policies don't seem very different; actions taken to protect French against English in France are reminiscent of those taken to protect French against English in Quebec. I think the similarities between the two situations are telling, but there are important differences as well. Even if there were good will on the part of a state to try, it would be very difficult to craft linguistic protectionism in a way that did not further disadvantage internal minority vernaculars. Global languages might be the ostensible target, but the primary effect may well be on smaller local languages. It is therefore disingenuous to try to ally the cause of linguistic protectionism to that of preservationism more broadly. The primary threat to small local languages is almost never a global language as such; it is almost always the local majority language or the local language of state.[14] All that can be said on behalf of language protectionism that cannot be said in favour of preservationism more generally is that the former rarely shores up a doomed language and thereby sacrifices the interests of the young. But that is because such policies are generally redundant in any event. The languages have both the advantage of being institutionalized in a modern state *and* the population and publication base to be safe from any real threat. Even without protectionism, that advantage is a powerful source of support for any language's persistence, above and beyond the security provided by mass literacy.

## 4. Defending Language Rights

None of this is to say that there are no good reasons for special measures to protect minority languages. Preservationism is not the only available defence for language rights. But other defences must be able to come to grips with the facts of language shift. Many languages have ceased to be spoken since the beginning

---

[14] Sometimes, as when English threatens American Indian languages, the threat does come from a global language, but arises primarily because it is *also* the local language of state.

of mass literacy, and many more will cease to be spoken as mass literacy spreads through Africa, South and South-east Asia, and the Pacific. This is perhaps to be regretted on aesthetic or cultural grounds, but on balance it is not to be regretted in terms of the lives of the persons most affected. Here I consider three defences of language rights that do not depend on preservationism; I call them present-tense language rights, linguistic egalitarianism, and counterbalancing.

The first defence, present-tense language rights, focuses attention not on the future but on the present. The currently living speakers of a minority language can face serious disadvantages, especially the adults coming into contact with the majority language for the first time. It may be that they cannot, or that they cannot reasonably be expected to, acquire the majority language and live in the society demarcated by that language.[15] It is surely unreasonable to govern them as if they spoke that language when they do not. At a minimum, the state governing such a population must attempt to make the governing comprehensible to the governed, whether through the provision of translators or by conducting official business in the minority language when appropriate. A state that as a matter of policy subjects those it governs to trials they cannot understand for violating laws they cannot understand acts unjustly.

It may turn out that, once interactions with the state are made comprehensible (via translation or via conducting the state business in the minority language to begin with), then the minority language can be sustained on its own. If the group speaking the language is fairly large, if the language is a written one, if perhaps it is used by many people elsewhere in addition to being used by the local group, if a range of lives can be lived in the language, then it may well turn out that the linguistic community is stable. Young people may not feel compelled or tempted to abandon it. In that case, this sort of language rights will be permanent despite being justified only in present-tense terms. By the time current speakers of the minority language die, their children and grandchildren will have the same kind of moral claims for language rights. The policies aim at the present not the future; but it will always be somebody's present.

But matters will not always turn out that way. Present-tense language rights will sometimes be transitional language rights, aiming to slow and ease—not stop—the switch from one language to another. They will sometimes be policies aimed at avoiding unfair and excessive disruption to older generations while younger ones assimilate. It is unreasonable to expect adults to simply cease living in their lifelong language. But the present is also always preparing the ground for somebody's future, and the need to insulate adults in the present must not be an excuse to prevent children from seeking a future in another language. This would sneak preservationism in by the back door, and would require using the children as mere means. The children have lives of their

[15] Alan Patten argues, I think persuasively, that it is to cases like this that Will Kymlicka's original argument for cultural rights most forcefully applies. See Kymlicka (1989) and Patten (2000).

own to lead, and should not be used as instruments to prop up an unsustainable language.[16]

The second defence, linguistic egalitarianism, has been ably articulated and in part defended by Alan Patten (2001), and I will not rehearse his arguments at length. He refers to it as the model of 'official multilingualism', and contrasts it with both language rationalization and language maintenance or preservation. 'A language is recognized in public life . . . when public services are offered and public business can be conducted in that language. The official multilingualism model maintains that each of the various languages spoken in the community should be accorded the same recognition' (Patten 2001: 695). That is, this model demands that a society's languages be treated equally, even though this might mean that language rationalization that would be desirable from the perspective of national solidarity or democratic politics will not take place, or might alternatively mean that language preservation will not take place. The defence proceeds in terms of fair processes rather than desired end-states.

Patten recognizes that it is individuals and not languages that have a right to equal treatment, and so he endorses some degree of per-capita prorating of the provision of services in the minority language. But he also argues that public recognition of a language's political status cannot be entirely prorated away. To have one's language formally recognized as equal to other languages by the state—most prominently by its inclusion in the list of the state's official languages—can help satisfy morally compelling interests in symbolic affirmation and identity promotion, in addition to the practical benefits conferred by the ability to communicate in one's own language.

It should be noted that, in Patten's formulation, linguistic egalitarianism takes the present-tense argument for granted (under the heading of 'communicative interests'). The reverse does not hold, however; a commitment to transitional language rights does not in itself require any commitment to the public symbolic recognition of a minority language.

Patten suggests that a fully-developed theory of language rights would require attention to both linguistic autonomy in the private sphere and public recognition of languages. He offers an account of the latter, and says that thinking about the moral claims at stake in public recognition first will help us sort out questions about linguistic autonomy later. The third non-preservationist defence of language rights reverses that order; it justifies public recognition as instrumentally

---

[16] Compare John Edwards: 'Just as the school exists as an arm of the state, so it is often singled out by language communities as the linchpin of their continuing cultural and linguistic identity. Wherever societal heterogeneity exists, schools may be asked to play a part—perhaps the central part—in maintaining and encouraging identities thought to be at risk. Schools and teachers have increasingly, in fact, played the role of agents of social change and have correspondingly experienced more difficulties since this does not always mesh well with their more traditional task of transmitting core or basic skills . . . Thirty years ago, a sensitive observer of the educational thrust of the Irish revival warned that "children's minds must not be made the battleground of a political wrangle," and another decried the use of children as "digits in the Irish revival statistics" ' (Edwards 1994: 11).

valuable in helping to maintain the political balance that protects and respects rights of linguistic autonomy. This argument—the one I will spend the balance of this chapter defending—rests on the need to *counterbalance* the predictable tendency of modern states to engage in unjust nationalizing projects.[17] We know, for reasons already discussed at length in section 2, that there are pressures for language consolidation that are not unjust, but arise from the transition to literacy, the competitive pressures created by other languages consolidating and creating a broader horizon of opportunities for their speakers, and so on. But we also know that modern states—certainly including democratic states, perhaps *especially* democratic states—often try to speed the process along, and often try to prevent the outcome that language consolidation still leaves two or more languages. The tendency of a modern state to try to turn its populace into a nation, which often entails linguistic homogeneity, is widespread and predictable. And these nationalizing projects are often coercive, violent, illiberal, and inhumane. They often violate individual rights of freedom of speech, association, religion, and so on that Patten refers to as linguistic autonomy.

One of the key concepts of constitutionalism—which is concerned with institutional design, not only with philosophical justifications—is counterbalancing. If we have good reason to expect that states will commit a particular kind of injustice, then we ought to try to design institutions that will lean against that tendency. That will often require us to design institutions that aren't demanded by justice in their own right, but are needed to prevent injustices from another direction. In the case of language, that may mean that linguistic minorities are provided with a level of government over which they have control, with control over some part of the state school system, or with guaranteed representation in the decision-making bodies of the central state.[18] It may also mean special provision in the military for minority-language units, to push against the centralizing tendency that armies have had. If that is impractical for security reasons—because the minority-language divisions are considered too likely to have divided loyalties—then that much more counterbalancing will be necessary in other contexts.

Counterbalancing is not an entirely free-standing justification for language rights. It depends on some account of what the injustices are that need to be leaned against. Earlier I described the policies available to state nationalizers as including both foul and fair means. How much counterbalancing justifies depends on the correct theory about which such means are foul and which are

---

[17] Here I draw on my book *The Multiculturalism of Fear* (Levy 2000) and on my article 'National Minorities Without Nationalism' (Levy forthcoming *a*).

[18] This last highlights the commonality between what I am calling 'counterbalancing' or 'constitutionalism' and what Kymlicka (1995*a*) uses as the justification for representation rights in *Multicultural Citizenship*. The difference is that I think the argument applies not only to guaranteed representation but also—and often more importantly—to what he calls self-government rights, but that the arguments he uses in defence of the latter do not succeed as they're based on either nationalist or cultural-preservationist premises.

fair. *Whatever* one's philosophical account of what justice demands with respect to language, counterbalancing may provide us with strategic reasons to provide more institutional weight and power for linguistic minorities than the account demands. This style of reasoning may, for instance, be used in conjunction with a pure negative-liberty account of language rights, with the present-tense account, or with linguistic egalitarianism, with different results that will be considered below. But the policies recommended by counterbalancing may not depend very much on the details of the particular account of language justice that lies beneath it. The kind of large-scale institutional over-correction that counterbalancing recommends will often make subtle differences between philosophical accounts irrelevant. I will return to this point after discussing how counterbalancing can work with different underlying justifications.

## Negative Freedom

I take it as obviously unjust to beat children who speak a minority language or to forbid private education, broadcasting, publishing, and personal names in it. Such actions violate core personal freedoms. While this is more controversial, I also take assimilation-by-conscription to violate individual liberty. No more than this is needed to trigger the need for counterbalancing in much of the world, because all of these policies are very much in use. If justice demands only the protection of the negative liberty to speak, use, publish in, and educate in the minority language in the privately funded private sphere, then the need for language rights may be limited in some states. Where freedom of speech, freedom of the press, and freedom of association are secure and vigorously protected in general, it is possible that linguistic freedom will be fully protected as a matter of course. The minority may still face the assimilative pressures of, for example, a monolingual state-funded educational system; but this is not a violation of negative liberty. If such a system is not a foul means, then there is no morally compelling need to counterbalance against its possibility.

It cannot simply be taken for granted that linguistic freedom is secure in liberal democracies; freedom for the majority language may coexist with restrictions on the minority, for instance when the minority language community is thought to pose a security threat to the state. But in the United States, for example, it is clear as a matter of constitutional law that minority-language private education, publishing, and speech may not be banned. Official English statutes pass constitutional review only in so far as they do not restrict these liberties. Linguistic freedom is protected incidentally, as a subset of liberal freedom of speech, the press, association, and contract.[19] Counterbalancing in

---

[19] *Pierce v. Society of Sisters*, 268 US 510 and *Meyer v. Nebraska*, 262 US 390, which respectively forbade laws banning private schools and laws against teaching in languages other than English, were decided in large part on freedom of contract grounds. Presumably if they had been heard during the Warren Court era rather than during the *Lochner* era, the same conclusions would have been reached

conjunction with a pure negative-liberty account of language rights may not justify any special provision for linguistic minorities in very liberal democracies.

## Present-Tense

If, however, the present-tense argument is right, then justice also demands some affirmative provision for some minority-language speakers, such as making documents and state services available in the minority language(s). These affirmative measures are less likely to be offered incidentally, and are accordingly more likely to require institutional arrangements to ensure their availability. Even an explicit constitutional commitment to bilingualism has not protected Canada from occasional judicial rulings against, for example, providing judicial proceedings in French (see Réaume 2000). Present-tense rights are likely to be even less secure for minorities that lack the institutional weight of francophones in Canada. Counterbalancing in conjunction with present-tense arguments are thus likely to justify at least some special provision for linguistic minorities even in free societies.

Here I should note that the normative approach I have elsewhere described as 'the multiculturalism of fear' (Levy 2000) is not synonymous with the negative-liberty approach even as modified by counterbalancing; it includes present-tense language rights as well. A very significant range of language rights can be justified using the counterbalancing-and-negative-liberty approach; but a concern with preventing state violence, cruelty, and coercion requires something more. The moral importance of making at least criminal proceedings comprehensible to the defendant seems to me very high. The criminal justice system exposes more citizens more often to the direct threat of violence and coercion than does any other branch of the state. We hem that system in with an unusual number of procedural guarantees that sometimes impede efficiency or truth-finding in order to protect against those threats. For similar reasons we should take especially vigorous action in that setting to protect those who cannot speak the state's language. And so, according to an approach that is concerned with the prevention of the evils that the state often visits upon ethnic minorities, some language rights are justified even in liberal democracies that scrupulously protect the basic negative liberties.

## Linguistic Egalitarianism

The demands made in the name of justice by linguistic egalitarianism are still more extensive than those made by the present-tense argument. But they are also somewhat different in kind; many of the institutions and rules that are available as part of counterbalancing strategies are demanded as part of the first-best

on other grounds, but as it now stands *Pierce* and *Meyer* are unusual in being *Lochner* cases that remain good law.

outcome by linguistic egalitarianism. To be sure, there are predictable tendencies on the part of states not to abide by the strictures of linguistic egalitarianism, so counterbalancing may be called for. But the balancing measures sought will often be the same as the provisions egalitarianism recommended in the first place.

## Institutional Convergence

Constitutional engineers have only relatively blunt tools at their disposal, at least when compared with the fine work done distinguishing philosophical theories. For this reason, it may not make a decisive difference which of these theories counterbalancing is combined with.

For instance, one of the policies that any kind of counterbalancing may call for in a given state is the central policy of linguistic egalitarianism, namely, recognition of minority languages as official languages and the entrenchment of that recognition. Such symbolic recognition cannot eliminate the trends and incentives that lead modern states down the path of enforced language consolidation. But the symbolic exclusion associated with official monolingualism matters. It matters not only in the insult to minority-language speakers, nor even only in the unjust practical barriers to communication it can create between members of the minority and the state. It also matters because a state's avowed self-understanding acquires normative force of its own. A state that is committed—say, by the terms of its constitution—to a nationalist and monolingual self-understanding might respect the legitimate linguistic autonomy of its citizens in the private sphere. But such constitutional commitments can, in part, structure the options that are perceived to be legitimate in ongoing politics. A state that is officially nationalist and monolingual might have a range of publicly acceptable views that range from toleration of minority languages when spoken in the private sphere to severe restrictions and prohibition. A state that is officially bilingual or multilingual will also have a range of publicly acceptable views; but the centre around which they vary will be quite different, and coercive monolingualism is much less likely to be in that range. That is not to say that official bilingualism or multilingualism guarantees that the actual language policies enacted will be just. Those policies may well err on the side of an unjust preservationism. But it seems to me that states' tendencies toward nationalism are pervasive enough that they are unlikely to err as severely in that direction as they often have in the other.[20]

There is a problem with this view of the potency of official symbolism: the old problem of tying the bell on the cat. Say that we agree that it would be

---

[20] If the end of the era of the modern state is upon us, as some hope and others fear, then this balance of probabilities may no longer be appropriate. But I confess this seems much less likely to me than it does to many. The kind of state the French Revolution bequeathed to us, and its characteristic faults, may well be with us for some time to come.

desirable to shift the centre around which publicly acceptable views on language vary in some particularly nationalist-Jacobin state like France or Turkey. Say that we agree that the constitutional commitments of the state, its official self-understandings, shape politics in ways that make it unlikely to fully respect linguistic autonomy and all too likely to commit severe injustices. We might then think that changing those constitutional commitments would help, that if the state endorsed multilingualism instead of monolingualism at the constitutional level then ordinary politics would shift too. But constitutional commitments don't magically appear; symbolic affirmation of multilingualism is hard to imagine unless the politics about language had *already* changed.[21] This may often mean that official language neutrality—shifting from one official language to none rather than from one to many—is the most that can plausibly be won by minorities. Of course, no state can *be* linguistically neutral. But removing the 'one nation, one language, indivisible' claims from foundational documents might at least open up the possibility of adopting minority-language policies through normal politics. Their presence is a barrier, as has recently been made clear in France. An important proposal for Corsican autonomy adopted through normal politics was rejected as incompatible with France's constitutional commitment to unitary nationalist republicanism.

In any event, symbolic recognition as an official language will likely be less important than more concrete institutions, for any variety of counterbalancing. Where this is feasible, the most important such institution is some variety of federalism or confederalism, with boundaries drawn so as to give speakers of the minority language(s) control over some provincial government(s) and—crucially—its education system. This provides the necessary bulwark against nationalizing projects by the central state. It is very likely that the province will over-protect its language. An advantage of this constitutionalist defence of language rights is that it allows us to admit this. We can think that robust Québécois autonomy on linguistic questions is legitimate and necessary without going through the intellectual contortions of trying to defend the details of Bill 101 and its progeny. It is in the nature of second-best solutions that not every aspect of them is justifiable.

Of course, the province may well engage in unjust nationalizing projects of its own, for all the familiar reasons. A balance of power among the two or three largest language groups in a state does not necessarily do anything to protect the smaller ones. It sometimes makes them worse off, since the local majority feels more vulnerable—and is thus more aggressive in its nationalization—than does the state-wide majority. Sometimes constitutional balances may be possible within a province: guaranteed representation in the provincial legislature, control over city or county or canton governments, and so on. Sometimes these smaller minorities ought to have a separate standing in the federation. In the

---

[21] This is just one instance of the problems with constitutional design in divided societies that Donald Horowitz discusses in Horowitz (2000).

United States and Canada, for example, Indian reservations have direct government-to-government relations with the centre instead of being understood as local governments within the State or Province.[22] Throughout, the aims ought to be, first, to prevent unjust and coercive assimilation, and second, to allow for voluntary language shift. The two are equal in their moral importance—individual freedom is restricted either by forced assimilation or by forced preservation—but the prevention of assimilation comes first in institutional design, because forced language consolidation has been so pervasive.

Even if fair institutions are designed and coercion and nationalization are prevented, widespread language shift and desuetude is to be expected. Linking the cause of minority language rights too closely to the goal of general language preservationism only makes the former seem implausible. But even after the language consolidation brought about by literacy and the modern state has run its course, even once we live in a world of hundreds of languages rather than thousands, there will be good reasons for some minority language rights.[23] Even if a language as a whole is relatively impervious to attacks by a modern state, its speakers are always persons who are all too pervious. Language rights were not needed to ensure the viability of Catalan under Franco and are not needed to protect the viability of Kurdish in Turkey today; they were and are needed to protect *individuals* against their states' nationalizing projects. We need not accept the unconditional defence of minority languages in order to justify the defence of those languages' speakers.

[22] I discuss this case at greater length in 'Indians in Madison's Constitutional order' (Levy 2002).

[23] We could almost say that there will be *better* reason, because it will be less likely that minority language rights result in the sacrifice of children's interests.

# 11

# The Antinomy of Language Policy

DANIEL M. WEINSTOCK

## 1. Setting the Stage

Language serves a number of functions in the lives of human beings. First, and perhaps most obviously, language allows people to communicate with one another. It is a tool that allows us to do business, to formulate and express our convictions and beliefs, to fall in love, and so on. Second, language provides people with access to cultures, and cultures perform a variety of functions in their lives. According to one prominent account that has been developed in the work of Will Kymlicka, cultures provide us with the range of options and evaluative grids that we require in order to develop our individual capacity for autonomous choice (Kymlicka 1989; 1995a). Third, languages are important to people's sense of who they are. They provide them with connections to the past, and thus serve to anchor their identities. The way in which the language they identify with is treated in the public sphere of the society in which they live thus becomes an important index of the recognition that their society affords them as distinct individuals. According to this view of the interest which humans have in language, I perceive my inability to use my language in the public sphere as somehow an affront to my integrity.

The problem for policy makers lies in the fact that, in certain contexts, these different functions underwrite quite different sets of language policies. The first, the 'communicative' function, militates, all things equal, for measures that facilitate the acquisition of languages that maximize a citizenry's communicative reach. The second, the 'cultural' function, supports policies that protect languages that underpin 'societal' cultures. And the third, the 'identity' stake, would support policies aimed at protecting ancestral tongues from the assimilative pressures of dominant languages, whether on the national stage or in the international context.

Versions of this chapter were presented to audiences at the Faculté de droit de l'Université de Montréal, at the Faculty of Law at McGill University, at the Philosophy Department of the University of Western Ontario, at the Philosophy Department of Carleton University, and at the Faculty of Law of the University of Toronto. I thank those present for providing me with questions and comments which have helped the chapter along immeasurably. I would also like to thank Joseph Heath, Will Kymlicka, and Alan Patten for extensive written comments.

Now, for citizens of powerful, linguistically homogeneous states whose forebears all spoke the same language as they presently do, these three functions can be tolerably well served by the same language. Though native speakers of English living in English-speaking countries are probably most able fully to realize their interests in these three functions, there are a number of 'global' languages (French, Spanish, Dutch) that allow their speakers to communicate with a vast number of the planet's inhabitants, while giving them access to a viable societal culture and affording them a connection to their historical roots. But consider the situation of, say, the Greek immigrant to Montreal. In her case, the three functions pull apart. Her identity stake in language would have her invest resources and incur opportunity costs in order to preserve Greek and to pass it on to her children. As a member of the societal culture in Quebec, she obviously has an interest in learning French, and in making sure that her children acquire fluency in it as well. And as a Canadian, a North American, and a resident of a global village in which English is increasingly becoming the lingua franca, she has an interest in being able to get by in English, and in making sure that her children do so as well. Assuming that there are limits on the capacity of the average person to acquire multiple languages and/or on the amount of resources that the average person can reasonably be expected to expend in doing so, she will be faced with the need to make difficult trade-offs.

But her deliberations as to how best to make these trade-offs are not conducted in a vacuum. Most multilingual states have enacted language policies that make some of the available strategies more difficult to pursue than others. By restricting the languages that are taught in public schools, by limiting the languages in which government services can be accessed, and through myriad other means, governments inflect the way in which its citizens will go about making the aforementioned trade-offs by assigning very different weights to the various values at stake.

What would a just language policy look like? An individualist public philosophy such as liberalism begins with a presumption favouring a policy of 'benign neglect'. It would hold that a variety of real but incommensurable values are at stake in the choices that people make as to how to distribute resources among these various values. The kind of autonomous life that liberals privilege involves making choices among incommensurable values without paternalistic intervention. And so, it might be claimed, the state ought simply to step back from legislating in the field of language, allow people to make the linguistic choices that best reflect their assessment of the rival goods in play, and let the linguistic chips fall where they may.

But, as has been pointed out by Alan Patten (2001) and by Will Kymlicka (1995a: 108–15), benign neglect is not a viable option as far as language is concerned. The state must communicate with its citizenry for a variety of reasons, and in order to do so efficiently it must choose a subset of the total set of languages spoken on its territory. The state can never be just an arbiter of linguistic preferences. It is itself a linguistic actor, and an important one at that. It simply cannot opt out of the linguistic arena.

I want in this chapter to argue that, while a policy of pure benign neglect is implausible, something of its spirit must be retained by language policies lest the states that enact them overstep the legitimate grounds of state action.

I will begin by arguing against three types of grounds that are often adduced for language policies that go beyond benign neglect in urging a significant degree of state paternalism with respect to individuals' linguistic choices. The first set of grounds points to the alleged 'intrinsic value' of particular languages and of particular linguistic communities, and to the need to preserve such languages and communities, even against the decisions of their own members. The second claims that the concatenation of individually unexceptionable linguistic decisions can give rise to unjust results. And the third holds that individual choices can fail to reflect people's actual linguistic preferences because, in an unrestricted context, there are dangers to their acting on their ideal preferences that they have a paramount interest in avoiding. I will then describe a fairly simple counterfactual contractualist test, one that attempts to adapt the liberal intuition that state coercion can legitimately occur only if it is in accordance with principles that all could accept from a suitably framed situation of choice.

## 2. Languages as Bearers of Intrinsic Value

Language policies inevitably involve either coercion or incentive-rigging by the state. At the more coercive end of the spectrum, they coerce members of linguistic minorities that are perceived as being particularly vulnerable into educating their children in one language rather than another, and into working and interacting with the officers of the state in that language as well. Other, more permissive language policies rig the incentives in ways that might be deemed problematic from the point of view of the hypothetical Greek immigrant to Montreal referred to above. They will make services and education available in the languages of two or more of the linguistic groups present on the territory over which they have jurisdiction, and will affirm the multilingual face of that territory. But, inevitably, the languages chosen for recognition and affirmation are those of the most powerful linguistic groups. From the point of view of our emblematic immigrant, such language policies impose costs that would not otherwise have existed on her pursuing a course that privileges the 'identity' stake she has in her ancestral language. In what follows, the former type of policy, which attempts to secure linguistic survival through coercion, will come under particularly close scrutiny. But we shall see that some of the reasons that we have for objecting to such policies from a liberal standpoint apply to the milder, 'incentive-rigging' type of policy as well.

The liberal intuition that people ought not to be coerced in the area of language choice is revealed by the uneasiness that we feel when we hear of the measures adopted by European nation-states in the nineteenth century in their most aggressive phases of 'nation-building'.[1] In order to ensure linguistic homogeneity over their whole territory, they ran roughshod over local languages and cultures, to the point of prohibiting the use of these languages in public education (Weber 1976; Bell 2001). The rationales invoked by high-minded nationalist thinkers today strike us as even worse than if such policies of cultural oppression had simply been justified by reference to the prerogatives of naked power. For example, John Stuart Mill, justifying the attempted eradication by the French of small languages, argued that it was actually in the interest of members of smaller, more benighted regional cultures that they be gently assimilated into the culture of the *métropole*, with its attendant greater riches and resources (Mill 1991).

Now, most language policies that aim to preserve languages from assimilative pressures involve some degree of coercion. In order to avoid the kind of condemnation that liberals rightly direct at the more egregious forms of nation-building, defenders of such policies must point to ethically relevant aspects of this kind of policy that allow us to distinguish them from nation-building policies. One difference that might be pointed to is that, while language policies such as those of the French aimed at linguistic homogenization, language policies geared at protecting languages against the assimilative pressures exercised by more powerful languages seek to preserve linguistic diversity. And, the argument continues, this is good because value inheres in each particular language that this kind of policy would help to preserve. Closely related, but importantly different in its implications, would be the observation that, while the language policies of the nation-builders of yore were tools through which the already powerful entrenched their unjust domination, the kinds of language policies that today protect vulnerable languages are tools that the oppressed deploy against mighty economic and political forces. On this view, these policies serve justice.

Were either of these ways of distinguishing policies aimed at language preservation and protection from nation-building policies warranted, they would shield such policies from the criticisms levelled at nation-building, while still justifying policies that override individual choice. On the first view, were languages and language communities bearers of intrinsic value, then there would be at least a prima facie case for preventing people from exercising their linguistic preferences when those preferences threaten the existence of a language. On the second view, it could be argued that, when people decide to invest their resources primarily so as to acquire proficiency in the language of the socio-economically dominant group, their preferences are an epiphenomenon

---

[1] I have analysed the idea of nation-building in greater detail in Weinstock.

of unjust social relations. On this view, justice does not require that their preferences be accorded any kind of supremacy by the state. Indeed, the opposite might very well be the case: justice might positively *require* that their preferences be overridden. Let me examine these two ways in which language policies might be distinguished and defended in turn.

The claim of those who follow the 'intrinsic value' route is that something of value is lost when a language and/or a culture disappear, and that this grounds a right to the use of minority languages in the public sphere regardless of whether or not the interests of individuals are in so doing realized.

What would it mean for language to have intrinsic value? It would mean that languages have value independently of the instrumental roles they perform in the lives of their users (or, indeed, non-users). As Denise Réaume (2000: 250–1), who has perhaps developed this view with the greatest sophistication, puts it, because it is a 'human accomplishment, and end, in itself', because it is a 'cultural inheritance' and a 'marker of identity', 'each language is itself a manifestation of human creativity which has value independent of its uses'. Inasmuch as particular languages have intrinsic value, the interests which people have in them cannot be reduced to their various instrumentalities as communicative tools and as 'contexts of choice'. People have reason to want to defend their languages against assimilative pressures even if it turned out to be the case that another language was a more efficient tool. She opposes her view to the influential argument developed by Will Kymlicka, according to which individuals require a stable societal culture in order to exercise the capacities required in order to lead an autonomous existence. She holds that Kymlicka's argument does not provide sufficiently robust a language right, since all it does is provide people with the right to *a* language and culture rather than with what in her view is wanted, namely, a right to *their* language and culture. For this, Réaume argues that we must be able to make out a case for the intrinsic value of individual linguistic communities.

I do not want to wade into philosophical thickets that the concept of intrinsic value involves.[2] Rather, I want to make two points about the use of the concept in the defence of minority language rights. First, the fact that something has intrinsic value does not in and of itself mean that it must in practical reasoning systematically trump 'merely' instrumental considerations. Consider the following example. Let us suppose that great works of art possess intrinsic value. Many works of art are also physical objects, such as wooden sculptures. Imagine that I am threatened with dying of exposure in a winter storm unless I use a magnificent wood sculpture that I have fortuitously stumbled upon as firewood to keep myself warm. My survival (hopefully) would justify me in using the sculpture to keep myself alive, its intrinsic value notwithstanding. (In case your intuitions are not sufficiently unambiguous in the case of the survival of just one person—a

---

[2]   The canonical modern formulation of the idea is in G. E. Moore's *Principia Ethica* (1903). For a forceful critique of the very concept of intrinsic value, see Thomson (1992). Moore is defended against Thomson's attacks in Zimmerman (1999).

philosopher at that!—you are free to add however many innocent children to the example that are required in order to make the point stick.) That is to say that the question of whether we should rank intrinsic value above instrumental value depends upon the specifics of the cases at hand. It may very well be that languages have intrinsic value, but that it would in certain cases nonetheless not be unreasonable to rank some instrumental value above its intrinsic value.

Second, and more importantly, appeal to intrinsic value does nothing to allay the concern that coercive language policies are illiberal. The reason is that, far from grounding an individual right to use language x or y, appealing to the intrinsic value *of languages* is actually a way of ascribing rights to languages or linguistic communities against their own members.[3] Now, remember that Réaume's intention in appealing to intrinsic value had been to provide a rationale for individuals being able to claim a right to use their own language in the public domain that might avoid some of the pitfalls associated with Kymlicka's approach. That argument, remember, has as its natural conclusion that individuals have a right to *a* culture, and thus to *a* language, rather than to whatever language they happen to have been raised in. If all languages and cultures have intrinsic value, then, presumably a right is generated that specifies the ability to access and use *particular* languages. But does such an argument really ground an individual right to particular languages? It does not. To see this, consider the canonical argument in the Western philosophical tradition for moral rights grounded in the intrinsic worth of persons, that of Immanuel Kant in the *Groundwork of the Metaphysics of Morals*. The argument in its broadest lines claims that, because each individual person has intrinsic worth (*dignity* rather than *price*), others are duty-bound not to treat persons as mere means. Now consider Herb, an individual person. If the Kantian argument goes through, it follows that Herb has a right against all others that they do not instrumentalize him and that they act positively so as to promote his rational nature. Other agents are saddled with correlative duties. In other words, the argument structure has it that agents have obligations towards that which bears intrinsic value.

The problem with the intrinsic value strategy for the defence of minority languages is, therefore, that if the argument upon which it is based goes through, it is not individual speakers of a language who have a right against others that they be allowed to use their language. Rather, minority languages *themselves* have rights against all others, *including their own speakers*, to have their intrinsic value affirmed. Minority languages, on other words, stand in this argument as does Herb in the Kantian argument, that is, as the beneficiary of a right. If we look at the argument from the point of view of individual persons, however, the argument underwrites not a right, but a duty. According to Zimmerman (1999: 204–5), 'intrinsic goods . . . have an intimate tie to morality, in that there is a moral *requirement* to favor them'. Now, at least as it had been articulated in

---

[3] I develop this point at much greater length in Weinstock (2000).

Réaume's argument, the appeal to intrinsic value was meant to address the problems associated with instrumental arguments such as Kymlicka's as defences of the rights of members of minority cultures. Such arguments, if successful, ground a right to *a* culture, whereas what is required is an argument justifying the right which people presumably have to *their* culture. But it is of the very nature of a right that right-holders can make use of their rights as they see fit, provided they do not in so doing infringe the rights of others. They have no such latitude in the case of a *duty*, however. To the extent that the intention of those who appeal to the intrinsic value of languages is to defend a right, it seems that the argument has overshot its mark.[4]

But this brings us back to the starting point. Remember that we had appealed to the intrinsic value strategy as a way of grounding an argument that would allow the defender of minority languages to oppose the nation-builder on moral grounds, while still being able to uphold threatened minority languages. And this strategy seems to have broken down. If cultures can have rights against their individual members, then on the face of it nation-builders can appeal to this fact just as protectors of minority languages can. An argument for cultural duties based upon the intrinsic value of culture and / or language runs into the same problems from the point of view of a broadly liberal political morality as the nation-building practices I briefly alluded to above. A liberal political morality would minimally have to affirm the moral supremacy of the individual. On this view, institutions, laws, and social practices have no irreducible value. They must ultimately find their justification in the positive difference that they make to individual human lives. Both the kinds of nation-building I have described, and laws and institutions that would impose duties upon individuals on behalf of cultures and/or languages, invert the liberal view of the relationship between individual and collective good, and this falls foul of the individualist liberal tenet.

Now, Réaume is free to accept the implication of this argument and to claim that the intrinsic value of languages and cultures requires that we do away with the priority accorded by liberals to the individual as against the collective. Nothing I have said in this section is meant to deny that linguistic communities have intrinsic value. My intention was simply to bring out the costs involved in the strategy favoured by Réaume. It implies that we do away with moral individualism, and that we accept that cultures and languages can have rights against their members. And this might justly be perceived by many people as too great a cost.[5]

---

[4] Albert Musschenga (1998) grasps the nettle and affirms that the intrinsic value of cultures grounds not rights but obligations.

[5] Réaume herself seems unwilling to take the illiberal step that would, in setting linguistic survival as a goal, ground a duty on the part of members of linguistic minorities. In her view, the end of linguistic *security* is more appropriate as a way of grounding an individual *right*. My intention in this paper has been to show that Réaume cannot have it both ways. Either she cleaves to the intrinsic value line of argument and ends up with an argument stronger than she wants, or she eschews appeal to intrinsic value and ends up with a discretionary language right, but without an argument as to why people *ought* to exercise that right in the way that she privileges, namely, to contribute to the viability of their language.

## 3. Language and Justice

Perhaps the case for language policies aimed at protecting languages against the choices of their own members can be made out by claiming that the results of unbridled individual choice would be unjust. In order to make out this claim, we need to be clearer on the kinds of processes that are presently at play in reducing the total number of viable languages on the planet today. Let me distinguish, ideal-typically, a number of routes which can all lead to the disappearance of individual languages or language groups.[6] First, languages might disappear simply because they are ill-equipped to deal with the requirements which modernity places upon them. Globalization increases the conditions for communicative efficacy that languages must satisfy. Modern conditions place all but an infinitesimal proportion of the planet's inhabitants in real or potential communication with a far greater number of people than would have been the case only a century ago. Languages that are geared to face-to-face communities thus seem particularly ill-equipped to meet these conditions. For example, languages which have not been codified as written tongues might be particularly vulnerable in this regard. The relatively late codification of aboriginal languages such as Inuktituk represents an attempt to pre-empt such processes. Let me refer to this as *Scenario I*.

Second, language groups have historically died out as a result of being explicitly targeted by the dominant linguistic group within a state embarked upon an aggressive phase of nation-building. This has principally been done through the legal prohibition of minority language instruction in public schools. I will refer to this kind of process as *Scenario II*.

Third, languages can be threatened by the costs, economic and otherwise, involved in the continued use and instruction of a minority language, in a context where another language offers a greater range of opportunities (*Scenario III*). One can imagine at least three sub-scenarios here. First, language shift can simply be a reflection of the unintended consequences of the operation of the market. Linguistic conventions emerge in an unplanned manner among members of a community, which might have as a side effect that some languages are driven out (*IIIa*). Second, language shift can reflect economic exploitation. In some societies, the means of production have been disproportionately held by members of a linguistic group, and the working classes and lumpenproletariat have been drawn from one or several others. At times, this economic exploitation is legally enshrined, as it was in apartheid South Africa. Here, linguistic change follows from economic injustice. Members of a disenfranchised linguistic group might choose to assimilate as a means of accessing economic opportunity unfairly monopolized by the dominant language group (*IIIb*).

---

[6] For two recent accounts of linguistic change that derive dramatically different normative conclusions from essentially the same empirical data, see Janson (2002) and Crystal (2000).

Finally, language shift can occur because of the state's official language policy. When a state declares that only one or some small subset of the total number of languages spoken on its territory will have the status of 'official' languages, it inflects the language choices that people will make by making it more difficult to organize instruction of non-official minority languages (even when such instruction is not prohibited altogether), by blocking those who do not speak the official languages from jobs in the public sector, and by making it more difficult for them to access public services efficiently (*IIIc*).

Determining whether a particular case of language shift is unjust and therefore deserving of some kind of redress by the state requires attending to the particulars of the case. In particular, we must be able to come to some determination of whether the processes that have given rise to language shift have been unjust. Some cases of language disappearance might be regrettable without being unjust. It would be overtaxing our institutions of justice intolerably to require of them that they never allow regrettable results. Now, clearly, Scenario I instantiates this kind of case. Cultures and languages are living, evolving phenomena that respond to myriad environmental pressures, and it is of the nature of such phenomena that, as the environment changes, so will particular languages' suitability to the environment. Though one should avoid lapsing into a crude 'survival of the fittest' model of linguistic change, one should also not deny that evolutionary explanations account, regrettably perhaps, for at least some unavoidable linguistic erosion. (It is no accident that the modern world, characterized as it is by modern means of communication and increasing globalization of markets and finance, is marked by a quite remarkable amount of linguistic *convergence*—according to some accounts only a few hundred of the thousands of languages that exist today are viable in the circumstances of modernity).

Conversely, Scenarios II and IIIb are clear cases of *injustice*. The kind of aggressive nation-building evoked by Scenario II violates the liberal-democratic tenet according to which individuals ought not to be treated as mere means toward collective ends. And societies in which linguistic change has occurred as in Scenario IIIb are ones in which linguistic choice has been made against a backdrop of egregiously unjust resource allocation. In these cases, redress is clearly called for, though whether the most appropriate form of state action should consists in inducements for oppressed groups to reclaim their languages is an open question. Arguably, cases corresponding to Scenario IIIb might require above all else that the state enact measures that will rectify the resource imbalance between groups. If it achieves this end, language choice could then occur on the basis of a fair baseline, and there is no guarantee that members of formerly oppressed groups would choose to reconstitute their cultures and languages. Respect for their agency requires that, once a fair baseline is set up, they be permitted to decide the matter for themselves.

Cases corresponding most closely to Scenario II in my view are those that most clearly call for redress at the level of language and culture. In such cases, the erosion of culture and language is no mere epiphenomenon of deeper economic forces. Rather, this erosion is directly willed by nation-builders. In this kind of case, measures directly targeted at enhancing a minority language group's ability to make viable use of its own language may be called for. Nation-building has historically been accompanied by a disparagement of 'local' languages and dialects as backward and uncivilized. The internalization over time of such attitudes by the groups against which they were initially directed might contribute to a situation in which no purely material distribution will succeed in redressing the harms caused by cultural and linguistic oppression. Measures aimed at undoing the directly cultural and linguistic dimensions of oppression might thus be required.

(In practice though, Scenarios II and IIIb tend to be intermingled. Cultural disparagement is most often an integral part of more general strategies of subjugation. It will in fact be rare to encounter historical instances of 'pure' economic exploitation, that is, of exploitation not tainted by overt, institutionalized cultural and linguistic contempt.)

Scenario IIIa is more controversial. There is very little consensus among philosophers or among the population at large about the fairness of market outcomes. Many liberal theorists believe that the market generates fair outcomes on the condition that initial resource endowments be fairly distributed. There are any number of ways of spelling out what such a fair initial allotment would be. According to Rawls's famous account, primary goods should be distributed in a manner that satisfies the 'difference principle'. According to Dworkin, resource bundles should pass the 'envy test'. It is unclear in any event how such theories would classify the 'resource' that is language. Should membership in one's own language group count as one of those resources which ought to be constrained by this or that resource-egalitarian principle, or should it count as one of the myriad goods which people spend their (initially fairly allocated) resources on in whatever way they see fit, as a function of their individual preference schedules? On the one hand, membership in a particular language group does not technically count as a Rawlsian primary good, as clearly it is not the type of resource which *all* people need, whatever their particular conception of the good. We cannot simply assume—to revert to Dworkinian language—that all rational persons will choose to use some of their initial resource endowment to insure against the possibility that they might find themselves speakers of an endangered language. It seems reductive, however, to claim that people are simply indulging an expensive taste when they choose to continue to speak and to bring up their young in a minority language. Perhaps language considered as a *distribuans* simply points to the limitations of resource-egalitarian conceptions of justice.

That membership in a language group can simply be considered neither as part of one's unalterable circumstances nor as a pure object of choice means that Philippe Van Parijs's (2002) claim that speakers of minority languages who must also acquire proficiency in the majority language should as a matter of justice receive compensation from speakers of the majority language because of the additional costs associated with learning two (or several) languages is at least problematic. (It does not, however, controvert Jonathan Pool's [1991a] suggestion that the *stability* of an official language regime in a multilingual context requires such compensation.) The argument that the costs of language training ought to be borne equally by all members of a society is clearly premised on the assumption that language is part of one's unchosen set of circumstances. The reality of the situation is, as we have seen, more complicated than that. (Such an approach would in any case have to be based upon a fuller reckoning of the benefits and burdens that asymmetrically multilingual societies involve. Van Parijs says nothing of the benefits which accrue to speakers of the minority language from having to learn and become proficient in more than one language.)

Another argument against language choice simply being determined by market forces and by majoritarian processes has been suggested by Will Kymlicka, and developed at greater length in a recent paper by Alan Patten (2001). It claims that, when we adopt a laissez-faire attitude to matters of language choice in societies comprised of a plurality of language groups, we de facto underwrite the tyranny of the linguistic majority. In their view, 'benign neglect' is both illusory and unjust. It is illusory because, as was noted above, the state cannot avoid being a linguistic actor. What *passes* as 'benign neglect' is on this view the unjustifiable de facto tyranny of the linguistic majority. For if we simply allow the weight of numbers to determine the language children will be taught in, or public services accessed, we will make it difficult, if not impossible, for minority languages to have status and visibility in the public sphere, and this will exert pressure upon minority languages just as surely as if the state had given the majority language official status. Scenario IIIa is on this view really no different from IIIc. What proponents of IIIc will deliberately, partisans of IIIa simply allow. But the result in both cases is on this view much the same.

The solution on this view is to adopt an official languages policy that attempts to deal fairly with the society's various language groups. They are to be given official recognition in the public arena, and in some cases language groups are to be empowered to enact laws and measures that will constrain their members into continuing to speak their language.

I see three problems with this argument. First, it is not clear that it will erase the arbitrariness that its proponents see in a policy of benign neglect. Second, it arguably adds deliberate symbolic harm to languages deemed unworthy of official status to the harm which benign neglect already allows. And third, it 'freezes' a society's linguistic composition at a certain stage of linguistic development, and forecloses the possibility that, as the society evolves, through immigration for instance, the choices made as to the languages to make 'official' will no longer reflect the linguistic 'facts on the ground'.

Why would a policy which gave official status to languages other than that of the majority not lead to greater fairness? The problem is that most societies in the world today contain a vast array of linguistic groups, more than can be encompassed by a multilingual official languages policy. Even a riotously multilingual polity such as India recognizes only 18 of the 42 languages other than English which are spoken by a million people or more.[7] In such a context, how can we in a principled manner decide which languages are to be granted the protections and prerogatives of official status? The criteria that tend to be used to decide all seem morally arbitrary. Length of historical establishment ends up in many contexts rewarding colonialism. (In the New World, the European groups that engaged in colonial plunder are called 'national minorities'. More recent arrivals are called 'immigrants'.) Number also seems a morally suspect criterion. For example, that there are so few members of various aboriginal peoples in North America is a lingering consequence of colonialism. Thus, a multilingual official languages policy reduces the number of people who are subjected to the arbitrary will of the majority, but it does not remove arbitrariness from the policy.

Now, it might be argued that reducing the number of people arbitrarily left out by a unilingual language policy constitutes moral progress. Numbers matter, one might claim, and so a multilingual policy that gives recognition to, say, the five most powerful language groups in a multilingual policy is preferable to one that recognizes only four.

Intuitions can diverge on this issue. However, to the extent that recognition of cultural specificities is a good that must be distributed justly, it could be countered that the justice of a society depends upon how it treats its weakest rather than its most powerful members with respect to this good. But even if we were to accept the 'numbers matter' claim, there are other problems attending a multilingual language policy that seem immune to such quantitative consideration.

For a start, just like official unilingualism, official bilingualism and multilingualism symbolically divide a society into two categories of citizen, those whose languages are affirmed by language policy and those whose languages are simply ignored (Bennett 2001). Similarly, policies of 'language maintenance' (as Patten terms them), which aim to protect minority languages from the assimilative forces exercised by continental or global languages, embody significant arbitrariness inasmuch as only the most powerful linguistic minorities can provide themselves with such policies. Typically, they require that a minority linguistic group be powerful enough to control the levers of state institutions. Language maintenance may very well succeed in protecting languages that would otherwise be vulnerable to assimilative pressures. But they do nothing to protect the languages of those linguistic minorities that are not powerful enough to enact and enforce such possibilities.

[7] This according to the *Ethnologue* database cited at http://theory.tifr.res.in/bombay/history/people/language/

What's more, an official languages policy states that, now and for ever, *these* will be the languages that will have pride of place in the public sphere of society. But societies evolve as a result of myriad forces acting upon them, some of them within the society's control (for example, immigration), others largely beyond its control (the various processes identified with 'globalization'). All of these forces can concatenate in a way that over time makes the choice of official languages for the society obsolete. When an official languages policy is enacted, and becomes part of the society's self-understanding, such evolution comes to be seen as a problem to be counteracted rather than simply as a change of neutral normative valence.

So it is simply false to say that official languages policies erase the stain of arbitrariness and majority tyranny which inheres in benign neglect. They merely alter the identity of the linguistic groups whose languages will be affirmed and promoted, but they do nothing to ensure that justice will thereby be done. What's more, official languages policies symbolically affirm the division of society into linguistically privileged and marginalized groups, whereas in a regime of benign neglect such linguistic division might simply be seen as the morally arbitrary result of market and majoritarian forces.

Let me take stock. The upshot of this section is that a case can be made for language protection, perhaps requiring that individual language choices be overridden, when the processes that have led to a language disappearing or becoming vulnerable are themselves unjust. Cultural oppression and humiliation has often been an integral part of policies of colonial oppression and exploitation, and of the subjugation of local languages and cultures in the context of nation-building. Restorative justice would here seem to require that measures of language protection be adopted at least until such a time that individuals' language choices can be taken to represent their autonomous choices rather than still bearing the taint of oppression.

At the opposite extreme, justice does not require that evolutionary processes that might lead to the disappearance of certain languages be counteracted. Such disappearances might be causes for regret, but not all that is to be regretted is unjust.

More controversial is the question of whether language changes that reflect the operation of market forces might in certain cases call for measures of distributive justice. At stake is the question of whether, in a resource-egalitarian context, language is to be seen as choice or circumstance. This is clearly a difficult question, the resolution of which far exceeds the bounds of this chapter.

Note that these arguments are based on processes that are clearly ideal types. Real-world cases will typically involve a combination of several of the scenarios that I have just sketched. Take the situation of French in North America. After the British conquest of 1780, the French communities were subjected for a time to policies of cultural subjugation. The infamous Durham Report is a pure example of cultural oppression masquerading as benevolent, Millean *noblesse oblige*. In the late nineteenth and early twentieth centuries, the vulnerability of

French was to a greater degree an epiphenomenon of the English economic domination of Canada. Today, the principal threat to French in Canada has to do with the emergence of a global market the lingua franca of which just happens to be the same as that of the people at whose hands French Canadians suffered colonial and economic exploitation. If the argument of the foregoing section is correct, the kinds of measures adopted by governments in Quebec since the early 1970s are justified to the extent that the lingering effects of colonialism and economic exploitation are still being felt. But they are more suspect as a means of countering the effects of the market. What is the extent of the vulnerability of French in North America today, and to what degree is this vulnerability a product of the oppression and exploitation of the past? These are questions that I cannot hope to answer here. The framework I have suggested in this section does not aspire to answer all the questions that might be posed concerning the injustice of this or that case of language disappearance, though perhaps it does allow us to be more perspicuous in the questions that we pose.

## 4. Language as a Public Good

I want briefly to consider one final argument that might be made for language policies that use coercive measures to preserve languages against the choices of the members of a linguistic community. It claims that, when people choose to devote all or most of their resources learning and passing on a communicatively more effective language to the detriment of languages that allow them to access a specific societal culture and/or ones that allow them to connect with their historical roots, their choices do not truly reflect their preferences. According to this argument, languages that are vulnerable to the assimilative pressures of communicatively more efficient languages are public goods that are susceptible to collective action problems. In a nutshell, the view is that speakers of a 'small' language would rather be able to live in their own language, but their ability to do so depends upon a sufficient members of their fellow speakers choosing to do so as well. The problem facing the individual deciding on how to use his resources acquiring languages is the following: if he chooses to learn and pass on to his children the 'smaller' language $S$ while his fellows decide to defect to the larger, communicatively more efficient language $E$, he ends up a loser on all fronts. There are not enough speakers of $S$ left, and he has deprived himself of the second-best outcome of being able to derive benefit from a language spoken by a vast number of people. In such a situation, it might appear rational, *even for an individual who would in an ideal world prefer to live in S*, to acquire proficiency in $E$ and to pass it on to his children, even if $S$ disappears as a result, his dominant motive being to avoid ending up a 'linguistic sucker'.

According to an account of the role of the state that has become widely accepted among defenders and practitioners of the welfare-state, a central function of the state is to ensure the provision of essential public goods which, though preferred by all, are vulnerable to collective action problems (Heath 2001). If smaller languages are like other public goods, preferred by all but chosen only by the foolhardy, then there is as much reason for the state to 'provide' language as there is for it to provide health or security.

There is, however, an important difference between language and other public goods that suggests that we should at least be cautious in accepting this argument too quickly. The kind of collective action problem that paradigmatic-ally calls for state action is one in which there is no question as to whether or not uncoordinated action is suboptimal. The different possible outcomes are ranked according to a single evaluative dimension. Suboptimal outcomes are suboptimal from everyone's lights. In Hobbes's classic case, the state of war is one that everyone has reason to want to quit.

The situation with respect to language is significantly different (Levy 2000: 118–21). As we saw at the outset of this chapter, decisions as to how to invest the limited resources that we can devote to language acquisition and transmission are made in the context of plural and contingently conflicting values. Communicative efficacy, contexts of choice afforded by societal cultures, and connection with one's roots all embody different and equally admirable values. Thus, to revert to the single case sketched above, when individuals make choices that collectively lead to $S$ disappearing, they find themselves less well-off then they might otherwise have been on the value scale that $S$ realizes, but they find themselves doing better on the value dimension that $E$ realizes than they would have been had they collectively devoted more resources to $S$. There is no single, higher-level dimension on the basis of which to determine which of these two outcomes is superior. It all depends on which of the plural values involved in language choice this or that individual happens to privilege.

Defenders of language policies that justify the overriding of individual lan-guage choices on the basis of an analogy with public goods thus make the assumption that communicative efficacy is systematically trumped in indi-viduals' 'authentic' preference schedules by (depending on the case) the desire to keep faith with one's historical roots or the wish to be part of a homogeneous societal culture. Now this assumption may end up being true as a matter of empirical fact, but it is certainly not an a priori truth, as the preference for life as against death, for health as opposed to disease, for security as opposed to con-stant threat come close to being. Yet this is the way that many theorists writing on the issue of language have treated it.

## 5. A Just Language Policy?

The upshot of the foregoing two sections is that the case for language policies aimed at protecting languages, even when this involves going against the choices of a language's own speakers, is weaker than many theorists who have emphasized the importance of culture and language for individual well-being have tended to assume.

I conceded earlier in this chapter, however, that the benign neglect that what would at first glance seem to be the natural upshot of this result cannot be maintained by the state. The state is an actor rather than simply a passive arbiter in the area of language. The business of government and of the courts must for reasons of practicability be carried out in some small subset of the total set of languages spoken on the territory.[8] Teachers must be trained and public education organized, and so on. If the state is to be more than simply an administrative irrelevance to its population, it must speak to its population so as to be understood and it must be able to comprehend when it is spoken to by its citizenry.

Clearly, some principles are required in order to govern the linguistic behaviour of the state. But benign neglect won't work, nor will appeal to the alleged intrinsic value of linguistic communities, to the justice of all cases of linguistic protection, or to the claim that, when speakers of minority languages choose to devote resources to learning and passing on languages other than their own, their choice does not actually reveal their 'true' preferences. How might a middle ground be found?

I want to suggest that states act justly in the area of language when they depart from the principle of benign neglect just enough to ensure that they will be able to communicate effectively with their citizenry, but no more. I will devote the rest of this chapter to fleshing out this very simple proposal.

Obviously, much of the work will have to be done fleshing out what is meant in the foregoing characterization by the term 'effectively'. Ideally, effective communication between the state and its citizens implies certain conditions being fulfilled by both communicating parties. The state must ensure that it communicates in a manner which makes plain to the average citizens what the rights and obligations created by the state's legislative action are, and that it explain how these obligations are to be fulfilled and these rights upheld. It must communicate in a manner that makes possible meaningful citizen participation in public debates about the legislative agenda. And it must develop means of responding to citizen input.

In order to communicate effectively, the state must satisfy some conditions that have been fairly well discussed by political philosophers, such as the condition of publicity (Kant 1970: 125–30; Gutmann and Thompson 1996: 95–127). But all the institutional openness and transparency in the world will come to naught if vast proportions of the population are unable to understand what the state is openly and transparently attempting to communicate. The linguistic requirement that the state communicate in a language or set of languages

---

[8] According to some accounts, translation costs account for 40% of the EU's total budget. This figure will increase beyond all reasonable limits when *élargissement* occurs.

most likely to ensure widespread uptake is thus also presupposed by the condition of effective communication.

Citizens must also satisfy certain conditions if effective communication is to take place. As has been pointed out by a number of political scientists in recent years, democratic life requires a not insignificant set of cognitive skills on the part of the average citizen. She must be able to draw valid inferences and detect the kinds of inferential fallacies that often infect the communication even of those among her political interlocutors who are in good faith, she must possess a considerable body of fairly technical knowledge, and the like (Lupia and McCubbins 1998; Elkins and Soltan 1999; *Critical Review* 1998). But she must obviously be in a position to understand at least one of the languages that the government speaks.

How can the linguistic fit between the government and its citizenry in multilingual societies come about? The path to linguistic congruence will lie somewhere between two extremes. On the one hand, the state can make use of its control of public education to enforce linguistic homogeneity. This is the traditional 'nation-building' approach, and we have seen that it faces insuperable moral difficulties. On the other, the state can cater to the linguistic diversity of its population by ensuring that laws and parliamentary debates are published in all of the languages present on its territory, by training a massively multilingual civil service, and so on. This would however be prohibitively costly. And it would also involve costs in terms of the society's democratic life, since there would be no guarantee that a multilingual society would be able to put in place the means for meaningful democratic deliberation among linguistic communities.

How should a liberal society determine where the right balance lies between these two extreme approaches? What is required is that we arrive at a determination of the best way in which to balance the various costs and benefits involved at either end of the continuum. How much of our individual linguistic freedom are we willing to sacrifice for the sake of reducing the different kinds of cost associated with the institutionalization of a truly multilingual society?

We cannot assume that there is one uniquely rational way to answer this question. Remember that individuals in a diverse society will arrive at a plurality of different ways of ranking the various values that are at stake in linguistic choice. Some will privilege investing resources in ensuring that they and their children remain linguistically and culturally connected to their historical roots, while others will emphasize the acquisition of 'global' languages such as English even when they are not the native languages of the 'societal culture' to which they belong. Others still will accord overriding importance to the linguistic integration of society around the language of the majority, so as to create a solidaristic society and a truly deliberative democracy.

Now, clearly, the rankings that individuals will make among these values will not be completely independent of the linguistic behaviour of the state to which they belong, or of the linguistic make-up of society as a whole. A speaker of language $L1$ in a society in which the vast majority of the population have $L2$ as a mother tongue will typically want to ensure that she and her children acquire sufficient proficiency in $L2$ to transact business, to follow and to take part in public debates, and the like, and this will likely be the case independently of whether or not the state enacts coercive legislation aiming at ensuring that speakers of languages other than $L2$ integrate linguistically. But there will nonetheless in such a society be aspects of individual rankings that are simply independent of such considerations. And, again granted the assumption that there are limits on the number of languages in which the average individual can acquire full proficiency and/or on the amount of resources, both real and in terms of opportunity costs, that an individual can reasonably be expected to devote to language acquisition, the fact that people have such independent preferences with respect to language will affect the degree of proficiency in $L2$ that they will strive to achieve. Those who value linguistic rootedness and/or communicative reach may tend to be satisfied with a 'working knowledge' of $L2$, while those who have chosen to acculturate will attempt to reach a more complete mastery, one that allows them, for example, to access the great works of literature and, over time, to come to 'identify' with the language and culture as well.

The state must thus find a fair way of governing its linguistic behaviour, given that its citizens legitimately rank the various values in different ways, and that they therefore also assess differently the costs associated with the different ways of achieving linguistic congruence between state and society.

My suggestion, in a Rawlsian spirit, is that the fairest perspective from which to assess these costs is from what one might call the 'least advantaged linguistic class' (Rawls 1971: 97–100). And clearly, those individuals upon whom different language regimes risk bearing hardest are those who at least in principle might want to divide the resources that they have at their disposal for language acquisition and transmission among a variety of languages, that is, those people who cannot have the various interests that human beings typically have in language served by the same language. (To revert to my earlier example, we can think of the Greek immigrant to Montreal who might want to preserve her ancestral tongue for reasons of identity, to acquire French so as to integrate into Quebec's societal culture, and to acquire English in order to extend her communicative reach in the global village.)

My claim is that, from the perspective of the least advantaged linguistic class, the most attractive language policy is one that goes no further in its imposition of the language of the majority than what is required in order for the state to be able to communicate effectively with its citizens. This would permit citizens in the least advantaged class to devote resources sufficient to acquiring working knowledge rather than full proficiency and identification, and thus to have resources left over for the realization of the other values that languages bear for them. From that perspective, while benign neglect is an impossible goal given the need for the state to communicate with its citizenry, the state should govern its linguistic behaviour in a manner that departs from benign neglect as little as possible, compatibly with the achievement of the state's communicative purposes.

What would this mean in practice? Obviously, much would depend upon the detail of specific cases. What is required for effective communication will differ in societies in which one massively dominant language coexists with a variety of much smaller ones (think of German and Turkish in Germany), and in societies in which there a plurality of languages spoken by significant numbers of people (think of India). The structure of government will also have an impact. The situation regarding the communicative needs of governments looks quite different in a federal state, where federal jurisdictions overlap significantly with linguistic ones, from that in a centralized state.

For the sake of simplicity, let's take the case of a society in which one language massively dominates the others. Clearly, there is a strong argument to be made for the government taking steps to ensure that all citizens have a working knowledge of that language. But the perspective of the least favoured linguistic group would militate against going any further than this by invoking one among of the various grounds of linguistic paternalism that were discussed earlier in this chapter. Thus, for example, if working knowledge of the language of the majority can be taught simply through language teaching and through broader access to the majority's culture as a whole, there is little reason for the state to prohibit schooling in languages other than that of the majority, provided that it includes learning the majority language as well. There will also be little reason for the state to intervene in areas that do not affect its ability to communicate effectively with its citizens. To generalize, a language policy governed, as justice seems to me to require that it ought to be, by the perspective of the least advantaged linguistic class will be marked by at least the three following principles:

1. *Minimalism*. Effective communication being the only independent linguistic goal that states legitimately pursue, states must use the least invasive means possible in its attainment, so as not to detract from its citizens' ability to act to as great a degree as possible on the basis of their rankings of the various goods at play. They must abstain from legislating about languages in areas that do not affect the state's ability to achieve this goal.
2. *Anti-symbolism*. Since the state privileges certain languages by virtue of their pragmatic efficacy rather than out of a concern for justice or intrinsic value, no symbolic significance is to be attached to the state's linguistic choice. States should abstain from any actions or pronouncements that can reasonably be taken to accord pre-eminence to native speakers of the majority language.
3. *Revisability*. As the state is committed to use language in a way that maximizes effective communication, it remains open to the possibility that its use of language may have to change so as to reflect the changing linguistic make-up

of society. Since societies are not on this view to be perceived as 'ontologically' linked to any particular language, the state's overriding interest is in using the mix of languages that best allows it to fulfil the pragmatic interest it has in ensuring effective two-way communication. And that can easily change over time. This will obviously be particularly relevant for immigrant societies that devolve power at least to some degree to the local level.

A language policy guided by these three principles would not amount to benign neglect. In most cases, it will advantage the language of the majority. But it will do so for pragmatic reasons to do with the organization of a functioning democracy, rather than because the majority linguistic community in question is seen as bearing 'intrinsic' value, or (if we set aside cases in which linguistic communities have been explicitly targeted for cultural oppression) because the defence of the language of the majority is uniquely just, or again because the state would thereby be allowing members of the majority to act on their 'real' preferences. And it would do so subject to the three principles that a restriction to pragmatic justification underwrites, principles that obviate the need for the state to be a linguistic actor rather than simply as a neutral linguistic arbiter, from lapsing into a justification of the tyranny of the linguistic majority.

## 6. Concluding Remarks

Language serves a variety of functions in people's lives. Until recently, political philosophers have paid scant attention to the way in which to construct a just language policy, despite the fact that the historical record clearly shows the lengths to which people are willing to go for the sake of language. Recent political philosophers have become more alive to the importance that culture and language play in people's lives, and have been correspondingly more willing to consider the ways in which our standard theories of justice must be adapted in order to have them contribute to the task of linguistic and cultural justice. But they have also been strangely one-dimensional in their appreciation of the full range of interests that people have in language. Strangely, they have tended to neglect what would seem to be the most obvious and fundamental aspect of language, namely, its instrumental nature, the fact that it allows us to communicate, and that, all things equal, we have an interest in communicating as broadly as possible (Corballis 2002). They have instead emphasized the importance of specific languages for individual identity and for nation-building, and, having done so, have developed impressive normative arguments for paternalistic languages policies geared towards the protection of particular languages, at times against the choices of the members of the linguistic communities involved.

Reckoning with the full range of values that language serves, and with the fact that human beings can exercise agency in ranking these values and acting on their rankings, forces us to reframe the debate to a considerable degree. I have tried to show that it should make us reconsider less paternalistic policies which, while they do not amount to the full abstentionism of benign neglect, depart from that policy as little as possible.

# 12

## Beyond *Person*ality: The Territorial and Personal Principles of Language Policy Reconsidered

DENISE G. RÉAUME

Language regulation regimes are commonly classified according to whether they exemplify the territorial model or the personality principle (Royal Commission on Bilingualism and Biculturalism 1967: Ch. 4; McRae 1975: 33; Laponce 1987; McRoberts 1989; May 2001: 178–9). This division picks out one particular feature of regimes: whether they regulate language use by territory, requiring people to adapt to the language of the place, or regulate in accordance with the linguistic preferences of speakers, wherever they reside. Described this thinly, neither model dictates very precisely a concrete policy on language, and indeed the literature displays a distinct lack of precision in the use of the two models to illuminate the concrete policies adopted in various jurisdictions. Starting from the analytical feature identified by the conventional distinction between the two models, I aim to build a more developed conceptual framework within which to place alternative language policies. This framework will not only relate the territorial/personal dimension of language policy to the preference for unilingualism or bilingualism, but will also excavate the underlying normative assumptions of each model.

Policy proposals grounded in territoriality tend to favour unilingualism: they aim at either converting a multilingual population into a unilingual one, or at least favouring one language above others (McRoberts 1989: 143). The personality principle is more friendly to a bilingual policy in a multilingual society, that is, a regime of language protections for speakers of more than one language. The connection between the territorial dimension of language policy and unilingualism is not a logical one, but the two features are combined often enough in the policy literature to make it worthwhile to use the combination as a policy model in order to investigate its normative underpinnings. The connection between the personality principle and bilingualism is also not, strictly

This chapter is based on a paper that was presented to the 2002 meeting of the Analytical Legal Philosophy Conference, held at Yale University, New Haven. I am indebted to the participants for a very lively discussion.

speaking, a logical one, but bilingualism will be the natural outcome of the adoption of the personality principle in any jurisdiction in which there are two or more language groups sharing territory. Exploring this connection will lead us naturally into a deeper exploration of the available justifications for such a policy.

How might these contrasting outcomes—the pursuit of territorial unilingualism or the adoption of bilingualism—be justified? I will distinguish between two broad types of justification—aggregative and rights-based—for the regulation of language use. Each hinges on a different understanding of the importance of a language to its speakers. Aggregative justifications are consequentialist and vary according to the end aimed at: economic efficiency, administrative convenience, and national unity (or at least social peace) are among the most prominent contenders. Such justifications conceive of language as a means to extraneous ends, and of people's interest in their language as reducible to a common denominator and able to be traded off against competing interests through a calculation of costs and benefits. It seems to me that most of the thinking about language policy to date has been largely in the aggregative mode (MacMillan 1998; Reid 1993; McRae 1975; Laponce 1987). By contrast, a rights approach must articulate a human interest in one's language that is sufficiently important to resist aggregation and to justify the imposition of obligations on others to protect that interest. The articulation of a rights framework for thinking about language protections has had to struggle to establish itself against the dominance of the aggregative approaches. The strongest evidence of this dominance is that both advocates of unilingualism and advocates of bilingualism often appeal to aggregative considerations as justification. The difficulty of this effort to define a conceptually distinct rights-based approach is compounded by the fact that language use is importantly different from other human interests traditionally deemed appropriate to a human rights analysis—where language protections exist, it is in large part for the sake of entire communities of speakers of a language, not for the sake of each individual speaker.

If the appeal to territory is tied to a preference for unilingualism, so too does it tend to be grounded in an aggregative justification. Likewise, the personality principle goes with bilingualism and at the same time makes the most sense constructed on a rights model. This mapping of regulatory scheme onto normative approach is not perfect; that is, it is not the case that all plausibly relevant aggregative justifications support territorial unilingualism, while only non-aggregative justifications support bilingualism. However, the affinities between each of the two models and the normative approach with which I have matched it are sufficiently strong to enable us usefully to treat territorial unilingualism as a predominantly aggregative approach and the personality principle as grounded in rights. Furthermore, while aggregative justifications can be offered for bilingualism, I think it is more difficult to come up with a valid rights-based justification for unilingualism. Thus, unilingualism requires an aggregative argument, even though not all aggregative arguments support unilingualism. And while aggregative considerations may sometimes militate in favour of bilingualism, their very contingency makes this a weaker form of argument. To line up unilingualism with aggregative justifications and bilingualism with rights-based arguments presents the models as conceptually and normatively distinct.

Arguments for territorial unilingualism proceed on the assumption that no valid rights claims stand in the way of such a policy, for it is in the nature of rights claims that they demand to be satisfied before aggregative considerations are allowed to enter the picture. Thus, as a comprehensive approach toward language policy, territorial unilingualism is viable only if there are no language rights. An examination of the understanding of the human interest in language implicit within the territorial unilingualism model will show it to be an impoverished one, and its flaws will point us in the direction of an alternative understanding that would ground a rights-based approach, thus pushing aggregative considerations to the margins of language policy. This will give us a start with the normative grounding of the personality model, but discussions of that model typically fall into an individual rights paradigm. This, I shall argue, makes it difficult to design a rights-based bilingualism policy that is both effective and justifiable. Thus, I propose an alternative to the personality principle that takes us beyond *personality* in the individualistic sense as the ground of language rights claims. I have begun elsewhere to develop this alternative account of language rights (Réaume 1988; 1994; 1991); my current concern is to provide a more elaborate account of the territorialism and personality models with which it competes and to use my account to help point up some of the conceptual and normative limits of those standard models of language policy.

Aggregative justifications underpinning the territorial model advanced in the literature misunderstand the nature of the interest in the use of one's own language. At the same time, the personality principle correctly diagnoses this problem with the territorial model, but is susceptible to an interpretation that is too individualistic. The proper understanding of the importance of language to its speakers makes it resistant to ordinary cost–benefit analysis, but that importance must be understood in terms that encompass an entire community of language speakers; it cannot be located solely in the individual speaker. So understood, the normative foundation of language protection extends to *each* viable linguistic community within a state or policy unit. Thus, a rights-based model is the best way to understand language issues. This explains the pull of the personality principle in political debate. This does not preclude resort to aggregative considerations once claims of right are satisfied, but does put them in their proper place in a comprehensive policy framework. But the social dimension of language use will sometimes mean that language use protections should not be fully individualized, that is, extended to each and every speaker under all circumstances. Instead, protection can be provided only where there are a sufficient number of speakers living in close proximity; this introduces a geographical dimension to language policy and to that extent borrows from the territorial idea. Nor can these rights always be fully universalized, that is, extended to the speakers of each language in a given territory. This explains the kernel of truth in the territorial model. In the final analysis, some protections will be tied to territory, but not in a way that need tie a given territory to a *single* language. In effect, language rights follow neither territories nor individuals, as suggested by the labels 'territorial model' and 'personality principle' respectively, but viable language communities. Thus, in designing a comprehensive language policy in a multilingual state, there is something to be learned from the appeals both to territory and to personality, but the kernel of truth in each model must be extracted from the rest of the conceptual or normative baggage that has conventionally characterized the territoriality and personality models.

## 1. Defining the Models

In developing contrasting models for language policy, we may distinguish three separate dimensions. The first refers to the root idea gestured towards in the labels 'territoriality' and 'personality': the role of geography in conditioning the availability of language services. The second dimension of each model further specifies its policy content, in particular whether it prescribes unilingualism or allows for bilingualism. The third aspect has to do with the justifications that can plausibly be offered for its combination of appeal to territoriality or personality and recommendation of unilingualism or bilingualism. To begin with, I will construct sharply contrasting models combining, on the one hand, territoriality, unilingualism, and aggregative justifications, and, on the other, personality, bilingualism, and rights-based justifications. These constructions are largely true to the debates in the policy literature, while making more explicit the basis for many of the disagreements in those debates. Ultimately, however, I shall argue that the first of these ingredients—the position on the relevance of geography to language entitlements—can be fruitfully uncoupled from the other elements of these opposing models and deployed in a more constructive manner. The first step in the analysis is to clarify the territoriality–personality dimension, and to elucidate the usual connections to unilingual or bilingual policy outcomes. The next section will then go on to explore the justifications that might be offered for each of the emerging models.

The territorial principle is usually said to describe a regime in which 'the rules of language to be applied in a given situation will depend on the territory in question' (McRae 1975: 33; see also McRoberts 1989: 143).[1] This does not take

[1] For similarly brief descriptions, see May (2001: 178), who maintains that 'the territorial language principle grants language rights that are limited to a particular territory'; MacMillan (1998: 4, 71), who argues that the territorial approach makes 'possession of language rights contingent upon geographic location'; and Reid (1993: 15, who describes the approach as one in which '[t]he territory in which each citizen lives determines the rights he or she will hold'.

us very far, though, since it does not, on its face, prescribe any particular content for a language regime. Most of the rules that govern us are rules promulgated within some territory and govern us as residents of that territory. As McRae (1975: 35) notes, the territorial base of the sovereign state has been taken for granted since the sixteenth century. All states are limited in their jurisdiction to a certain territory and have sovereignty within that territory. That tells us nothing about what the rules of a given state should allow or disallow, encourage or discourage. In particular, this description does not specify whether the rules within a territory foster unilingualism or allow for bilingualism. This content-independent description is therefore easily conflated with the question of jurisdiction over language matters—which legislative authority has the power to regulate language use.[2] This confusion is particularly endemic in debates in federal systems of government (Cook 1969; Leslie 1986); proposals to devolve jurisdiction over language matters exclusively to provinces or regional governments are sometimes treated as instantiations of the territorial principle, whether the recommendation is that the local authority should enforce unilingualism or promote bilingualism (Reid 1993: 30).

The collapse of the territoriality idea into a question of jurisdiction renders it analytically useless: since every state's jurisdiction is defined territorially, every country's language policy is to this extent territorial. By this reckoning it is hard to imagine what would count as a non-territorial policy. Further, to focus on jurisdiction pushes the normative debate in a procedural rather than a substantive direction. The question of which level of government is best placed to decide language policy is very different from the question of what policy should be settled upon, whoever does the deciding. Each question invokes a different order of normative argument for its resolution. Jurisdiction in the formal legal sense must be treated as a backdrop against which any particular model of language policy is to be considered. The territoriality idea must refer to something else if it is to make a contribution to language policy. The appeal to territory, as a basis for language policy, is better understood as tying official provision for the use of a particular language to the existence of a geographical concentration, of some degree, of users of that language. Services are provided, for example, in geographically defined regions within a given jurisdiction in which there is such concentration, but not elsewhere.

As with territoriality, the personality principle is somewhat sketchily articulated in the literature. May's (2001: 179) brief description is characteristic: 'the personality principle . . . attaches language rights to individuals, irrespective of their geographical position'.[3] This definition gestures toward some fundamental differences between the personality principle and the territorial approach, but

[2] This weak version of the model is explicitly articulated in Kloss (1965: 52–73). See also McRae (1975) who follows Kloss on this point.
[3] See also MacMillan (1998: 71), who says the principle 'recognizes an individual entitlement to government services in one's official language, independent of the territory in which one resides'; McRae (1975: 33), according to whom the personality principle requires 'that the rules

276 DENISE G. RÉAUME

fails fully to flesh out the conceptual features of the model and, for that reason, again obscures some of the important normative questions needing attention. The initial contrast turns on the relevance of geography: the personality principle is premised on the idea that services in a particular language should be available to speakers wherever they happen to reside, without need for a certain threshold number of speakers in a given geographical area to trigger the entitlement, whereas an appeal to territoriality is an appeal to geographically concentrated numbers as the foundation for the provision of services. Thus stated, the personality principle simply denies the relevance of geography that is asserted by the territoriality model, and insists on what Laponce (1987: 160) calls the 'transportability' of entitlements: whatever rights are recognized by the model move around with the right-holders.

This position on geography unambiguously builds in at the ground floor a commitment to bilingualism. The personality idea anticipates the presence of more than one language group in a jurisdiction and, by making explicit reference to the provision of services in one's *own* language, it starts off with some minimal content in the direction of bilingualism. Whereas there is a tight connection between the personality principle and bilingualism, the link between territoriality and unilingualism is logically looser, but is nevertheless often treated as natural in the policy literature. To say that there must be some level of geographical concentration of speakers of a particular language before services will be provided in that language does not necessarily imply that within any given region there will be services for only one language community. Depending on how regions are defined, there may often be sufficient concentrations of more than one language group in a given region, in which case the idea of territoriality would be consistent with a policy prescription in favour of bilingualism. Nevertheless, the territoriality idea is most often invoked in conjunction with the argument that unilingualism should be promoted within the territory in question. This makes the definition of territorial boundaries crucial to the model; we can neither construct nor assess the normative arguments in favour of territorial unilingualism without knowing the territorial boundaries within which it is proposed. And here advocates often fall back on, often without argument, existing jurisdictional boundaries. As I shall argue in the next section, it is this move that pushes advocates of this model to adopt aggregative justifications for it.

'Territorial unilingualism', then, designates a model that advocates unilingualism within a given territory.[4] It holds that each territory needs a language it can

[about language use] will depend on the linguistic status of the person or persons concerned'; Reid (1993: 24), who describes it as 'treat[ing] language rights as intrinsic to each individual' which 'remain in effect in every part of the country, regardless of local demographics'; Laponce (1987: 165), who says it 'establishes language as a right equally as portable as the right to vote or the right of religious expression'.

   [4] Philippe Van Parijs (2000a: 244) uses the label 'territorial separation' to designate the same approach.

call its own and vice versa.[5] Anyone wanting to make her or his home within a given territory must adapt to the language of the place. Jean Laponce, perhaps the model's chief proponent, is the most explicit about this, proclaiming that 'Territorial solutions stem from the principle that languages in contact should be separated as much as possible by means of fixed frontiers . . .' (Laponce 1987: 172).[6] Even those who rely on the weaker, jurisdictional version of territorialism acknowledge that territorialism and unilingualism tend to go together in practice (Reid 1993: 15–16; MacMillan 1998: 71). This approach starts from the undeniable human phenomenon that grounds the idea of territoriality: speakers of the same language tend to group themselves together geographically. From this is derived the prescription that, in an ideal world, state boundaries would coincide with or follow 'natural' linguistic boundaries, so that everyone within a given state territory would speak the same language. The geographic territory over which the state has jurisdiction would coincide with the territory over which one language holds sway. Newcomers would be regarded as exceptional, and required to assimilate to the language already 'in possession' of a given territory.

However, while it is true that there is a geographical concentration to language use, speakers of a language often do not group themselves neatly. In the real world, if we drew boundaries around all and only those who speak a given language we would end up with some very oddly shaped territorial units, if we could do it intelligibly at all.[7] Thus, we cannot realistically use linguistic boundaries to define states, and the model is not so utopian as to advocate comprehensive boundary redrawing to make states match linguistic population concentrations. Instead, the model takes existing boundaries as given, and attempts to realize the ambition of 'one language / one territory' by prescribing language use within existing territories as legally defined. Instead of 'one language/one territory' (where there is a common language, there should be one state), we get 'one territory/one language' (where there is one state, there should be a common language).

The territorial unilingualism model must therefore decide what to do about states that happen to include more than one language group. There are two possible options consistent with the prescription of unilingualism: (1) where possible, divide the larger state into different linguistic regions, or (2) choose one

[5] Perhaps the clearest proponent of this strong version of the territoriality approach is Laponce (1987). Van Parijs (2000a) seems equally supportive, relying heavily on Laponce.

[6] However, even he fudges the point occasionally, sliding from defining territorialism by reference to the maintenance of fixed boundaries to saying that within a territory, 'The dominant group can thus use the existing boundaries either to protect the minority or to protect itself' (Laponce 1987: 173), as though we were merely talking about the jurisdiction any territory's government has to suppress or protect minority languages as it chooses.

[7] Van Parijs (2000a), supporting territorial separation in the Belgian context, has the luxury of working with an example that does involve definable territories exhibiting substantial linguistic homogeneity. He notes that this condition is necessary for this approach to 'work smoothly', but does not say much about the appropriate policy in regions less neatly divided up linguistically.

language as the favoured one for the entire territory. The former strategy represents a watered-down version of the yearning for the perfect coincidence of linguistic and political borders. Sometimes, as is partially true in Canada and more fully exemplified in Switzerland and Belgium, a federal structure is used to achieve the division of a larger territory into linguistic sub-regions, with provincial boundaries and a range of legislative powers following linguistic dividing lines. However, the mapping of territory onto linguistic communities is as likely to be imperfect in federal states as in any other context, thus threatening to reproduce the problem of bizarrely shaped units that divide people who share a wide range of interests apart from linguistic ones.

This repeated problem of oddly shaped political units, whether experienced nationally or regionally, leads to advocacy of the second strategy: adoption of one language over others as the preferred language of a particular territory. If we cannot map state boundaries onto existing linguistic communities, we can manipulate language use within existing territories to produce linguistic uniformity. The natural choice of favoured language of advocates of territorialism is the language of the majority within a given territory.[8] Applied to a unitary state as a whole, this produces state-wide unilingualism; in federal systems, the territorialist prescription usually recommends a mixture of language policies—regional unilingualism in a setting of bilingual federal structures (Laponce 1987: 175). I shall argue below that this apparent accommodation of a degree of bilingualism is unstable as long as the regime takes its inspiration from the territorialist model as it has developed.

If the personality model starts with a conviction that language use protections are a personal entitlement and derives from that a commitment to bilingualism whenever members of more than one linguistic community coexist within a society, the territorial unilingualism model seems to start from a conviction that unilingualism is a good thing, and proceeds to a search for a territory within which to instantiate it. This insight gives us the starting point for articulating the deeper normative underpinnings of each model.

## 2. The Interest in Language: Why Does Language Matter to People?

### The Territorial Unilingualism Model

What normative framework might account for the policy of uniformity and majoritarianism that characterizes the territorial unilingualism model? Two different bases may be advanced for the assumption that unilingualism is superior

---

[8] For an outline, in the context of Canadian political history, of the tendency of territorial solutions to produce majoritarian outcomes reinforcing homogeneity rather than pluralism, see Cook (1969).

to bilingualism. The first is grounded in aggregative considerations of convenience and efficiency.[9] Uniformity, it might be argued, maximizes ease of communication within the country and therefore contributes to efficiency in commercial affairs and the administration of government. It keeps costs down and productivity high. This account of the principles of language regulation locates the point or value of language in its instrumental usefulness as a means of communication. It is wholly ancillary to the other ends of individuals and society, and therefore can be regulated in order best to further those ends. The majoritarianism of this approach falls out from its aggregative, consequentialist vision. Where there is a dominant language, the choice of that language is rendered salient. Its convenience for a majority of the population is all the justification its choice needs. This treats the interests of people in speaking a particular language as appropriately subject to aggregation and trade-off against competing interests. If there are more speakers of English than of French in a given territory, for example, we maximize benefits by choosing English. The loss to speakers of one language is outweighed by the gain to the speakers of the other. The loss might be understood as the trouble of having to adapt to another language, or as the cost of having to leave the jurisdiction, or finally, as the cost of ineffective communication with others and the resulting reduction of opportunities. However conceptualized, it can be reduced to a common denominator with and traded off against the benefits otherwise accruing from linguistic uniformity.

A second version of this story places the justification for territorial unilingualism not in efficiency but in the social benefits of cohesion, or at least the avoidance of the social conflict that often accompanies the mixing of two or more language groups. A common language is looked to as the basis for solidarity, making up for the lack of other unifying characteristics.[10] Fostering linguistic commonality will be conducive, it is sometimes thought, to political stability and a greater willingness of citizens to bear the reciprocal sacrifices necessary for the common good. Van Parijs, taking his inspiration from Mill, rephrases this position, 'No viable democracy without a linguistically unified demos' (2000a: 236), but while 'democracy' may sound like a more high-minded goal than social unity, they amount to much the same thing. Democracy is interpreted by Van Parijs as 'a common space for discussion and decision-making' (2000a: 237). In other words, in order that everyone may participate in the same debates about public policy, all must use the same language. In any event, the choice of the majority language as the tool selected in pursuit of unity or democratic debate betrays an aggregative framework. The benefits to those in the majority of choosing their language are deemed to outweigh the costs to the

---

[9] This is one advantage of unilingual territorialism referred to in passing by McRae (1975: 49).

[10] This appeal to a common language as a basis for solidarity is a constant theme of the Larose Report. See Commission des états généraux sur la situation et l'avenir de la langue française au Québec (2001).

minority. More people more quickly and easily will be able to be brought into the network through choice of the majority language, and it is the end—unity or common ground in debate—that is important. The rest will be eventually absorbed, their loss merely transitional. On either of these versions, the loss to minority language speakers is not treated as particularly onerous, or, to the extent that it is, the greater numbers on the other side justify its imposition.[11]

This model works smoothly, whatever suspicions there might be about its fairness to the losers, as long as the territorial boundaries of existing states are treated as given. But why should they be? The model provides no answer. The arbitrariness of existing boundaries rises to the surface when the model is used to try to justify the combination in a single state of two different language groups divided, in a federal system or otherwise, into separate regions. One vision of Canada, for example, sees it as a federation of French-speaking Quebec and nine English-speaking provinces. Yet the aggregative tendencies of the underlying justification for territorial unilingualism undermines the existing way of carving up the territory. As long as the account operates within the existing provincial boundaries, the majoritarian logic of the aggregative approach produces a bilingual Canada of a sort: two language communities contained within the same state, each contained within its own provincial borders. However, if we consider Canada to be the relevant territorial unit of analysis instead, an efficiency-based cost–benefit calculation ought to dictate a policy of linguistic uniformity nationwide. Nationally, English speakers outnumber francophones three to one. Likewise, if linguistic uniformity fosters social cohesion, the prognosis is poor for Canada–wide cohesion if there are two competing foundations for identification and allegiance coexisting within the relevant unit.

Since the human interests considered capable of aggregation by this model cut across existing political boundaries, there is no reason within the model for the cost–benefit analysis to be confined to the residents of any particular political unit. Although this tension is most acute when federalism is used to try to negotiate language difference, the problem is just as capable of arising on the international stage, and is likely increasingly to do so given globalization trends. Ultimately, why shouldn't everyone on the planet speak the same language if it will increase efficiency or ensure world peace?

Advocates of a minority-language community can only argue against this logic by arbitrarily reasserting and trying to fortify the existing jurisdictional boundary between linguistic regions. It is easy to see how this fosters separatist ambitions, since this is the surest way to short-circuit the majoritarian logic of the pan-Canadian vision. But if we shift focus to the geographical territory of

---

[11] A variation on this version is Laponce's (1987) advocacy of territorial unilingualism for the sake of preserving languages in contact with others with more adherents. Here the end is survival of a particular language rather than solidarity amongst all residents of the territory, but that end is taken to justify the cost inflicted on those within that territory who happen to speak another language: their interests must be sacrificed to the greater good of the survival of the favoured language.

Quebec, we find regions that could make a claim to status as anglophone provinces, or at least municipalities (Janda 1998);[12] the potential for near-infinite regress is evident. The secessionist argument tries to appeal to the ideal of one language/one territory—that states should follow language communities—but it confronts anew the reality that language communities often cannot be geographically divided very neatly. Further fragmentation can be prevented only by arbitrary reliance on existing boundaries, but it is, of course, just such arbitrary insistence on the boundaries that define Canada as the relevant unit of language policy that begins this process. In other words, an aggregative territorialist model does not seem to provide a very stable basis for language policy: it pushes in the direction of one language across one legal sense of the relevant territory, provoking by way of resistance successive attempts at secession by sub-units in order to create new legal territories. Without an independent account of why particular political boundaries should matter for purposes of language policy, there is no principled way to choose between these radically different alternatives.

To call attention to the machinations of language policy in a federal state trying to negotiate the coexistence of two or more language groups is also to flag the limits of the equation of aggregative arguments with unilingualism. It is common enough for a federal state to adopt a policy of bilingualism at the national level even as provinces or states pursue a territorialist policy favouring the majority language at the local level (McRae 1975: 41). An aggregative model can provide some explanation for such a regime, but I shall argue that it is not very secure, nor very satisfying. These problems highlight the inadequate conception of the interests at stake in designing language policy in any aggregative justification—even one in favour of bilingualism. A policy of territorial unilingualism is all the more problematic.

Pierre Trudeau (1986: 31) gestured toward an aggregative explanation of bilingualism in advocating it for Canada because 'each of [the French and English] linguistic groups has the power to break the country'. For breakdown to be avoided, some concessions in respect of language are necessary, according to this story. Unilingualism might be the generally efficient or unity-inducing state of affairs, but, if a minority has the numerical or perhaps economic strength to impose sufficient costs should unilingualism be foist upon them, pragmatic and instrumental considerations of social peace and political stability militate in favour of accommodating their demands. The assumption behind Trudeau's claim is simply that the costs of breakdown exceed those of accommodating the linguistic minority; hence the balance, in this case, is in favour of bilingualism. More generally, Kenneth McRae has offered a framework for assessing a range of mixed territorial/personal regimes that is entirely aggregative. He outlined

[12] It is this demographic reality of anglophone minority clusters within Quebec that fuels the partition movement of Quebec—the movement amongst some anglophones to reject Quebec sovereignty in the event of a declaration of independence in order to remain attached to the Canadian state.

a variety of 'goals' that may be served by either imposing uniformity or allowing scope for some use of a minority language, and then sketched some of the circumstances in which unilingualism may be more conducive to the achievement of these goals and when inclusion of a personality-based policy would do a better job (McRae 1975). Van Parijs (2000a: 239) takes this kind of argument one step further, arguing that linguistic diversity can have beneficial consequences such as encouraging experimentation which may ultimately be in the general interest, or creating a brake on mobility of people where too much mobility may be destabilizing, which consequences may offset the advantages of unilingualism.

Since this sort of justification depends on calculating the costs and benefits of a particular policy, everything depends on the balance in actual concrete circumstances. This should mean that the question of which accommodations should be provided at any given point in time is constantly up for grabs. A minority that has a great deal of power at one point in time may decline in influence, thus reducing the cost of imposing unilingualism. Similarly, a minority might go from obscurity and docility to a position of power and influence. However, this sits only uneasily with the constitutionalization of language policy, as in Canada. The value of convenience and national unity are the sorts of political objectives the weight of which can fluctuate over time; it therefore makes little sense to constitutionally entrench the balance as it exists at a particular point in time. This would merely require cumbersome constitutional amendments in order to redress a shift in the balance as needed. Thus, an aggregative account seems a poor account of a system that gives constitutional protection to the use of more than one language. If there is no account available that makes sense of the inclusion of language protections in a constitutional bill of rights, then perhaps this aspect of Canadian policy needs rethinking. On the contrary, if there is a plausible account of constitutionalized language rights, this casts doubt on the satisfactoriness of an entirely aggregative justification for language policy.

The aggregative account of bilingualism may appear plausible on the surface, but it must deal with a central nagging question, one which will come back to haunt the territorial unilingualism model. How are we to understand the disruptiveness of minority communities, a disruptiveness sufficient to require concessions in order to preserve the peace? If valid language policy is just a matter of maximizing facility of communication within the country, the minority would seem to be irrational and obstructionist to stand in the way of linguistic efficiency or national unity. Who do they think they are to stand in the way of the greatest good for the greatest number? Even more mysterious must be the motivation of those in the minority who take the view that the original arrangement never was or is no longer satisfactory and who seek independence for that part of the country populated by the minority. Why sacrifice the greater good for the sake of a mere alternative means of communication? To pose the questions is to expose the flaw in the argument that language policy is grounded wholly in considerations of efficiency. The minority desire to carry on its own language tradition, whether through protections within a bilingual state or through separation, is not irrational or mysterious. It is not like a diehard preference for imperial units of measure even though convenience has tipped the balance in favour of the metric system. In other words, understood in instrumental terms, the interest in language is altogether too thin to motivate the language struggles that are familiar to multilingual countries and to explain people's attachment to their mother tongue.

Language enables us to do many things that have meaning and value independently of the language in which they are accomplished. It is therefore instrumental in achieving these independent ends; this instrumental value can be severed from any particular language and manipulated to achieve unilingualism as these efficiency arguments do. But language also has an intrinsically valuable dimension for its speakers beyond the extraneous ends to which it can be put. It is itself a human creation or accomplishment, participation in which is an end in itself. Each language is a manifestation of human creativity that has value independently of its practical uses. Although it may express ideas, concepts, myths, traditions that have equivalents in other languages, it is a unique form of expression and valuable as such. This is the understanding of the importance of language that makes sense of the idea that protecting one's language is worth even some sacrifice of other worthwhile objectives to which use of another language would be more conducive. It is this aspect of the importance of language that is ignored by the efficiency account of the appropriate principles of language regulation.

The social cohesion argument gestures towards a richer understanding of the importance of language. It glimpses the special importance to its speakers that makes language a binding force between people capable of motivating trust, cooperation, and mutual sacrifice. But the territorialist version of the argument turns a blind eye to the value *each* community places on its *own* language in order that it may purport to justify exclusive imposition of the *majority* language in a given territory.[13] But why should we think that linguistic affiliation can be so easily manipulated, that no wrong is done in the attempt? To the extent that language forms an aspect of identity and provides a basis for belonging—as the social cohesion argument claims it does—it does so organically, as an outgrowth of the communal life of a group of people. People who already enjoy this sense of belonging within a given language community are not likely to relinquish it easily in pursuit of ready-to-wear solidarity with members of another community.

---

[13] Van Parijs (2000a: 239–40) is an exception in that he is sensitive to the fact that injustice and not just harm is done in forcing a minority community to abandon its language. However, his understanding of the nature of the injustice is coloured by his largely instrumentalist conception of the value of language; it is only because members of the minority will, in the short run, suffer various sorts of disadvantage because they cannot communicate well in the majority language that an injustice is done to them. For a criticism of such exclusively instrumentalist accounts, see Réaume (2000).

To force them to do so is likely to produce merely an ersatz national unity. While the social cohesion account implicitly recognizes the intrinsic value of its language to the majority, whose language is the selected instrument of social cohesion, it expects minority groups to treat identification with a language purely instrumentally, as something to be done for the sake of a greater sense of collective purpose. It provides no account of why we should expect a minority to value its language any differently from the way the majority does. If we take seriously the implicit understanding of the importance of language in the social cohesion account, it renders suspect the pursuit of a policy of territorial unilingualism.[14] In fact, as we shall see, the social cohesion account of the importance of language actually gives us a better starting point for developing a satisfactory version of the personality model, but this may ultimately lead to the rejection of unilingualism.

## The Personality/Bilingualism Model

Conventional analyses of the personality principle do not ground it in an assessment of costs and benefits, assessed globally. Instead language use is treated as a personal entitlement, capable of enforcement by individuals wherever they are and whatever the circumstances, regardless of the impact on aggregate welfare. The rejection of an aggregative, consequentialist approach places this model within a human rights framework. What kind of a story do we have to tell about the rationale for language protections in order to make a plausible case that they are grounded in human rights? Human rights are moral rights, grounded in important human interests (Green 1987: 647). A right to something exists if and only if some person's interest is sufficient reason for holding others to be under a duty to provide or secure it (Raz 1984a: 194–214; 1986: Ch. 7; 1984b). Moral rights defy the aggregative logic of other kinds of moral argument. To say that I have a right to personal security, for example, is to say that my security deserves protection even in the face of substantial benefits accruing to others from its violation. It may not be absolute, but it is immune to unrestricted, routine cost–benefit analyses. The challenge, then, in demonstrating that language protections are human rights protections is to articulate a set of human interests in language that have this character.

Thus, in order to make the case that language protections are rights-based, we must be able to argue that there is a vital human interest in language, one capable of justifying the imposition of duties on others to secure that interest. So far, the personality idea as we have described it merely stipulates that one should be able to use one's language wherever one resides within a given jurisdiction. This focus on portability leaves open the question of why such portability might be worth protecting, and the policy literature does not take us very far in filling in such an account. Many discussions of the personality model presuppose

---

[14]  At least it does so on what I take to be the safe assumption that some form of linguistic cleansing is not an acceptable means by which a multilingual territory can be rendered unilingual.

a heavily individualistic account of the interest in language and couple it with a classic negative liberty analysis of the rights it advocates. A negative liberty approach is necessary to deal with the intractable problems of conflict that an individualistic account of language rights creates, but, in the long term, it renders the effectiveness of the model doubtful. The individualistic approach ties language rights to persons in a particular way, adopting a conception of personality that creates problems for the model. In the next section, I will propose an alternative model that has a 'personality' dimension in that it ties entitlement to personal attributes, but allows us to go beyond a focus on individual persons.

Discussions of the personality principle often begin by situating it within a classical individual rights framework, conceptualizing a language right as protection for the individual's choice of language. This puts linguistic freedom on a par with freedom of expression and religion. So, for example, McRae (1975: 36) identifies the transition from state-established religions to freedom of individual conscience as the triumph of the personality principle in the context of religious difference. The implication is that the personality principle would apply to language analogously. Similarly, Laponce (1987: 165) analogizes between individual language rights and the right to vote or the right to freedom of religious expression. These rights—freedom of conscience, the right to vote, freedom of expression—do all have portability in common, but they exhibit other conceptual features as well. This model is additionally characterized by a commitment to universality as well as by an appeal to the sanctity of individual choice. In other words, these rights are portable because they are universal, and they are universal because individual autonomy in respect of important aspects of how one leads one's life is valuable. This kind of story about the justification of human rights is too well known to require elaboration. It is undoubtedly the case that it has some role to play in a comprehensive account of language regulation. For much the same reasons that a state should not dictate religious belief or observance, compelling people to use one language rather than another is normatively suspect. And most states do give some place to an individual choice model by refraining from interfering in their citizens' choice of language in their everyday lives, even if they see this as guaranteeing freedom of expression and protection against discrimination rather than the recognition of language rights per se. This model also incorporates another important element: it conceptualizes personal rights as negative liberties. Others must refrain from interfering with one's exercise of choice of language, on this model, but need incur no positive obligations in order to facilitate that choice.

As long as freedom of linguistic choice is interpreted merely as a negative liberty, the analogy to other classical, universal human rights is perfectly apt. The negative model also fits the classical human rights model by applying equally to the speakers of all languages whatever territory they find themselves in, and whatever language is the object of choice, whether mother tongue or any other. However, if confined to this individualistic, negative liberty version, the personality model cannot provide very secure protection for minority language use. Majorities do sometimes go so far as to seek formally to prohibit the use of minority languages, but they rarely have to in order to accomplish the de facto dominance of the majority language, even the ultimate elimination, through assimilation, of minority languages. A negative liberty right would restrict language use protections to the private sphere, and it is common knowledge in language policy circles that this is a recipe for the decline of minority language groups over the long run.[15] There are many freedoms of which one person's exercise does not in any way prevent another's like exercise. Religious worship, for example, can be privately carried on simultaneously in any number of religious communities so that each enjoys equal freedom. Freedom of religion can be substantially confined to the private sphere without curbing its expression. By contrast, if the freedom to use one's own language is understood as a negative liberty, exercisable only in the private sphere, this means only in interactions between speakers of the same language, which threatens to restrict vastly the normal domains or contexts of language use. By its nature, language is capable of being used to conduct any sort of communication between people in any of the contexts that make up daily life. In a linguistically mixed population, but one in which one language group has a numerical or marked social advantage, the disadvantaged group will find its opportunities for linguistic free expression severely restricted.[16] Yet some interaction between groups is often necessary and always useful in some respects.[17] This virtually forces the vulnerable group to become bilingual, and creates incentives to defect to the other group where there are greater social and economic opportunities. A policy encouraging ultimate linguistic uniformity on the territoriality model could easily be mounted without running foul of a principle of freedom of language choice understood as a mere negative liberty—it would simply take a few generations to realize.

So while we may assume that the human interest in autonomy is as important in the realm of language choice as in many other spheres and that this is sufficient to give rise to duties of non-interference, a language policy grounded exclusively in such negative rights will not sustain minority language communities over the long run. Long-term security requires the imposition of positive obligations to facilitate language maintenance amongst the minority. Can the interest in choice understood as an aspect of individual autonomy do the more ambitious

[15] As Lacordaire wisely noted, 'Entre le fort et le faible c'est la liberté qui opprime, et la loi qui affranchit' (quoted by McRae 1975: 48). See also Laponce (1987: 156).

[16] The most obvious difficulty is for a linguistic community that is very substantially outnumbered by another, and this is the most common situation in which the inadequacies of a negative liberty model will be felt. But the experience of francophones in Montreal in securing the ability to work in French is instructive. Francophones were not outnumbered by anglophones, but the greater economic power of anglophones meant that business owners and managers expected everyone to speak English. For a recent analysis of these struggles, see Levine (1990).

[17] Laponce (1987: 151) comments, 'I do not have to "pray" or be of the same race as my neighbours, but I do have to "speak" to them'.

work of grounding positive obligations of support? It seems doubtful. It is no accident that an individualistic conception of the entitlement goes together with a negative liberty interpretation, for a more positive interpretation is likely to give rise to endemic conflict.

The individual choice model treats language as an object of choice, on a par with one's choice of occupation or marriage partner (Laponce 1987: 150). Prima facie, it also treats each chooser as well as each instance of choice, whatever the language chosen and whatever the social context of choice, as equally valuable. It is entirely possible to be this even-handedly respectful of all such choices when all that it required is non-interference, but the move into the realm of positive obligations is bound to produce conflict between individual choices. When language groups intermingle there will be contact between speakers of different languages. If each has the right that others accommodate her choice of language, there is no positive obligation that can be imposed in the interests of one party without violating the duty holder's right not only to non-interference, but also to the same positive accommodation from her interlocutor. Such conflict is not only inevitable, but likely to be common.[18] While one cannot dismiss an account of rights simply because it gives rise to the potential for conflicts of rights—after all, what account doesn't?—there does seem something defective about an account that pervasively gives rise to irresolvable conflict. That rights conflict is endemic in this model is amplified when one remembers that, understood individualistically, the human interest protected inheres equally in each speaker of each language. Thus, in a *multi*lingual society, the conflicting interests of the speakers of scores of different languages would have to be mediated in dozens of contexts of interaction on a daily basis.

It may be possible to refine the individual choice model to deal adequately with this problem of endemic conflict. To subject only the government to positive obligations is one step in this direction. To confine choice to certain contexts, or to develop a more nuanced hierarchy of language related rights so that one can decide which ones trump others in situations of conflict, would make the model more plausible as well. However, the task does seem Herculean, each of millions of forms of conflict requiring justification for the particular type and extent of limitation called for in that circumstance. In the end, one suspects we would end up so far from the model's starting point—that each instance of choice by each language user in each context of choice is equally valuable—that one would be entitled to wonder whether we still had an account of the

---

[18] Even if the right to choose is held to give rise only to positive obligations against the government rather than against other individuals, the potential for conflict does not entirely disappear since the government communicates with citizens only through people who are themselves individuals whose right to choose is equally valuable. Depending on the substance of the positive accommodations argued for in a fully fleshed out model of this sort, government agencies may also often find themselves in the situation of not being able to accommodate a speaker of one language without having to violate the rights of another.

individual right to freedom of linguistic choice. The account of the limits on the right would vastly dwarf the account of the right itself. Rather than pursue all these issues here in order fully to test the viability of the individual choice model, I propose to shift away from such a heavily individualistic focus and suggest that another approach may be more fruitful. This approach is consistent with the central portability feature of the personality model, and therefore stands in opposition to a territorial model, but it understands the importance of language in a non-individualistic way.

## 3. Beyond *Personality*

We have seen that an individual choice model, while grounded in a valid conception of the human interest in language use, is unlikely to be able to justify more than entitlements in the form of negative liberties, and this is inadequate protection for the long-term maintenance of a language. In a sense, the strength of the individual choice model—that it applies to each individual and each instance of choice—is also its weakness, since it is this universality that creates the potential for endemic rights conflict that requires scaling down entitlements. There is another approach to language policy in place in some jurisdictions that implicitly moves away from this individualistic conception of the interest in language. My aim in this section is to sketch the features of this approach and articulate its normative foundations. I hope to show that this alternative approach can solve some of the problems created by the individual choice model while remaining within a human rights framework.

Language protections often do not take the form of affording a right of individual choice, understood as a universal entitlement. Even when granted to individuals, they may be limited to the use of specific languages rather than allowing a full range of choice. Examples from the Canadian regime will illustrate. This approach protects language use through group-specific rights or rules; it also affords positive rights to the use of the protected group's language in certain contexts. The approach picks out a specific language community for protection and involves the creation of rules that apply only to those in that group. The existence of a constitutional right held by French and English minority communities, but no others, to education in their own language is an example of this technique. This kind of approach may go further, delegating authority to institutions within a specific community to create the group-specific rules that will govern it. The inclusion of management rights over minority-language schools, requiring the creation of school boards run by the minority community, is an example of this variant. This approach also goes beyond the recognition of negative liberties. The very enactment of group-specific provisions is a positive act rather than merely a form of non-interference. But more in the way of positive accommodation is needed. Group-specific rules or institutions that merely protect against interference will do no better than the individual choice model in protecting minorities from the long-term pressure to assimilate.[19] Group-specific regimes, such as the Canadian system, usually do provide affirmatively for the accommodation of minority languages. For example, federal legislation must be enacted in both languages; speakers of either official language have the right to federal government services in either language. In ways such as these, the state must adapt to the citizen's language, not merely refrain from requiring the citizen to use a specific language.

A group-specific regime exhibits the portability feature of the personality model, but not because it grants individual rights. Rather, it conditions entitlement or susceptibility to regulation on some personal attribute, in this case being part of a specific language community. The condition pertains across the jurisdiction under examination and therefore may apply to persons situated anywhere in the state, thus making entitlements portable, but gives the notion of 'personality' a different gloss. An aspect of personality is the basis for enjoying the protection, but the personal attribute that triggers entitlement is not fully universal; only some will qualify.[20] Individual choice may play some role in the exercise of the entitlement, but the value at stake must be something other than individual autonomy to make sense of the group-specificity of this approach. For example, Canadians have a right to use either French or English in proceedings before federal courts. It is up to the individual to choose to invoke this right, but it makes no sense to see it as an exercise of individual autonomy in a universal sense. What reason could there be for thinking that each individual, whatever her or his language, has an interest in the choice between French and English?

Thus, this approach treats language as sufficiently important to justify *positive* measures in support of *particular* languages. Further, the idea of delegating some regulatory authority to the community itself seems to appeal to some conception of autonomy—to letting the members of a protected community determine the rules that shall govern them. The task now is to determine what, if any, normative approach would ground these features. In particular, what conception of rights would justify protecting the language interests of speakers of particular languages? The shift in this approach away from a fully individualized understanding of the

---

[19] A group-specific rights model is often advocated as a way of creating normative separation between communities, and, where separation is possible, each community may thereafter respect the other simply by refraining from interfering in its practices. However, complete separation between linguistic communities is often neither possible nor desirable. Some communication must take place across linguistic lines, raising the question of whose terms will govern.

[20] Note, however, that the foundation for entitlement can be more or less exclusive. Criteria that are entirely objective and beyond individual control, such as mother tongue, are more exclusive than subjective criteria that allow for choice, such as subjective identification with a specific language community. The difference between the millet system in the Ottoman empire and the short-lived Estonian group autonomy scheme illustrates these alternatives. For an analysis of these regimes, see McRae (1975: 36–8) and Laponce (2000: 171–2) on the Estonian scheme. See also Van Parijs (2000a: 242–3).

interest in language should point us in the direction of looking for a collective interest capable of justifying the imposition of obligations.

This shift of focus allows us to see the maintenance of a language community as the complex group practice that it is. Individuals are, of course, involved in that practice and it is through their individual choices that the practice is either maintained or abandoned. But each individual's role through each individual choice should not be given exaggerated importance. What gives each individual's choices value is the fact that they collectively constitute participation in the larger group enterprise. It is in and through participation with others in the creation and sustaining of a language and the cultural forms it is used to create that value is created.[21] It is that larger enterprise that should take centre stage in the analysis, and its value cannot be reduced to what it 'does' for individuals as individuals, whether that is understood as satisfying their choices, opening doors for them, or preserving them from the hardships of change. A language is sustained as countless individual acts of participation cumulate and conjoin on an hourly, daily, weekly basis. These individual acts—large and small, organized and informal, for public consumption or private enjoyment—converge, diverge, cross-cut, build on one another, and simply swirl around us with dizzying complexity. To follow them all and even try to protect the integrity of each for its own sake would be impossible. But individual protection is unnecessary to provide adequate space for the community, as a whole, to carry on.

The ensemble of all the day-to-day contributions can usefully be thought to constitute and reveal a collective choice by the members of a language community to carry on the heritage that is its language (Réaume 1995: 117). It is not as individually chosen by each and every chooser on each and every occasion that language is valuable, but as the collective choice of members of a community exercising that choice through their continuing participation in the use and maintenance of their language. It is the value of such collective choice that grounds a specific group's claims to protection for the use of their language. Such an approach requires that we develop a notion of equality or equal respect owed by members of one community to another. Some such conception of equality is the bedrock of rights theory. This is not difficult to articulate at the communal level. The creation and development of a complex human good such as a language community is a work of enormous human creativity. It is intrinsically valuable to its members as such. To deny the value of others' language is to insult their community. It is to treat the creative way of life that one community has fashioned for itself as less worthy of respect than that of another. This notion of equal respect simply parallels the story of the relationship between individuals. As individuals, we must respect the life choices and projects of other individuals because they ascribe value to them as expressions of their conception

[21] Elsewhere I have argued that an appreciation of the participatory nature of the interest in language use should lead us to treat language rights as group rights rather than individual rights (Réaume 1988; 1994).

of the good. Communities need be no less respectful of the choices and life projects of other communities.

An analysis of language use as a group practice, given value through the participation of many, helps explain the group-specificity of this model of language policy. In the first instance, in order for protection to be claimed for the use of a particular language, there must be a group whose language it is. That there may be some individual speakers of a particular language within a jurisdiction is insufficient to attract attention. The number of speakers must be sufficient to constitute a viable language community. In most states under normal circumstances the groups that meet this viability condition will be readily identifiable and relatively stable. It is therefore not surprising that they should be identified by name in language rights legislation, as with the specific according of rights to the French and English in Canada. It might be preferable to confer rights on groups in a more general way—not by identifying specific communities but by providing criteria for viability, letting any community that now qualifies or may come to qualify seek recognition. Perhaps if and when a conception of group rights such as this comes to be more generally accepted we will move in this direction. That would be to make the criteria for language rights more universal, but not in a way that takes us back to an individualistic approach—it would permit any group to qualify, but only groups would be eligible.

Once we are satisfied that a particular group exists, in the sense of being viable, the idea of communal choice comes into play to round out the explanation of the group-specificity of language claims. We provide support or accommodation for *this* language because *this* language community has chosen to conduct its life in that language. This argument builds on accounts of ethnicity as a source of identity that eschew belief in the fixed and eternal nature of culture and the deterministic accounts of its role in identity formation (Nagel 1994; May 2001: Ch. 1).[22] There is nothing primordial or necessary about linguistic identity. The belief that there is simply substitutes for an argument for why the commitments that people do have should be respected. It is not because their language is 'in their blood' that a group's linguistic heritage deserves recognition, but because the group chooses to maintain its allegiance to that heritage. This basis in communal autonomy does a better job of accounting for the normativity of group-specific rules than Kymlicka's approach. Kymlicka (1995a: Ch. 5) attempts to provide an explanation of the value of particular cultures capable of grounding group-specific rules in part through the argument that people are deeply attached to their culture and are reasonably entitled to expect that it will continue. The deep-attachment argument can easily be read in a way that takes us back to an individual choice model, with its attendant difficulties;

---

[22] May (2001: Ch. 1) provides a useful survey of the contrast between primordialist and situationalist accounts of ethnicity, and stakes out a plausible middle ground. May's focus, however, is on providing an account of what ethnicity *is*; mine is on why its particular instantiations in particular populations should be respected.

the reasonable-expectation argument requires an account of what makes such expectations reasonable, and this too could be fleshed out in an individualistic fashion. People are usually deeply attached to their language, but it is their collective attachment that can be understood as an exercise of communal autonomy requiring accommodation by others. And it is a particular history created and shared by the group that gives rise to reasonable expectations of continuity.

Yet, as the individual choice model shows, to include positive supports for the use of one's language gives rise to the problem of conflict between rights claims. Can a group-specific rules model deal with conflict more successfully? The focus on groups instead of individuals helps. It is not that the problem of conflict disappears with the shift of focus, but rather that the shift enables us to see that security for each of two (or more) language communities does not typically require micro-regulation at the level of individual interactions—the level at which conflict is most destructive to the viability of a rights-based account.

Considering the collective dimension of the human interest in language turns questions of linguistic accommodation into questions, in the first instance, of the relationship between language communities rather than the relationship between individuals across a linguistic divide. In working through the details of concrete issues in any given jurisdiction, the matter may ultimately come down to a final consideration of the justice of some particular imposition on some particular individual, but we should end rather than begin there. Starting from the macro level we are likely to find that we can do a great deal of accommodating without coming close to infringing on legitimate individual interests in freedom of linguistic choice. This is important, because to say that one of the human interests in language is a collective one does not mean that there is not also an individual interest. The analysis above has already identified a legitimate, though limited, individual interest in freedom of language choice. Any comprehensive account of a just language policy will want to avoid trenching on these individual rights as much as it tries to articulate the demands of justice between communities.

Macro or community-level thinking encourages us to think in terms of long-term planning around language issues rather than short-term, and of intervening to influence the flow of general currents in language behaviour rather than prescribing discrete individual acts. Precisely because of the complexity and richness of the existence of a language community, there is no need to police every interaction between individuals. To remain healthy, it is not necessary for members of one language group to conduct their lives exclusively in their own language. It is necessary for policy makers to keep an eye on the conditions that work against the ability of speakers of a particular language to use their language in a wide variety of contexts. The more such conditions are allowed to proceed unchecked, the sooner the point will be reached at which freedom to choose to carry on in any meaningful way will be lost to the community as a whole. But these conditions can be significantly controlled without unfairness to individuals. In the nature of things it is mainly by using the language amongst themselves that members of a linguistic minority will foster the conditions making it possible to carry on doing so. If there does not already exist a viable community of people committed to the continuance of the language, insistence that others provide life support is absurd. A language is a living, organic thing; it cannot be artificially preserved without changing its character.

Against this backdrop of the community's own efforts to sustain itself, other communities sharing the same soil and political institutions can do a great deal to help. The main place to begin is with measures that make the institutional structures of government and perhaps other leading institutions equally open to members of both language communities. This will often require the creation of quasi-parallel structures: one operating in one language, the other in another. Some level of personal bilingualism within the population of both communities will undoubtedly be necessary to grease the wheels of such a system, but this does not seem too onerous to expect as an empirical condition of success.[23] In any event, wise policy makers will act to encourage the necessary level of personal bilingualism in order to make possible the other measures needed. The social and political structure of a given country as well as its history of 'sticking points' will determine the precise accommodations in these institutional structures that will best allow for freedom of linguistic choice as between its communities. Such measures go considerably beyond non-interference with the language practices of the other group, but this seems the minimum required by any conception of substantive equality between communities.

Measures designed to facilitate coexistence might well include one or both of the kinds of group-specific accommodations I have outlined. Some might consist of direct group-specific entitlements, such as the guarantee of government services to members of the minority community in their own language. Such a scheme requires governments to think in terms of structuring the civil service so that it has sufficient numbers of minority-language speakers and that they can be deployed effectively to provide the services needed to the minority community. There may also be contexts in which it is more appropriate to create separate institutions within which the minority can manage its own affairs. I have already mentioned the managerial control over minority-language schools given to parents in the Canadian system. The main point is that a great deal of work can be done in these directions without any interference with the majority's own right to linguistic security. The organization of the civil service so that minority-language speakers may be served in their own language does not deprive majority-language speakers of the like service. Creation of minority-language school boards does not interfere with the operation of majority-language boards. Language use may be competitive at the margins, but, considered from the point

---

[23] Although Van Parijs (2000a: 241) seems to suggest otherwise, his empirical assumptions are not better grounded than mine. Personal bilingualism is not that difficult, as minority-language communities everywhere prove daily. What makes it seem difficult to majority-language speakers is the absence of support for second-language learning, and, one suspects, an ideology of superiority.

of view of the mutual accommodation of two language communities, it is not that difficult to see how their interactions can be organized so that they both thrive. No doubt in the development of a comprehensive system of language regulation we will ultimately come to the point where the demands of one group cannot be met without infringement on the like interest of another group, and such conflicts will require careful attention. The attraction of using a communal rather than an individual lens to think about these questions is that we do not derail the entire exercise from the start with the bogeyman of pervasive rights conflict.

## 4. Conclusion: Transcending Territorialism and Personality

The aggregative justifications underlying the territorial model trivialize the interest in language and treat is as fungible; the personal model, interpreted both positively and individualistically, construes the interest in language as an interest in individual choice and gives it exaggerated importance, engendering pervasive conflicts of rights in contexts involving interaction between language groups. But we can learn from the shortcomings of both of these justificatory approaches. Language interests should not be subjected to a majoritarian calculus, but a plausible rights-based model must temper the individualism of conventional human rights analysis by focusing on a language group's collective choice to maintain its linguistic way of life as deserving of the respect of other language communities.

My analysis grounds language rights firmly in a non-aggregative, rights-based form of argument. Language rights are grounded in the interests in linguistic security of viable communities, as communities, wherever they are. That my account is rights-based allies it with theories of individual rights and sets it against the aggregative foundation of the territorial model. Yet the fact that enjoyment of linguistic security is not individualizable sets these rights apart from traditional human rights. The need for a viable community of language speakers in order to provide the material and conceptual base for the protection of language use gives the right to linguistic security a superficial resemblance to some aspects of the territorial model. Since language speakers tend to congregate geographically, and some services must be provided physically, there will be a territorial element to the delivery of some language protections. But location in a particular territory is only indirectly connected to the crucial element in a claim to the protection of linguistic security, which is the existence of a viable language community. Communities exist in geographical space, but there is no reason to think that any given territory can accommodate only one linguistic community (Magnet 1986: 195). Thus, the central truth of the relevance of territory is freed from the ideology of one territory/one language. Likewise, we can acknowledge the kernel of truth in the social unity justification of unilingualism, namely, that the importance to a community of its language goes beyond the language's instrumental uses as a means of communication, while extending that recognition to each viable community instead of arbitrarily affording it only to the majority in each territory.

This analysis suggests that the distinction between territorial and personality models of language policy is misleading. The salient divide is between aggregative justifications for unilingualism and rights-based justifications for bilingualism. The former needs a territory within which to be implemented, but the approach stands or falls on the propriety of its conception of the interest in language as capable of such aggregation. A rights-based bilingualism model can be grounded in individual choice as the label 'personality' suggests, but need not be. I have suggested that a more successful approach would treat communal interests as grounding the rights recognized. Since communities tend to be less mobile than individuals, we would expect to see some concrete accommodations given a territorial scope, thus giving territory some relevance on both sides of the aggregative/rights-based policy divide.

# 13

# What Kind of Bilingualism?

ALAN PATTEN

## 1. Two Principles of Bilingualism

The term 'bilingual' can be applied to individuals, to societies, and to institutions. Individuals are called 'bilingual' if they can speak two languages with a reasonable level of proficiency. We label a society 'bilingual' if there are two languages spoken within the territory of that society. Finally, institutions are termed 'bilingual' if they *recognize* two languages. Under institutional bilingualism, public services are offered in two different languages and public business can be conducted in either language.

Bilingual societies face several important and difficult problems of public policy. Most basically, they must decide whether or not to adopt some form of institutional bilingualism. They must decide whether to operate schools, hospitals, courts, legislatures, unemployment offices, and so on, in both of the languages spoken on their territory, or whether they are better off designating one of the languages as the 'official' language and requiring all public institutions to operate in it.

When a bilingual society does opt for some form of institutional bilingualism, it must make several additional choices. Regimes of institutional bilingualism can vary along a number of different dimensions (McRae 1975: 42–6). One question, for instance, is whether the recognition of the two languages should be strictly equal or whether there should be some difference in rights or status between the majority language and the minority one (if there is a clear majority/minority division). Another is whether bilingualism ought to be applied to the full set of domains of public language use or just to some of them (for instance, to schools and courts but not to the health service). A third issue arises in federal systems: should institutional bilingualism be a requirement of both levels of government or just of one?

In this chapter I will focus on a fourth question faced by bilingual societies opting for some form of institutional bilingualism. Looking around the

A first draft of this chapter was written while I was a visiting fellow at the Center for Human Values, Princeton University. Thanks to members of the Fellows' Seminar for their comments and especially to Chris Eisgruber for serving as my discussant. Earlier drafts were also presented at the University of Toronto and to an ECPR workshop in Turin, Italy. I'm grateful to all those in attendance at these events and to Will Kymlicka for written comments on the first draft.

world at some of the different countries that recognize more than one language in their public institutions, one quickly notices two different approaches. In some cases, both languages are recognized across the country, so that no matter where a speaker of one of these languages is in the country he can interact with public institutions in his own language. A person has the same language rights with respect to education, public services, the courts, and so on, no matter where in the country he resides. In other cases, however, an attempt is made to identify regional patterns of language use within the country, with an eye to varying language rights from region to region according to local conditions. Under this approach, the language rights that you can claim depend on where in the country you happen to be living.

The principle that citizens should enjoy the same set of language rights no matter where they are in the country is commonly referred to as the 'personality principle'. The opposing principle, that language rights should vary from region to region according to local conditions, is generally labelled the 'territoriality principle'. On the first principle, language rights follow *persons* wherever in the state they may choose to live; on the second, your language rights depend on what part of the *territory* of the state you find yourself in.[1] The aim of this chapter will be to assess the comparative strengths and weaknesses of these two principles. Supposing that a society has decided to adopt some form of institutional bilingualism, then under what circumstances should it prefer the personality principle, and when should it opt for the territoriality principle?

It is very hard to find a pure case of either the personality principle or the territoriality principle anywhere in the world. Most regimes of bilingualism include at least some language rights that remain invariant across the territory of the state and at least some that vary from region to region according to local conditions. There are, however, significant differences amongst various regimes of institutional bilingualism in the degree to which they emphasize one or the other principle.

Belgium and Switzerland are perhaps the clearest examples of institutionally multilingual countries that have embraced the territoriality principle. Belgium is divided into four language districts, each recognizing a distinct set of language rights. The provinces of Wallonie and Flanders are, for the most part, institutionally unilingual, operating in French and Dutch respectively. The capital, Brussels, is institutionally bilingual. And in an area of Wallonie near the border with Germany, certain minority language rights are extended to German-speakers. In Switzerland, most important decisions concerning language policy are made at the cantonal level, and the majority of cantons have adopted policies of unilingualism reflecting the language usage of the local majority population.

---

[1] The distinction between these two principles is now standard in the literature on language rights. See for example Royal Commission on Bilingualism and Biculturalism (1967: Ch. 4), Kloss (1971: 264–7), McRae (1975), Laponce (1984), Nelde, Labrie, and Williams (1992), Van Parijs (2000*a*), and Réaume (this volume).

Canada and South Africa, by contrast, are good examples of countries that give greater emphasis to the personality principle. For instance, the Canadian Charter of Rights and Freedoms includes provisions guaranteeing minority language education and the provision of federal public services, in either English or French, that apply across the country, subject only to a 'where numbers warrant' proviso that is triggered at very low levels of demand (secs 16–23).[2] The South African Constitution of 1997 recognizes eleven official languages and includes a right to education in the official language of one's choice, limited only by the requirement that the education be 'reasonably practicable' (secs 6, 29(2)).

One reason to investigate the normative underpinnings of the two principles of institutional bilingualism is to better understand the choices made in these different cases and in other comparable ones. Why is more weight attached to one principle in some cases and more to the other in others? Are the choices made in each of these societies defensible, or could an argument be made in some of them that the balance should be readjusted in favour of one or the other principle? The mix between personality and territoriality is hotly contested in many of these societies. In Canada, for instance, the weight given to the personality principle has been attacked by anglophone commentators in English-majority provinces for imposing an excessive burden on the majority English-speaking population, and by francophone commentators throughout the country for failing to do enough to protect the French language. In Belgium, the Brussels area is the flashpoint of a conflict between proponents of the two principles. Proponents of territoriality have reaffirmed the institutional unilingualism of Flanders in the face of a growing availability of services in French in the suburbs of Brussels. An exploration of the normative basis of the two principles can help us to better understand these and other conflicts and perhaps to provide some guidance in resolving them.

The chapter will not defend a general preference for one or other of the two principles. In general, I think that the personality principle is appropriate in some cases; the territoriality principle in others. The main aim will be to try to say something more precise about the conditions under which each principle should be preferred. My claim will be that a preference for territoriality requires the satisfaction of one or other of two conditions that will be explained in the course of the chapter. Either territoriality must be necessary to bring about a common public language within some relevant political unit, or it must be necessary to prevent a vulnerable language community from deteriorating to the point that it no longer offers an adequate context of choice to its members. Where neither of these conditions is met, then, in general, the personality principle should be regarded as normatively preferable.

A choice between the two principles will inevitably depend, in part, on considerations of stability. Multilingual societies can be subject to a high degree

---

[2] For consideration of the levels of demand needed to trigger the minority language education provisions, see Supreme Court of Canada (1990; 2000).

of instability arising from conflict between the different linguistic groups. Drawing on the enviable Swiss experience of stability, some political scientists have suggested that the territoriality principle can help to avoid or at least to regulate this kind of group conflict (McRae 1975: 50–1; Nelde, Labrie, and Williams 1992).[3] Good fences, as the old adage has it, make for good neighbours (McRae 1975: 51). Just as the principle of *cuius regio eius religio* helped to bring an end to the Reformation-era wars of religion in Germany and Switzerland, the territoriality principle may have similar consequences in multilingual societies around the world.

The analysis that I develop here will follow a different path. Although stability considerations are clearly important, it is also important to know whether stability is grounded in a set of arrangements that are just or reasonable on their own merits. An analysis that abstracts from stability considerations can help us to select from the various stable equilibria that are feasible, or could be made so, in a given society. In reflecting on the conclusions of the analysis, however, we should not rule out the possibility of a conflict with stability that necessitates falling back to the second-best.

Rather than highlighting stability, my strategy will be to analyse the choice between the two principles in terms of a number of important interests that individuals have in connection with language policy—interests in 'public access', 'social mobility', 'democratic participation', and 'identity' (sections 4–7). Before examining these interests, I offer a more precise statement of the territoriality principle than I have so far given (section 2) and I discuss why the choice between the two principles is a matter of some controversy (section 3). In a concluding section of the chapter (section 8), I pull together the different elements of the framework that has been constructed and I briefly illustrate it through some comments on the Canadian and Belgian cases.

## 2. Refining the Territoriality Principle

Consider a very simple case of societal bilingualism, as depicted in Fig. 13.1. In this case, speakers of the country's two languages, A and B, are neatly concentrated into two unilingual regions. Intuitively, this case seems like a strong candidate for the application of the territoriality principle: there could legitimately be some variation in language policy between the two regions.

---

[3] The Swiss jurist Walther Burckhardt offered the classic formulation of this claim: 'It is now a tacitly recognized principle that each locality should be able to retain its traditional language regardless of immigrants of other languages, and consequently that linguistic boundaries once settled should not be shifted, neither to the detriment of the majority nor of minorities. It is trust in this tacit agreement that provides a foundation for peaceful relations among the language groups. Each group must be sure that the others do not wish to make conquests at its expense and diminish its territory, either officially or by private action' (Burckhardt 1931: 806; cited in McRae 1983: 122).

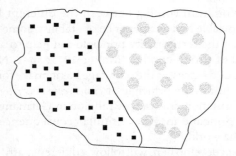

■   Concentration of *A*-speaking population

◉   Concentration of *B*-speaking population

FIGURE 13.1  Perfect concentration

This variation could take two distinct forms. According to a principle of *jurisdictional territoriality*, language policy choices should, as far as possible, be made by political institutions that operate at the regional level. Suppose, for instance, that the country under consideration has a federal constitution and that the two linguistic regions correspond perfectly with two units or provinces of the federation. Under the principle of jurisdictional territoriality, language policy decisions should, as far as possible, be made by the political institutions of the province rather than by institutions of the central state.

To make this formulation of the territoriality principle more precise, it is necessary to flesh out the 'as far as possible' qualifier. A first step in doing this is to notice that it would be impossible for *all* language policy decisions to be made at the provincial level. *Ex hypothesi*, the two regions are not separate states but are joined together into a single federal state. It follows that there is a central government retaining at least some areas of jurisdiction. When the central government operates within its areas of jurisdiction, it must do so in some language(s) or other, and this means that it cannot help but make certain language policy decisions.

Faced with this constraint, there seem to be two ways of understanding 'as far as possible'. First, we might say that the principle of jurisdictional territoriality is in effect to the extent that each province has the authority to make language policy decisions with respect to its own areas of jurisdiction. There is no right retained by the central government to determine language policy in provincial areas of responsibility. Thus, if education is a provincial matter, then it is the province, not the central government, that has the authority to make decisions about the language of education. Call this *weak jurisdictional territoriality*.

By contrast, under *strong jurisdictional territoriality*, not only do provinces retain the right to make language policy in their own areas of jurisdiction, but the areas of jurisdiction themselves are to be assigned, wherever possible, to the provincial level of government. Thus, in our example, there would, according to this principle, be two provinces, each having significant areas of jurisdiction and each possessing the authority to make decisions about language policy in those areas. When the principle of strong jurisdictional territoriality is in effect, the state is highly decentralized and the province is sovereign over questions of language within its areas of responsibility.

A second way in which language policy could vary between the two regions points to a distinct formulation of the territoriality principle. Under a principle of *unilingual territoriality*, public institutions operate exclusively in the language spoken in the region in which they are situated. Schools, hospitals, courts, government offices, and so on, located in the A-speaking region of the country operate exclusively in A and those located in the B-speaking region operate exclusively in B. Some institutions will apply to the whole territory of the state—for instance, the legislature of the central government, and the state's highest court—and their language rules will not be determined by this principle. But, for any institution having responsibilities corresponding to a specific part of the territory of the state, the principle of unilingual territoriality would be operative.

Unlike jurisdictional territoriality (in both its weak and strong variants), unilingual territoriality does not depend on political authority over language decisions being arranged in any particular way. The principle is as applicable to unitary states as it is to federal ones and, in the latter, it applies in central government areas of jurisdiction as well as in provincial ones. Suppose, for instance, that education is considered a responsibility of the central government. The principle of unilingual territoriality would still require that all public schools located in the A-speaking region operate in language A and those located in the B-speaking region operate in language B.

If we just focus on the provincial level, the implications of the unilingual and jurisdictional territoriality principles would likely be very similar, at least in the simple case before us. Provincial governments that have the authority to make language policy in their own areas of jurisdiction would likely opt for institutional unilingualism if their citizens all spoke the same language. But even here it is worth noting the difference between the two versions of the territoriality principle, if only for analytic purposes. A provincial government would not *necessarily* opt for institutional unilingualism; and to this extent the two versions of the principle are not the same. It is conceivable, for instance, that A-speaking citizens might pressure their provincial government to offer public education in B as well as A, if fluency in B was a key to economic opportunity in other parts of the country or world.

One way of summarizing the difference between the jurisdictional and unilingual variants of the territoriality principle would be to say that the two answer different questions. Jurisdictional territoriality is one possible answer to the question: 'Who ought to have the authority to make some decision about language policy?'. Unilingual territoriality, by contrast, is a possible answer to the question: 'What substantive decisions about language policy should be made by those who have the authority to make them?'. The two versions of the principle travel together in so far as answering the first question in a particular way will lead to predictable policy outcomes. But in so far as a given answer to the 'who should have authority?' question leaves open the 'how should that authority be exercised?' question, the two are best treated as distinct.

The remainder of this chapter will focus on the second of these two questions. In practice it is the more fundamental of the two, since demands for a particular allocation of jurisdictional authority are often predicated on the assumption that such an allocation would be more or less hospitable to unilingual territoriality. To assess such demands, it is important to have some view on the legitimacy of calls for unilingual territoriality. For the purposes of the chapter, then, when I refer to the principle of territoriality I will mean the principle of unilingual territoriality. I wish to contrast this answer to the 'how should authority over language policy be exercised?' question with the answer given by the personality principle.

## 3. Locating the Controversy

In Switzerland, most cantons have a very high degree of linguistic homogeneity and, where they do not, it has generally been possible to draw a boundary within the canton that does manage to separate neatly the different linguistic groups (McRae 1983: 49–62, 123). Where a country can be divided into a set of perfectly homogeneous Swiss-style cantons, then most people would not seriously object to an application of the territoriality principle in which public institutions are operated exclusively in the language of the local canton (or cantonal district). It is rare, however, to find cases that approach Swiss levels of territorial concentration, let alone real-world instances of societal multilingualism that involve the degree of neat separation imagined in Fig. 13.1. It is in the standard cases—the cases where the different language communities are territorially intermixed and there is no way of drawing or redrawing cantonal boundaries to eliminate local linguistic heterogeneity—that the controversy over the territoriality principle begins.

There are two important variations on this more complex kind of situation. The first is illustrated in Fig. 13.2. In this case, the country's two language groups are imperfectly concentrated into two regions. In one region, language A predominates but there are pockets of B-speaking populations. In the other, the reverse is true.

The other kind of situation of interest is illustrated in Fig. 13.3. In this case, one language, language B, predominates throughout much of the country, but there are significant concentrations of A-speaking in certain areas. The A-speakers are scattered in such a way that it is possible to designate certain bilingual districts in

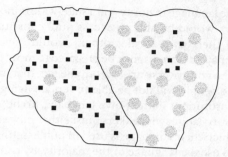

■  Concentration of *A*-speaking population
●  Concentration of *B*-speaking population

FIGURE 13.2  Imperfect concentration

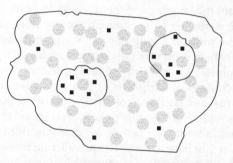

■  Concentration of *A*-speaking population
●  Concentration of *B*-speaking population

FIGURE 13.3  Bilingual districts

which both languages are spoken by significant numbers of people. But, although many *A*-speakers live in these bilingual districts, some do not.

In both these cases, the territoriality principle becomes controversial in a way that is theoretically interesting. In the Imperfect Concentration case, the territoriality principle would recommend the establishment of two institutionally unilingual regions. Each of these regions would have its own local majority and minority. Minority-language speakers would be expected either to accommodate themselves to the use of the majority language in public-institutional settings or to move to the region in which their language is in the majority. In the Bilingual Districts case, the territoriality principle would call for institutional unilingualism throughout the country, except for designated bilingual districts in which both languages are institutionally recognized. Under this scenario, there is a state-wide language majority and a state-wide minority. Some minority-language speakers would be able to access public institutions in their own language and in their own locale; others would have to accommodate themselves to the majority language or be prepared to move to a bilingual district.

In both cases, the controversy arises from the fact that, under the territoriality principle, some people will not be able to remain living where they are *and* deal with public institutions in their own language. To be able to access public institutions, minority-language speakers must either move to a different district of the state, in which their language is used in public settings, or they must be willing and able to use the language of the majority. By contrast, under the personality principle, both languages would be recognized across the country and nobody would be forced to choose between staying where they are and using their own language in dealing with public institutions.

To assess the relative merits of the territoriality and personality principles, we need some sense of how reasonable it is ask members of a linguistic minority to either leave or adopt the language of the majority in dealings with public institutions. I take it that moving to another part of the state has significant costs, especially when the move is a long one. Although moving is not difficult for some people, for others it involves giving up employment and employment qualifications, abandoning networks of family, friends, and community, and enduring the psychological hardships of leaving a place that one considers 'home'. For these reasons, we do not normally regard the possibility a minority has of exiting to be sufficient to justify policies that would otherwise be unreasonable towards that minority. We do not, for example, think that the freedom a religious minority might have to move to a jurisdiction that is more congenial to their religion makes it acceptable for the jurisdiction they live in now to treat their religion unfavourably.[4]

The key question then, in my view, is how reasonable it is to ask members of a language minority to use the majority language in public settings. This is obviously an important question, not just for adjudicating between the personality and territoriality principles, but also for assessing whether a bilingual society should introduce any form of institutional bilingualism in the first place. Although readers may want to test the arguments that follow against their intuitions about this more fundamental problem, my remarks will mainly focus on the choice between personality and territoriality. I assume that, where it is reasonable to expect members of the minority to use the majority language in public settings, the territorial principle is acceptable. Where it is not, the personality principle should be preferred.

The reasonableness of the expectation, in turn, depends on the various ways in which members of the minority and majority groups would be advantaged

---

[4] Even when there is freedom to move from territory to territory, the principle of *cuius regio eius religio* seems objectionably illiberal today. For discussion of this principle from a liberal point of view, see Barry (2001: 25).

and disadvantaged by the policies associated with the territoriality principle. With this problem in mind, I turn now to a consideration of four different interests that people have in connection with language policy. I call these the interests in 'public access', 'social mobility', 'democratic participation', and 'identity'. For each interest, I consider the distribution of advantage and disadvantage under various empirical scenarios.

To keep the exposition as uncluttered as possible, I will mainly have in mind the Imperfect Concentration case. The terms 'minority' and 'majority' thus refer to the local majorities/minorities that would be created by the unilingual districts established under the territoriality principle.[5] Although most of what I say can be applied straightforwardly to the Bilingual Districts case, the language of majority/minority has to be interpreted differently there and I will leave it to the reader to make the necessary changes.

## 4. Public Access

The choice between the personality and territoriality principles is a choice about what rules and practices of language use should be adopted by public institutions such as schools, courts, legislatures, government offices, and the like. In developing a framework for analysing this choice, an obvious place to start is with the communication that takes place between members of the public and those institutions themselves. The interest in public access is the interest that people have in being able to access public services and participate in the conduct of public business. Since the ability to access public institutions depends on the ability to communicate in the context of those institutions, this interest is clearly relevant to language policy.

Under the personality principle, both minority and majority language speakers have their interest in public access satisfied. Since public institutions operate in both languages, no member of either language group is prevented from accessing public institutions by an inability to communicate in public settings.

By contrast, under the territoriality principle, minority language speakers will have difficulty accessing public institutions if they are unable to speak the majority language fluently. People with little or no knowledge of the majority language will clearly struggle in public settings and are vulnerable to having their rights and interests, and those of their children, overlooked. Even people who have achieved a reasonable degree of competence in the majority language may face some obstacles under the regime of majority-language unilingualism

[5] A local linguistic minority may or may not be a state-wide minority or a minority in an international context. English-speakers in Quebec count as a minority in the terminology I will adopt, even though English-speakers are in the majority in Canada, and in North America, and English is a dominant international language. In the arguments to follow, nothing of substance rests on whether a group gets labelled a 'minority' or 'majority'.

that would be in effect under the territoriality principle. In highly stressful contexts, such as a court of law or hospital, or in contexts requiring a special, technical vocabulary, such as dealing with tax officials, even fairly competent speakers of a public language may have difficulty accessing the information or help they need or communicating their point of view.

A focus on the interest in public access, then, would seem to dictate an unambiguous preference for personality over territoriality. To the extent that facilitating communication in the context of public institutions is all that matters, personality clearly outperforms territoriality. The personality principle allows both majority- and minority-language speakers to access public institutions, whereas the territoriality principle is liable to exclude at least some members of the minority-language community.

An argument based solely on the interest in public access turns out to be quite weak, however. The main reason for this is that people have a capacity to learn new languages. Members of the minority-language community who do not already speak the majority language can be assisted to do so through an intensive programme of language training and education. To the extent that this programme is successful, even members of the language minority will be able to access public institutions under the territoriality principle: they will be able to do so in the majority language.

In response to this proposal, it might be objected that a programme of language education is likely to be time-consuming and, at best, only partially successful. It is typically very difficult for adults to learn a new language and, while they are in the process of trying to do so, they will face a considerable disadvantage if public institutions refuse to communicate with them in their own language.

This argument suggests that territoriality should be phased in gradually and gently but not that it should rejected altogether. In contrast with adults, children are typically very good at learning new languages, and so a policy of making everyone competent in the majority language could be aimed especially at them and have a reasonable likelihood of success. So long as current adult members of the language minority are given certain transitional accommodations in public settings, adopting the territoriality principle would not be objectionable from the standpoint of the interest in public access.

## 5.  Social Mobility

Of course, to argue that there is a way of squaring territoriality with the interest of language minorities in public access is not yet to give a positive reason for preferring territoriality. As I pointed out, the principle of personality is also compatible with accommodating the interest in public access, and it does not involve going to the considerable trouble of teaching everyone the majority language. A defence of the principle of territoriality would need to identify some more positive arguments.

One such set of arguments appeals to the interest that all individuals have in social mobility. This is the interest they have in a 'context of choice' that includes valuable options and opportunities embracing the full range of human activities (Kymlicka 1995a: 82–4). Access to a context of choice is a condition of individual autonomy, and more generally of individual well-being. Since people are different, and they frequently revise their ends, there needs to be a variety of options and opportunities if all individuals are to flourish.

Competence in the language(s) in which opportunities and options are offered is a precondition of having this context of choice. Without competence in the language spoken by those around her, a person will encounter difficulties in finding a job, doing business, making friends, practising a religion, and so on. For any given individual, this linguistic precondition can be satisfied in two different ways. There can be a sufficiently healthy context of choice operating in her own native language. Or she can achieve sufficient competence in a second language in which there is an adequate context of choice available.

Adapting some of Will Kymlicka's terminology, I will say that a language supports a 'societal culture' when an adequate context of choice is available in that language.[6] To say that there is a francophone societal culture in Quebec, for instance, is to say that a French-speaker in Quebec has access to an adequate range of options and opportunities operating in the French language. To say that there is no Italian-speaking societal culture in the United States, by contrast, would be to deny that an Italian speaker in that context has an adequate range of Italian-language options and opportunities. To enjoy social mobility, an Italian-speaker in the United States must learn English and access the English-language societal culture that dominates the country. As these examples suggest, an individual's interest in social mobility can be satisfied in two different ways. There can be a societal culture operating in a language that the individual speaks. Or the individual can integrate into a societal culture by learning the language in which it operates.

A defence of the territoriality principle appealing to the interest in social mobility can take two different forms. It might be argued that territoriality is necessary to secure the social mobility of members of the linguistic minority. Or the claim might be that territoriality helps to secure the social mobility of members of the majority. Let us consider each of these arguments in turn.

The first of the arguments is the more straightforward. Suppose that the majority language supports a societal culture but the minority language does not. Suppose further that the minority language community is sufficiently small and fragmentary that there is little chance that public policy could transform it into a viable societal culture. Under these conditions, the best policy from the

---

[6] Kymlicka (1995a: 76). Kymlicka defines a societal culture as a 'culture which provides its members with meaningful ways of life across the full range of human activities'.

point of view of the interest in social mobility would be to encourage members of the language minority to acquire the majority language. Only this way, given the assumptions that have just been made, can those individuals have access to an adequate context of choice. The argument for territoriality consists in the claim that unilingualism would be the best way of encouraging members of the language minority to learn the majority language. When public institutions such as schools and government offices operate exclusively in the majority language, then members of the minority, especially children, are likely to learn that language very effectively.

The main weakness of this argument is its last step. Although it is true that territoriality is likely to be effective at integrating minority-language speakers into the majority-language societal culture, this might also be true under the personality principle. Since minority-language speakers do not enjoy social mobility in their own language, there is already a strong incentive for them to learn the majority language. It is possible that all, or almost all, members of the minority-language community can be made to acquire the majority language with only minimal assistance from public policy. It might be the case, for instance, that a robust curriculum of second-language education in the majority language in a school system (and broader institutional context) that is otherwise available in the minority language would be sufficient to make the majority-language societal culture accessible to minority-language speakers. Under these circumstances, the interest in social mobility would be compatible with either territoriality or with an application of the personality principle that involved adequate second-language teaching in the majority language.

Still, this first argument from social mobility does help us to identify some specific empirical conditions in which a preference for territoriality is clearly indicated. Three conditions must be satisfied:

- the majority language supports a societal culture;
- the minority language does not support a societal culture; and
- minority-language speakers will acquire the linguistic competence they need to access the majority-language societal culture only if the territoriality principle is adopted.

A second argument appealing to the interest in social mobility requires the introduction of a further distinction: the distinction between what I shall term 'secure' and 'vulnerable' societal cultures. A secure societal culture is one that remains intact as a societal culture even in the face of a range of different demolinguistic shocks and changes. In a secure societal culture, there could be fairly significant demographic changes, or a fairly significant number of people who shift to another language, and the language community would still be able to offer its members an adequate context of choice. A vulnerable societal culture is one that is insecure. Even fairly minor changes in demographics, or a modest accumulation of individual decisions to use another language, can leave such a culture in a position where it is unable to provide an adequate context of choice to its members.

Vulnerable societal cultures raise a specific concern from the point of view of the interest in social mobility. The concern is that competition between several languages will end up undermining a vulnerable societal culture. Attracted by the options and opportunities that it provides, some members of the vulnerable culture may increasingly choose to live aspects of their lives in the more secure language. The unilingual members of the vulnerable culture will, as a result, become stranded: their own language community will no longer be able to afford them an adequate context of choice, and they would not have the linguistic capacities to access options and opportunities in the other language.[7]

The argument for the territoriality principle appeals to the possibility that the majority language societal culture may be vulnerable. Suppose that the following conditions are satisfied:

- it is likely that adopting the personality principle would trigger, or fail to counteract, demo-linguistic changes that leave the majority language community unable to support a societal culture;
- these changes would not occur under the territoriality principle; and
- some majority-language speakers are unilingual, and it is unlikely that they can be made proficient in the minority language.

When these conditions are met, a concern for the interest in social mobility of majority members indicates a preference for territoriality. Under the principle of personality, the minority language would tempt enough people, interacting in key domains of language use, away from the majority language to undermine the social mobility of unilingual majority-language speakers.

It might be objected that the third condition runs counter to my remarks in the previous section about the possibility of teaching people new languages. If the majority-language community is vulnerable, then the best course of action may not be to prop it up by adopting the territoriality principle, but to embark on an intensive programme of language training aimed at ensuring that *all* members of

---

[7] I discuss this kind of case further in Patten (2001: 707–8). The concern with language vulnerability and 'survival' is central to Laponce's (1984: Ch. 6) defence of the territoriality principle. See also Van Parijs (2000a). Laponce has relatively little to say about why ensuring language survival should be prioritized, commenting only that he is working on the presumption that language is a 'value in itself', in which 'the polis has its cement and its soul', rather than a 'simple, interchangeable instrument of communication' (1984: 144). Van Parijs devotes more attention to the normative issues raised by language policy decisions—emphasizing the relationship between respect and language recognition (2000a: 239–40)—but he does not specifically relate these normative considerations to a defence of language survival as a political aim. The idea of language as the intrinsically valuable 'soul' of the polis, and the appeal to considerations of 'respect', suggest that the animating normative principle for these writers is closer to what I term 'identity' than 'social mobility'. I analyse the identity argument in section 7 below.

the majority-language community are able to enjoy social mobility in the minority language. The main response to this objection should be to concede that the empirical conditions needed for this version of the social mobility argument to go through are indeed very demanding. Given that the first condition reflects the power and attraction of the minority language for members of the majority, it is unlikely that it will be satisfied in conjunction with the third condition.

This concession should be qualified in two ways, however. It is possible that different sections of the majority community may have very different propensities to be fluent in the minority language. Knowledge of the minority language may be disproportionately concentrated in an urban middle class oriented around white-collar employment. Competence in the minority language may be considerably less common amongst working-class majority members or amongst those who live away from the metropolis, and training these majority-language speakers in the minority language may be fairly difficult if they do not have much exposure to it. Under these kinds of circumstances, the third condition may not be impossible to satisfy.

The second qualification is connected with the possibility of transitional accommodations. In discussing the interest in public access, I stressed the importance of making transitional accommodations for the language minority if the territoriality principle is adopted. Although children would be educated in the majority language under this approach, certain public services would continue to operate in the minority language for some transitional period, and it would still be possible to conduct some public business in that language. In the case under consideration, however, where the personality principle is adopted and the majority-language community is imperilled, it is not clear what a scheme of transitional accommodations would look like. Securing social mobility for unilingual members of the majority is not just a matter of keeping some public offices open that operate in the majority language; it means ensuring that a whole range of options and opportunities—in the economy and society—are available in that language. Short of introducing the territoriality principle, there may be no way of accomplishing this as a transitional measure.

## 6. Democratic Participation

To the extent that democratic participation is equated with the act of voting, the interest in democratic participation does not seem to introduce any new requirements of communication that are not already analysable as part of the interest in public access discussed earlier. Democratic participation would require a ballot printed in a language spoken by the voter, and this requirement could, in principle, be addressed either by an application of the personality principle or by adopting the territoriality principle and ensuring that the language minority becomes competent in the majority language.

Many political theorists maintain, however, that democratic participation is not just a matter of periodically casting one's vote on the basis of antecedently given opinions and preferences. Democracy, they argue, also involves participation in an ongoing process of deliberation and discussion that takes place away from the formal political arena. In the course of this process, citizens exchange reasons and are sometimes moved to change their opinions and preferences on the basis of reasons offered by others. When the time to vote does arrive, citizens are guided by opinions and preferences that reflect the most compelling reasons that they and their fellow citizens are able to identify.

This view of democratic participation is clearly an ideal rather than a description of actual democracies as we know them. In practice, democratic citizens do not always participate in the informal, deliberative life of their political community and, even when they do, their voting behaviour is often not guided by the best reasons that they and fellow citizens succeed at identifying. Still, to the extent that the ideal is an attractive one, it is worth investigating which conditions help a political community to approach the ideal and which ones work to frustrate it.

In considering the choice between the territoriality and personality principles, one such condition stands out. The political community should not be segmented into several self-contained sub-communities, within which public deliberation and discussion take place, but whose members do not deliberate across communal lines. In a segmented political community, citizens are exposed to the most compelling reasons identified in their own sub-community but not necessarily to the most compelling reasons that are identified in their political community more generally, since they are ignorant of the discussions and deliberations going on in other sub-communities. We can contrast this with an integrated community in which there are mechanisms for circulating reasons around the community that are sufficiently elaborate and comprehensive to establish points of possible contact between any given pair of citizens.

A standard worry, classically formulated by John Stuart Mill, is that the presence of several distinct language communities would have the effect of segmenting a political community into two deliberative sub-communities. In Mill's view, 'Among a people without fellow-feeling, especially if they read and speak different languages, the united public opinion, necessary to the working of representative government, cannot exist' (Mill 1991: 428). Societal bilingualism will mean that people cannot (and will not) communicate across communal lines, and so a 'united public opinion' will not form.[8] The reasons that are identified as most compelling in one segment of society will not be brought into dialogue with those that seem most compelling in the other.

The consequences of this danger of segmentation for the choice between territoriality and personality depend on how the units of democratic decision making

---

[8] For contemporary statements of this worry, see Van Parijs (2000a: 236–7) and Kymlicka (2001a: 212–16).

are defined. Suppose that the state is federal and that the federal units are defined in a way that concentrates language groups into their own units as much as possible. Under these conditions, an argument for the territoriality principle is that it can help to break down barriers to inter-communal deliberation within each jurisdictional unit. The assumption here is that, when public institutions such as schools and government offices operate exclusively in the majority language, members of the minority, especially children, are likely to learn that language very effectively. With a common language, one significant cause of segmentation would be removed. Members of one language group would not be cut off from members of the other by an inability to communicate with one another or to access common media.

This argument for territoriality faces two possible objections. The first is identical to a problem encountered in the previous section. If the minority language community is a sufficiently marginal one, then it may not be necessary to resort to territoriality to induce minority members to learn the majority language. Their incentive to learn the majority language may already be so considerable that a programme of second-language teaching in the majority language is all that would be necessary. Under these circumstances, the interest in democratic participation would be compatible either with territoriality or with an application of the personality principle that involved adequate second-language teaching in the majority language. As with the social mobility argument, this objection should not lead us to reject a democratic argument for territoriality altogether but to understand more clearly an empirical condition that would have to be satisfied for the argument to be forceful. It must be the case that minority-language speakers would acquire sufficient competence in the majority language to participate in community-wide political deliberations only if the territoriality principle is adopted.

The other possible objection draws attention to the broader political framework in which the territoriality principle is to be implemented. The jurisdiction adopting territoriality is not, in our discussion, an independent state but a unit in a larger federation. In this federation, there are other units in which the majority language is the same as the local minority language. By focusing exclusively on facilitating democratic deliberation within the unit, the argument for territoriality seems to ignore the importance of deliberation at the federation-wide level.

The main response to this objection should be to question whether there is a *trade-off* between facilitating democratic deliberation locally and facilitating it nationally. Using territoriality to encourage the local language minority to acquire the majority language does not suddenly disable them from speaking their own minority language and thus does not undermine their capacity to participate in national political deliberations.

Of course this response does not address the problem of facilitating national deliberation. Realistically, there may be no perfect solution to this problem.

When a state contains several viable societal cultures, it may not be possible to establish a common language of political discussion and deliberation. The experience of second-language teaching in places such as Canada, Belgium, and Switzerland, for instance, should not lead one to be too optimistic about the prospects for success of this response to the problem of segmentation.

Under these circumstances, it is important to look for other ways of eliminating segmentation besides the creation of a common-language community. One response might be to establish cross-linguistic channels that are sufficiently elaborate and comprehensive so as to integrate the political community into a single deliberative body. This might involve, for instance, the activity of individually bilingual go-betweens and/or an extensive reliance on translations of discussions and deliberations taking place in the other language community. Another response might involve redefining the boundaries of the political community through a significant devolution of power to political units in which a common-language community is present or could be brought about (see the principle of strong jurisdictional territoriality discussed in section 2 above) (Van Parijs 2000a: 244–5). These solutions would probably work best in tandem, so that the cross-linguistic channels of deliberation would need only to support the democratic decision making of the residual political community remaining after certain powers and areas of jurisdiction had been devolved.

Even in tandem, these responses are unlikely to be as successful as the establishment of a common-language community. But under some conditions they probably represent the best that can be done from the standpoint of realizing the interest in democratic participation. And adopting the territoriality principle would not, as far as I can see, get in the way of efforts like these to facilitate democratic deliberation.

## 7.  Identity

So far the proposed framework for analysing the choice between the personality and territoriality principles has been entirely concerned with language as an instrument of communication. The two principles have been evaluated on the basis of their respective capacities to facilitate communication in the contexts of public institutions, the economy and society, and the informal political arena. A common claim in the literature on language rights, however, is that language is not just a tool of communication (see, for example, Laponce 1984: 144). It is claimed that for some people language is a central and defining feature of identity. What difference does this identity dimension make for the choice between the personality and territoriality principles?

To say that language is central to some individual's identity, I take it, is to say something about her attitudes and preferences. It involves, for instance, some or all of the following dispositions. The individual self-identifies with the (local) community of speakers of her language. She is proud of the language and the cultural achievements that have been expressed through it. She takes pleasure in using the language and encountering others who are willing to use it. She enjoys experimenting with the language and discussing its intricacies and subtleties with co-linguists. She hopes that the language community will survive and flourish into the indefinite future. In some contexts, she feels respected and affirmed when others address her in her language and denigrated when others impose their linguistic preferences on her. And so on.

Arguments for or against particular language policies that appeal to identity considerations presumably wish to claim that some of these attitudes and preferences should be accommodated. The claim, for example, is that the pleasure that people derive from using and experimenting with their language is something valuable, and thus the conditions that give rise to it ought, as a matter of language policy, to be fostered and maintained. Likewise, it may be argued that the preference that some have for the survival and flourishing of their language community in the future should be satisfied. Or it might be claimed that public institutions should be designed and operated in ways that make people feel respected and affirmed rather than denigrated.

Suppose, for instance, that the majority-language community is vulnerable in the sense defined earlier. Imagine, in addition, that members of the majority have a strong language-based identity, whereas minority-language speakers do not. Under these conditions, an identity argument would seem to support the territoriality principle. Territoriality would help to secure the majority-language community, and this would satisfy the attitudes and preferences of those in the majority without imposing any costs on the minority (assuming that transitional arrangements are made).

An obvious problem with this argument is its assumption that the minority-language speakers do not have a language-based identity.[9] If we relax this assumption, the identity argument becomes harder to read. Adopting the territoriality principle would advance the identity-related interests of those in the majority but set back those same interests for members of the minority.

One possible response to this identity conflict would simply be to side with the majority. On this view, given a choice between helping the majority and helping the minority, policy makers should help the majority, simply because they are the more numerous. The attitudes and preferences of more people are being accommodated when language policy attends to the identity of the majority than when it attends to the minority's identity.

But this argument is obviously too crude. One problem is that it takes no account of the degree to which the attitudes and preferences of members of the respective groups are already being satisfied. Imagine that the attitudes and

---

[9] Interestingly, this assumption may be more reasonable for (some) immigrants. For a brief comparison of the claims of immigrant and 'national' language groups, see Patten (2001: 696–7, 711).

preferences of those in the majority enjoy a reasonably high level of satisfaction, whereas the level of accommodation for those in the minority is very low. Is it really plausible to think that language policy makers should lavish even more attention on the majority and further disadvantage the minority? Anyone who thinks that justice requires some attention to the position of the worst-off should think not. A second problem with the majoritarian solution lies in its assumption that language policy must help *either* the majority *or* the minority. Perhaps a language policy could be devised that gives some attention to the identity interests of *both* groups, distributed according to some idea of equality or fairness?

These problems point to a different and more sophisticated way in which the identity argument might be developed for cases in which both the majority and the minority have a language-based identity. Language policy might be designed according to a criterion of equal satisfaction of everyone's attitudes and preferences. Suppose, for instance, that everyone has the same identity-related attitudes and preferences with respect to his or her own language but that the majority-language community is much more vulnerable than the minority one. Adopting the territoriality principle might be defended on the grounds that it leaves everyone with a roughly equal level of satisfaction of their attitudes and preferences. The minority-language community is (by assumption) independently secure and thus its members' identity-related attitudes and preferences are satisfied to some degree. Through the adoption of territoriality, the majority-language community is made secure too, and so its members can expect a degree of satisfaction that is comparable with those in the minority.

Although this way of resolving the identity conflict is much more appealing than the crude majoritarian solution, I think it is still flawed. The problem is that the equal-satisfaction standard caters too much to existing preferences and attitudes. Some people have preferences and attitudes that are rather easy to satisfy in the sense that they do not require many resources or much attention from public policy. Other people, by contrast, have preferences and attitudes that are very 'expensive' to satisfy. For them to achieve the same level of satisfaction as others, considerable resources must be devoted to their projects and/or significant attention must be given by public policy. This might be because the satisfaction of those preferences and attitudes requires expensive raw materials or tools or because it involves large numbers of people adopting or maintaining a practice, something they can be induced to do only through significant expenditures or institutional pressures.

The objection is that it seems unfair to ask those with the less expensive preferences and attitudes to subsidize those with the more expensive ones. And this is exactly what the equal-satisfaction standard would imply. Those with easy-to-realize identities would have to forgo resources, and accept inconvenient institutional arrangements, so that those who adopt harder-to-achieve identities will have the same chance of succeeding as they do. Underlying this claim of unfairness is the thought that people should be treated as if they had some control over what identities they have. There is nothing wrong with adopting an expensive identity but one should not expect others to bear the cost. One can legitimately claim one's fair share of resources and then devote those resources to realizing hard-to-achieve preferences and attitudes. But one is not entitled to *additional* resources just because one does not enjoy the same level of success as those with less expensive attitudes and preferences.

If this argument is correct, then the mere fact that one person's identity-related preferences and attitudes are not realized to the same degree as another's is not, on its own, sufficient grounds on which to make a claim for public assistance. Since this outcome may have arisen under what Rawls calls 'fair background conditions', we cannot conclude that there is anything necessarily objectionable about it (Rawls 1993: 195–200). Consider, for instance, a person who is complaining that the language policy adopted by his state is unfair to his language community. If the grounds for the complaint are that his language community ends up less successful than the other one, then the complaint is vulnerable to the argument I have been making. Merely pointing to a particular undesired outcome for one's language community is not enough to establish unfairness, since it is possible that the outcome arose in a context in which everyone had a fair share of resources and public assistance.

This way of responding to the person's complaint, however, suggests a third and much more promising way of making the identity argument. To see this, suppose that the complaint is made in a context in which one particular language is being systematically promoted by public institutions and the other is not. Imagine, for instance, that public institutions exclusively recognize the majority language. Under these circumstances, speakers of the minority language might make a complaint that does not rely on any claim concerning the relative success of their language community. They might complain that it is unfair for public institutions to assist one language community and not the other. When public institutions align themselves with one particular way of life in this way, then it can reasonably be objected that the background conditions under which individuals strive for the realization of their identities are unfair.

In some areas of policy, the best response to this unfairness would probably be for public institutions to withdraw from the promotion of particular ways of life altogether. Public institutions establish fair background conditions in which different identities can compete for success by helping *nobody*. For better or worse, this strategy of withdrawal is not available to language-policy makers. Since public institutions must operate in some language or other, it is impossible to avoid promoting certain languages.

When withdrawal is impossible, the closest that public institutions can come to establishing fair background conditions is to attempt a policy of 'even-handedness' (Carens 2000: Ch. 1). Under such a policy, public institutions attempt to give everyone some roughly equivalent help with their way of life. In the language case, this would involve offering public services, and making it possible to conduct public business, in both the majority and the minority language. Unless these provisions are made for the minority language, speakers of that language could reasonably complain that the exclusive attention and assistance given to the majority language does not leave them with a fair opportunity to realize their own identity-related preferences and attitudes.

What are the implications of this identity argument for the choice between the territoriality and personality principles? An objection to the territoriality principle is that it seems to violate the fair background-conditions requirement. Under the territoriality principle, language policy helps to secure and promote the language of the majority and, to this extent, accommodates the preferences and attitudes of those in the majority with a language-based identity. At the same time, the territoriality principle offers no assistance at all to those in the minority with a language-based identity. By recognizing only one language, public institutions are helping the majority language to flourish and maintain itself without giving any comparable assistance to those who define their identity in terms of the minority language. A bearer of a minority-language-based identity could reasonably object that he does not have a fair chance to realize the preferences and attitudes associated with his identity. By contrast, under the personality principle, this unfairness is absent. Public institutions operate in both the majority and the minority language and to this extent offer roughly equal kinds of assistance to bearers of minority-language and majority-language identities.

It seems to me, then, that a defensible version of the identity argument would indicate a general preference for personality over territoriality. Two important caveats should be mentioned, however. The first is that I have not offered a detailed account of fairness and language policy but have instead simply relied on the assumption that territoriality—which devotes no resources at all to the minority language—would be incompatible with such an account, whatever its precise contours turn out to be. Although this seems like a reasonable assumption, it is worth pointing out that a minority's fair share of resources may not entitle it to anything like the same level of public recognition as the majority enjoys. If a group's entitlement to resources is prorated according to its size (or the level of demand for services in the group's language), and there are economies of scale in the provision of public services in a particular language, then fairness is compatible with a lesser level of recognition of the minority group than of the majority group. For this reason, it seems appropriate for the personality principle to be qualified by a 'where numbers warrant' proviso.

The other caveat concerns the amount of weight that should be attached to the identity argument, even in the defensible 'fair background conditions' formulation that I have proposed here. It is natural to wonder what should be done when an analysis of the communication-related interests indicates a preference for the territoriality principle, whereas the identity-related interests, as I have argued, are more supportive of the personality principle. I will try to pull together the various strands of the discussion in the next section. For now, let me just emphasize that nothing in the argument of the present section is meant to suggest that the identity-related interests are more urgent than the communication-related ones. In fact, although I will not argue it here, my own view is that a person's interests in being able to access public institutions, in having an adequate context of choice, and in being able to participate in democratic deliberations are more urgent than her interests in having access to a fair share of identity-related resources.

Where there is a sharp conflict between the two kinds of interests, then, I would tend to privilege the communication-related ones. That said, an exploration of the identity argument is still important for assessing those cases in which both the personality and the territoriality principle can be reconciled with the individual's communication-related interests. In these cases, I claim, a consideration of the identity argument indicates a preference for the personality principle.

## 8. Discussion

Looking back at the arguments of the four previous sections, we can draw several general conclusions. One conclusion is that there are two main kinds of cases in which territoriality may be appropriate:

- cases in which territoriality is necessary to bring about a common public language; and
- cases in which territoriality is necessary to prevent people from being cut off from an adequate context of choice because of a deterioration in their language community.

In the first kind of case, the argument for territoriality appeals to considerations of democracy and/or social mobility. Territoriality is regarded as necessary to establish an integrated deliberative community and/or to ensure access to a societal culture for members of the language minority. In the second kind of case, the accent is on preserving social mobility for members of the language majority. Territoriality is deemed to be necessary to avert a situation in which unilingual members of the majority get stranded by the deterioration of their language community.

Unless at least one of these conditions is satisfied, my argument indicates a general preference for the personality principle. Absent the satisfaction of one of the conditions, the interests in public access, social mobility, and democratic deliberation are all satisfied under the personality principle, or could be made to be satisfied through a programme of second-language education in the majority language. Even if these interests would also be satisfied under the territoriality principle, the identity argument tilts the balance of reasons in favour of the personality principle.

Two qualifications should be added to these general remarks. The first is that any application of the personality principle should include a 'where numbers warrant' proviso. Where a language community is tiny, the 'fair share' of resources that it can legitimately claim will not be sufficient to finance a significant level of provision of services in that language, given economies of scale. This qualification is consistent with the common-sense intuition that territoriality is particularly appropriate for jurisdictions that have a very high degree of linguistic homogeneity.

The other qualification is connected with the costs of moving faced by the language minority under a regime of territoriality. In general, I argued, these costs are fairly significant, and so the possibility of moving cannot be regarded as sufficient compensation for a policy that is otherwise unreasonable. It is possible to imagine cases, however, in which the costs of moving are quite low. If the language districts are small enough, and close enough together, then moving may just involve relocating to a different part of the same town or city. Under these circumstances, even if an analysis of the language-related interests indicates a preference for the personality principle, it would seem acceptable for a jurisdiction to opt for the territoriality principle instead.

Finally, by way of conclusion, let me offer a brief comment on the Belgian and Canadian cases. I do so in order to illustrate the framework I have been developing rather than in the hope of saying anything definitive about these complicated controversies. A full analysis of these cases would obviously require a more detailed empirical investigation than I am prepared to offer here.

As I mentioned near the start of the chapter, the Belgian controversy has recently focused on the language rights of French-speakers living in Flanders in the suburbs of Brussels. Although Belgium is one of the main examples of a country that has adopted the territoriality principle, French-speakers in certain suburban communes in Flanders enjoy access to French-language 'facilities' (schools, government offices). Whereas Flemish public opinion is generally opposed to this exception to the territoriality principle, French-speakers have increasingly adopted the language of minority rights to defend their facilities.

My framework points to several empirical questions that should be asked in assessing this conflict. One concerns the propensity of French-speaking residents of Flanders to learn Dutch. Is this propensity too weak under a linguistic regime that recognizes the facilities? Would it increase significantly were the facilities to be abandoned? Although a knowledge of Dutch is probably not necessary for the social mobility of French-speakers (because of the proximity of French-dominant Brussels), the interest that all citizens of Flanders share in securing the conditions of deliberative democracy make it reasonable to expect that French-speakers living in Flanders will also learn Dutch. This expectation seems especially relevant in the Belgian context, in light of the highly decentralized character of the Belgian state. The other question concerns the impact of the facilities on linguistic transfers from Dutch to French in the Brussels area. Do the facilities encourage these transfers? Are there (significant numbers of) Dutch-speakers who lack proficiency in French and are, in this sense, 'left behind' by such transfers? And is the rate of any such transfers likely to reach a level where it risks undermining the capacity of Flemish societal culture to offer an adequate context of choice to the Dutch speakers who are left behind?

Canada, as I mentioned earlier, is one of the leading examples of a country that has opted for the personality principle (especially in federal institutions). In assessing this policy, it is convenient to look separately at the recognition of French outside Quebec and at the recognition of English in Quebec.

The francophone communities outside Quebec are characterized by a very high level of individual bilingualism, and so the members of those communities can typically enjoy social mobility in the English language and participate in the common political life of their province.[10] At the same time, the anglophone communities outside Quebec are extremely secure. It would seem, then, that neither of the conditions that would indicate a case for abandoning the personality principle is present in these cases. At best, it could be argued that some areas of the country are very homogeneously anglophone. For this reason, the 'where numbers warrant' proviso in Canada's application of the personality principle seems appropriate.

The case of anglophones in Quebec is somewhat more complicated. Increasingly, members of the anglophone community in Quebec enjoy a high level of individual bilingualism.[11] They are thus able to access francophone societal culture and participate in French-language political deliberations. On the other hand, it cannot be said that the French-language societal culture in Quebec enjoys a high level of security. And a surprisingly high proportion of Quebec francophones are unilingual.[12] The risk that demo-linguistic changes would undermine the social mobility of some francophones cannot, therefore, be entirely discounted. At the same time, despite Canada's adherence to the personality principle, there is evidence that French has overwhelmingly become the language of public life in Quebec.[13]

The degree to which the French language in Quebec is vulnerable is a matter of considerable empirical controversy. My own judgement is that it is not near

[10] According to the 1996 Canadian Census, 84% of francophones outside of Quebec consider themselves bilingual (Statistics Canada 1997).

[11] 62% of anglophones in Quebec consider themselves bilingual (Statistics Canada 1997).

[12] 34% of francophones in Quebec consider themselves bilingual. I call this figure 'surprising' because it is often suggested that English has penetrated into francophone life in Quebec to a much greater extent. One finds this suggestion both amongst critics of French language rights, who suggest that 'they all speak English anyways', and amongst more serious commentators such as May (2001: 230), who incorrectly states that francophones in Quebec are 'invariably bilingual'.

[13] A 1997 study estimated that 87% of the whole Quebec population over 18, born in Quebec or who had immigrated before 1995, used mainly French in public (Conseil de la langue française 1999).

enough the threshold of vulnerability required by the social mobility argument to justify the federal government abandoning its commitment to the personality principle, but I will not seek to justify that view here.[14] What the framework I am proposing does tell us is that this is the right sort of empirical question to be asking.

[14] One of the most pessimistic predictions that I am aware of is that French will become a minority language on the island of Montreal within about 15 years (Termote 2000, cited in Commission des état généraux sur la situation et l'avenir de la langue française au Québec 2001: 200). This conjecture needs to be put in context, however. 1. English is also declining in importance in Montreal. It is the languages of recent immigrants ('Allophones' as they are called) that are growing in importance. The widespread use of immigrant languages is a phenomenon that is observed in many North American cities and does not mean that immigrants will not eventually assimilate into the dominant societal language—French in the case of Quebec (see Jedwab 1996: 95, cited in Arel 2001: 88). 2. The prediction is for the *island* of Montreal (which now corresponds to the city). It thus excludes a number of the heavily francophone off-island suburbs—which are sometimes closer to downtown Montreal than the heavily anglophone or Allophone on-island suburbs that are counted. 3. The prediction is for the language spoken at home, not for the language used in public (where French is quite predominant). The normative reason for caring about vulnerability directs us to be more concerned about the latter (which affects the social mobility of the francophone population) than the former. 4. The past 25 years have witnessed considerable legal, institutional, and social change in Quebec and in Montreal (see for example Levine 1997). It is difficult to be confident about projections into the future based on linguistic behaviour during a period of such significant transition. Even if we accept Termote's projection, it is far from clear that things would change very much were the federal government to abandon the personality principle. As the Larose Report (Commission des états généraux 2001: 201) argues, the main factors behind the changing linguistic landscape of the island of Montreal are urban sprawl, high levels of immigration, and a low birth-rate amongst francophones—none of which is connected with the federal government's policy of offering services in English as well as French.

# References

ACKERMAN, BRUCE (1980). *Social Justice and the Liberal State* (New Haven: Yale University Press).

ALLEMANN-GHIONDA, CRISTINA (ed.) (1994). *Multikultur und Bildung in Europa* (Berne: Peter Lang).

ANDERSON, BENEDICT (1983). *Imagined Communities* (London: Verso Books).

—— (1991). *Imagined Communities*, revised edn (London: Verso).

ANDERSON, ELIZABETH (1999). 'What is the Point of Equality?', *Ethics*, 109/2: 287–337.

AREL, DOMINIQUE (2001). 'Political Stability in Multinational Democracies: Comparing Language Dynamics in Brussels, Montreal and Barcelona', in Alain-G. Gagnon and James Tully (eds), *Multinational Democracies* (Cambridge: Cambridge University Press), 65–89.

ARNESON, RICHARD (1982). 'The Principle of Fairness and Free-Rider Problems', *Ethics*, 92: 616–33.

AUDI, ROBERT (2000). *Religious Commitment and Secular Reason* (Cambridge: Cambridge University Press).

BADER, VEIT-MICHAEL (ed.) (1997). *Citizenship and Exclusion* (New York: St Martin's Press).

BAKER, COLIN (2001). *Foundations of Bilingual Education and Bilingualism*, 3rd edn (Clevedon: Multilingual Matters).

—— and PRYS JONES, S. (eds) (1998). *Encyclopedia of Bilingualism and Bilingual Education* (Clevedon: Multilingual Matters).

BAKER, KEITH and DE KANTER, ADRIANA (1981). *Effectiveness of Bilingual Education: A Review of the Literature* (Washington, DC: US Department of Education).

—— —— (eds) (1983). *Bilingual Education: A Reappraisal of Federal Policy* (Lexington, MA: Lexington Books).

BANTON, MICHAEL (2000). 'What Foundations for the Management of Cultural Pluralism?', in J. Dacyl and C. Westin (eds), *Governance of Cultural Diversity* (Stockholm: Swedish National Commission for UNESCO), 253–77.

BARBOUR, STEPHEN and CARMICHAEL, CATHIE (eds) (2000). *Language and Nationalism in Europe* (Oxford: Oxford University Press).

BARNARD, F. (1965). *Herder's Social and Political Thought: From Enlightenment to Nationalism* (Oxford: Clarendon Press).

BARRETO, AMILCAR ANTONIO (2001). *The Politics of Language in Puerto Rico* (Gainesville: University Press of Florida).

BARRY, BRIAN (2001). *Culture and Equality* (Cambridge, MA: Harvard University Press).

BASCH, LINDA, GLICK SCHILLER, N., and SZANTON BLANC, C. (1994). *Nations Unbound: Transnational Projects, Postcolonial Predicaments and Deterritorialized Nation-States* (London: Routledge).

BAUBÖCK, RAINER (1995). *Transnational Citizenship: Membership and Rights in International Migration* (Aldershot: Edward Elgar).

—— (1999). 'Liberal Justifications for Ethnic Group Rights', in C. Joppke and S. Lukes (eds), *Multicultural Questions* (Oxford: Oxford University Press), 133–57.

—— (2000). 'Why Stay Together? A Pluralist Approach to Secession and Federation', in W. Kymlicka and W. Norman (eds), *Citizenship in Diverse Societies* (Oxford: Oxford University Press), 366–94.

—— (2001). 'Cultural Citizenship, Minority Rights and Self-Government', in Alex Aleinikoff and Douglas Klusmeyer (eds), *Citizenship Today: Global Perspectives and Practices* (Washington: Carnegie Endowment for International Peace), 319–48.

—— (2003). 'Public Culture in Societies of Immigration', in Bernhard Peters (ed.), *Migrant Categories, Groups and Collective Identities* (Avebury: Ashgate).

BECKERMAN, WILFRED and PASEK, JOANNA (2001). *Justice, Posterity, and the Environment* (Oxford: Oxford University Press).

BELL, DAVID A. (2001). *The Cult of the Nation in France* (Cambridge, MA.: Harvard University Press).

BENNETT, FRED (2001). 'Multicultural Citizenship or Citizenship in a Multicultural Polity', Ph.D. thesis (Ottawa: University of Ottawa).

BERRY, JOHN (1998). 'Official Multiculturalism', in J. Edwards (ed.), *Language in Canada* (Cambridge: Cambridge University Press), 84–101.

—— (2000). 'Sociopsychological Costs and Benefits of Multiculturalism', in J. Dacyl and C. Westin (eds), *Governance of Cultural Diversity* (Stockholm: Swedish National Commission for UNESCO), 297–354.

BILLIG, MICHAEL (1995). *Banal Nationalism* (London: Sage).

BJELJEC-BABIC, RANKA (2000). '6,000 Languages: An Embattled Heritage', *The UNESCO Courier*, April.

BLAIR, PHILIP (2000). 'The Content of the European Charter for Regional or Minority Languages', paper presented at the ECMI Conference 'Evaluating Policy Measures for Minority Languages in Europe', Flensburg, 23–4 June.

BLAKE, MICHAEL (2000). 'Rights for People, Not for Cultures', *Civilization*, August/ September: 50–3.

—— (2002). 'Diversity, Survival, and Assimilation', *Journal of Contemporary Legal Issues*, 12/2: 627–60.

BLATTBERG, CHARLES (2000). *From Pluralist to Patriotic Politics* (Oxford: Oxford University Press).

BLOEMRAAD, IRENE (2002). 'The North American Naturalization Gap: An Institutional Approach to Citizenship Acquisition in the United States and Canada', *International Migration Review*, 36/1: 193–228.

BLOMMAERT, JAN (1996). 'Language and Nationalism: Comparing Flanders and Tanzania', *Nations and Nationalism*, 2: 235–56.

—— (ed.) (1999). *Language Ideological Debates* (Berlin: Mouton de Gruyter).

BOURDIEU, PIERRE (1991). *Language and Symbolic Power* (Cambridge: Polity Press).

BRANCHADELL, ALBERT (1999). 'Language Policy in Catalonia: Making Liberalism Come True', *Language and Communication*, 19: 289–303.

BRIMELOW, PETER (1996). *Alien Nation: Common Sense about America's Immigration Disaster* (New York: Harper).

BRUBAKER, ROGERS (1996). *Nationalism Reframed: Nationhood and the National Question in the New Europe* (Cambridge: Cambridge University Press).

—— (1998). 'Myths and Misconceptions in the Study of Nationalism', in J. Hall (ed.), *The State of the Nation: Ernest Gellner and the Theory of Nationalism* (Cambridge: Cambridge University Press), 272–306.

BURCKHARDT, WALTHER (1931). *Kommentar der schweizerischen Bundesverfassung vom 29. mai 1874*, 3rd revised edn (Bern: Stämpfli).

BUTLER, YUKO GOTO, ORR, JENNIFER EVELYN, BOUSQUET GUTIÉRREZ, MICHELE, and HAKUTA, KENJI (2000). 'Inadequate Conclusions from an Inadequate Assessment: What Can SAT-9 Scores Tell Us about the Impact of Proposition 227 in California?', *Bilingual Research Journal*, 24/1–2: 141–55.

CALLAN, EAMONN (1997). *Creating Citizens: Political Education and Liberal Democracy* (Oxford: Oxford University Press).

CANOVAN, MARGARET (1996). *Nationhood and Political Theory* (Cheltenham: Edward Elgar).

CARENS, JOSEPH (1997). 'Liberalism and Culture', *Constellations*, 4/1: 35–47.

—— (2000). *Culture, Citizenship and Community: A Contextual Exploration of Justice as Evenhandedness* (Oxford: Oxford University Press).

CASAL, PAULA (1999). 'Environmentalism, Procreation, and the Principle of Fairness', *Public Affairs Quarterly*, 13/4: 363–75.

CASTLES, STEPHEN (2000). *Ethnicity and Globalization: From Migrant Worker to Transnational Citizen* (London: Sage).

CHAMBERS, JACK and TRUDGILL, PETER (1980). *Dialectology* (Cambridge: Cambridge University Press).

CHAMBERS, SIMONE (1996). *Reasonable Democracy: Jurgen Habermas and the Politics of Discourse* (Ithaca: Cornell University Press).

—— (2001). 'A Critical Theory of Civil Society', in Simone Chambers and Will Kymlicka (eds), *Alternative Conceptions of Civil Society* (Princeton: Princeton University Press), 90–110.

CHRISTIANO, THOMAS (1996). *The Rule of the Many* (Boulder: Westview).

CHURCH, JEFFREY and KING, IAN (1993). 'Bilingualism and Network Externalities', *Canadian Journal of Economics*, 26: 337–45.

CLYNE, MICHAEL (1998). 'Managing Language Diversity and Second Language Programmes in Australia', in S. Wright and H. Kelly-Holmes (eds), *Managing Language Diversity* (Clevedon: Multilingual Matters), 4–29.

COCHRAN, DAVID CARROLL (1999). *The Color of Freedom: Race and Contemporary American Liberalism* (Albany: SUNY Press).

COHEN, JOSHUA (1997). 'Deliberation and Democratic Legitimacy', in Robert Goodin and Philip Pettit (eds), *Contemporary Political Philosophy: An Anthology* (Oxford: Blackwell), 143–55.

COLE, PHILLIP (2000). *Philosophies of Exclusion: Liberal Political Theory and Immigration* (Edinburgh: Edinburgh University Press).

COMMISSION DES ÉTATS GÉNÉRAUX SUR LA SITUATION ET L'AVENIR DE LA LANGUE FRANÇAISE AU QUÉBEC (2001). *Le français, une langue pour tout le monde: une nouvelle approche stratégique et citoyenne* (Québec: Gouvernement du Québec). Available at: www.etatsgeneraux. gouv.qc.ca/pdf/COM1-021_Rapport_final.pdf

CONGRESS OF LOCAL AND REGIONAL AUTHORITIES OF EUROPE (1998). *Recommendation 43 on Territorial Autonomy and National Minorities* (Strasbourg: Council of Europe).

CONNOLLY, WILLIAM (1995). *The Ethos of Pluralization* (Minneapolis: University of Minnesota Press).

CONSEIL DE LA LANGUE FRANÇAISE (1999). *Le Français, langue d'usage public au Québec en 1997: Rapport synthèse* (Québec: Conseil de la langue française). Available at www.clf.gouv.qc.ca/Publications/PubB149/B149.PDF

CONVERSI, DANIELE (1997). *The Basques, the Catalans and Spain* (London: Hurst).

COOK, RAMSAY (1969). *Provincial Autonomy, Minority Rights and the Compact Theory, 1867–1921*, Studies of the Royal Commission on Bilingualism and Biculturalism, No. 4 (Ottawa: Information Canada).

CORBALLIS, MICHAEL C. (2002). *From Hand to Mouth. The Origins of Language* (Princeton: Princeton University Press).

CORSON, DAVID (1995). 'Norway's Sámi Language Act: Emancipatory Implications for the World's Aboriginal Peoples', *Language in Society*, 24: 493–514.

—— (1998). *Changing Education for Diversity* (Buckingham, England: Open University Press).

—— (2001). *Qulliq Quvvariarlugu: Policy Options for Bilingual Education in the Territory of Nunavut: A Report to the Government of Nunavut* (Iqaluit: Nunavut).

COSTA, JOSEP (forthcoming 2003). 'Catalan Linguistic Policy: Liberal or Illiberal?', *Nations and Nationalism*, 9/3.

—— and WYNANTS, S (1999). 'Catalan Linguistic Policy Act: External Protection or Internal Restriction?', paper presented at the conference 'Nationalism, Identity and Minority Rights', University of Bristol, September.

COULOMBE, PIERRE (1995). *Language Rights in French Canada* (New York: Peter Lang Publishing).

—— (2000). 'Citizenship and Official Bilingualism in Canada', in W. Kymlicka and W. Norman (eds), *Citizenship in Diverse Societies* (Oxford: Oxford University Press), 273–93.

COUNCIL OF EUROPE (1998a). *Conference Proceedings of the 'Conférence internationale sur la Charte européenne des langues régionales ou minoritaires'*, Strasbourg, 26–7 March 1998 (Strasbourg: Council of Europe).

—— (1998b). *Conference Proceedings of the 'Conference Implementation of the European Charter for Regional or Minority Languages'*, Innsbruck, 14–15 December (Strasbourg: Council of Europe).

COWAN, MARIANNE (1963). *Humanist Without Portfolio: An Anthology of the Writings of Wilhelm von Humboldt* (Detroit, MI.: Wayne State University Press).

CRAWFORD, JAMES (1989). *Bilingual Education: History, Politics, Theory and Practice* (Trenton, NJ.: Crane Publishing Co.).

—— (1992a). *Hold Your Tongue: Bilingualism and the Politics of 'English Only'* (Reading, MA.: Addison-Wesley).

—— (ed.) (1992b). *Language Loyalties: A Source Book on the Official English Controversy* (Chicago, IL.: University of Chicago Press).

—— (1994). 'Endangered Native American Languages: What Is To Be Done and Why?', *Journal of Navajo Education*, 11/3: 3–11.

—— (2001). *At War with Diversity: US Language Policy in an Age of Anxiety* (Clevedon: Multilingual Matters).

CRITICAL REVIEW (1998). *Special Issue on 'Public Ignorance'*, 12/4.

CRYSTAL, DAVID (2000). *Language Death* (Cambridge: Cambridge University Press).

CULLITY, GARRETT (1995). 'Moral Free Riding', *Philosophy and Public Affairs*, 24: 3–34.

CUMMINS, JIM (1996). *Negotiating Identities: Education for Empowerment in a Diverse Society* (Toronto: California Association for Bilingual Education).

—— (1999). 'Alternative Paradigms in Bilingual Education Research: Does Theory Have a Place?', *Educational Researcher*, 28/7: 26–32.

CUMMINS, JIM (2001). *Language, Power and Pedagogy: Bilingual Children in the Crossfire* (Clevedon: Multilingual Matters).

DANOFF, MALCOLM, COLES, GARY, MCLAUGHLIN, DONALD, and REYNOLDS, DOROTHY (1978). *Evaluation of the Impact of ESEA Title VII Spanish/English Bilingual Education Program* (Palo Alto, CA.: American Institute for Research).

DE BRIEY, LAURENT and VAN PARIJS, PHILIPPE (2002). 'La justice linguistique comme justice coopérative', *Revue de philosophie économique*, 5: 5–37.

DE SWAAN, ABRAM (1993). 'The Evolving European Language System: A Theory of Communication Potential and Language Competition', *International Political Science Review*, 14/3: 241–55.

—— (2001). *Words of the World* (Cambridge: Polity Press).

DE VARENNES, FERNAND (1996). *Language, Minorities and Human Rights* (The Hague: Kluwer Law International).

—— (1999). 'Les droits de l'homme et la protection des minorités linguistiques', in H. Guillorel and G. Koubi (eds), *Langues et Droits* (Brussels: Bruylant), 129–41.

—— (2001). 'Language Rights as an Integral Part of Human Rights', *MOST Journal on Multicultural Societies*, 3/1. Available at www.unesco.org/most/v13n1var.htm

DEVEAUX, MONIQUE (2001). *Cultural Pluralism and Dilemmas of Justice* (Ithaca: Cornell University Press).

DICKER, SUSAN (1996). *Languages in America* (Clevedon: Multilingual Matters).

—— (2000). 'Official English and Bilingual Education: The Controversy Over Language Pluralism in U.S. Society', in J. Kelly Hall and W. Eggington (eds), *The Sociopolitics of English Language Teaching* (Clevedon: Multilingual Matters), 45–66.

DIGIACOMO, SUSAN (1999). 'Language Ideological Debates in an Olympic City: Barcelona 1992–1996', in J. Blommaert (ed.), *Language Ideological Debates* (Berlin: Mouton de Gruyter), 105–42.

DRYZEK, JOHN (1990). *Discursive Democracy* (Cambridge: Cambridge University Press).

—— (2000). *Deliberative Democracy and Beyond: Liberals, Critics, Contestations* (Oxford: Oxford University Press).

DUNBAR, ROBERT (2001). 'Minority Language Rights in International Law', *International Comparative Law Quarterly*, 50/1: 90–120.

DURAND, CHARLES (2001). *La mise en place des monopoles du savoir* (Paris: L'Harmattan).

DWORKIN, RONALD (1981). 'What is Equality?', Parts I and II, *Philosophy and Public Affairs*, 10/3: 185–246 and 10/4: 283–345.

—— (2000). *Sovereign Virtue: The Theory and Practice of Equality* (Cambridge, MA: Harvard University Press).

THE ECONOMIST (2001). 'A World Empire By Other Means', 22 December, 64–6.

EDWARDS, JOHN (1985). *Language, Society and Identity* (Oxford: Blackwell).

—— (1994). *Multilingualism* (London: Routledge).

—— (2001). 'The Ecology of Language Revival', *Current Issues in Language Planning*, 2/2–3: 231–41.

EISENBERG, AVIGAIL (1995). *Reconstructing Political Pluralism* (Albany: SUNY Press).

ELKINS, STANLEY and SOLTAN, KAROL EDWARD (eds) (1999). *Citizen Competence and Democratic Institutions* (University Park: Penn State Press).

ERIKSEN, THOMAS HYLLAND (1993). *Ethnicity and Nationalism. Anthropological Perspectives* (London: Pluto Press).

EUROPEAN PARLIAMENT (1999). *Rules of Procedure* (14th edn), Official Journal, L 202, 02/08/1999, P. 0001–0108.

FEINBERG, WALTER (1998). *Common Schools/Uncommon Identities: National Unity and Cultural Difference* (New Haven: Yale University Press).

FELDMAN, ALICE (2001). 'Transforming Peoples and Subverting States: Developing a Pedagogical Approach to the Study of Indigenous Peoples and Ethnocultural Movements', *Ethnicities* 1/2: 147–78.

FERGUSON, CHARLES A. (1959). 'Diglossia', *Word*, 15: 325–40.

FERMIN, ALFONS (2001). *The Justification of Mandatory Integration Programmes for New Immigrants*, ERCOMER Research Paper 2001/01 (Utrecht: European Research Centre on Migration and Ethnic Relations).

FISHMAN, JOSHUA (1972). *The Sociology of Language* (Rowley, MA: Newbury House).

—— (1989). *Language and Ethnicity in Minority Sociolinguistic Perspective* (Clevedon: Multilingual Matters).

—— (1991). *Reversing Language Shift: Theoretical and Empirical Foundations of Assistance to Threatened Languages* (Clevedon: Multilingual Matters).

—— (2001). *Can Threatened Languages Be Saved?* (Clevedon: Multilingual Matters).

FLERAS, ANGIE (1994). 'Multiculturalism as Society-Building. Blending what is Workable, Necessary and Fair', in M. Charleton and P. Baker (eds), *Cross-Currents: Contemporary Political Issues* (Scarborough: Nelson), 26–42.

—— and ELLIOT, JOHN (1991). *Multiculturalism in Canada: The Challenge of Diversity* (Scarborough: Nelson).

FLETCHER, GEORGE (1997). 'The Case for Linguistic Self-Defense', in Jeff McMahan and Robert McKim (eds), *The Morality of Nationalism* (New York: Oxford University Press), 324–39.

FRASER, NANCY (1992). 'Rethinking the Public Sphere: A Contribution to the Critique of Actually Existing Democracy', in Craig Calhoun (ed.), *Habermas and the Public Sphere* (Cambridge, MA: MIT Press), 109–42.

GALSTON, WILLIAM (1991). *Liberal Purposes: Goods, Virtues, and Duties in the Liberal State* (Cambridge: Cambridge University Press).

—— (1995). 'Two Concepts of Liberalism', *Ethics*, 105: 516–34.

GARCIA, OFELIA (1995). 'Spanish Language Loss as a Determinant of Income among Latinos in the United States: Implications for Language Policies in Schools', in J. Tollefson (ed.), *Power and Inequality in Language Education* (Cambridge: Cambridge University Press), 142–60.

GAUTHIER, DAVID (1986). *Morals by Agreement* (Oxford: Oxford University Press).

GELLNER, ERNEST (1983). *Nations and Nationalism* (Oxford: Blackwell Publishers).

—— (1997). *Nationalism* (New York: New York University Press).

GLAZER, NATHAN (1983). *Ethnic Dilemmas: 1964–1982* (Cambridge, MA.: Harvard University Press).

—— (1997). *We Are All Multiculturalists Now* (Cambridge, MA: Harvard University Press).

GLENDON, MARY-ANN and BLANKENHORN, DAVID (eds) (1995). *Seedbeds of Virtue: Sources of Competence, Character and Citizenship in American Society* (Lanham, MD: Madison Books).

GOBARD, HENRI (1966). *L'aliénation linguistique. Analyse tétraglossique* (Paris: Flammarion).

GREEN, LESLIE (1987). 'Are Language Rights Fundamental?', *Osgoode Hall Law Journal*, 25: 639–69.

—— and RÉAUME, DENISE (1990). 'Second Class Rights? Principles and Compromise in the Charter', *Dalhousie Law Journal*, 13: 564–93.

GRILLO, RALPH (1989). *Dominant Languages: Language and Hierarchy in Britain and France* (Cambridge, MA: Harvard University Press).

GRIMES, BARBARA (ed.) (1998). *Ethnologue: Languages of the World*, 11th edn (Dallas: Summer Institute of Linguistics).

GRIMM, DIETER (1995). 'Does Europe Need a Constitution?', *European Law Journal*, 1/3: 282–302.

GRIN, FRANÇOIS (1994). 'Combining Immigrant and Autochthonous Language Rights: A Territorial Approach to Multilingualism', in T. Skutnabb-Kangas and R. Phillipson (eds), *Linguistic Human Rights: Overcoming Linguistic Discrimination* (Berlin: Mouton de Gruyter), 31–48.

—— (1996a). 'Conflit ethnique et politique linguistique', *Relations Internationales*, 88: 381–96.

—— (1996b). 'The Economics of Language: Survey, Assessment, and Prospects', *International Journal of the Sociology of Language*, 121: 17–44.

—— (1997). 'Diversité linguistique et théorie économique de la valeur', in J. Hatem (ed.), *Lieux de l'intersubjectivité* (Paris: L'Harmattan), 155–74.

—— (1999a). *Compétences et récompenses. La valeur des langues en Suisse* (Fribourg: Éditions universitaires).

—— (1999b). *Language Policy in Multilingual Switzerland: Overview and Recent Developments* (Flensburg: European Centre for Minority Issues).

—— (2000a). 'The Economics of Diversity Governance', in J. Dacyl and C. Westin (eds), *Governance of Cultural Diversity* (Stockholm: Swedish National Commission for UNESCO), 355–78.

—— (2000b). *Evaluating Policy Measures for Minority Languages in Europe: Towards Effective, Cost-Effective, and Democratic Implementation*, Report No. 6 (Flensburg: European Centre for Minority Issues).

—— (2002a). 'La Suisse comme non-multination', in M. Seymour (ed.), *États-nations, multinations et organisations supranationales* (Montréal: Liber), 265–81.

—— (forthcoming 2002b). 'Language Planning and Economics', *Current Issues in Language Planning*.

—— and DAFTARY, FARIMAH (eds) (forthcoming 2003). *Nation-Building, Ethnicity and Language Politics in Transition Countries* (Budapest: Open Society Institute, LGI).

—— and VAILLANCOURT, FRANÇOIS (1997). 'The Economics of Multilingualism', *Annual Review of Applied Linguistics*, 17: 43–65.

GUTMANN, AMY and APPIAH, K. ANTHONY (1996). *Color Conscious: The Political Morality of Race* (Princeton: Princeton University Press).

GUTMANN, AMY and THOMPSON, DENNIS (1996). *Democracy and Disagreement* (Cambridge, MA: Harvard University Press).

HABERMAS, JÜRGEN (1994). 'Struggles for Recognition in the Democratic Constitutional State' in A. Gutmann (ed.), *Multiculturalism: Multicultural and Multilingual Policies in Education* (Princeton: Princeton University Press), 107–48.

—— (1995). 'Citizenship and National Identity', in Ronald Beiner (ed.), *Theorizing Citizenship* (Albany: SUNY Press), 255–82.

—— (1996). *Between Facts and Norms: Contributions to a Discourse Theory of Law and Democracy* (Cambridge, MA: MIT Press).

HEATH, JOSEPH (2001). *The Efficient Society* (Toronto: Viking-Penguin).

HEATH, SHIRLEY BRICE (1977). 'Language and Politics in the United States', in M. Saville-Troike (ed.), *Linguistics and Anthropology: Georgetown University Round Table on Language and Linguistics* (Washington, DC: Georgetown University Press), 267–96.

HECHTER, MICHAEL (2000). *Containing Nationalism* (Oxford: Oxford University Press).

HELD, DAVID (1995). *Democracy and the Global Order: From the Modern State to Cosmopolitan Governance* (London: Polity).

HEUGH, K., SIEGRÜHN, A., and PLÜDDERMANN, P. (eds) (1995). *Multilingual Education for South Africa* (Johannesburg: Heinemann).

HOFFMAN, EVA (1990). *Lost in Translation: A Life in a New Language* (New York: Penguin Books).

HOFFMANN, CHARLOTTE (1999). 'Language Autonomy and National Identity in Catalonia', in D. Smith and S. Wright (eds), *Whose Europe? The Turn towards Democracy* (Oxford: Blackwell/Sociological Review), 48–78.

HOLBOROW, MARNIE (1999). *The Politics of English: A Marxist View of Language* (London: Sage).

HOLLINGER, DAVID (1995). *Postethnic America. Beyond Multiculturalism* (New York: Basic Books).

HOROWITZ, DONALD (1985). *Ethnic Groups in Conflict* (Berkeley: University of California Press).

—— (2000). 'Constitutional Design: An Oxymoron?', in Ian Shapiro and Stephen Macedo (eds), *Designing Democratic Institutions*, NOMOS 42 (New York: New York University Press), 253–84.

HROCH, MIROSLAV (1985). *Social Preconditions of National Revival in Europe: A Comparative Analysis of the Social Composition of Patriotic Groups among the Smaller European Nations*, trans. Ben Fowkes (Cambridge: Cambridge University Press).

HUTTENBACH, HENRY R. (ed.) (1990). *Soviet Nationality Policies: Ruling Ethnic Groups in the USSR* (London: Mansell).

IVISON, DUNCAN, SANDERS, WILL, and PATTON, PAUL (eds) (2000). *Political Theory and the Rights of Indigenous Peoples* (Cambridge: Cambridge University Press).

JANDA, RICHARD (1998). *La double independence: La naissance d'un Québec nouveau et la renaissance du Bas-Canada* (Montréal: Éditions Varia).

JANSON, TORE (2002). *Speak. A Short History of Languages* (Oxford: Oxford University Press).

JEDWAB, JACK (1996). *The English Fact in Montreal* (Montréal: Éditions Images).

JERNUDD, BJÖRN (2001). 'Language Planning on the Eve of the 21st Century', paper presented at the '2n Congrés Europeu sobre Planificació Lingüística', Andorra, 14–16 November.

JOHNSTON, JAMES (2002). 'Liberalism and the Politics of Cultural Authenticity', *Politics, Philosophy and Economics*, 1/2: 213–36.

KANE, JOHN (1997). 'From Ethnic Exclusion to Ethnic Diversity: The Australian Path to Multiculturalism', in I. Shapiro and W. Kymlicka (eds), *Ethnicity and Group Rights* (New York: New York University Press), 540–71.

KANT, IMMANUEL (1970). 'Perpetual Peace: A Philosophical Sketch' [original 1795], in H. Reiss (ed.), *Kant's Political Writings* (Cambridge: Cambridge University Press).

KAUL, INGE, GRUNBERG, ISABELLE, and STERN, MARK A. (eds) (1999). *Global Public Goods: International Cooperation in the 21st Century* (Oxford: Oxford University Press).

KLOSS, HEINZ (1965). 'Territorialprinzip, Bekenntnisprinzip, Verfügungsprinzip: Über die Möglichkeiten der Abgrenzung der volklicken Zugehörigkeit', *Europa Ethnica*, 22: 52.

—— (1971). 'Language Rights of Immigrant Groups', *International Migration Review*, 5/2: 250–68.

—— (1977). *The American Bilingual Tradition* (Rowley, MA: Newbury House).

KONTRA, MIKLOS, PHILLIPSON, ROBERT, SKUTNABB-KANGAS, TOVE, and VÁRADY, TIBOR (eds) (1999). *Language: A Right and a Resource Approaching Linguistic Human Rights* (Budapest: CEU Press).

KRASHEN, STEPHEN (1999). *Condemned without Trial: Bogus Arguments against Bilingual Education* (Portsmouth, NH: Heinemann).

KRAUS, PETER A. (2000). 'Political Unity and Linguistic Diversity in Europe', *Archives Européennes de Sociologie/European Journal of Sociology*, 41: 138–63.

KYMLICKA, WILL (1989). *Liberalism, Community and Culture* (Oxford: Clarendon Press).

—— (1995a). *Multicultural Citizenship* (Oxford: Oxford University Press).

—— (ed.) (1995b). *The Rights of Minority Cultures* (Oxford: Oxford University Press).

—— (1997). 'Do We Need a Liberal Theory of Minority Rights?', *Constellations*, 4/1: 72–87.

—— (1998). *Finding Our Way* (Toronto: Oxford University Press).

—— (1999). 'Theorizing Indigenous Rights', *University of Toronto Law Journal*, 49: 281–93.

—— (2001a). *Politics in the Vernacular: Nationalism, Multiculturalism, Citizenship* (Oxford: Oxford University Press).

—— (2001b). 'Western Political Theory and Ethnic Relations in Eastern Europe', in Will Kymlicka and Magda Opalski (eds), *Can Liberal Pluralism Be Exported?* (Oxford: Oxford University Press), 13–105.

—— (2002). 'Justice and Security in the Accommodation of Minority Nationalism', in Alain Dieckhoff (ed.), *Nationalism, Liberalism, and Pluralism* (Lanham, MD: Lexington Books).

—— and NORMAN, WAYNE (eds) (2000). *Citizenship in Diverse Societies* (Oxford: Oxford University Press).

LAGERSPETZ, EERIK (1998). 'On Language Rights', *Ethical Theory and Moral Practice*, 2/1: 181–99.

LAITIN, DAVID (1977). *Politics, Language and Thought: The Somali Experience* (Chicago: University of Chicago Press).

—— (1989). 'Linguistic Revival: Politics and Culture in Catalonia', *Comparative Studies in Society and History*, 31/2: 297–317.

—— (1992). *Language Repertoires and State Construction in Africa* (Cambridge: Cambridge University Press).

—— (1993). 'The Game Theory of Language Regimes', *International Political Science Review*, 14/3: 227–39.

—— (1994). 'The Tower of Babel as a Coordination Game: Political Linguistics in Ghana', *American Political Science Review*, 88: 622–34.

—— (2000). 'Language Conflict and Violence', *Archives Européennes de Sociologie*, 41/1: 97–137.

——, SOLÉ, CARLOTA, and KALYVAS, STATHIS (1994). 'Language and the Construction of States', *Politics and Society*, 22: 5–29.

LANGTAG (Language Plan Task Group) (1996). *Towards a Language Plan for South Africa* (Pretoria: Ministry of Arts, Culture, Science and Technology).

LAPONCE, JEAN (1984). *Langue et Territoire* (Québec: Presses de l'Université Laval).

—— (1987). *Languages and Their Territories* (Toronto: University of Toronto Press).

LEAP, WILLIAM (1981). 'American Indian Languages', in C. Ferguson and S. Heath (eds), *Language in the U.S.A.* (Cambridge: Cambridge University Press), 116–44.

LEHNING, PERCY and WEALE, ALBERT (1997). *Citizenship, Democracy and Justice in the New Europe* (London: Routledge).

LESLIE, PETER (1986). 'L'aspect politique et collectif', *Cahiers de Droit*, 27: 161–70.

LEVINE, MARC V. (1990). *The Reconquest of Montreal: Language Policy and Social Change in a Bilingual City* (Philadelphia: Temple University Press).

—— (1997). *La Reconquête de Montréal* (Montréal: VLB Éditeur).

LEVY, JACOB T. (2000). *The Multiculturalism of Fear* (Oxford: Oxford University Press).

—— (2002). 'Indians in Madison's Constitutional Order', in John Samples (ed.), *James Madison and the Future of Limited Government* (Washington, DC: Cato Institute).

—— (forthcoming *a*). 'National Minorities Without Nationalism', in Alain Dieckhoff (ed.), *Nationalism, Liberalism, and Pluralism* (Lanham, MD: Lexington Books).

LEVY, NEIL (2001). 'Why Regret Language Death?', *Public Affairs Quarterly*, 15: 373–84.

LIND, MICHAEL (1996). *The Next American Nation* (New York: Free Press).

LOPEZ, MARK HUGO (1996). 'The Educational and Labor Market Impacts of Bilingual Education in the Short and Long Run: Evidence from the National Education Longitudinal Study of 1988 and High School and Beyond', Ph.D. thesis (Princeton: Department of Economics, Princeton University).

LUPIA, ARTHUR and MCCUBBINS, MATTHEW (1998). *The Democratic Dilemma* (Cambridge: Cambridge University Press).

MCCARTY, TERESA (2002). *A Place to be Navajo: Rough Rock and the Struggle for Self-Determination in Indigenous Schooling* (Mahwah, NJ: Lawrence Erlbaum Publishers).

MACEDO, DONALDO (1994). *Literacies of Power: What Americans are Not Allowed to Know* (Boulder, CO: Westview Press).

MACEDO, STEPHEN (2000). *Diversity and Distrust: Civic Education in a Multicultural Democracy* (Cambridge, MA: Harvard University Press).

MCKAY, SANDRA and WONG, S. (1988). *Language Diversity: Problem or Resource?* (Boston, MA: Heinle and Heinle).

MACMILLAN, MICHAEL C. (1991). 'Linking Theory to Practice: Comments on *The Constitutional Protection of Language*', in D. Schneiderman (ed.), *Language and the State* (Cowansville, QUE: Éditions Yvon Blais), 59–68.

—— (1998). *The Practice of Language Rights in Canada* (Toronto: University of Toronto Press).

MCRAE, KENNETH (1975). 'The Principle of Territoriality and the Principle of Personality in Multilingual States', *International Journal of the Sociology of Language*, 4: 33–54.

—— (1983). *Conflict and Compromise in Multilingual Societies. Vol. 1: Switzerland* (Waterloo, ON: Wilfrid Laurier University Press).

—— (1986). *Conflict and Compromise in Multilingual Societies. Vol. 2: Belgium* (Waterloo, ON: Wilfrid Laurier University Press).

MCRAE, KENNETH (1997). *Conflict and Compromise in Multilingual Societies: Vol. 3: Finland* (Waterloo, ON: Wilfrid Laurier University Press).

MCROBERTS, KENNETH (1989). 'Making Canada Bilingual: Illusions and Delusions of Federal Language Policy', in David P. Shugarman and Reg Whitaker (eds), *Federalism and Political Community: Essays in Honour of Donald Smiley* (Peterborough: Broadview Press), 141–71.

—— (1997). *Misconceiving Canada: The Struggle for National Unity* (Toronto: Oxford University Press).

MAGGA, OLE (1996). 'Sámi Past and Present and the Sámi Picture of the World', in E. Helander (ed.), *Awakened Voice: The Return of Sámi Knowledge* (Kautokeino: Nordic Sámi Institute), 74–80.

MAGNET, J. E. (1986). 'The Future of Official Language Minorities', *Cahiers de droit*, 27: 189–202.

MARGALIT, AVISHAI (1997). *The Decent Society* (Cambridge: Harvard University Press).

—— and RAZ, JOSEPH (1995). 'National Self Determination', in W. Kymlicka (ed.), *The Rights of Minority Cultures* (Oxford: Oxford University Press), 79–92.

MARSHALL, DAVID (1986). 'The Question of an Official Language: Language Rights and the English Language Amendment', *International Journal of the Sociology of Language*, 60: 7–75.

MARTINIELLO, MARCO (1998). 'Wieviorka's View on Multiculturalism: A Critique', *Ethnic and Racial Studies*, 21: 911–16.

MAY, STEPHEN (ed.) (1999a). *Indigenous Community-Based Education* (Clevedon: Multilingual Matters).

—— (1999b). *Critical Multiculturalism: Rethinking Multicultural and Antiracist Education* (London: Routledge Falmer).

—— (2000). 'Accommodating and Resisting Minority Language Policy: The Case of Wales', *International Journal of Bilingual Education and Bilingualism*, 3/2: 101–28.

—— (2001). *Language and Minority Rights: Ethnicity, Nationalism and the Politics of Language* (Harlow/London: Longman/Pearson Education).

—— (2002a). 'Multiculturalism', in D. Goldberg and J. Solomos (eds), *A Companion to Racial and Ethnic Studies* (Oxford/Cambridge: Blackwell), 124–44.

—— (2002b). 'Developing Greater Ethnolinguistic Democracy in Europe: Minority Language Policies, Nation-States, and the Question of Tolerability', *Sociolinguistica*, 16, 1–13.

—— (2002c). 'Indigenous Rights and the Politics of Self-Determination: The Case of Aotearoa/New Zealand', in S. Fenton and S. May (eds), *Ethnonational Identities* (London: Palgrave Macmillan), 84–108.

MAYER, THOMAS (1993). *Truth versus Precision in Economics* (Aldershot: Edward Elgar).

MEHTA, UDAY (1999). *Liberalism and Empire* (Chicago: University of Chicago Press).

MENCHACA, M. (2001). *Recovering History, Constructing Race: The Indian, Black and White Roots of Mexican Americans* (Austin: University of Texas Press).

MILL, JOHN STUART (1991). *Considerations on Representative Government* [original 1861], in *On Liberty and Other Essays* (Oxford: Oxford University Press), 203–467.

MILLER, DAVID (1995). *On Nationality* (Oxford: Oxford University Press).

—— (1999). 'Social Justice and Environmental Goods', in A. Dobson (ed.), *Fairness and Futurity: Essays on Environmental Sustainability and Social Justice* (Oxford: Oxford University Press), 151–72.

—— (2000). *Citizenship and National Identity* (Cambridge: Polity Press).

—— (2002). 'Doctrinaire Liberalism Versus Multicultural Democracy', *Ethnicities*, 2/2: 255–9.

MILLS, CHARLES (1997). *The Racial Contract* (Ithaca: Cornell University Press).

MISCEVIC, NENAD (ed.) (2000). *Nationalism and Ethnic Conflict: Philosophical Perspectives* (LaSalle, IL: Open Court).

MOORE, GEORGE EDWARD (1903). *Principia Ethica* (Cambridge: Cambridge University Press).

MOORE, MARGARET (2001). *The Ethics of Nationalism* (Oxford: Oxford University Press).

MORAN, RACHEL (1990). 'Language and the Law in the Classroom: Bilingual Education and the Official English Initiative', in K. Adams and D. Brink (eds), *Perspectives on Official English: The Campaign for English as an Official Language of the USA* (Berlin: Mouton de Gruyter), 285–92.

MÜLHÄUSLER, PETER (2000). 'Language Planning and Language Ecology', *Current Issues in Language Planning*, 1: 306–67.

MUSSCHENGA, ALBERT (1998). 'Intrinsic Value as a Reason for the Preservation of Minority Cultures', *Ethical Theory and Moral Practice*, 1: 201–25.

NAGEL, JOANE (1994). 'Constructing Ethnicity: Creating and Recreating Ethnic Identity and Culture', *Social Problems*, 41/1: 152–76.

NARAYAN, UMA and HARDING, SANDRA (eds) (2000). *Decentering the Center: Philosophy for a Multicultural, Postcolonial, and Feminist World* (Bloomington: Indiana University Press).

NASH, MANNING (1989). *The Cauldron of Ethnicity in the Modern World* (Chicago, IL.: Chicago University Press).

NELDE, PETER (1997). 'Language Conflict', in F. Coulmas (ed.), *The Handbook of Sociolinguistics* (London: Blackwell), 285–300.

——, LABRIE, NORMAND, and WILLIAMS, COLIN H. (1992). 'The Principles of Territoriality and Personality in the Solution of Linguistic Conflicts', *Journal of Multilingual and Multicultural Development*, 13/5: 387–406.

NENTWICH, MICHAEL and WEALE, ALBERT (eds) (1998). *Political Theory and the European Union: Legitimacy, Constitutional Choice and Citizenship* (London: Routledge).

NETTLE, DANIEL and ROMAINE, SUZANNE (2000). *Vanishing Voices: The Extinction of the World's Languages* (New York: Oxford University Press).

NICKEL, JAMES (1995). 'The Value of Cultural Belonging: Expanding Kymlicka's Theory', *Dialogue*, 33: 635–42.

NIC SHUIBHNE, NIAMH (2002). *EC Law and Minority Language Policy: Culture, Citizenship and Fundamental Rights* (The Hague: Kluwer International Law).

NOZICK, ROBERT (1974). *Anarchy, State and Utopia* (New York: Basic Books).

OKIN, SUSAN (1999). *Is Multiculturalism Bad for Women?* (Princeton: Princeton University Press).

OLDFIELD, ADRIAN (1990). *Citizenship and Community: Civic Republicanism and the Modern World* (London: Routledge).

ONG, AIHWA (1999). *Flexible Citizenship: The Cultural Logics of Transnationality* (Durham: Duke University Press).

Ó RIAGÁIN, DÓNALL (ed.) (1998). *Vade-Mecum. A Guide to Legal, Political and Other Official International Documents Pertaining to the Lesser Used Languages of Europe* (Dublin/Brussels: European Bureau for Lesser Used Languages).

ORTIZ DE URBINA, ARACELI (2000). 'In Praise of Mulilingualism: An Interview with Joseph Poth [then head of UNESCO's Languages Division]', *The UNESCO Courier*, April.

OZOLINS, ULDIS (1993). *The Politics of Language in Australia* (Cambridge: Cambridge University Press).

PAREKH, BHIKHU (2000). *Rethinking Multiculturalism: Cultural Diversity and Political Theory* (London: Macmillan).

PARFIT, DEREK (1986). *Reasons and Persons* (Oxford: Oxford University Press).

PATTANAYAK, DEBI (ed.) (1990). *Multilingualism in India* (Clevedon: Multilingual Matters).

PATTEN, ALAN (2000). 'Liberal Egalitarianism and the Case for Supporting National Cultures', in Nenand Miscevic (ed.), *Nationalism and Ethnic Conflict* (Chicago / La Salle: Open Court Publishing), 197–217.

—— (2001). 'Political Theory and Language Policy', *Political Theory*, 29: 691–715.

PETTIT, PHILIP (2000). 'Minority Claims under Two Conceptions of Democracy', in D. Ivison, P. Patton, and W. Sanders (eds), *Political Theory and the Rights of Indigenous Peoples* (Cambridge: Cambridge University Press), 199–215.

PHILLIPS, ANNE (1995). *The Politics of Presence: Issues in Democracy and Group Representation* (Oxford: Oxford University Press).

—— (2000). 'Feminism and Republicanism: A Plausible Alliance', *Journal of Political Philosophy*, 8 / 2: 279–93.

PHILLIPSON, ROBERT (1992). *Linguistic Imperialism* (Oxford: Oxford University Press).

—— (2000). *Rights to Language: Equity, Power, and Education* (Mahwah, NJ: Lawrence Erlbaum Publishers).

—— (2001). 'English for the Globe, or Only for Globe-Trotters?', paper presented at the Conference of the Austrian Academy of Sciences 'Die Kosten der Mehrsprachigkeit— Globalisierung und sprachliche Vielfalt', Vienna, 7–9 June.

PICKUS, NOAH (1998). 'To Make Natural: Creating Citizens for the Twenty-First Century', in Noah Pickus (ed.), *Immigration and Citizenship in the 21st Century* (Lanham, MD: Rowman and Littlefield), 107–40.

PILLER, INGRID (2001). 'Naturalization Language Testing and its Basis in Ideologies of National Identity and Citizenship', *International Journal of Bilingualism*, 5 / 3: 259–77.

POGGE, THOMAS W. (1989). *Realizing Rawls* (Ithaca: Cornell University Press).

—— (1997). 'Group Rights and Ethnicity', in W. Kymlicka and I. Shapiro (eds), *Ethnicity and Group Rights*, NOMOS 39 (New York: New York University Press), 187–221.

POOL, JONATHAN (1991*a*). 'The Official Language Problem', *American Political Science Review*, 85: 495–514.

—— (1991*b*). 'A Tale of Two Tongues', unpublished manuscript (Seattle: Department of Political Science, University of Washington).

POOLE, ROSS and KUKATHAS, CHANDRAN (eds) (2000). Special Issue on 'Indigenous Rights', *Australasian Journal of Philosophy*, 78 / 3.

PORTER, ROSALIE PEDALINO (1996). *Forked Tongue: The Politics of Bilingual Education*, 2nd edn (New Brunswick, NJ: Transaction Publishers).

PORTES, ALEJANDRO and RUMBAUT, RUBEN (2001). *Legacies: The Story of the Immigrant Second Generation* (Berkeley: University of California Press).

PURVIS, A. (1999). 'Homeland for the Inuit', *Time Magazine*, Canadian edn, 15 February: 34–5.

RAMÍREZ, J., YUEN, S., and RAMEY, D. (1991). *Final Report: Longitudinal Study of Structured English Immersion Strategy, Early-Exit and Late-Exit Transitional Bilingual Education Programs for Language-Minority Children* (San Mateo, CA: Aguirre International).

RAWLS, JOHN (1971). *A Theory of Justice* (Cambridge, MA: Harvard University Press).

—— (1972). *A Theory of Justice* (Oxford: Clarendon Press).

—— (1993). *Political Liberalism* (New York: Columbia University Press).

—— (1999). *Collected Papers* (Cambridge, MA.: Harvard University Press).

RAZ, JOSEPH (1984a). 'On the Nature of Rights', *Mind*, 93: 194–214.

—— (1984b). 'Right-Based Moralities', in J. Waldron (ed.), *Theories of Rights* (Oxford: Oxford University Press), 182–200.

—— (1986). *The Morality of Freedom* (Oxford: Clarendon Press).

RÉAUME, DENISE (1988). 'Individuals, Groups, and Rights to Public Goods', *University of Toronto Law Journal*, 38: 1–27.

—— (1991). 'The Constitutional Protection of Language: Survival or Security?', in David Schneiderman (ed.), *Language and The State: The Law and Politics of Identity* (Cowansville: Éditions Yvon Blais), 37–57.

—— (1994). 'The Group Right to Linguistic Security: Whose Right, What Duties?', in Judith Baker (ed.), *Group Rights* (Toronto: University of Toronto Press), 118–41.

—— (1995). 'Justice Between Cultures: Autonomy and the Protection of Cultural Affiliation', *U.B.C. Law Journal*, 29: 117–41.

—— (2000). 'Official-Language Rights: Intrinsic Value and the Protection of Difference', in Will Kymlicka and Wayne Norman (eds), *Citizenship in Diverse Societies* (Oxford: Oxford University Press), 245–72.

REICH, ROB (2002). *Bridging Liberalism and Multiculturalism in American Education* (Chicago: University of Chicago Press).

REID, SCOTT (1993). *Lament for a Notion: The Life and Death of Canada's Bilingual Dream* (Vancouver: Arsenal Pulp Press).

RENAN, ERNEST (1990). 'What is a Nation?' [original 1882], in H. Bhabha (ed.), *Nation and Narration* (London: Routledge), 8–22.

RHEE, JOHN (1999). 'Theories of Citizenship and their Role in the Bilingual Education Debate', *Columbia Journal of Law and Social Problems*, 33: 33–83.

RICENTO, THOMAS (1996). 'Language Policy in the United States', in Michael Herriman and Barbara Burnaby (eds), *Language Policies in English-Dominant Countries* (Clevedon: Multilingual Matters), 122–58.

RODRIGUEZ, RICHARD (1982). *Hunger of Memory: The Education of Richard Rodriguez* (New York: Bantam Books).

ROEMER, JOHN (1986). 'Equality of Resources Implies Equality of Welfare', *Quarterly Journal of Economics*, 101: 751–84.

ROMAINE, SUSAN (1995). *Bilingualism*, 2nd edn (Oxford: Blackwell).

ROSENBLUM, NANCY (ed.) (2000). *Obligations of Citizenship and Demands of Faith: Religious Accommodation in Pluralist Democracies* (Princeton: Princeton University Press).

ROSSELL, CHRISTINE and BAKER, KEITH (1996). 'The Effectiveness of Bilingual Education', *Research in the Teaching of English*, 30: 7–74.

ROYAL COMMISSION ON BILINGUALISM AND BICULTURALISM (1967). *Final Report. Vol. 1: The Official Languages* (Ottawa: Queen's Printer).

RUBIO-MARÍN, RUTH (2000). *Immigration as a Democratic Challenge: Citizenship and Inclusion in Germany and the US* (Cambridge: Cambridge University Press).

SAFRAN, WILLIAM (1999). 'Nationalism', in J. Fishman (ed.), *Handbook of Language and Ethnic Identity* (Oxford: Oxford University Press), 77–93.

SANDEL, MICHAEL (1996). *Democracy's Discontent* (Cambridge, MA: Harvard University Press).

SAN MIGUEL, GUADALUPE and VALENCIA, RICHARD (1998). 'From the Treaty of Guadalupe Hidalgo to Hopwood: The Educational Plight and Struggle of Mexican Americans in the Southwest', *Harvard Educational Review*, 68: 353–412.

SCHIFFMAN, HAROLD (1996). *Linguistic Culture and Language Policy* (London: Routledge).

SCHLESINGER, ARTHUR (1992). *The Disuniting of America* (New York: Norton).

SCHMIDT SR., RONALD (2000). *Language Policy and Identity Politics in the United States* (Philadelphia: Temple University Press).

SCHMIDTKE, OLIVER (2002). 'Naïve Universalism: The Neglected Questions in Brian Barry's Culture and Equality', *Ethnicities*, 2/2: 268–73.

SCHMITTER, PHILIPPE (2000). *How to Democratize the European Union . . . and Why Bother?* (Lanham, MD: Rowman & Littlefield).

SCHWARTZ, LEE (1990). 'Regional Population Redistribution and National Homelands in the USSR', in Henry R. Huttenbach (ed.), *Soviet Nationality Policies: Ruling Ethnic Groups in the USSR* (London: Mansell).

SCHWARTZ, WARREN (ed.) (1995). *Justice in Immigration* (Cambridge: Cambridge University Press).

SCOTT, JAMES C. (1998). *Seeing Like A State* (New Haven: Yale University Press).

SECADA, W. and LIGHTFOOT, T. (1993). 'Symbols and the Political Context of Bilingual Education in the United States', in M. Arias and U. Casanova (eds), *Bilingual Education: Politics, Practice, and Research* (Chicago: The National Society for the Study of Education/University of Chicago Press), 36–64.

SEN, AMARTYA (1992). *Inequality Re-examined* (New York: Russell Sage).

SHACHAR, AYELET (2001). *Multicultural Jurisdictions: Preserving Cultural Differences and Women's Rights in a Liberal State* (Cambridge: Cambridge University Press).

SHAPIRO, IAN and KYMLICKA, WILL (eds) (1997). *Ethnicity and Group Rights* (New York: New York University Press).

SHELL, MARC (1993). 'Babel in America: The Politics of Language Diversity in the United States', *Critical Inquiry*, 20: 103–27.

SIMONNOT, PHILIPPE (1998). *Trente-neuf leçons de théorie économique* (Paris: Gallimard).

SKINNER, QUENTIN (1998). *Liberty Before Liberalism* (Cambridge: Cambridge University Press).

SKUTNABB-KANGAS, TOVE (1999). 'Linguistic Diversity, Human Rights and the "Free" Market', in M. Kontra *et al.* (eds), *Language: A Right and a Resource* (Budapest: Central European University Press), 187–222.

—— (2000). *Linguistic Genocide in Education or World Diversity and Human Rights* (Mahwah, NJ: Lawrence Erlbaum Publishers).

—— and PHILLIPSON, ROBERT (with RANNUT, MART) (1994). *Linguistic Human Rights: Overcoming Linguistic Discrimination* (Berlin & New York: Mouton de Gruyter).

SPINNER, JEFF (1994). *The Boundaries of Citizenship: Race, Ethnicity and Nationality in the Liberal State* (Baltimore: John Hopkins University Press).

SPINNER-HALEV, JEFF (2000). *Surviving Diversity: Religion and Democratic Citizenship* (Baltimore: John Hopkins University Press).

STATISTICS CANADA (1997). '1996 Census: Mother Tongue, Home Language and Knowledge of Languages', *The Daily*, 2 December. Available at www.statcan.ca/Daily/English/971202/d971202.htm#ART1

STRUBELL, MIQUEL (1998). 'Language, Democracy and Devolution in Catalonia', *Current Issues in Language and Society*, 5: 146–80.

TAMIR, YAEL (1993). *Liberal Nationalism* (Princeton, NJ: Princeton University Press).

TARAS, RAY (1998). 'Nations and Language-Building: Old Theories, Contemporary Cases', *Nationalism and Ethnic Politics*, 4/3: 79–101.

TAYLOR, CHARLES (1992). 'The Politics of Recognition', in A. Gutmann (ed.), *Multiculturalism and the 'Politics of Recognition'* (Princeton, NJ: Princeton University Press), 25–73.

—— (1993). 'Why Do Nations Have to Become States?', in Guy Laforest (ed.), *Reconciling the Solitudes* (Montreal: McGill-Queens University Press), 40–58.

—— (1994). 'The Politics of Recognition', in A. Gutmann (ed.) (2edn), *Multiculturalism: Examining the Politics of Recognition* (Princeton, NJ: Princeton University Press), 25–73.

—— (1997). 'Nationalism and Modernity', in Jeff McMahan and Robert McKim (eds), *The Morality of Nationalism* (New York: Oxford University Press), 31–55.

—— (1998). 'The Dynamics of Democratic Exclusion', *The Journal of Democracy*, 9: 143–56.

—— (1999). 'Nationalism and Modernity', in R. Beiner (ed.), *Theorizing Nationalism* (New York: SUNY), 219–45.

TERMOTE, MARC (2000). 'Perspectives démolinguistiques pour Montréal et le Québec. Implications politiques', paper presented to the 'Commission des états généraux sur la situation et l'avenir de la langue française au Québec', Montréal, 11 December.

THOMAS, WAYNE and COLLIER, VIRGINIA (1997). *School Effectiveness for Language Minority Students* (Washington, DC: National Clearinghouse for Bilingual Education).

THOMSON, JUDITH JARVIS (1992). 'On Some Ways in Which a Thing Can Be Good', *Social Philosophy and Policy*, 9: 96–117.

THORNBERRY, PATRICK (1991). *International Law and the Rights of Minorities* (Oxford: Clarendon Press).

—— (1994). 'International and European Standards on Minority Rights', in Hugh Miall (ed.), *Minority Rights in Europe: The Scope for a Transnational Regime* (London: The Royal Institute for International Affairs and Pinter), 14–21.

TODAL, JON (1999). 'Minorities within a Minority: Language and the School in the Sámi areas of Norway', in S. May (ed.), *Indigenous Community-Based Education* (Clevedon: Multilingual Matters), 124–36.

TOYNBEE, A. (1953). *A Study of History*, Vols. 7–9 (London: Oxford University Press).

TRESVIÑA, JOHN (1992). 'Bilingual Ballots: Their History and a Look Forward', in James Crawford (ed.), *Language Loyalties: A Source Book on the Official English Controversy* (Chicago: University of Chicago Press), 257–63.

TRUDEAU, PIERRE ELLIOT (1986). *Federalism and the French Canadians* (Toronto: Macmillan).

TULLY, JAMES (1995). *Strange Multiplicity: Constitutionalism in an Age of Diversity* (Cambridge: Cambridge University Press).

—— (2002). 'Caricatures of Multiculturalism', *Ethnicities*, 2/2: 273–77.

UNESCO (1953). *The Use of Vernacular Languages in Education*, Monographs on Fundamental Education, No. 8 (Paris: UNESCO).

UNITED NATIONS (1948). Universal Declaration of Human Rights, adopted and proclaimed by General Assembly resolution 217 A (III) of 10 December 1948 (New York: United Nations).

VAILLANCOURT, FRANÇOIS (1978). 'La Charte de la langue française au Québec. Un essai d'analyse', *Canadian Public Policy/Analyse de politiques*, 4: 284–308.

—— and GRIN, FRANÇOIS (2000). 'The Choice of a Language of Instruction: The Economic Aspects', unpublished manuscript (Washington, DC: Report to the World Bank Institute).

VAN PARIJS, PHILIPPE (1995). *Real Freedom for All. What (if Anything) Can Justify Capitalism?* (Oxford: Clarendon Press).

—— (1996). 'Free Riding versus Rent Sharing. Why even David Gauthier Should Support an Unconditional Basic Income', in F. Farina, F. Hahn, and S. Vanucci (eds), *Ethics, Rationality and Economic Behaviour* (Oxford: Oxford University Press), 159–81.

—— (1999). 'Mills, Rawls, Machiavel: Quelle philosophie politique pour une démocratie plurilingue?' *La Revue nouvelle*, 9, 90–108.

—— (2000a). 'Must Europe be Belgian? On Democratic Citizenship in Multilingual Polities', in Catriona MacKinnon and Iain Hampsher-Monk (eds), *The Demands of Citizenship* (New York/London: Continuum), 235–53.

—— (2000b). 'The Ground Floor of the World. On the Socio-Economic Consequences of Linguistic Globalisation', *International Political Science Review*, 21/2: 217–33.

—— (2001). 'Real Freedom, the Market and the Family. A Reply', *Analyse & Kritik*, 23/1.

—— (2002). 'Linguistic Justice', *Politics, Philosophy & Economics*, 1/1: 59–74.

VIROLI, MAURIZIO (1995). *For Love of Country: An Essay on Patriotism and Nationalism* (Oxford: Oxford University Press).

VON HUMBOLDT, WILHELM (1988). *On Language: The Diversity of Human Language Structure and its Influence on the Mental Development of Mankind* [original 1836], trans P. Heath (Cambridge: Cambridge University Press).

WALDRON, JEREMY (1992). 'Superseding Historical Injustice', *Ethics*, 103/1: 4–28.

—— (1993). *Liberal Rights* (Cambridge: Cambridge University Press).

WALKER, BRIAN (1999). 'Modernity and Cultural Vulnerability: Should Ethnicity be Privileged?', in R. Beiner (ed.), *Theorizing Nationalism* (New York: SUNY), 141–65.

WEBER, EUGEN (1976). *Peasants Into Frenchmen: The Modernization of Rural France* (Stanford: Stanford University Press).

—— (1979). *Peasants Into Frenchmen: The Modernization of Rural France* (London: Chatto and Windus).

WEINSTEIN, BRIAN (1983). *The Civic Tongue: Political Consequences of Language Choices* (New York: Longman).

—— (1990). *Language Policy and Political Development* (Norwood, NJ: Ablex Publishers).

WEINSTOCK, DANIEL (2000). 'Doit-on recourir aux droits collectifs pour défendre une culture?', *Terminogramme*, 95–6.

—— (forthcoming). 'Four Kinds of (Post-)Nation Building', in Michel Seymour (ed.), *The Fate of the Nation-State* (Montreal: McGill-Queens' Press).

WICKSELL, KNUT (1958). 'A New Principle of Just Taxation', in R. A. Musgrave and A. T. Peacock (eds), *Classics in the Theory of Public Finance* (London: Macmillan), 72–188.

WIEVIORKA, MICHEL (1998). 'Is Multiculturalism the Solution?', *Ethnic and Racial Studies*, 21: 881–910.

—— and OHANA, JOCELYNE (eds) (2001). *La différence culturelle Une reformulation des débats* (Paris: Balland).

WILLIAMS, MELISSA (1998). *Voice, Trust and Memory: Marginalized Groups and the Failings of Liberal Representation* (Princeton: Princeton University Press).

—— (2000). 'The Uneasy Alliance of Group Representation and Deliberative Democracy', in W. Kymlicka and W. Norman (eds), *Citizenship in Diverse Societies* (Oxford: Oxford University Press), 124–52.

WILLIG, A. (1985). 'A Meta-Analysis of Selected Studies on the Effectiveness of Bilingual Education', *Review of Educational Research*, 55: 269–317.

—— (1987). 'Examining Bilingual Education Research through Meta-Analysis and Narrative Review: A Response to Baker', *Review of Educational Research*, 57: 363–76.

WOOLARD, KATHLEEN (1989). *Double Talk: Bilingualism and the Politics of Ethnicity in Catalonia* (Stanford, CA: Stanford University Press).

WRIGHT, SUSAN (2000). *Community and Communication: The Role of Language in Nation State Building and European integration* (Clevedon: Multilingual Matters).

WURM, STEPHEN A. (2001). *Atlas of the World's Languages in Danger of Disappearing* (Paris: UNESCO).

YOUNG, IRIS MARION (1990). *Justice and the Politics of Difference* (Princeton: Princeton University Press).

—— (2000). *Inclusion and Democracy* (Oxford: Oxford University Press).

YUVAL-DAVIS, NIRA and WERBNER, PNINA (eds) (1999). *Women, Citizenship, and Difference* (London: Zed Books).

ZENTELLA, ANA CELIA (1997). 'The Hispanophobia of the Official English Movement in the US', *International Journal of the Sociology of Language*, 127: 71–86.

ZIMMERMAN, MICHAEL (1999). 'In Defense of The Concept of Intrinsic Value', *Canadian Journal of Philosophy*, 29: 389–410.

# Index

*Note*: A small 'n' following a page reference indicates a footnote.

accent 63, 154
accommodation rights 105
  equal citizenship 108–11
  history 105–7
  immigration 107–8
  language of school instruction 115–21
  minorities 106–8
  unchosen inequalities 111–13, 113–15
aesthetic value, and linguistic diversity 195–6
affirmative action, and minority languages 246
Arneson, Richard 196, 205
assimilation 226
  cultural 253
  language loss 210, 211, 213, 215–16, 217,
    218, 219
  linguistic 211, 232
  minorities 131
  as violation of liberty 245
Atkins, J. D. C. 131
Australia, multiculturalism 133
Austro-Hungarian Empire, and language
  justice 84–5
autonomy 97, 98
  linguistic 243–4

Barry, Brian 86–8, 95–6
Basque Country 4, 100
Belgium 4, 7
  language policy 18, 22
  minority language rights 132–3
  official language 25
  territorial principle 29–30, 297, 298, 319–20
benign neglect 109, 251–2, 260
  language policy 32–3, 265
bilingual ballot, and American Hispanics 76–8
bilingual education 120, 130, 136, 143–7, 236
bilingualism 272
  asymmetric 167
  definitions of 296
  democratic participation 310–13
  identity 313–18
  institutional 296–8, 304, 305–6
  language justice 167, 276
  personality principle 271–2, 286, 297, 298
  social mobility 307–10

  territorial principle 299–302
  value of programs of 94
  *see also* multilingualism
Billig, Michael 138
biodiversity, and language loss 10, 44–5, 190,
  192–3, 207–8
bio-linguistic diversity 192
boundaries, national 99–100
Bourdieu, Pierre 126
Burckhardt, Walther 299 n. 3

Canada 4, 7
  bilingualism 281
  boundary changes 100
  language policy 5 n. 6, 18, 20–1, 22, 22–3
  language rights 30, 56 n. 2, 58 n. 6, 67 n. 22,
    134, 148
  minority protection 59, 60–1
  multiculturalism 133
  official language 25
  personality principle 29, 298, 320–1
  private language usage 23
  territorial unilingualism 280, 281
  *see also* Quebec
Canadian Charter of Rights and Freedoms
  (1982) 56 n. 2
Carens, Joseph 93, 100
Casal, Paula 203
Catalonia 4, 96–7
  boundaries 100
  language justice 82–3, 87
  language policy 18, 96
  linguistic nationalism 138–9
Chambers, Simone 15
Church, Jeffrey 160
citizenship
  equality of 108–11
  identity 11–12, 13
  multicultural 11–13
class:
  accent 63 n. 15
  least advantaged linguistic 268–9
Clinton, Bill 19
collective rights, and language rights 30–1
colonization, and language loss 85, 222–3

common language 39–42
communication:
    effective state 265–8
    language patterns 38
communicative interests, and language loss
        214–16
communitarianism 11
community, membership of 11
compensation regimes, and language justice
        158–60
compensatory justice 112, 113 n. 12
    language 80–1, 82–4, 102
constitutionalism 244
constitutions, and language rights 247–9
convergence:
    institutional 247–9
    linguistic 37, 38, 43
cooperative justice 154–6
Corsica 7
cost-benefits, of language learning 157–8
cost sharing, and language justice 156–7, 167
costs, and limitations of language rights 75–6
Council of Europe 3–4, 35 n. 31
Council of Ministers (EU), language policy 20
counterbalancing, and minority language rights
        243–5
Croatia 58 n. 4
Crystal, David 211
cultural diversity 12
cultural identity 64
    language 67
    state promotion of 113–14
cultural membership 107
cultural protection, and language rights 56–9
culturalism, liberal 88–92
culture:
    language 52–3
    liberalism 90–1
    function of 250
    judgements of 109
    preservation of 215
    value of 197–8

democracy:
    common language 39–40
    communal identity 11–12
    deliberative 13–16
    difference 185
    dominant language 70–1
    effective communication 265–8
    ethnolinguistic 149
    legitimacy 14

literacy 233–5
transnational 9–10
unilingualism 279–80
vote-centric 13–14
voting 30, 65, 76–8
see also liberal democracy
democratic participation, and language
        policy 310–13
democratization, and linguistic diversity 3
Denmark, and compensatory language
        justice 83
dialect 210 n. 1
difference, and diversity 178
difference principle 154
DiGiacomo, Susan 139
diglossia 43
discrimination 154
    language loss 218, 220–4
    language rights 63–5, 67
    minority language speakers 136
    official languages 225–6
disestablishment, linguistic 32, 55
diversity:
    academic research 174–5, 176–7
    conflictual nature of 178–9
    cost-benefits of 187–8
    cultural 12
    difference 185
    diversitism 187–8
    diversity clover 174–5
    language rights 178–83, 183–7
    management of 178, 178–9, 181–2, 185
    objective 179, 180
    policy choices 185, 187–8
    policy intervention 180, 181
    rights 180–3
    social intervention 169–70
    subjective 179–80
    terminology 173
    threatened character of 179
    transdisciplinary approach 182–3
    unifying concept 169, 178, 187
    value of 170, 171–2
    see also linguistic diversity
dominant languages 4, 5, 7, 8, 97, 126–8
    duty to learn 70–3
    immigrants 71, 72–3
    racial policy 131–2
    right to learn 68–70, 78–9
    social mobility 135–8
    unilingualism 279
Dworkin, Ronald 109, 112, 183 n. 19

eastern Europe, linguistic diversity and ethnic
    conflict 3–4
ecology of language 192
economics, and language diversity 172
ecosystem, and language loss 192–3
education:
    bilingual 120, 130, 136, 143–7, 236
    choice of language of instruction 115–21
    costs 57–66, 259–60
    language 70, 143–7
    language policy 21–3, 36
    language preservation 239–40
    language repertoires 98–9
    language rights 65, 66, 70
    minority languages 147–9
    public 118
    right to 69
Edwards, John 243 n. 16
efficiency, and language justice 160–1
egalitarianism, linguistic 243–4, 246–7
English First, principle of 118–19, 120–1
English Only movement (USA) 60, 94, 120–1,
    136 n. 10
enlargement, territorial and language policy 24–5
environment, linguistic 178
environmentalism, and language loss 192–3
equal rights 183
equality 220
    citizenship 108–11
    protection of language groups 64
    see also inequalities
equivalence, and minority language rights 147–9
Estonia, language policy 18
Ethiopia, language policy 18
ethnic conflict, and linguistic diversity 3–4
ethnic minorities 106–8, 129
    external protections 142–3
    see also minority language rights
ethnicity 171, 173
European Charter for Regional or Minority
    Languages (1992) 3–4, 182–3
European Convention on Human Rights 64 n. 16
European Court of Justice, language policy 20
European Parliament, language policy 20
European Union:
    language policy 17, 20, 25
    language rights 76 n. 33, 182
    linguistic diversity 4, 9–10
    linguistic minorities 59 n. 8, 60 n. 10, 62 n. 12
    official languages 25, 71 n. 28
    private language usage 23

exit, and minority languages 149–51
external protections 142–3

fairness, principle of 199–201
    free-rider problem 205–6
    intentional production condition 203–5
    voluntary acceptance condition 201–3
Finland, and language policy 22 n. 25, 148
Fishman, Joshua 125
Flanders 4, 132–3
Framework Convention for the Protection of
    National Minorities (1995) 3–4
France 6–7, 24, 25, 27
Franco, Francisco 38
freedom, negative 245–6, 285–6
free-rider problem, and public goods 205–6

Galbally Report (Australia 1978) 133
Gauthier, David 161, 165
genocide, linguistic 42
geography:
    language loss 236
    language policy 274
    see also territorial principle
Germany 6–7, 184
Ghana 83
Glazer, Nathan 150
globalization, and subjective diversity 180
government:
    effective communication 265–8
    language policy 17–18
    language of school instruction 115–21
    minority languages 241
    promotion of cultural groups 113–14
Green, Leslie 44
group rights 89, 124, 288–94

Hawaii 25
Hebrew 93
Hispanics:
    accommodation rights 105
    bilingual ballot 76–8
    disadvantaged 105, 106, 107
    language justice 105
    self-image 108
    social mobility 136
    unchosen inequalities 107, 107–8, 111–12
history:
    accommodation rights 105–7
    injustice 222–4
    linguistic fait accompli 132–4

minority language rights 125–6
 presentism and minority languages 126–8
 sanitization 128–32
homogeneity, language, *see* language
  consolidation
human rights:
 language protection 284–7
 linguistic 33–6

identity 177–8
 civic 11–12, 13
 cultural 64, 67, 113–14
 language 13, 56–7, 88, 95, 139–43, 313–14
 language loss 213–14
 language policy 313–18
 language preservation 45–6
 markers of 95
 minority rights 142
 national 5, 31, 41
 political 11–12
immigration:
 accommodation rights 107–8
 diversity 175–6
 dominant language 71, 72–3
 immigrant languages 184, 186
 immigrant minorities 183–4, 185
 integration 7–9
 language groups 27
 language policy 24
 language shift 7–8
 right to education 69
imperialism 85, 222–3
India 25, 84, 148, 261
indigenous languages 10
indigenous peoples, and minority language
  rights 149
Indigenous Peoples, Draft Declaration of
  (1993) 85
individual choice, and linguistic diversity 198
individual rights, and language rights 30–1
inequalities:
 chosen 112
 unchosen 106, 107–8, 111–12, 113–15, 116
institutions, and minority language rights 247–9
instrumental language rights 62–7, 70, 72
 bilingual ballot for Hispanics 76–8
 limitations 73–6
 purpose of 74–5
 right to learn dominant language 68–70
international law 34–5, 148
Inuit, and minority language rights 134

Israel, and Hebrew 93
Italy 4, 25

Japan 25
judiciary:
 courts, and language rights 62, 65
 language policy 19–21, 35
jurisdictional territoriality, principle of 300–2
justice:
 distributive 154–6
 language policy 265–9
 language shift 258–63
 linguistic diversity 80
 *see also* language justice

Kant, Immanuel 255
King, Ian 160
Kloss, Heinz 26, 27

language:
 functions of 250
 identity 13, 88, 95, 139–43, 313–14
 intergenerational transfer 90, 91
 intrinsic value of 252–6, 283
 nationalism 52–3, 138–9, 140–1
 private usage 23–4
 public good 195, 263–4
 role of 213
 social interaction 65
language change, *see* language consolidation;
  language loss; linguistic change language
  communities 93–5
language consolidation 98, 210–11, 235–6
 literacy 231–2
 nationalism 233–5, 244, 253
 pressures for 231, 235
 process of 238, 257–8
 the state 244
language death, *see* language consolidation;
  language loss language distribution 191
language groups, *see* linguistic diversity
language injustice 206–7
 liberalism 219–20
 linguistic diversity 216–18
 literacy 237–7, 242
 minority languages 207
 morality of 211
 official languages 224–5
 patterns of 192
 revival policies 239–41
 types of 210–12

language injustice (*cont.*)
  unequal advantage 225–8
  *see also* language justice; language protection
language justice 153
  bilingualism 167, 276
  compensatory approach to 80–1, 82–4, 102,
    128, 134, 158–60
  cooperative 154–6
  cost-benefits of language learning 157–66
  cost sharing 156–7, 167
  distributive justice 154–6
  efficiency 160–1
  language loss 190
  liberal culturalist approach to 81, 88–92, 102
  liberal democratic approach to 81, 92–102
  maximin relative benefit 161–2
  measurement of 157–66
  nationalist approach to 81, 84–8, 102
  policy implications 167–8
  unequal advantage 225–8
  *see also* language injustice
language learning:
  costs 57–66, 259–60
  *see also* education
language loss 191
  assimilation 210, 211, 213, 215–16, 217,
    218, 219
  causes of 189, 191, 218–20, 220–1, 222–4
  communicative interests 214–16
  discrimination 220–2, 222–4
  environmental correlations 192
  geography of 236
  identity 213–14
  language justice 190
  liberalism 213, 219–20
  literacy 237, 242
  official languages 224–5
language policy 16–17
  aggregative justifications 271
  benign neglect 32–3, 251–2, 265
  coercive 252, 253
  cohesion 281, 283, 283–4
  content 274, 275
  courts 19–21, 35–6
  democratic participation 310–13
  diversity 42–8, 182, 253
  education 21–3, 36
  fairness 260–1
  geography 274
  group-specific approach 288–94
  identity 313–18
  illiberal 255

immigration 24
individual choice model 286–8
individual vs. collective rights 31
internal usage in government 17–18
jurisdiction 275
jurisdictional territoriality 300–2
justice 265–9
language protection 43–8, 252–6, 261, 262,
    264–5
legislatures 19–21
linguistic convergence 37
linguistic human rights 33–6
minority languages 43–5
models for 274–8
multilingualism 251
nation-building 37–42
nationalism 96–7
naturalization 24, 71, 77
official languages 25, 33, 258, 262
personality principle 19, 22, 271
political boundaries 280–1
private usage 23–4
privileged languages 36
procedural approaches 49–51
public good 263–4
public services 17–19, 305–6
requirements of a just 268–9
rights-based approach 271
social mobility 39, 40, 306–10
stability 298–9
territorial enlargement 24–5
territorial principle 19, 22, 271, 274–5, 276
language protection 57–8, 185–6, 228–9, 236–41,
    242–3, 271, 273–4
  group-specific approach 288–94
  human rights 284–7
  individual-choice model 286–8
  language policy 252–6, 262, 264–5
  liberalism 212
language protectionism 241
language revival 94, 239–40
language rights:
  collective 30–1
  cultural protection 56–9
  defending 241–5
  deliberative democracy 13–16
  discrimination 63–5, 67
  diversity 178–87
  education 65, 66, 70
  financial costs 75–6
  growth of interest in 10–11
  individual 30–1

instrumental 62–7, 70, 72
judiciary 62, 65
language communities 274
liberalism 125
limitations 73–6
minorities 29, 78
multicultural citizenship 11–13
multinational states 67 n. 23
nationalist perspective 191 n. 2
neglect of 6–7, 52
non-instrumental 56–62, 66, 67
norm-and-accommodation 28, 29, 33
official language rights 28–9
personality principle 29
presentism 126–8
prioritizing 74
promotion-oriented 26–7, 34, 54, 55
public schools 115–21
purpose of 74–5
social mobility 135–8
territorial principle 29–30
tolerance-oriented 26–7, 54, 55
voting 65, 76–8
see also minority language rights
language shift 16, 149–51, 237, 241–2, 257–8
encouraging 8–9
immigration 7–8
justice 258–63
see also language consolidation; language loss
language transfer 90, 91, 161
Laponce, Jean 277
legislatures, and language policy 19–21
legitimacy, democratic 14, 76, 151–2
Levy, Neil 197
liberal democracy, and language justice 92–102
liberalism 11
benign neglect 32
cultures 90
inequality 225–6
judgement of cultures 109
language justice 86–7, 219–20
language loss 213, 219–20
language preservation 212
language rights 78, 125
liberal culturalism 88–92
limits on parents' discretion 98–9
linguistic competence 154, 164 n. 18
linguistic conflict 3–4, 76, 215–16
linguistic diversity 61, 198
biodiversity 190, 192, 207–8
costs of 156–7
decline of 190, 216–18

democratization 3
economics 172
ethnic conflict 3–4
fairness principle 199–206
individual choice 198
justice 80, 216–18
language policy 42–8, 253
minorities 4–6
minority languages 42
multicultural citizenship 13
official languages 4
political controversy 3–10
political theory 16, 123–5, 151–2
production of 200–1
public good 193–9, 202–3, 206–9
science 196–8
threatened character of 179
value of 190, 195–8
see also language consolidation; language loss
linguistic human rights 33–6
Linguistic Normalization, Law of (Catalonia 1983) 96–7
Linguistic Policy Act (Catalonia 1998) 96–7
literacy:
democracy 233–5
language 232–3
language consolidation 231–2
language loss 237–7, 242
nationalism 233
literacy programmes, and nation-building 38
López, Mark Hugo 94

maintenance, language 43–8
majoritarianism 99
majority languages, perception of 124–5
see also dominant languages
Maori 94, 134
market forces, and language choice 259–60, 262
maximin relative benefit, principle of 161, 165–6
May, Stephen 85, 88, 94, 236–7
Mill, John Stuart 38, 101, 253, 311
minorities:
academic interest in 172–3
accommodation rights 106–8
assimilation 131
conflict 178–9
cultural rights 92
definition of 177
deliberative democracy 15, 16
discrimination 220–2
disruptiveness of 282–3
diversity clover 174–5

minorities (*cont.*)
  ethnic 106–8, 129
  immigrant 183–4, 185
  integration 91
  language loss 42–5
  language protection 57–8
  language revival 94
  language of school instruction 115–21
  liberal culturalism 89–90
  linguistic diversity 4–6
  national 106–8, 129, 183–4
  protection of 59–60
  typology of 173–4
  unequal advantage 225–8
  *see also* minority language rights
minority cultures, unchosen inequalities 106,
    107–8, 111–12
minority language rights:
  affirmative provisions 246
  bilingual education 143–7
  counterbalancing 243–5
  defending 241–5
  equivalence 147–9
  ethnic minorities 149
  exit from language 149–51
  historical sanitization 128–32
  history 125–6
  identity 142
  indigenous peoples 85, 149
  institutional convergence 247–9
  linguistic egalitarianism 243–4, 246–7
  linguistic fait accompli 132–4
  minority language education 147–9
  national minorities 149
  nationalism 138–9, 151–2
  negative freedom 245–6
  personality principle 133
  political consequences 151–2
  political legitimacy 151
  political theory 123–5
  present-tense 242–3, 246
  social mobility 135–8
  territorial principle 132
minority languages 55, 177
  affirmative action 246
  communicative ranges 239
  compensatory justice 82
  desire to learn 83, 84
  exit 149–51
  government 241
  group-specific protection 288–94

instrumental value 142
jurisdictional boundaries 280–1
language injustice 207
language policy 43–5
linguistic diversity 42
literacy 231–2
loss of 42–5, 240–1
official languages 225–6
personality principle 285–6
presentism 126–8
proscription 131–2
public good 124, 263–4
recognition of 184
revival policies 239–40
social mobility 238–9
threats to 200
unthreatened 207
value of 45, 254–6
monolingualism, *see* unilingualism
Moore, G. E. 254 n. 2
multiculturalism 8, 12–13, 133, 176 n. 4
multilingualism 226, 236
  compensatory language justice 83, 84
  costs 266–7
  language policy 251
  literacy 231–3
  minority groups 5
  official 243
  *see also* bilingualism
multinational societies 69
multinational states, and language rights 67 n. 23

nation building, and language policy 37–42,
    127–8
nation states, and minority language rights 151–2
national identity, and language 5, 39, 41
national language groups 27
national languages 126–8
  imposition of 127
  racial policy 131–2
national minorities 3–4, 106–8, 129, 183–4
  external protections 142–3
  minority language rights 149
nationalism 173
  language 52–3, 138–9, 140–1
  language conflicts 76
  language consolidation 233–5, 244, 253
  language minorities 234
  language policy 96–7
  linguistic 138–9
  minority language rights 138–9, 151–2

regional languages 5–6
  sub-state 41
nationhood, and language 6
Native Americans, language rights 130–1
naturalization, and language policy 24, 71, 77
Netherlands, and compensatory language
    justice 83
New Zealand 94, 134
Nickel, James 214, 215
non-instrumental language rights 56–62, 66, 67
norm-and-accommodation language rights 28,
    29, 33
Northern Ireland 4
Norway, and compensatory language justice 83,
    128, 134
Nozick, Robert 201

objective diversity 179–80
official languages 33, 54–5, 126–7, 177, 243, 247,
    258, 262
  criteria 261
  cultural protection 58
  discrimination 225–6
  language injustice 224–5
  language loss 224–5
  language policy 25, 33, 258, 262
  language rights 28–9
  learning as civic duty 70–1
  linguistic diversity 4
Ottoman Empire, and nationalist approach to
    language justice 84–5

Parfit, Derek 205
particularism 11
Patten, Alan 214, 243, 260
personality principle 133, 265–6, 284–8
  application of 318–19
  bilingualism 271–2, 276, 286, 297, 298
  definition 29
  democratic participation 310–13
  identity 313–18
  language policy 19, 22, 271
  language rights 29
  public access 305–6
  rights justification 272
  social mobility 306–10
political theory, and linguistic diversity 16, 123–5,
    151–2
politics, and language justice 92–3, 96, 97, 103, 128
Pool, Jonathan 160
presentism, and language rights 126–8

preservation, language 43–7, 57
promotion-oriented language rights 26–7, 34,
    54, 55
Proposition 227 (California 1998) 21, 57–8, 99,
    117, 118, 147
public education, and minority language
    provision 147–9
  see also education
public good:
  aesthetic value 195–6
  characteristics of 194
  collective production of 194–5
  compulsoriness 202–3
  concept of 193–4
  contributor's dilemma 205
  definition 194, 202
  financing of 205 n. 9
  free-rider problem 205–6
  intentional production condition 203–5
  language as 195, 263–4
  language policy 263–4
  linguistic diversity as 193–9, 202–3, 206–9
  minority languages 124, 263–4
  non-excludability 202
  paying for 195, 196
  value of 196, 197
public schools, choice of language of
    instruction 115–21
public services, language policy 17–18, 18–19
Puerto Rico 4, 7, 25

Quebec 4
  boundary changes 100
  cultural change 93
  language policy 22, 22–3, 24, 96
  minority protection 59, 60, 60–1

racial policy, and national language 131–2
racism, and minority language speakers 136
Rawls, John 112, 199
Réaume, Denise 85, 254
regional languages 4–6
Renan, Ernest 141
rights:
  collective 30–1
  cultural 92
  diversity 178–83
  equal 183
  group rights 89, 124, 288–94
  human 33–6, 284–7
  individual 30–1

rights (*cont.*)
   personality principle 285
   *see also* accommodation rights; language
      rights; minority language rights
Roemer, John 111
Russia 7, 18

science, and linguistic diversity 196–8
Scotland 4
second languages 64, 70
   cost-benefits of learning 157–66
   difficulties learning 63
   duty to learn 79
social interaction, impact of accent 63
social mobility:
   language policy 39, 40, 306–10
   minority language rights 135–8
   minority languages 238–9
South Africa, and official language 25, 148,
     184, 298
South Tyrol 4
Soviet Union, and compensatory language
     justice 84
Spain 4, 7
   boundary changes 100
   Catalonia and language justice 82–3
   duty to learn official language 71 n. 29
   language policy 20
   linguistic competence 64 n. 18
   linguistic nationalism 138–9
   official language 25, 69 n. 26
   *See also* Basque Country; Catalonia
Stalin, Joseph 99
state, the:
   effective communication 265–8
   language consolidation 244
   language policy 251–2
   national language 127
subjective diversity 179–80
suffrage, and language rights 76–8
Swaan, Abram de 195
Sweden, and language policy 23, 83, 128
Switzerland 7
   language policy 6 n. 6, 22, 24
   minority language rights 133
   official language 25
   territorial principle 29, 30, 297, 299, 302

Tamir, Yael 93
taxation, and creation of language
     communities 93, 95

Taylor, Charles 45–6
territorial principle 132, 299–302
   aggregative justification 272
   appropriateness of 318, 319
   bilingualism 297
   conditions for 298
   definition 29
   democratic participation 310–13
   difficulties with 302–4
   identity 313–18
   language policy 19, 22, 271, 274–5, 276
   language rights 29–30
   public access 305–6
   social mobility 306–10
   territorial unilingualism 273, 278–84
   unilingualism 271, 276
territorialization, and language use patterns 42–3
tolerance-oriented language rights 26–7, 54, 55
translation, limitations 75
transnational democracy, and language 9–10
transnationalism, immigrant 8
Trudeau, Pierre 281
unilingual territoriality, principle of 301–2
unilingualism 144, 235, 272–3
   aggregative justifications 272–3, 279, 281
   benefits 157
   civic identity 13
   cohesion 281–2
   eastern Europe 3
   justifications of 279–80
   literacy 231
   territorial 273, 278–84
   territorial principle 271, 276–7, 277–8

United Kingdom 6–7
   *See also* Scotland; Wales
United States 4, 6–7
   bilingual education 144–5
   bilingual programs 94
   boundary changes 100
   compensatory language justice 84
   English Only movement 60, 94, 120–1,
     136 n. 10
   language education 70
   language history 129–30
   language policy 17, 19, 20, 21, 23–4, 25, 39
   minority language rights 130, 245
   Native American languages 130–1
   official language 25
   Proposition 227 (California) 21, 57–8, 99, 117,
     118, 147

recognition of language rights 62
Spanish-speaking citizens 105
voting and language rights 30
*see also* Hispanics
universalism 11

value, intrinsic vs. instrumental 254–5
Van Parjis, Philippe 195
Varennes, Fernand de 127, 148, 149
voting, and democracy 13–14, 30, 65, 76–8

Waldron, Jeremy 151
Wales 7
minority language rights 137, 137–8
Welsh language 86, 87, 90
Welsh-language preservation 47–8
Wallonia 132–3
Weber, Max 98, 141
Weinstein, Brian 124
Wilson, Woodrow 85

Yugoslavia 7